Global Media Perceptions of the United States

Global Media Perceptions of the United States

The Trump Effect

Edited by Yahya R. Kamalipour

ROWMAN & LITTLEFIELD
Lanham • Boulder • New York • London

Published by Rowman & Littlefield
An imprint of The Rowman & Littlefield Publishing Group, Inc.
4501 Forbes Boulevard, Suite 200, Lanham, Maryland 20706
www.rowman.com

6 Tinworth Street, London SE11 5AL, United Kingdom

British Library Cataloguing in Publication Information Available

Library of Congress Control Number: 2020946240

ISBN 978-1-5381-4241-7 (cloth)
ISBN 978-1-5381-4243-1 (electronic)

This volume is dedicated to my family, to the COVID-19 essential workers (especially physicians and nurses), and to the families of the over 800,000 coronavirus victims who have lost their lives around the world.

Greed has poisoned men's souls, has barricaded the world with hate, has goose-stepped us into misery and bloodshed. We have developed speed, but we have shut ourselves in. Machinery that gives abundance has left us in want. Our knowledge has made us cynical. Our cleverness, hard and unkind. We think too much and feel too little. More than machinery we need humanity. More than cleverness we need kindness and gentleness. Without these qualities, life will be violent and all will be lost.

—Charlie Chaplin, The Final Speech, 1940

No other planet in the solar system is a suitable home for human beings; it's this world or nothing. That's a very powerful perception.

You probably don't need more weapons than what's required to destroy every city on earth. There's only 2,300 cities. So, the United States, by that criteria, only needs 2,300 nuclear weapons—well, we've got more than 25,000!

—Carl Sagan, The Cosmos, 1980

Capitalist society is based upon the exploitation of labor. A small minority owns everything; the working masses own nothing. The capitalists command. The workers obey. The capitalists exploit. The workers are exploited. The very essence of capitalist society is found in this merciless and ever-increasing exploitation. Capitalist production is a practical instrument for the extraction of surplus value.

—Nikolai Bukharin, 1918

Perception is more important than reality. If someone perceives something to be true, it is more important than if it is in fact true. This doesn't mean you should be duplicitous or deceitful, but don't go out of your way to correct a false assumption if it plays to your advantage.

—Ivanka Trump, The Trump Card, 2010

I'm a bit of a P. T. Barnum. I make stars out of everyone.

—Donald Trump, 1991

Every time we turn our heads the other way when we see the law flouted, when we tolerate what we know to be wrong, when we close our eyes and ears to the corrupt because we are too busy or too frightened, when we fail to speak up and speak out, we strike a blow against freedom and decency and justice.

—Robert F. Kennedy, 1961

Contents

MEXICO

NIGERIA

PAKISTAN

POLAND

RUSSIA

TURKEY

Foreword

Cees Hamelink, University of Amsterdam

Whatever one may think about the 45th United States president it would seem to me that most people worldwide could agree on the classification of Donald Trump in the category of "bullies." Bullies are the figures who from classrooms to family dinners, and from work floors to political assemblies manage to provoke their fellow human beings with a level of self-confidence and intimidating authority, putting themselves always first and blaming everyone else for things that go wrong.

The classical image of the bully is someone whose behavior is unpredictable (even by himself) and often borders on recklessness and irresponsibility. Yet the bully may be for some the perfect role model, while others grade the bully as a seriously deranged personality. The bully has ardent followers and equally ardent opponents. The bully divides the world into those who love him and those who hate him.

In human evolutionary history the bully has a special place. As a free rider, the bully is considered a danger to the fitness of the group. Christopher Boehm (2012) has documented how in hunter-gatherer egalitarian societies alpha-male social predators were policed by their own band-level communities. There is an interesting lesson to be learned from our predecessors and the way they neutralized risks to their survival. As Noam Chomsky writes in his chapter, the most important question in our time is whether organized human life will survive. In the beginning of the twenty-first century, humanity faces the existential risk of extinction. Whereas neoliberal globalization and global connectivity may suggest global togetherness, polarized fragmentation continues to be the crucial characteristic of contemporary human life around the globe. A deeply polarized human species is unable to provide protection against the existential risk it faces today. We cannot afford bullies that recklessly contribute to global polarization thus speeding up human extinction. The neutralization of bullies was in earlier times the result of a communicative process.

We have always been a gossiping species. We like to discuss the doings of others and while enjoying it discover the disrupting forces in our communities. In modern society, the media have become the standard forums for debating what our moral codes are or should be. As Boehm writes, "All human groups frown on . . . undue use of authority, cheating that harms group cooperation, major lying" (2012, 34). Therefore, human groups communicate about these acts and seek to identify the bully and understand how to socially control his behavior. The evolution of human communication has been guided by the need and the capacity of "thinking together." Human communication is motivated by mutualism and reciprocity. We request from others information that is helpful to us, and we offer others information that is useful to them. We also share information and emotions with others because we want to be linked to them. Thus, communication was used to send warning signals in cases of imminent danger. The collective hunting of our predecessors demanded cooperation and a fair distribution of the loot, which implied the suppression of bullies. Cooperative foraging needed expertise which developed and expanded through information sharing. From earliest times on, hominins and later humans were information junkies: constantly seeking and receiving information.

It is important here to take note of the narrative structure of human communication. We do things (like hunting, cultivating the land, building settlements, fighting wars) and from beginning to end we tell each other stories about what we are going to do and about what we did. Storytelling is an essential condition to make human action possible. It is imperative that we learn how the storytelling forums in different countries deal with this if we want to know how we view each other in the global arena. The study in front of you assists us enormously in getting some idea of the wide variety of mediated perceptions on the role of the United States and its president. It is the great contribution of Yahya Kamalipour to bring all these stories together and provide us with the challenge to learn how the world gossips about the alpha male in the White House and to what extent his actions are promoting or endangering the fitness and resilience of the world community.

REFERENCE

Boehm, C. (2012). *Moral Origins*. New York: Basic Books.

Acknowledgments

In the course of editing this timely book on *Global Media Perceptions of the United States: The Trump Effect*, I have greatly benefited from the kind support and cooperation of nearly thirty-five accomplished media scholars in 18 countries, representing every continent. My sincere gratitude goes to the contributing authors of this book, for without their genuine interest and continued support, this project could not have come to fruition.

At Rowman & Littlefield, I am grateful to acquisition editors Elizabeth Swayze and Natalie Mandziuk for their keen enthusiasm and kind interest in this exciting project. The excellent creative, production, and marketing teams at R&L, especially Alden Perkins, also deserve to be noted for their valuable contributions to the overall design, layout, structure, and promotion of this book.

Also, I would like to express my appreciation to my former colleague and friend Professor Yueqi Zhang of Purdue University Northwest for conceptualizing the cover image and to my wife, Mah, and daughters, Shirin and Niki, for suggesting improvements. Of course, the art design experts at Rowman & Littlefield deserve credit for revising and finalizing the cover image.

Finally, I am indebted to my wife, children, and family members for their unconditional love, emotional support, and understanding throughout this project, which is paved with good intentions and best hope for a more cohesive and prosperous America and a peaceful world.

Introduction

If it is widely assumed that the new President cannot move forward simply because of a narrow victory, there can easily develop a sense of unease and uncertainty, adversely affecting every sector of American society, our economy and the perception of other nations.

—Richard V. Allen, US National Security Advisor to President Ronald Reagan

The 45th president of the United States of America, Donald J. Trump, has shaken up national and international orders, treaties, and norms, resulting in significant transformations that will continue to rearrange the social, political, economic, and nation-to-nation relationships for years to come. The consensus seems to be that his out-of-the-box worldview, unusual policies, unorthodox conducts, and braggadocio personality have resulted in a highly polarized America and fractured world.

A unique feature of Trump is that he stands up for what he believes in and seems to rely more on his own intuition than on his advisors. One of his hallmarks is that, unlike his predecessors, he tends to be spontaneous by saying or tweeting what he thinks perhaps without worrying about the impacts or consequences of his utterances. He is astonishingly self-confident and all-knowing and, has, on several occasions, declared himself as the only person who (1) can fix everything, (2) knows more than the generals, (3) can do practically anything, (4) can even shoot somebody on a New York street without losing any supporters, (5) can make stars, (6) is the chief law enforcement officer of the United States, and (7) has total authority in decision-making!

I recall that in 1983, President Ronald Reagan was labeled as the "Teflon President," but considering the myriad of misbehaviors, misinformation, and misuse of presidential power, Donald Trump wins the real "Teflon President" label. Despite his impeachment by the House, his questionable dealings with Ukraine, his reported sexual misconducts, and other legal troubles and lawsuits, nothing has stuck to him. It is safe to say that Trump seems to be even tougher than Teflon.

As an avid observer of contemporary events, I credit President Trump for being able to attract media attention masterfully and consistently by providing tantalizing news bites and often controversial and even insulting statements, since he declared his candidacy in 2016. Whether by design or coincidence, one cannot find even a day in which the US media have not covered Trump. The barrage of media coverage has resulted in numerous special programs, comedy segments, and feature stories. Moreover, reminiscent of the partisan press in the post-colonial era, the contemporary US media could be divided into Trump supporters (e.g., Fox News, Breitbart News, *The National Enquirer*, and evangelical media outlets) and those critical of his conducts and disruptive policies (e.g., CNN, CNBC, MSNBC, *New York Times*, and *Washington Post*).

TRUMP-RELATED BOOKS

In 2016, most media, political pundits, and exit polls didn't believe Trump was going to win the elections. In his book, *Why We're Polarized* (2020), Ezra Klein argues that even his team didn't believe he was going to win. But he won the electoral college even though 61 percent of voters said, in Election Day exit polls, that he was unqualified to hold the presidency, and the consensus was that Hillary Clinton would be the next president. Writers and commentators are still trying to understand why and how a businessman and former television series host—with no political experience—was able to occupy the White House.

Interestingly, within the last four years (2016–2020), nearly one hundred books have focused, wholly or partially, on President Trump, most of them highly critical of his presidency. As of this writing and amid President Trump's impeachment proceedings, his hawkish former National Security Advisor, John Bolton, has announced a new book, *The Room Where It Happened: A White House Memoir*, which reportedly sheds new light on the Ukrainian scandal and behind-the-scene dealings. In his memoir, Bolton confirms that Trump conditioned nearly $400 million in military aid to Ukraine on politically motivated investigations of the 2020 Democratic candidate, Joe Biden and his son.

THE TWITTER PRESIDENT

To bypass the traditional media and communicate directly with his constituents, Trump has successfully adopted Twitter, @realdonaldtrump, as his main channel of communication and hence has earned the title of the "Twitter President." For instance, as his Senate's impeachment trial was in progress, he reportedly posted more than 140 times on Twitter on Wednesday, January 22, 2020.

According to *USA Today* (2020), President Trump celebrated his acquittal on two articles of impeachment by taunting Democrats via Twitter. Just minutes after the Senate trial vote, Trump tweeted out a thirty-second video of a *Time* magazine cover with the blaring headline: "How Trumpism Will Outlast Trump." It included mock Trump campaign signs for the next several presidential elections. Indeed, regardless of his reelection in 2020, Trumpism will continue to impact America and the world at large.

REVOLT AGAINST THE MEDIA

President Trump and his supporters tend to routinely dismiss unfavorable media coverage and applaud those who present favorable coverage. Although the concept of "fake news" is not new, it has been repeatedly used by Trump and his supporters to discredit the mainstream media to the extent that it has become a part of daily discourse in the United States and elsewhere. The critical reporters and media outlets are labeled as "liars," "the opposition party," "fake news," and "the enemy of the people."

Another popular concept concocted by the Trump administration, particularly his surrogates, is "alternative facts," which is used to justify or put a spin on factual reports. According to the *Washington Times* (2019), "President Trump has broken the press in America. Or at least he has left it bruised and battered."

TRUMP'S STATE OF THE UNION ADDRESS

As a charismatic individual and former television personality, host of *The Apprentice* (a reality television series), and student of theatrics, Trump understands the value of entertainment and has acquired firsthand insight into the American media; therefore, knows how to attract attention and gain daily coverage. He masterfully incorporates showmanship and entertainment in his public speeches and campaign events, including in his final State of the Union address on Tuesday, February 4, 2020. Illustrative of the highly partisan and divisive Washington and national politics, he refused to shake hands with the House Speaker Nancy Pelosi, who presided over the president's impeachment by the House of Representatives. His well-delivered, well-rehearsed, and well-orchestrated speech included the following elements: (1) nationalism, (2) self-aggrandizement, (3) suspense, (4) emotional appeal, (5) economic success, (6) bestowing the Presidential Medal of Freedom on his supporter and far-right conservative radio personality Rush Limbaugh, (7) reuniting a military sergeant with his family, (8) boasting about assassinating the top Iranian military commander Qassim Suleimani in Iraq, (9) recognizing a self-declared Venezuelan opposition leader, Juan Guaidó, (10) rejecting socialism, (11) depicting Democrats as radicals, and (12) recognizing several African Americans for their accomplishments. Finally, after his address and to everyone's surprise, Pelosi ripped up a copy of Trump's speech, which overshadowed the post–State of the Union media coverage. It should be noted that this was perhaps the best speech delivered during Trump's presidency. He adhered to the teleprompter and, unlike many of his earlier speeches, did not ad-lib or deviate from the written script.

TRUMP'S IMPEACHMENT

On December 18, 2019, President Donald Trump became the third president in US history to be impeached by the House of Representatives based on two articles, abuse of power and obstruction of Congress, which were approved in mostly party-line votes.

On February 5, 2020, the impeachment trial was conducted by the Senate, without any witnesses, and ended with a "not guilty" verdict in mostly party-line votes.

On February 6, 2020, President Trump delivered an acquittal victory speech in the White House, in which he thanked his supporters and sharply slammed his opponents. According to the *Atlantic* magazine (Graham 2020), Trump targeted his enemies, including: "A group that included not only Democrats like Nancy Pelosi and Adam Schiff, but also former FBI Director James Comey and current Republican Senator Mitt Romney, he was vindictive. The charges were 'bullshit.' His adversaries were evil, vicious, corrupt 'dirty cops.'"

US IMAGE ACCORDING TO PEW RESEARCH CENTER REPORT

A must-read, the comprehensive 2017 Pew Research Center report, based on the Global Attitudes Survey of 37 countries, is quite relevant to the contents of this book and highlights the declining perceptions of the United States and Trump around the world. Below are two of the many tables included in the report.

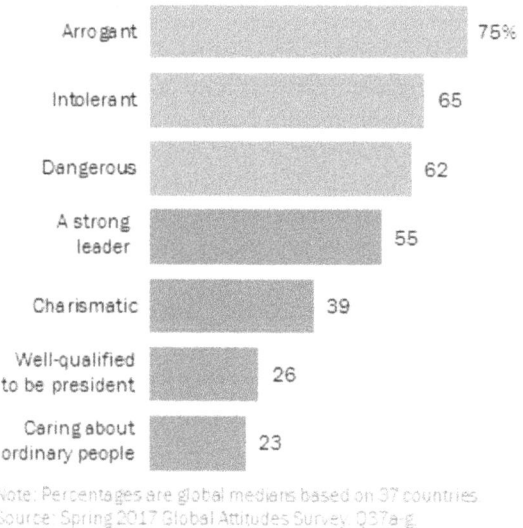

Global views of Trump's characteristics

% saying they think of President Donald Trump as ...

Arrogant	75%
Intolerant	65
Dangerous	62
A strong leader	55
Charismatic	39
Well-qualified to be president	26
Caring about ordinary people	23

Note: Percentages are global medians based on 37 countries.
Source: Spring 2017 Global Attitudes Survey. Q37a-g.

PEW RESEARCH CENTER

Figure I.1   Global views of Trump's characteristics
Pew Research: https://www.pewresearch.org/global/2017/06/26/u-s
   -image-suffers-as-publics-around-world-question-trumps-leadership/

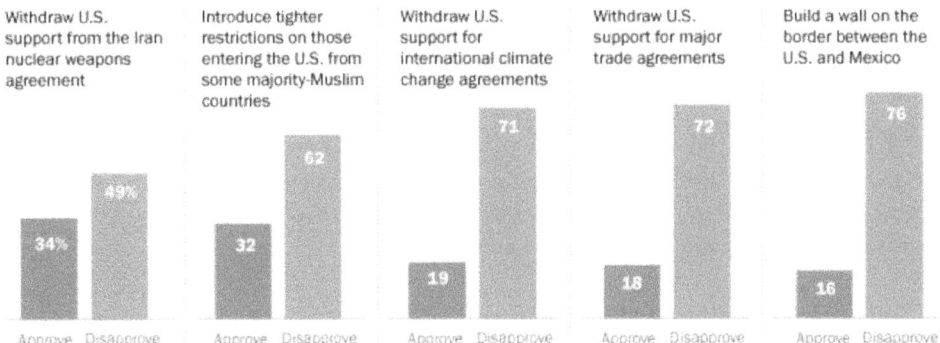

Widespread disapproval of Trump's signature policy proposals

___ *of President Donald Trump's proposed policy to ...*

| Withdraw U.S. support from the Iran nuclear weapons agreement | Introduce tighter restrictions on those entering the U.S. from some majority-Muslim countries | Withdraw U.S. support for international climate change agreements | Withdraw U.S. support for major trade agreements | Build a wall on the border between the U.S. and Mexico |

Approve 34% / Disapprove 49%

Approve 32 / Disapprove 62

Approve 19 / Disapprove 71

Approve 18 / Disapprove 72

Approve 16 / Disapprove 76

Note: Percentages are global medians based on 37 countries.
Source: Spring 2017 Global Attitudes Survey. Q38a-e.

PEW RESEARCH CENTER

Figure I.2   **Widespread disapproval of Trump's signature policy proposals**
Pew Research: https://www.pewresearch.org/global/2017/06/26/u-s-image-suffers-as-publics-around-world-question
-trumps-leadership/pg_2017-06-26-us_image-00-5/

AIMS OF THIS BOOK

In view of the tumultuous national and global environments and controversial views of Donald J. Trump's presidency, this timely book aims to inform interested readers, students, scholars, politicians, and media professionals of various nations' perceptions and media coverage of the United States.

The aim of this book is to present the US image around the world as it is portrayed through the media of 19 countries. A new image which is reflective of the new realities ushered in by President Trump and his unorthodox style of leadership, conduct, and behavior.

Thirty-five accomplished and prominent media, communication, and journalism scholars—representing 18 countries—have methodically researched and assessed their respective country's perceptions of the United States and Trump through content and discourse analysis of their major national newspapers and social media.

Unmatched by any previous publication, this book provides a valuable and much-needed global perspective of the United States through the eyes of other peoples and cultures as portrayed in the media of diverse countries around the world.

Writing Styles

One of the key advantages of an edited volume is that it offers readers and researchers broad and multidimensional perspectives that typically are absent, or presented one-dimensionally, in a single-authored or coauthored book. You will note that the writing styles of each section vary, but, nonetheless, they collectively present significant research results that will allow readers to gain a reasonably informed and well-grounded perspective about the global perceptions and media coverage of other countries regarding the United States and Trump. My own belief is that one cannot avoid variations in such a multifaceted and diverse book project.

In any case, advantages and disadvantages, together, potentially can lead to lively discussions; critical analysis; further research; exposure to diverse thoughts; exposure to diverse writing/communication styles; and an appreciation for the complexity of the global media, journalism, and communication.

Target Audience

This book will be a valuable resource for domestic and international readers interested in learning about current public opinion, media coverage, and overall perceptions of the United States and Trump around the world, including:

- media and communication professionals
- educators
- researchers
- politicians
- students
- journalists
- governmental organizations
- nongovernmental orgazinations
- interested readers

This multicultural and global volume will be also an excellent required or supplemental book in courses such as (1) global/international communication, (2) global studies, (3) global journalism, (4) political communication, (5) cultural studies, (6) intercultural communication, and (7) other related graduate or undergraduate courses.

Structure of This Book

Readers will note that the length of chapters varies, depending on the analysis and time frame of the research regarding the national media coverage of the United States and Trump in each country.

Except "The American Context" section, in which three notable media scholars provide the necessary background and foundation for both domestic and international readers, the rest of the 16 countries appear in alphabetical order, starting with Australia and ending with Turkey.

A TUMULTUOUS AND VULNERABLE WORLD

A global game of power shift and balance is unfolding in front of us. Isolationism, nationalism, and autocratic behaviors are undermining the liberal world order that the United States set up and has promoted since the end of World War II. International treaties are unraveled. The old-fashioned dichotomy of "Us vs. Them" is revived. Hate and intercultural conflicts are on the rise. And several global hotspots are in an explosive mode.

In addition to the ongoing conflicts in the Middle East, Asia, Africa, and Latin America, a highly contentious Democratic Party primary election across America resulted in two leading candidates, Joe Biden and Bernie Sanders. On April 8, 2020, Sanders ended his presidential race and later endorsed Biden, making Biden the presumptive Democratic candidate who will challenge Trump in the November 2020 presidential elections. At the same time, a highly contagious Coronavirus (COVID-19), originated in Wuhan, China, is rapidly spreading throughout the United States and the world. According to the published reports, the disease has already crippled people's daily routines in 200 countries, overwhelmed the medical facilities, infected over 2.6 million, and has killed over 180,000 people around the world. Unfortunately, the virus continues to relentlessly spread throughout the world; hence, by the time this book is published, the reported statistics may be much higher. As of April 18, 2020, the most impacted countries, having the highest infected individual and death rates, are the United States, Spain, Italy, France, Germany, United Kingdom, China, Iran, and Turkey.[1] Of these, Iran has been in an alarming situation due to the unprecedented and extensive economic and trade sanctions imposed by Trump.

We are indeed facing extraordinary and unparalleled times. The global impact of the COVID-19 pandemic has been profound, wide-ranging, disruptive, and damaging to all economic, political, environmental, and social sectors, particularly the health care industry. This epidemic is illustrative of the fact that regardless of our geographic location, nationality, race, religion, gender, ethnicity, and political ideology, we are highly interconnected, interdependent, and indeed vulnerable and helpless. The coronavirus has affected the lives of millions of people across the world, disrupting their daily lives, work, interactions, and relationships. Tourist attractions, museums, restaurants, schools, and businesses are closed, and the stock market has plunged to its lowest level in recent history; thereby, impacting all individuals and institutions around the world.

In addition, a myriad of persisting global problems, including deforestation, ozone depletion, environmental pollution, climate change, war and conflict, terrorism, overpopulation, human rights violations, economic inequality, migration, refugee crisis, poverty, clean water shortage, militarization, nuclear weapons, and natural disasters impact all inhabitants of the earth. To reverse course, clearly, all governmental, private, and nongovernmental organizations must devise new and practical approaches to address these alarming human challenges based on sound strategies, cooperation, collaboration, mutual respect, mutual understanding, and kindness. Regardless of our religion, language, race, gender, nationality, culture, wealth, level of education, and political affiliation, we are all in this and any future pandemic together.

As the Persian poet and philosopher Saadi Shirazi (1204–1292) said:

> Human beings are parts of a body, created from the same essence.
> When one part is hurt and in pain, the other parts remain restless.
> If the misery of others leaves you indifferent,
> You cannot be called a human being.

In short, global problems require global solutions. To build a better tomorrow, governments and global corporations must seriously rethink and reexamine their failed, counterproductive, and disastrous policies of the past by changing their self-centered approaches, short-sighted actions, and exploitative conducts that have resulted in our current sad state of affairs.

---

1. Source: https://covid19info.live/.

The protection, stability, prosperity, and preservation of humanity dignity and planet earth should be our main priorities.

Yahya R. Kamalipour
Greensboro, North Carolina
July 2020

REFERENCES

Graham, D. A. (2020, February 6). Charity toward none, malice toward all: Donald Trump takes a post-impeachment victory lap. *Atlantic.* Retrieved from https://www.theatlantic.com/ideas/archive/2020/02/trumps-vindictiveness/606214/.

Klein, E. (2020). *Why we're polarized.* Simon & Schuster.

USA Today. (2020, February 5). Donald Trump celebrates impeachment acquittal by taunting Democrats with video. Retrieved from https://www.usatoday.com/story/news/politics/2020/02/05/impeachment-trump-taunts-democrats-after-senate-acquitttal/4626030002/

Washington Times. (2019, December 15). Missteps, selective coverage drive Trump supporters into full revolt against press. Retrieved from https://www.washingtontimes.com/news/2019/dec/15/trump-supporters-revolt-against-media-pew-research/

THE AMERICAN CONTEXT

1

America and the World

The Plight of Organized Human Life

Noam Chomsky, University of Arizona

The following is an edited and updated text of Professor Chomsky's speech at St. Olaf College, May 4, 2018, which has been reviewed and approved by him and, because of its relevance to the theme of this book, is intended to provide an American perspective on several significant contemporary issues impacting human life across the globe.

INTRODUCTION

What I would like to do is to focus on just one question. The most important question that has ever been asked in human history, a question that should be uppermost on everyone's mind, has been hanging over our heads for many years, and is becoming more urgent every year. It has now reached the point that the question will be answered in this generation. Your challenge is to answer it, and it can't be delayed. The question is "whether organized human life will indeed survive and not in the distant future."

The question was raised clearly to everyone with eyes open on August 6, 1945. I was then roughly your age and happened to be at a summer camp. I was a counselor and in the morning an announcement came over the loudspeaker saying that the United States had obliterated the city of Hiroshima with a single bomb, the atom bomb. People listened with a few expressions of relief and then everyone went on to their next activity: baseball game, swimming, or whatever it might be.

I was horrified both by the news and by the casual reaction. So utterly horrified that I just took off and went off into the woods for a couple of hours to think about it. It was perfectly obvious, if you thought for a second, not only about the horrible events, but that humans in their glory had achieved the capacity to destroy everything, not quite at that time, but it was clear that once the technology was established, it would only be developed further to escalate and soon reach the point of becoming what Daniel Ellsberg in his recent book, an essential reading incidentally, calls *The Doomsday Machine*, an automatic system set up so that virtually everything becomes annihilated. And as he points out, we have indeed constructed such a machine and we are living with it.

NUCLEAR WAR

Coming forward until today, leading specialists on these topics echo much the same double concern, but now in more stark and urgent terms than in 1945. One of the leading US nuclear specialists, former defense secretary William Perry, has been touring the country recently with the message that he is, as he puts it, "doubly terrified." Terrified by the severe and mounting threat of nuclear war and even more so by the lack of concern about the possible termination of organized human life. And he is not alone. Among others is General Lee Butler, formerly head of the US Strategic Command, which controls nuclear weapons and nuclear weapons policy. He recently reflected with deep remorse on his many years of service in implementing plans for what is sometimes called "omnicide crime" far surpassing genocide. Crime of wiping out just about every living organism. He writes that we have so far survived the nuclear age "by some combination of skill, luck, and divine intervention, and I suspect the latter in greatest proportion" (Cohen 2013). And he adds a haunting question: By what authority do succeeding generations of leaders in the nuclear weapon states usurp the power to dictate the odds of continued life on our planet and most urgently why does such breathtaking audacity persist at a moment when we should stand trembling in the face of our folly and united in our commitment to abolish its most deadly manifestations?

You should definitely read Ellsberg's book, *The Doomsday Machine*, in which he outlines his shocking firsthand account of America's nuclear program in the 1960s, mostly based on classified documents, from inside the government at the highest planning level for many years and describes it as a chronicle of human madness, and that's accurate enough. The record should really be studied carefully. It's shocking that sometimes it's due to the reckless acts of leaders, sometimes we escaped by sheer accident. I'll give you a couple of examples, but there are actually hundreds, literally. For example, in 1960, when it was discovered that the Russians might have missiles, or soon might have missiles, the first early-warning system was set up to detect missile attack. The first day the system went into operation, it provided to high leaders the information that the Russians had launched a missile attack with 99.9% certainty. Fortunately, people didn't react the way they're instructed to react. It turned out that there had been some miscalculations and the radar hit the moon and bounced back, which was not expected.

CUBAN MISSILE CRISIS

A couple of years later, in 1962, came what's been called rightly the most dangerous moment in history (by historian and Kennedy advisor Arthur Schlesinger), the Cuban Missile Crisis. The background is worth studying—won't have time to go into it, but it is reckless acts of leaders, including our own leaders. At the peak moment of threat of the Cuban Missile Crisis, which came extremely close to terminal disaster, at that moment there were Russian submarines outside the quarantine areas that John F. Kennedy had established, and they were under attack by US destroyers that were dropping depth-bombs on them. The conditions in the submarines were such that the crew could not really survive much longer because they were not designed for service in the Caribbean, they were designed for the far north. The United States didn't know it at the time, but they had missiles with nuclear warheads and the captains at some point decided, look, since they're dropping bombs on us—they had no contact with anyone—there must be a nuclear war so we might as well send off the Ultimate Weapon. That would have been the end. There would have been retaliation and then we were finished. To send off the missiles, it required the agreement of three submarine commanders. Two agreed and one refused and that's one of the reasons that we're still here.

In 1979, the National Security advisor, Zbigniew Brzezinski, was literally on the phone ready to call President Jimmy Carter saying that there was definite information of a massive Russian missile attack when he got a call saying it was an error, so he didn't call. A year later, Ronald Reagan became the president and one of his first acts was to start a program to probe Russian defenses. The objective was to determine what kind of defenses the Russians had against our attack. The official wording was to practice command and staff procedures with particular emphasis on the transition from conventional to non-conventional operations including use of nuclear weapons. The idea was to simulate air and naval attacks on Russia, and all of this was made public to see how the Russians would react, including simulated nuclear attacks.

At the time, it was thought that the Russians would figure out that it's simulated and wouldn't react. When the Russian archives came out, it turns out they took it very seriously just as we would certainly have done. One of the leading US intelligence analyses, in a monograph entitled *The War Scare Was for Real*, concludes that they took it extremely seriously. In the midst of this, the Russian detection systems, which are far more primitive than ours, did detect an ongoing US missile attack. The protocol is for the human being who receives it—in this case, his name happened to be Vladimir Petrov—is supposed to send that information up to the Russian high command and they decide whether to release a totally destructive missile attack on us. He just decided not to do it, probably he thought it wasn't serious. This is another reason that we are alive, and we can add him to the role of honor. This goes on time after time. There have been literally hundreds of cases that came very close.

THE DOOMSDAY CLOCK

The Bulletin of Atomic Scientists established what they call a "Doomsday Clock" shortly after the atomic bombing. What they do is every year a group of physicists, strategic analysts, and nuclear specialists get together to try to assess the threats to the world and set the minute hand of the Doomsday Clock a certain number of minutes before midnight. Midnight means "say goodbye, we are finished." The first setting in 1947 was seven minutes to midnight. It reached the most frightening setting of just two minutes to midnight in 1953 when what was easy to anticipate in 1945 had happened. First, the United States and then the Soviet Union carried out tests of hydrogen bombs that are vastly more destructive than an atomic bomb. In fact, the atom bomb is just used as a trigger to set it off with its huge destructive capability. That meant that human intelligence had reached a point that we could destroy all life, no problem. Then, the minute hand reached 2 minutes. Since then it has oscillated but in recent years it has been approaching midnight again. In January 2017, right after Donald

Trump's inauguration, the minute hand was advanced to two and a half minutes to midnight. In January 2018, after Trump was in the White House for only one year, it was advanced another half-minute to 2 minutes to midnight.[1] That's a sign that we have now matched the closest point to terminal disaster in the nuclear age, or ominously close to it. A couple of months later, President Trump's nuclear posture review was released, which raises the dangers further. I presume if the clock was set now, it might move another half minute to midnight.

ENVIRONMENT

Let me focus on the current crises which are very real and how they are being handled and what we might do about them to avoid disaster. First, something else.

Since 1945, we have been somehow surviving the nuclear age, quite miraculously, and we can't count on miracles going on forever. But what we didn't know in 1945 was that humans were entering another epoch. A new one, which is no less ominous, what geologists call the Anthropocene. A new geological epoch in which human activity is destroying the environment. There have been debates among scientists about when to date the onset of the Anthropocene, but last year the World Geological Society determined that a proper time to set it is right after World War II, the same time as the nuclear age. The reason is because of the sharp escalation at that point in human activities which were significantly damaging and will soon destroy the environment for organized life. The Anthropocene carries with it automatically a third major epoch, which is called the sixth extinction. You look through millions of years of history, there have been periods when some of them caused the mass extinction of the animal life. The last one was 65,000 years ago when an asteroid hit the earth, destroyed about 75% of animal life, ended the age of the dinosaurs, and opened a way for small mammals to survive. They ultimately became us. We are determined to become another asteroid intent on destroying most animal life on Earth and we are well advanced in this process. So, there are three major epochs that we have been living with: The nuclear age, the Anthropocene, and sixth extinction, which are all accelerating.

Let's just ask how dangerous is the Anthropocene. I'll give you a couple of recent illustrations from some of the leading scientific journals, recent articles, starting with *Nature*, a leading British journal. The title of the article is "Global warming's worst-case projections look increasingly likely." It reports that a new study based on satellite observations finds that temperatures could rise nearly 5 degrees centigrade by the end of this century. The odds that temperatures will increase more than four degrees by 2100, in the current scenario, increased from 62% to 93%. In other words, pretty near certain.

THE PARIS AGREEMENT

Let's go back to the Paris Agreement or Paris negotiations, December 20, 2015. The hope was in the international negotiations that the temperature rise could be kept to 1.5-degree centigrade rise; they considered that 2% might be tolerable. Instead, we are heading to 4 to 5 percent with very high confidence.

---

1. According to *Newsweek*, on January 23, 2020, "the metaphorical clock is now set at 100 seconds before midnight (20 seconds closer to catastrophe)." https://abcnews.go.com/US/doomsday-clock-decision-looming-scientists-gauge-nuclear-climate/story?id=68299493

Still quoting from the major science journals, according to the World Meteorological Organization, concentrations of carbon dioxide in the atmosphere surged at record-breaking speed in 2016 to the highest level in 800,000 years. The abrupt changes in atmosphere witnessed in the past 70 years, the Anthropocene, are without precedent in the geological record. Globally, the average concentration of CO_2 reached over 400 parts per million, up from 399.4 parts per million in 2015, which has been considered the upper tolerable limits. Now, we are beyond the concentrations of CO_2, which is 150% above the preindustrial level. The rapidly increasing atmospheric levels of CO_2 and other greenhouse gases have the potential to initiate unprecedented changes in climate systems leading to severe ecological and economic destruction. The last time the Earth experienced a comparable concentration of CO_2 was somewhere around 3 to 5 million years ago. At that point, the temperature was 2 to 3 degrees Centigrade above now and the sea level was 30 to 60 feet higher than it is now. That's what we're moving to in the near future. In fact, we're going beyond because the prediction is 4 to 5 degrees Centigrade. I will leave the effects to your imagination.

Here's a final example from *Science*, a leading American journal. Even slightly warmer temperatures less than anticipated in coming years will start melting permafrost, which in turn threatens to trigger the release of huge amounts of greenhouse gases trapped in ice. There's twice as much carbon in permafrost as in the atmosphere. This will then trigger the release of huge amounts of methane, which is far more lethal than CO_2, even though shorter persistence. And that accelerates other processes now clearly underway, like the rapid melting of polar ice. And polar ice, as it melts it reduces the reflective surface for the sun's rays and creates more absorbent surfaces of the dark seas. So, that escalates warming quickly, perhaps to a nonlinear process in which everything blows up. For example, West Antarctica contains enough ice to raise sea level more than 10 feet.

The prospects are extremely serious, and they are really awesome, which raises an obvious question about what we are doing about it and how we are reacting. Well, the world is actually taking some steps, inadequate, but at least they are doing something. There is a commitment and states and localities in the United States are also taking steps, which is quite important. But what is of prime importance, of course, is the federal government, the most powerful institution in human history. So, what is it doing? It has withdrawn from the international efforts and, beyond that, it is committed to increasing the use of the most destructive fossil fuels. So, our federal government, for which we are responsible, is dramatically leading a race to destruction while we sit and watch.

That is pretty astounding and it should be the screaming headline in every day's newspaper. This ought to be the main topic of study in every class; there's never been anything like it, and astoundingly, it does not receive anything like the needed attention. Another doubly terrifying phenomenon. We should be asking, among other things, what this tells us about our society and about our culture and what we are immersed in. Remember all of this is imminent; we are approaching this rapidly. In this century, your task is to do something about it rather than ignoring what's going on.

RENEWABLE ENERGY

In the meantime, one of our chief competitors in destroying the planet, the Saudi Arabian dictatorship, has just announced plans to spend $7 billion this year (2018) to build seven new solar plants and big wind farms as a part of an effort to move from oil, which destroys everything, to renewable energy. This is Saudi Arabia and that highlights how lonely we are in our race to destruction. Even the extreme reactionary dictatorship, Saudi Arabia, which lives on oil, refuses to join us in our unique insanity which is dedicated to destroying organized human life. And it is not just the current administration; the entire Republican party leadership agrees. Going back to the 2016 primaries, every single candidate denied that what was happening is happening, with the exception of those who are called the sensible moderates, like Jeb Bush, who said it's all kind of uncertain but we don't have to do anything about it because we're producing more natural gas, thanks to fracking. In other words, we are making it worse. The other sensible moderate adult in the room—as it was called—was the governor of Ohio, John Kasich, who agreed that anthropogenic global warming is taking place, but he added that we are going to burn coal in Ohio and we're not going to apologize for it. On ethical grounds, that's the worst of all. Think about it.

MASS MEDIA

Well, what about the media? They totally ignored this spectacle. Every crazy thing you can imagine was discussed extensively in the massive coverage of the primaries, but not the fact that the entire leadership of the party was saying "let's quickly destroy ourselves." Nothing; go back and check. Almost no comment about it. The denialism of the leadership is having an effect on public opinion. So, Republican voters have been climate change skeptics for a long time, way beyond anything in the world. But it has gotten far more extreme since Trump took office and the numbers are pretty shocking. So, by now, half of Republican voters deny that global warming is taking place at all. Only 30% think humans may be contributing to global warming. I don't think I can find anything like that among any significant part of the population anywhere in the world. It should tell us something: that there's a lot to do for those who hope that maybe organized human life will survive. We're not talking about a remote future. Just think about the numbers I gave you before. We are talking about something imminent.

OBEY THE LAW

Let's put that aside for a moment and go back to the growing threat of nuclear war. Are these ominous developments inexorable so should we just throw up our hands in despair and say, okay, we are finished, have a nice time, goodbye? That's not at all true. There are very plausible answers in every existing case. Diplomatic options are always open and there are quite straightforward general principles that can be quite effective.

One principle is simple: Obey the law. Not a radical idea, almost unheard of, but it could have some consequences. So, what is the law? Well, there is something called the US Constitution, which people are supposed to honor and revere. The Constitution has parts, such as Article 6, for example, that says that valid treaties are the supreme law of the land and every elected official is required to observe them. What's the most important treaty of the modern period? Unquestionably, it's the United Nations Charter. Its Article 1 requires us to keep to peaceful means to resolve international tensions and disputes and to refrain from "the threat or use of force" in international affairs. And I stress *threat* because it's violated all the time by every president and every high political leader. Every time you hear the phrase "all options are open" that's violating the supreme law of the land. If anyone cares.

THE IRAN DEAL AND MIDDLE EAST

Let's look at the couple of examples. Iran is an important example. There is a good deal of talk about the possibility that Iran may be violating the joint comprehensive agreement (JCPOA) or the Iran deal.[2] There is no evidence for that claim. US intelligence says they're observing it. The International Atomic Energy Agency, which carries out inspections, says they're observing it completely. There is a lot of discussion about it. Let's talk about something else. Is the US violating the agreement? The answer is simple: The US is radically violating the agreement and has been all along. The agreement states that all participants, including the US, are not permitted to impede in any way Iran's reintegration into the global economy, particularly the global financial system, which we pretty much control because everything works through New York. We are not permitted to interfere in any way with the normalization of trade and economic relations with Iran. We are doing that all the time and in fact are proud of it. All violations of the agreement are ignored on a principle that's kind of interesting based on the prevailing tacit assumption that the United States just stands above the law, including its own laws. So, we don't have to observe our laws or any other laws because we are just unique, and we do what we like. See if you can find an exception to that in the discourse on this topic. Well, in a couple of days, President Trump will probably withdraw from the treaty, possibly that's a gift to the hardliners in Iran telling them they should maybe return to nuclear programs and that's an opening for the new National Security advisor, John Bolton, and for Benjamin Netanyahu, both of whom have called for bombing Iran right away, even while they fully respect the terms of the agreement that we violate quite publicly. There is no secret about it and the consequences could be horrendous.

But there happen to be ways of blocking those consequences. Namely by a very simple device of respecting our own law. In fact, the supreme law of the land. Again, see if you can find a suggestion that we should obey the Constitution? And ask yourself what the answer tells us.

Are there peaceful options? Very obviously. In this case we could join the rest of the world by permitting the agreement to continue to function. Or better, we might turn to improvement of the agreement, one thing that Trump has vociferously demanded. And there is a good way to do that. One obvious proposal for improving the agreement, which is ignored entirely, is to move towards establishing a nuclear weapons-free zone in the region. There are such agreements in various parts of the world, including Latin America, a sensible step toward mitigating the threat of a nuclear disaster.

So, what about a nuclear weapons-free zone in the Middle East? If that were established, with the kind of inspections we know to be effective, it would end any conceivable Iranian threat that you could imagine. So, is there a problem of establishing it? Well, actually there is one problem, but it's not the one that comes to mind. There is no problem convincing Iran because they've been calling for it for years, vociferously. The Arab world is in favor of it because they initiated and proposed it 25 years ago. The rest of the world agrees as well.

There is one exception, the United States. The United States refuses to allow it to proceed. It comes up every couple of years at the annual review meetings of the nonproliferation treaty countries. It's continually brought up—and vetoed by the United States, most recently by President Obama in 2015. And the reasons are perfectly clear to everyone: the US will not permit Israeli nuclear weapons to be even examined by the international agency, let alone dis-

---

2. On May 8, 2018, the United States withdrew from the 2015 landmark "Iran Nuclear Deal" and Trump imposed maximum sanctions on Iran, which has resulted in unprecedented domestic hardships and shortages of products and services.

mantled. The US can't even admit that it knows—as everyone does—that Israel has nuclear weapons. Under US law, that would ban all US aid to Israel.

Therefore, we can't proceed with this very simple way of eliminating any nuclear threat from Iran or anyone else in the region. Also not discussed is that the United States and Britain have a special obligation, a unique obligation, to pursue a nuclear weapons–free zone in the Middle East. The reason is United Nations Security Council Resolution 687, which was initiated by the US and Britain, in 1991, which called on Iraq to terminate its nuclear weapons programs. In fact, the US and Britain relied on this resolution, in 2003, when they were trying to concoct some pretext for their planned invasion of Iraq. So, they appealed to this resolution and said we think Iraq is violating it, which in fact they weren't, and they had plenty of evidence that they weren't. If you read that resolution, Article 14, it commits the signers to work for a nuclear weapons–free zone in the Middle East. So, the US and Britain are uniquely committed to working for this by the Security Council Resolution that they initiated. Well, again, check to see if it's ever discussed.

So, in short, the US willingness to observe US law could bring this crisis to a very quick end and could even move on to a better solution. For example, if we were willing to observe Security Council resolutions such as 687, which we ourselves instituted. And more generally to observe the Constitution and end the illegal threats of force by every recent president and other high officials and end our constant violations of the Iran nuclear agreement. So, there are easy answers to this crisis: obey the law; that would end the crisis. Again, I advise you to search to see how often this is discussed and what that implies about our educational system and culture, media, universities, and so on.

NORTH KOREA

Let's turn to another major threat, North Korea. There has been a proposal on the table for some years about how to reduce the threat in Northeast Asia, called double freeze, which was initiated by China, supported by North Korea and Russia, and has general support throughout the world. The idea is that North Korea should freeze its weapons and nuclear programs and in return the United States should call off the threatening military maneuvers that the US constantly carries out on North Korea's border, including flights on the border by our most advanced nuclear-capable bombers warning of the threat of the total obliteration of North Korea, constantly happening. It's no joke for the North Koreans. They have a little memory that we may want to forget. At the end of the Korean War when it was more or less settled, the US bombing was so intense that there was nothing left to bomb, literally. And so, the Air Force started destroying major dams. If you read the Air Force history, they exult about this, which happens to be a crime for which people were hanged at Nuremberg, but again we are above the law.

North Korea can remember, and when advanced nuclear bombers are flying there it evokes a memory. So double freeze is one possibility. Double freeze could easily open the way to further negotiations, and at this point the record becomes important. You can find it in the scholarly records, if not the press. There have been successes in negotiations. In 2005, the Bush administration was pressured by the international community to return to negotiations, which were extremely successful. North Korea agreed to abandon all nuclear weapons and existing weapons programs and to allow international inspections and, in return for that, the US agreed to establish a consortium that would provide North Korea with a light-water reactor for medical use. The US would also issue a nonaggression pledge and an agreement that the two sides would respect each other's sovereignty, exist peacefully together, and take steps to normalize relations.

Instantly, the Bush administration renewed the threat of force, froze the North Korean funds and foreign banks, and disbanded the consortium that was to provide North Korea with a light-water reactor. According to the leading US scholar Bruce Cummings, the sanctions were specifically designed to destroy the September pledges [and] to head off an accommodation between Washington and Pyongyang. That was 2005. Well, I have been searching the press for some time to see if these facts can even be reported, breaking the constant refrain that North Korea has broken all agreements and so cannot be trusted. I urge you to try too. You'll learn a lot. Well that path could be pursued again. But as we know there are even better options and it's worth taking a closer look at them.

THE TWO KOREAS AND TRUMP

On April 27, North and South Korea signed a historic document, the Panmunjeom Declaration for Peace, Prosperity and Unification of the Korean Peninsula. It's worth reading it carefully. In this Declaration, the two Koreas "affirmed the principle of determining the destiny of the Korean nation on their own accord . . . to completely cease all hostile acts against each other in every domain . . . [to] . . . actively cooperate to establish a permanent and solid peace regime on the Korean Peninsula . . . to carry out disarmament in a phased manner, [to achieve] the common goal of realizing, through complete denuclearization, a nuclear-free Korean Peninsula . . . to strengthen the positive momentum towards continuous advancement of inter-Korean relations as well as peace, prosperity and unification of the Korean Peninsula." They further "agreed to actively seek the support and cooperation of the international community [meaning, the US] for the denuclearization of the Korean Peninsula."

It's important to read those words and their import is very clear. What they are saying is the US should back off and allow the two Koreas to achieve peace, disarmament, unification, and complete denuclearization on their own accord. In other words, the United States should accept the call for support and cooperation in this endeavor by the two parts of the Korean Nation to determine their destiny on their own accord. To put it simply, the Declaration is a polite letter saying, "Dear Mr. Trump: declare victory, if you want to, prance around in public, but please go away and let us move towards peace, disarmament, and unification without disrupting the process."

The plea could hardly be clearer. The general interpretation here is quite revealing: it complicates Washington's strategy. As the *New York Time* explains, "Mr. Trump will find it hard to threaten military action against a country that is extending an olive branch." It is entirely true that threatening military action, which happens to be a criminal act, is hard when the target is extending an olive branch. So, we have some problems.

THE 2016 US ELECTIONS

Case after case, we find that there are peaceful diplomatic options. Can't be certain that they will work, but they should always be prioritized in accordance with our international obligations and in accordance with the supreme law of the land. Is it hopeless? No, far from it, we have plenty of evidence to prove that. So, let's go back to a very important date in modern history: November 8, 2016. Several events happened that are significant. The least significant of them was the one that gets most of the media coverage, the election of Donald Trump. It's a little bit unusual, but it's not that out of the norm if a billionaire with a huge amount of campaign spending and huge media support wins the presidency. But something really surprising did happen, the Bernie Sanders campaign. That broke with practically all of American political history. For well over a century, American elections have been mainly bought, literally. You can predict the outcome of an election, with high confidence, by just looking at campaign funding. There is extensive and detailed academic study of this topic both for the presidency and Congress, mainly by political scientist Thomas Ferguson, including Trump's election.

What happened in November 2016 was different. For the first time, a candidate came very close to winning the nomination and would have won the nomination probably if the Democratic party managers had not manipulated affairs to keep Bernie Sanders out. And he did it without any campaign funding from major sources: no corporate funding, no wealth, and no media support—he was either ignored or denigrated in the media. That's a real breakthrough. What's more, he ended up becoming by far the most popular political candidate in the country. Look at the polls, including those announced by Fox News. In fact, he was well above any other political figure in popularity. In a democratic society, the most popular political figure in the country who just carried off a remarkable break in well over a century of political history would be highly prominent in the media. You hear him occasionally, but you should make your own judgments.

That's a more important event that took place in November 2016.

THE PARIS NEGOTIATIONS

Here's another important event, which didn't get covered but should have. At that time, the world was carrying out the successor negotiations to the Paris negotiations. The Paris negotiations on climate change, in December 2015, aimed at a verifiable treaty to do something about this ominous threat. They couldn't reach a treaty for one reason; the Republican Party would not permit it. So, they couldn't have a treaty but only a voluntary agreement.

The following year, in 2016, they were meeting again to try to put some teeth in the treaty. On November 8, the day of American elections, the World Meteorological Organization, at the meeting taking place in Marrakesh, Morocco, released a study on the very dire state of the climate change. Then the election results came in and the meeting basically stopped. The question before the international world was: Can the world survive when the most powerful country in history is taken over by a political party that not only denies what is happening, but is committed to accelerating the race to destruction. They kind of hoped that maybe China would save the world from disaster. Just think about that for a moment. Maybe China will save the world from the disaster that the Republican Party is bringing to the world.

CONCLUSION

The fact is there are plenty of things that can be done. The success of Senator Sanders's campaign and particularly the aftermath of that could make a difference, but it doesn't happen on its own. It takes serious engagement.

Let me go back to the beginning. Your generation, that's you, is facing the most awesome question that has ever arisen in human history. The question is "will organized human life survive?" and we are talking about the near future. The fact is we can't escape it. There are plenty of opportunities. Whether you like it or not, it's up to you to determine the fate of the human species. It is an awesome responsibility and it's one that cannot be evaded.

REFERENCES

Cohen, N. (2013, September 29). Review of command and control by Eric Schlosser, *The Guardian*. Retrieved from https://www.theguardian.com/books/2013/sep/29/command-control-eric-schlosser -review

Ellsberg, D. (2018). *The doomsday machine: Confessions of a nuclear war planner*. Bloomsbury Publishing.

Independent (2017, December 6). Worst-case global warming predictions are the most accurate, say climate experts. Retrieved from https://www.independent.co.uk/environment/global-warming -temperature-rise-climate-change-end-century-science-a8095591.html.

Washington Post (2018, April 27). The full text of North and South Korea's agreement, annotated. Retrieved from https://www.washingtonpost.com/news/worldviews/wp/2018/04/27/the-panmmunjom -declaration-full-text-of-agreement-between-north-korea-and-south-korea/

THE AMERICAN CONTEXT

2

How Americans See the World

What Research Tells Us

John V. Pavlik, Rutgers, the State University of New Jersey

INTRODUCTION

How Americans see the world is a complex matter. American worldviews are not monolithic. Although there are identifiable overall patterns and trends, the nature of the views vary along a variety of dimensions, including demographics, location, and general attitudes including political party affiliation or identity and religion. American worldviews vary by subgroup, by topic, and by country or region of the world they are considering.

How Americans view the world matters. It is important and has consequences. American global views matter for multiple reasons. American worldviews may significantly shape how America engages with the world. America has an outsized impact on the world for several reasons, including its role as a leading consumer of goods and a producer of fossil fuels, which contribute greatly to the world's carbon footprint and climate change. America's military presence globally is profound and depends at least in part on how its people see the world. How Americans see the world affects its engagement with the world's refugee crisis. And American worldviews contribute to its approach to international trade and trade policies, or at least the actions of its elected leadership or those it elects to those positions, including the US president. These are just a few of the reasons why American worldviews matter.

This chapter is based on far more than simply anecdotal evidence or examples or the views of a selected set of leaders such as political or governmental officials, or the opinions of the author. Instead it draws upon systematic data especially public opinion polls. This chapter examines what research in the form of public opinion surveys and other data sources tells us about American worldviews.

The chapter is organized into three main parts. First, the chapter begins by looking at overall patterns in Americans' worldviews. This discussion examines both general international attitudes and opinions of Americans as well as how they view what America's role in the world should be. This is the foundation for and frames more specific American world-views, beliefs, and knowledge.

Second, the implications of American worldviews are considered. This discussion considers how American worldviews may affect US international engagement, including militarily, regarding climate change, and in terms of international trade and human migration or refugees.

Third, patterns and variations by region and country in American worldviews are considered. Within this discussion, the views of Americans about the world are analyzed in terms of multiple dimensions. The discussion examines how these views vary by subgroup (e.g., demographics, geographic location, political affiliation, religious affiliation) within the overall American population, and in comparison, to the people of other nations. Patterns based on topical areas are examined. Importantly, the impact of Trump and historical context is considered. Situating current perceptions into a broader historical context helps to establish the trajectory of those views (e.g., are they shifting, becoming more or less favorable, stronger or weaker).

WHAT THE DATA TELL US

This chapter draws upon survey research and other data to describe and analyze the views and knowledge Americans have of countries around the world. Sources include the global research survey data collected by the Pew Research Center, survey data from the World Public Opinion organization, and multiple surveys conducted by the Center for International Security Studies at the University of Maryland and other organizations such as Gallup.

OVERALL AMERICAN WORLDVIEWS

How Americans view the role of the United States in the world is a foundation for how the nation engages in world affairs. Survey data indicate there are important differences between how the US public and that of the rest of the world view engagement in international conflict (Council on Foreign Relations, 2012). Since 2007, most Americans (77%) have agreed there are times when it is necessary to use military force to maintain world order (Pew, 2012). This is substantially higher than much of the rest of the world. Among the 22 countries Pew surveyed, the average level of approval for military force is just over one-half (61%).

Moreover, some Americans are particularly hawkish with regard to the use of conventional or nuclear bombs as preemptive weapons. Notably, the United States is the world's only country to have ever deployed a nuclear weapon in a war, which it did in Japan in WWII (Allen, 1969). A 2019 survey of 3,000 Americans reveals that a third (33%) of Americans would support a preemptive nuclear or conventional weaponry strike on North Korea under certain conditions (Denyer, 2019). In particular, if North Korea were to test a long-range missile that could reach the United States, a third of those surveyed would support the use of a preemptive nuclear or conventional weaponry strike even if it resulted in the death of one million civilians (Haworth, Sagan, & Valentino, 2019). Conducted by the Bulletin of the Atomic Scientists and British research firm YouGov, the survey was conducted in February of 2019 just after the Hanoi summit between Trump and North Korea's leader Kim Jong Un, which failed to produce a nuclear agreement between the nations (Wu, 2019). Another 2019 survey however, indicates most Americans are much less hawkish if civilian casualties are likely, depending on how the question is asked. "In the survey, 80 percent of Americans strongly or somewhat agreed with the idea that civilians should never be the object of attack in war. Many expressed disbelief at the question itself, seeing the very idea of attacking a civilian city as un-American" (Carpenter & Montgomery, 2019).

American worldviews are also tempered by the widely held belief in the importance of adhering to international law, even if unpopular among political leaders. Americans have stated the United States generally should follow international law. As the Council on Foreign Relations has reported, "Americans believe that their nation is obliged to abide by international law." A 2009 WorldPublicOpinion.org (WPO) poll posited to US respondents the subject of international law: "As you may know there are a number of international laws based on agreements between most nations, including our own. These govern a wide set of issues ranging from fishing rights to the use of military force." Those surveyed were then asked to choose between two positions on international law. More than two-thirds (69%) chose the one that said: "Our nation should consistently follow international laws. It is wrong to violate international laws, just as it is wrong to violate laws within a country." Less than one-third (29%) agreed that, "If our government thinks it is not in our nation's interest, it should not feel obliged to abide by international laws."

CLIMATE CHANGE

Climate change and the role of human activity in it has become a global flashpoint in the 21st century. Most world leaders accept the consensus of scientific research, not to mention the commonsense view, that climate change is real, and caused by human activity, especially the rampant burning of fossil fuel since the advent of the industrial age. Yet a few, led most visibly by US President Donald J. Trump, largely deny and reject this logical and evidence-based view. Trump has gone so far as to withdraw the United States from the Paris Climate Accord (Wikipedia, 2019).

The Chicago Council on Global Affairs conducted a poll in June 2016 to assess American views on Trump's action. The survey found that more than two-thirds (71%) of American adults favor US participation in the Paris Agreement (Mooney, 2016). A November 2016 poll by the Yale Program on Climate Change Communication found a similar percentage (69%) of US registered voters favored US participation in the Paris Agreement (Smeltz, Kafura, & Martin, 2016). A survey conducted June 2–4, 2017, by Washington Post/ABC found that a similar percent (59%) of American adults opposed Trump's decision to withdraw the United States from the Paris Agreement (Clement and Dennis, 2017). Almost half (42%) said they felt withdrawal from the accord would harm the US economy. The survey revealed a sharp divide along partisan lines, with two-thirds (67%) of Republicans supporting Trump's decision, and less than a quarter (22%) of independents and less than a tenth (8%) of Democrats supporting it.

REFUGEE CRISIS

Another vital arena of global public opinion is views regarding the world's refugee crisis. According to a United Nations report, there are more forcibly displaced persons—nearly 71 million—worldwide than at any time since WWII (UNHCR Nations Refugee Agency, 2019). The refugee crisis is largely a consequence of armed conflicts and the global climate crisis, which has produced not only global warming but also extreme weather and adverse climate conditions, such as drought, famine, and flooding as well as rising sea levels.

Regarding international public opinion about the refugee crisis, Ipsos research has conducted a series of international surveys since at least 2011. According to the most recent Ipsos survey (Skinner & Gottfried, 2017) on this topic, three-quarters (75%) of those persons surveyed in 25 countries "believe that immigration has increased in their country over the last five years," according to the Ipsos Global @dvisor survey.

Conducted among online adults aged under 65 in 25 countries worldwide, these views are similar to the previous year when 78% said immigration had increased in their country. However, views have shifted significantly since 2011. Germany and Sweden have seen the largest increase in the number of people thinking immigration has increased. In those countries the percentage reporting they see higher rates of immigration, "up 22 and 24 percentage points from 2011 to 85% and 90% respectively" (Skinner & Gottfried, 2017).

Meanwhile, Ipsos reports, "Britain and the United States are the two countries which have had the largest positive change (regarding views per immigration) since 2011. In Britain, two in five (40%) now say immigration has had a positive impact (up from 19% in 2011) while 35% in the United States say the same (up from 18% in 2011)" (Skinner & Gottfried, 2017).

AMERICAN VIEWS TOWARD WORLD REGION AND COUNTRIES

As the findings reported above suggest, an important way in which American worldviews vary is by region of the world and by country. Americans view some regions and nations with a higher level of respect, greater warmth, and more affinity. Some regions and countries the American public sees as far more problematic, with less affinity and warmth, and even as inferior. Moreover, these views vary substantially by subgroup, such as political affiliation or identity (e.g., Republican or Democrat, conservative or liberal).

Mexico and Canada are the United States' closest neighbors, sharing thousands of miles of common border. For many Americans, Mexico is a proxy for Latin America in general, subsuming into how it sees that country virtually all of the Spanish-speaking or Portuguese-speaking Western Hemisphere, including Central and South America. And as such, American views of Mexico/Latin America are in dramatic contrast to its views of its neighbor to the north.

Schoultz (1998) documents that since its founding the United States has tended to perceive Latin America as a fundamentally inferior neighbor. Americans often consider Latin American nations as unable to manage their affairs and that they remain "stubbornly underdeveloped." He states that this perception of inferiority has been apparent from the earliest days of the United States. John Quincy Adams, sixth president of the United States (1825–1829), who first established diplomatic relations with Latin America, said that Hispanics are "lazy, dirty, nasty and in short I can compare them with nothing but a parcel of hogs" (Schoultz, 1998: 1).

These words clearly demonstrate the principles that continue to characterize many widely held contemporary American views of Mexico, including those of US President Donald J. Trump, who has often used the word "nasty" to disparage those he does not like, including Mexicans. While on the campaign trail in 2015, Trump claimed Mexico was deliberately sending murderers and rapists into the United States. Then, he echoed these sentiments in 2018 when he described "caravans" of migrants making their way to the United States via Mexico and that in those caravans, "Women are raped at levels that have never been seen before" (Jacobs, 2018). Trump's views both reflect and shape those of his core constituency or base and tend to legitimize or affirm those racist views.

Trump has articulated these views in a variety of settings including campaign rallies and even in the Oval Office. He has made similar remarks about some Caribbean nations and much of Latin America, alleging that rapists, murderers, and gangs heavily populate the region (Kirby, 2018).

Trump has likewise slammed dark-skinned immigrants in general as dangerous, uneducated, and destined to be a drain on the United States and therefore largely undesirable as immigrants. In early 2018 Trump reportedly labeled the African continent, especially sub-Saharan Africa, as characterized by mostly "shithole nations" (Kirby, 2018). A *New York Times* report described a White House meeting about immigration in which Trump complained Haitians "all have AIDS" and Nigerian immigrants would never "go back to their huts" (Kirby, 2018).

Africa and the Middle East

American views of African nations are mixed. Somewhat favorable views pertain to North Africa, a region often linked to the Middle East known by the acronym, MENA, or the Middle East and North Africa. Largest and arguably most important from an economic perspective among the North Africa nations is the Republic of Egypt, home to an ancient civilization dating to at least 6000 BCE. With a current population of about 95 million, Egypt is a predominantly Sunni Muslim country with Islam as its state religion (Egypt State Information Service, 2016). With regard to the Egyptian population, approximately 85–90% are Muslim, 10–15% Coptic Christian, and 1% other Christian denominations.

A Gallup survey of Americans conducted in late January 1991 showed about two-thirds (66%) of the US adult population viewed Egypt favorably. The percentage was relatively unchanged by February 2001 (65%). Following the attacks of 9/11, US views of Egypt dropped notably, with only about one-half (54%) holding favorable views of the country, according to Gallup surveys. The percentage of Americans viewing Egypt favorably reached a low point in 2011 after the Arab Spring, when just 40% held positive views (Skinner, 2011). The percentage has increased since then, reaching more than half (57%) in a February 2019 poll. Gallup polls of American views regarding other parts of Africa are limited. Surveys taken regarding South Africa from 1989 to 1991 show only one-third (about 33%) of US adults holding a favorable view. Views had become more favorable by 2001, when more than half (57%) of Americans viewed South Africa favorably. More recent Gallup survey data regarding American views of Egypt are not available as of this writing.

A national survey of American adults taken after the 2010 earthquake in Haiti reflects the general attitudes Americans have long held toward that nation. Following the devastating earthquake, it was reported that a growing number of Haitians were seeking entry into the United States. A *USA Today*/Gallup poll found that most Americans think the United States should not increase the number of Haitian immigrants it accepts. Views are divided along political lines. More than half (57%) of Democrats and independents are in favor of increasing the number of immigrants from Haiti (Morales, 2010). Meanwhile more than two-thirds (67%) of Republicans (67%) are opposed.

Pew Research reports that the negative views Trump has advanced with regard to Latin America are echoed among the American public, although in some areas attitudes are mixed. Lologgia (2018) states, "As the Trump administration proposes changes to the North

American Free Trade Agreement (NAFTA), Americans have sharply different feelings about the two countries that, along with the US, are part of that agreement." About one-third (39%) report warm feelings toward Mexico, while about one-third (34%) feel coldly, and just a quarter (26%) hold neutral views, according to a Pew Research Center survey of 4,581 US adults conducted between July 30, 2018, and August 12, 2018.

In contrast to the United States' immediate neighbor to the south, American views are much more favorable toward Canada. The same Pew Center survey found that more than two-thirds of Americans (67%) report warm feelings toward Canada, and more than half (52%) say they have a very warm feeling. Just one in ten (12%) report feeling coldly toward Canada.

Canada and Scandinavian Nations

American views of another northern world region, Scandinavia, are, as regarding Canada, highly positive. Americans long have viewed Scandinavian nations, including Denmark, Finland, Norway, and Sweden, and their people in largely favorable terms. In contrast to his overall views toward immigration and his specific opposition to immigrants from Africa, the Caribbean, and Latin America, Trump has proposed that America try to encourage more Norwegians to migrate to the United States. Many observers have noted how Trump's favorable views of the world, as well as those of his substantially white supremacist base, tend to feature countries and regions populated largely by persons of Caucasian ethnic backgrounds, while his negative views tend to be directed at countries whose populations are much more apt to include persons of color. Trump's racist views are echoed among his base. As reported by the *Washington Post*, racial resentment fueled the nearly half (41%) of white millennials who voted for Trump, reveals a GenForward survey of August 31, 2017, to September 16, 2017, which included 1,816 respondents between 18 and 34 (GenForward, 2017; Lopez, 2017; Fowler, Mendenica, & Cohen, 2017).

Just as they hold generally favorable views of Scandinavia, Americans also tend to hold positive views of the United Kingdom (U.K.) or Great Britain, as well as many European countries. Approximately nine out of ten (wavering between 87% and 90% from 1989 to 2019) Americans have held favorable views of the U.K. since the late 1980s, indicate Gallup polling data (2019a). One of the most polarizing contemporary issues in the U.K. since the rise of populism in that country (and much of the world) is the proposed exit of that nation from the European Union (E.U.), known as Brexit (a portmanteau of Britain and exit). A 2016 poll indicates that more than three-fourths (80%) of Americans favor the U.K. exit from the E.U. (Sola, 2016). "The data comes from polls posted through May and June (2016) in 123 articles on the website of *The Independent*, a liberal British newspaper with a global online readership. Polling and quiz company Apester powered the polls and analyzed votes from 359,217 users." It is important to note that this set of polling data is not scientifically collected and does not derive from a random survey; but rather the results represent the views of self-selected poll participants. Therefore, generalizing from these results is not justifiable from a social science perspective, but they may suggest certain possible patterns for further research investigation.

Germany

American views toward Germany, another important European ally, are similarly strong (Poushter & Castillo, 2019). "In the US, seven-in-ten say that relations with Germany are good, a sentiment that has not changed much in the past year. Germans, on the other hand, are much more negative: 73% say that relations with the US are bad, a 17-percentage-point increase since 2017." Still, "Nearly three-quarters of Germans are also convinced that a foreign policy path independent from the US is preferable to the two countries remaining as close as they have been in the past. But about two-thirds in the US want to stay close to Germany and America's European allies."

One aspect of Scandinavia many Americans historically have viewed with skepticism if not outright hostility is its socialist domestic policies. Americans have tended to view socialism as a proxy for communism, which many have seen negatively and even as an existential threat. Much of this viewpoint traces to the Cold War if not before, and possibly to anti-Semitism (Zelizer, 2019). Socialism and communism have been seen by some as the antithesis of what American values are all about, especially among more conservative political circles as well as among the most religiously conservative, especially Christian Evangelicals, a group to which is Trump is closely aligned and from which he enjoys strong support (Morris, 2019).

Socialism

But these skeptical views toward socialism are changing. Recent poll data from the Gallup organization indicate since the 1940s American attitudes toward socialism have become much more favorable. According to a Gallup poll of US adults in 2019, although half (51%) of US adults say socialism would be bad for the country, nearly half (43%) say it would be a good thing (Younis, 2019). These sentiments contrast with a 1942 Roper/Fortune survey that showed just a quarter (25%) said socialism would be a good thing for the country and the remainder said socialism would be a bad thing for the United States (40%) or had no opinion (34%) (Younis, 2019).

Views of socialism continue to divide along political fault lines. Almost half (47%) of Democrats polled by Gallup in 2018 view socialism positively (Newport, 2018). In contrast, less than one-fifth (16%) of Republicans are positive toward socialism. Meanwhile, the portion of Democrats who view capitalism positively has declined from over half (56%) in 2016 to less than half (47%) in 2018. This contrasts with Republicans who overwhelmingly view capitalism as positive (71% in 2018; unchanged from 2010) (Newport, 2018). Views toward capitalism, communism, and socialism have long been intertwined among the American public.

Russia

Russia, or the Russian Federation officially, represents another important country regarding US international engagement, and one most Americans view largely in terms of its communist politics. A 2018 NBC News/Survey Monkey poll shows that the majority of Americans view Russia as unfriendly and the enemy of the United States (Bustos, 2018). Conducted July 9–15, 2018, the survey of 5,300 US adults showed that less than a quarter (23%) view the Eastern European nation as friendly and just one in twenty (5%) view Russia as "an ally to our country." Most Americans view Russia as either unfriendly (43%) or an enemy of the United States (25%).

In just a year, Americans' views of Russia have shifted notably downward. In a Gallup poll taken in 2017, more than a quarter (28%) of Americans viewed Russia favorably (Bowman, 2017). Negative views have been on the rise since the fall of the Soviet Union in 1989, when almost two-thirds (62%) of the American public viewed Russia favorably. Republicans are more apt to see Russia favorably (35%) than Democrats (16%). Bowman (2018) attributes these patterns largely to Trump's relatively favorable tweets and other pronouncements on Russia.

How Russians and Americans see each other have been largely in parallel since at least 2006, according to Pew Center Research data (Poushter, 2018). In 2006, slightly less than half of Americans (44%) and Russians (41%) viewed the other country favorably. Views improved slightly until they peaked in about 2012 with more than half (56%) of Russians and almost half (49%) of Americans viewing the other nation favorably. Views have declined among both populations since then, although slightly more Russians viewed America favorably just after the election of Trump (41%). By 2018, only a quarter (26%) of Russians) hold a favorable view of the United States and only a fifth (21%) of Americans see Russia favorably.

Americans are deeply divided with regard to the question of whether President Trump colluded with Russia on the 2016 election. A national poll shows a nearly even split in views toward allegations of collusion, an issue that contributed to an investigation under the direction of Robert Mueller, former director of the Federal Bureau of Investigation (FBI), as well as the impeachment proceedings of the US Congress. Half (49%) say they believe the Trump campaign colluded with Russia during the 2016 campaign and half (48%) say they believe the campaign did not (Kadvany, 2018). Trump himself has repeatedly denied any allegations of collusion, although adding a somewhat peculiar caveat. "There is no collusion, and even if there was, it's not a crime," Trump said in an interview in December of 2017 with the *New York Times* (Schmidt, 2017). Opinions divide along demographic and regional lines as well. In Alabama and North Dakota, for instance, two very conservative, less educated, and strongly Christian and Republican states, four-fifths (78%) say they think the Trump campaign did not collude with Russia (Kadvany, 2018; Gelman, 2014; Bureau of US Census, 2019). By contrast, in more progressive, Democratic, and more educated states the vast majority believe his campaign did collude; nearly three-quarters of those in Rhode Island (72%) and almost nine in ten in Hawaii (85%) say collusion happened. Along straight political affiliation lines, less than one in ten (9%) Republicans believe collusion happened whereas almost nine in ten (86%) Democrats believe it did.

North Atlantic Treaty Organization (NATO)

Trump has repeatedly called the North Atlantic Treaty Organization (NATO) "obsolete" and criticized its member states for not meeting their financial obligations. Despite Trump's criticisms, Americans have maintained their strong supportive of NATO, which they have held since its formation in 1949. NATO was created as a mechanism to prevent Soviet and now Russian aggression against America's European allies. In February of 2017, four-fifths (80%) of the American public told Gallup pollsters they think the alliance should be maintained, with two-thirds (63%) saying our support should continue at the current level of commitment. In something of an about face, in late 2019 Trump modified his public view of NATO, blasting French President Emmanuel Macron for calling into question the leadership of NATO (noting "the brain death of NATO"), and describing Macron's statement as a "very, very nasty statement essentially to 28 countries" (Rogers & Karni, 2019).

Israel and Palestine

Among the more conflicted and contentious arenas of US global views is how Americans view Israel and Palestine, which intersect with their views toward Judaism, Islam, Christianity, and the Middle East in general. Doherty (2019) reports that "Americans have more favorable views of the Israeli and Palestinian peoples than of their governments," according to a 2019 Pew Research Center survey. "And as previous surveys on this subject have shown, there are substantial partisan differences in these attitudes." The US public overall holds favorable views of both the Israeli people; two-thirds, 64%, hold very or somewhat favorable views of the Israeli people; while less than half, 41%, hold positive views of the Israeli government. About half of the US public holds favorable views of the Palestinian people (46%) and only a fifth (105) hold such views of the Palestinian government. Republicans, the more conservative party of the United States, are far more likely than Democrats to sympathize with Israel than the Palestinians. Still, most in both parties hold favorable views of Israel's people. Three-fourths (77%) of Republicans and Republican-leaning independents hold favorable views. Meanwhile, more than half (57%) of Democrats and Democratic leaners (57%) hold favorable views toward the Palestinian government.

Islam

Data indicate American views of the world, at least regarding some countries and topics, have shifted since the election of President Donald J. Trump. This is apparent in several arenas, including American views regarding Muslims and Islam.

"In general, Americans continue to express mixed views of both Muslims and Islam. But on some measures, opinions about Muslims and Islam have become more positive in recent years," reports the Pew Research Center (2017). Americans have expressed "warmer" feelings toward Muslims than in the past. Moreover, fewer Americans say Islam is "more likely than other religions to encourage violence among its followers." A Pew survey in December 2016 showed that just under half (49%) of "Americans said Islam is not more likely than other religions to encourage violence among its followers, while 41% said it is more likely to encourage violence." This is a decrease of 9 percentage points from September 2014.

"Half of US adults say Islam is *not* part of mainstream American society" (Pew Research Center, 2017). Overall opinions about Muslims split largely along partisan lines, however. Republicans view Muslims less positively than they generally do members of other major religious groups. Meanwhile, "70% of Republicans say Islam is more likely than other religions to encourage violence, compared with 26% of Democrats who say the same." Overall, half the US public says there is a "natural conflict" between Islam and democracy (Pew Research Center, 2017).

Saudi Arabia

With a population of 33.4 million, the Kingdom of Saudi Arabia (KSA) is an Islamic nation in the Middle East on the Arabian Gulf[1] (Royal Embassy of Saudi Arabia, 2012). The United States has long viewed KSA as a strategic ally and a key source of oil, but KSA has seen its favorability among the American public steadily decline over the past several decades. A Gallup poll taken in August of 1991 showed a majority (56%) of Americans held a favor-

---

1. According to the historical documents, the region's body of water has been known as the Persian Gulf, named after the Persian Empire (present-day Iran). Since the 1960s, rivalry between Persians and Arabs, along with the growth of Arab nationalism and evolving Western political and economic interests, has prompted an increasing use of the term *Arabian Gulf* when referring to the region's body of water. https://www.strausscenter.org/hormuz/about -the-persian-arabian-gulf.html

able view of KSA. By February of 2001 that support was down to just under half (47%) of the American public. After the attacks of 9/11, support fell dramatically, to barely a quarter (27%) in February of 2002. Favorability remained relatively flat until 2017 when it peaked at nearly half (41%) in February 2017. It has since declined again to about a quarter (29%) in February 2019, after the Saudi assassination of Saudi journalist Jamal Khashoggi in October of 2018 (Coskun, 2018). Trump has often defended the KSA, despite the country's admission of guilt in the assassination of Khashoggi (Miller, 2019).

Afghanistan

Regarding Afghanistan, a Muslim-majority nation with which the United States has engaged in armed conflict since the early 2000s, American views long have been largely negative. Over the intervening two decades these views have shown a gradual decline, with the pattern continuing since Trump's election. According to an annual Gallup poll (2019a) of American views of foreign nations, in February 2002 about two-thirds (68%) of American adults said they had an unfavorable (34%) or very unfavorable (34%) view of Afghanistan. About a quarter (26%) of the US public held a favorable (22%) or very favorable (4%) view of Afghanistan in 2002. A small portion (4%) of those surveyed holds no opinion toward the nation.

Views toward Afghanistan have generally deteriorated since then, with three quarters (77%) holding unfavorable (48%) or very unfavorable (29%) views as of February 2019. Less than one fifth (19%) hold favorable (16%) or very unfavorable views (3%). A small portion (4%) of Americans still holds no opinion.

In contrast to Afghanistan, American views of India have not been in decline since the election of Trump. Instead, American views of India have remained relatively favorable in recent years. Two decades ago, Americans held a much less favorable view of India. In a March 2000 Gallup survey, less than half (47%) of Americans held a favorable view of India (Gallup, 2019a). Those views have become steadily more favorable in the intervening years. By 2010, about two-thirds (66%) of Americans viewed India favorably. By February 2016, three-quarters (75%) of Americans viewed India favorably. By February 2019, the portion was largely unchanged, though slightly lower (72%).

American views regarding China, officially the People's Republic of China, the world's most populous country with more than 1.4 billion persons, have also shifted downward since the election of Trump (Demographia, 2013). Data from 2019 indicate American views of China, a communist nation, have turned sharply negative, against the backdrop of Trump's trade war with that country (2019).

China

Since Trump initiated a trade war with China, the two countries have imposed a series of tariffs on each other. As of mid-2019, the United States had imposed taxes (i.e., tariff) on excess of $250 billion in Chinese goods, and China had imposed taxes on $110 billion worth of American goods (Wiseman, 2019). A possible new trade agreement between the countries was announced in December 2019, although whether the agreement will ultimately go into effect and whether it will affect American views of China remains to be seen.

Based on a national poll of 1,503 Americans between May 13, 2019, and June 18, 2019, Pew Research Center survey data show that Americans say economic connections between the United States and China are poor. And, amid these economic concerns, unfavorable opinions of China have "reached a 14-year high. Today, 60% of Americans have an unfavorable opinion of China, up from 47% in 2018 and at the highest level since Pew Research Center began asking the question" (Silver, Devlin, & Huang, 2019). Americans also increasingly see China as a threat. About one-fourth of Americans (24%) cite China as the nation that poses the greatest threat to the United States in the future, double the number that said so in 2007. Both China and Russia are seen by a quarter (24%) of people as the countries most threatening to the United States. The sole other nation to register concern among at least 10% (12%) of the American public is North Korea.

Cuba

Another country with whom American views have shifted downward since Trump's election is Cuba, the communist island nation located just 90 miles to the south of Florida. American views toward Cuba have markedly declined since Trump took occupation of the White House. A Gallup survey from March of 1996 showed that American attitudes toward the island nation were largely unfavorable, with just one-tenth (10%) of the adult US population seeing Cuba favorably. The portion of the US adult population that held positive views toward Cuba rose during the administration of President Barack Obama, who began working toward the normalization of relations between the two countries, which have been at odds since the 1959 revolution in Cuba. American views of Cuba peaked in favorability in February 2016 when more than half of US adults (54%) held favorable views of the communist country. Since his 2016 election, President Trump has advanced an increasingly hostile foreign policy toward Cuba, imposing new economic sanctions on that nation and other negative policies as well as many negative tweets about the country (Reuters, 2019; Sabatini, 2019). Gallup polls show that favorable American views of Cuba have begun to drop, falling to less than one-half (46%) by February of 2019 (Gallup, 2019a).

Implications of American Worldviews

American worldviews have important real-world implications and potential consequences. Echoing the views of his largely Evangelical and conservative, white nationalist base, a compelling case in point is the interconnected nature of American foreign policy toward Iran, officially the Islamic Republic of Iran, and the views of the American public toward that nation. President Trump has advanced a foreign policy agenda in the Middle East that among other things has shifted military support away from the Kurds in the battle against ISIS in Syria, and ramped up the perceived threat of Iran to the United States, and the world order, especially as an alleged sponsor of terrorism.

Iran

As the Trump administration withdrew the United States from the Iran nuclear deal and imposed increasingly heavy economic sanctions on Iran, it anticipated the Iranian public would pressure its government through mass protests in response to economic pain. Yet a series of "new surveys of the Iranian public conducted by The Center for International and Security Studies at the University of Maryland (CISSM) not only deflate this view, they show that US efforts are having the opposite effect from what is intended" (Ramsay, 2019). CISSM has conducted surveys of Iranian public opinion since 2014. In 2019, CISSM conducted surveys in May, August, and October. The surveys were conducted with 3,000 randomly selected respondents via telephone interviews administered by IranPoll, a Toronto-based organization.

Gallup polls of American views of Iran conducted regularly since 1989 show that the US public has held largely negative and unchanged views of Iran over that time. Also known as Persia, Iran represents an important force in the Middle East. Located on the Persian Gulf, Iran is a nation with a population of some 78 million, has a significant economy, and is a major source of the world's oil supply (CIA, 2007). In 1989, more than four-fifths (89%) of the American public held an unfavorable view of Iran. The portion of Americans with a negative view of Iran has been nearly constant since then, never dipping below 79% (1991, 2003, 2018), and never reaching higher than 87% (2013). In 2019, four-fifths (82%) of the US public reported holding a generally negative view of Iran, largely the same level as over the past two decades, although this is a slightly greater portion (79%) than did so in 2017 (Gallup, 2019b).

CONCLUSION

American worldviews are a complex and changing phenomenon. Survey research demonstrates that most Americans view the United States' place in the world order as important. Yet, there is a sharp political divide over what the US level of international engagement should be. Republicans generally are opposed to immigration, especially from the Global South, and have limited interest in concerted action against climate change, such as is advocated in the Paris Agreement. Democrats generally favor action against climate change, and are much more supportive of the welcoming of refugees, regardless of origin or religious affiliation. Moreover, American views diverge from much of the world with regard to the legitimacy of the use of military force to advance world order, with Americans substantially more supportive of military engagement than much of the world. Further, Republicans generally support preemptive military strikes against nations such as North Korea, whereas Democrats or Democrat-leaning Americans are much less hawkish, regardless of the conditions.

American views of specific regions and countries vary widely and diverge along partisan and other lines. In particular, US views are generally far more favorable when looking north than toward the Global South although there are exceptions such as the generally negative views held by most Americans toward Russia. Republicans tend to be stronger in support of Israel, whereas Democrats show empathy for the Palestinians as well.

The Trump effect on US public opinion is most apparent when looking at American attitudes toward the Middle East, China, and Latin America. Trump has advanced a foreign policy agenda that has posited an increased threat to the United States from Iran, China, and Latin America. Americans views of Iran have not shifted notably, having been largely negative since 1989, although they have ticked slightly more downward since Trump's taking office. Meanwhile, Americans' views of China have deteriorated greatly in recent years as Trump has advanced his trade war with that country and imposed a series of tariffs as well as frequently negative tweets. American views toward Latin America have been largely negative for the entire history of the United States, and have continued in their general negative tone under the Trump administration, with the most likely impact of the Trump presidency in this area to be the reinforcement of those views and the polarization of Republicans and Democrats/ Independents along immigration and refugee lines.

The global consequences of these American worldviews are profound. The general pattern carries substantial implications for US foreign policy, the use of military force, the nature of international trade, how the United States confronts the world's refugee crisis and climate change.

This chapter has offered a framework for understanding American views and how they may further evolve in the impeachment environment and with the approach of the 2020 presidential election and possible new leadership in Washington, D.C. The data suggest that although some patterns in American worldviews have held since the very beginnings of the American republic, others have been more fluid and shaped by US leadership, such as it were, especially that of the US president.

REFERENCES

Allen, L. (1969). The nuclear raids. In Basil Liddell Hart (Ed.), *History of the Second World War*. Volume 6 (pp. 2566–2576). Purnell.

Bowman, K. (2017). Americans' views on Russia, NATO, and foreign policy under President Trump. *Forbes*. https://www.forbes.com/sites/bowmanmarsico/2017/03/13/americans-views-on-russia-nato-and-foreign-policy-under-president-trump/

Bureau of US Census. (2019). 2013–2017 American Community Survey 5-Year Estimates. *factfinder.census.gov*. https://www.census.gov/newsroom/press-kits/2018/acs-5year.html

Bustos, S. (2018, July 18). Most Americans view Russia as US enemy, unfriendly, shows new NBC News poll. *USA Today*. https://www.usatoday.com/story/news/world/2018/07/18/poll-russia-us-enemy/794640002/

Carpenter, C., & Montgomery, A. H. (2019, June 27). Americans want their leaders to obey the laws of war new research claims that the US public doesn't care about protecting enemy civilians. It is wrong—and dangerous. *Foreign Policy* https://foreignpolicy.com/2019/06/27/americans-want-their-leaders-to-obey-the-laws-of-war/

Central Intelligence Agency (CIA). (2007). The world factbook—Iran. CIA. Retrieved 14 December 2019 from https://web.archive.org/web/20120203093100/https://www.cia.gov/library/publications/the-world-factbook/geos/ir.html

Clement, S., & Dennis, B. (2017, June 5). Post-ABC poll: Nearly 6 in 10 oppose Trump scrapping Paris agreement. *Washington Post*.

Coskun, O. (2018, October 6). Exclusive: Turkish police believe Saudi journalist Khashoggi was killed in consulate—sources. Reuters. Retrieved 13 December 2019 from https://www.reuters.com/article/us-saudi-politics-dissident/exclusive-turkish-police-believe-saudi-journalist-khashoggi-was-killed-in-consulate-sources-idUSKCN1MG0HU?il=0

Council on Foreign Relations. (2012). *Public opinion on global issues: A web-based digest of polling from around the world*. CFR. Retrieved 8 December 2019 from http://www.americans-world.org/default.cfm

Demographia. (2013). *Demographia world urban areas*, 9th ed. Retrieved 14 December 2019 from https://web.archive.org/web/20130501024602/http://demographia.com/db-worldua.pdf

Denyer, S. (2019, June 25). One third of Americans would support a preemptive nuclear strike on North Korea, researchers say. *Washington Post*. https://www.washingtonpost.com/world/one-third-of-americans-would-support-a-preemptive-nuclear-strike-on-north-korea-researchers-say/2019/06/25/25ed1314-9711-11e9-a027-c571fd3d394d_story.html

Doherty, C. (2019). A new perspective on Americans' views of Israelis and Palestinians. Pew Research Center. Retrieved 7 December 2019 from https://www.pewresearch.org/fact-tank/2019/04/24/a-new-perspective-on-americans-views-of-israelis-and-palestinians/

Egypt State Information Service (2016, March 4). Population in censuses by sex & sex ratio (1882–2006). Retrieved 13 December from http://www.sis.gov.eg/newvr/egyptinfigures/Tables/1-%20%D8%A7%D9%84%D8%B3%D9%83%D8%A7%D9%86/9.pdf

Fowler, M., Mendenica, V. E., & Cohen, C. J. (2017, December 15). Why 41 percent of white millennials voted for Trump. *Washington Post*, Retrieved 8 December 2019 from https://www.washingtonpost.com/news/monkey-cage/wp/2017/12/15/racial-resentment-is-why-41-percent-of-white-millennials-voted-for-trump-in-2016/

Gallup. (2019a). Country ratings. Gallup.com. Retrieved 13 December 2019 from https://news.gallup .com/poll/1624/Perceptions-Foreign-Countries.aspx

Gallup (2019b). Iran. Gallup.com. Retrieved 8 December 2019 from https://news.gallup.com/poll/ 116236/iran.aspx

Gelman, A. (2014). The twentieth-century reversal: How did the Republican states switch to the Democrats and vice versa? *Statistics and Public Policy*. 1: 1–5. CiteSeerX 10.1.1.309.9174.

GenForward. (2017). GenForward September 2017 toplines. GenForward.com Retrieved 8 December 2019 from http://genforwardsurvey.com/assets/uploads/2017/10/September-2017-Final-Toplines.pdf

Haworth, A. R., Sagan, S. D., & Valentino, B. A. (2019, June 24). What do Americans really think about conflict with nuclear North Korea? The answer is both reassuring and disturbing. *Bulletin of the Atomic Scientists*. Special issue: Space: Military frontier or arms control opportunity? *75*(4). Retrieved 11 December 2019 from https://tandfonline.com/doi/full/10.1080/00963402.2019.1629576

Jacobs, B. (2018, April 5). Trump defends Mexican rapists claim during conspiracy-laden speech. *The Guardian*. Retrieved 7 December 2019 from https://www.theguardian.com/us-news/2018/apr/05/ trump-mexico-caravan-voter-claims-speech-west-virginia

Kadvany, E. (2018). How Americans view Russian role in the US election. TheStacker.com. Retrieved 11 December 2019 from https://thestacker.com/stories/338/msn-polling-how-americans-view-russian -role-us-election

Kirby, J. (2018, January 11). Trump wants fewer immigrants from "shithole countries" and more from places like Norway. Vox. Retrieved 8 December 2019 from https://www.vox.com/2018/1/11/16880750/ trump-immigrants-shithole-countries-norway

Lologgia, J. (2018). Americans have mixed views of Mexico, "warmer" feelings toward Canada. Pew Research Center. Retrieved 8 December 2019 from https://www.pewresearch.org/fact-tank/2018/08/28/ americans-have-mixed-views-of-mexico-warmer-feelings-toward-canada/

Lopez, G. (2017). The past year of research has made it very clear: Trump won because of racial resentment. Vox. Retrieved 8 December 2019 from https://www.vox.com/identities/2017/12/15/16781222/ trump-racism-economic-anxiety-study

Miller, H. (2019, June 23). "Trump defends Saudi Arabia partnership despite Khashoggi killing: I'm not 'a fool.'" *HuffPost*. Retrieved 13 December 2019 from https://www.huffpost.com/entry/trump-saudi -arabia-khashoggi_n_5d0fba7de4b0aa375f4e5db2

Mooney, C. (2016, November 21). Trump wants to dump the Paris climate deal, but 71 percent of Americans support it, survey finds. *Washington Post*.

Morales, L. (2010). Americans lean against letting more Haitians into US. Gallup. Retrieved 8 December 2019 from https://news.gallup.com/poll/125372/americans-lean-against-letting-haitians.aspx

Morris, A. (2019, December 2). False Idol: Why the Christian Right worships Donald Trump. *Rolling Stone*. https://www.rollingstone.com/politics/politics-features/christian-right-worships-donald -trump-915381/

Newport, F. (2018). Democrats more positive about socialism than capitalism. Gallup.com. Retrieved 10 December 2019 from https://news.gallup.com/poll/240725/democrats-positive-socialism -capitalism.aspx

Pew Research Center. (2012). Global attitudes survey. Pew Research Center. Retrieved 8 December 2019 from https://www.pewresearch.org/global/

Pew Research Center. (2017). How the US general public views Muslims and Islam. Pew Research Center. Retrieved 13 December 2019 from https://www.pewforum.org/2017/07/26/how-the-u-s -general-public-views-muslims-and-islam/

Poushter, J. (2018). 6 charts on how Russians and Americans see each other. Pew Research Center. Retrieved 11 December 2019 from https://www.pewresearch.org/fact-tank/2018/10/04/6-charts-on -how-russians-and-americans-see-each-other/

Poushter, J., & Castillo A. (2019). Americans and Germans disagree on the state of bilateral relations, but largely align on key international issues. Pew Research Center. Retrieved 14 December 2019 from https://www.pewresearch.org/global/2019/03/04/americans-and-germans-disagree-on-the-state -of-bilateral-relations-but-largely-align-on-key-international-issues/

Ramsay, C. (2019, October 29). New surveys show Trump's Iran policy has opposite of intended effect. *Baltimore Sun.* https://www.baltimoresun.com/opinion/op-ed/bs-ed-op-1030-iran-policy-20191029 -67bxz7x5sbfavp5vfytnbwn4xq-story.html?fbclid=IwAR1LtUBCrq8ZGls3cP0073VLHAE8zyp DUH3TObo6HbKYJftDCLitG0ETj1s

Reuters. (2019, April 30). Trump threatens "full" embargo on Cuba over Venezuela policy. Reuters. Re- trieved 13 December 2019 from https://www.reuters.com/article/us-venezuela-politics-trump-tweet/ trump-threatens-full-embargo-on-cuba-over-venezuela-security-support-idUSKCN1S62PD

Rogers, K., & Karni, A. (2019, December 3). In tense exchange, Trump and Macron put forth duel- ing visions for NATO. *New York Times.* Retrieved 14 December 2019 from https://www.nytimes .com/2019/12/03/us/politics/trump-nato-summit.html

Royal Embassy of Saudi Arabia. (2012). About Saudi Arabia: Facts and figures. The Royal Embassy of Saudi Arabia, Washington, DC. Archived from the original on 17 April 2012. Retrieved 14 Decem- ber 2019 from https://web.archive.org/web/20120417231457/http://www.saudiembassy.net/about/ country-information/facts_and_figures/

Sabatini, C. (2019, July 24). Trump doubles down on failed Cuba policy. *New York Times.* https://www .nytimes.com/2019/07/24/opinion/trump-cuba-embargo-venezuela.html

Schmidt, M. S. (2017, December 28). Excerpts from Trump's interview with the *Times. New York Times.* from https://www.nytimes.com/2017/12/28/us/politics/trump-interview-excerpts.html

Schoultz, L. (1998). *Beneath the United States: A history of U.S. policy toward Latin America.* Harvard University Press.

Silver, L., Devlin, K., & Huang C. (2019). US views of China turn sharply negative amid trade ten- sions. Pew Research Center. Retrieved 13 December 2019 from https://www.pewresearch.org/ global/2019/08/13/u-s-views-of-china-turn-sharply-negative-amid-trade-tensions/

Skinner, G., & Gottfried, G. (2017, September 13). Global views on immigration and the refugee crisis. Ipsos.com. Retrieved 13 December 2019 from https://www.ipsos.com/en/global-views-immigration -and-refugee-crisis

Skinner, J. (2011, December 10). Social media and revolution: The Arab Spring and the occupy move- ment as seen through three information studies paradigms. Association for Information Systems AIS Electronic Library (AISeL): 3.

Smeltz, D., Kafura, C., & Martin K. (2016, November). Growing support in US for some climate change action. Chicago Global on Public Affairs. Retrieved 8 December 2019 from https://www .thechicagocouncil.org/sites/default/files/pos_climatechange_nov2016.pdf

Sola, K. (22 June 2016). "Brexit poll shows 80% of Americans think Britain should leave EU." *Forbes.* https://www.forbes.com/sites/katiesola/2016/06/22/brexit-poll-shows-80-of-americans-think-britain -should-leave-eu/#5e5462257433

UNHCR Refugee Agency. (2019, June 19). *Global trends report.* UNHCR. Retrieved 13 December 2019 from https://www.unhcr.org/ph/figures-at-a-glance

Wikipedia (2019). United States withdrawal from the Paris Agreement. Wikipedia.org Retrieved 8 Decem- ber 2019 from https://en.wikipedia.org/wiki/United_States_withdrawal_from_the_Paris_Agreement

Wiseman, P. (2019). Survey: Trade war dims Americans' view of China. PBS.org. Retrieved 13 Decem- ber 2019 from https://www.pbs.org/newshour/world/survey-trade-war-dims-americans-view-of-china

Wu, W. (2019, March 30). At Hanoi summit, Donald Trump asked Kim Jong-un to hand over North Korea's nuclear weapons. *South China Morning Post.* https://www.scmp.com/news/asia/east-asia/ar ticle/3003952/hanoi-summit-donald-trump-asked-kim-jong-un-hand-over-north

Younis, M. (2019). Four in 10 Americans embrace some form of socialism. Gallup.com. Retrieved 10 De- cember 2019 from https://news.gallup.com/poll/257639/four-americans-embrace-form-socialism.aspx

Zelizer, J. E. (2019, October 29). Trump needs to demilitarize his rhetoric: Anti-Semitism in the US is nothing new. Still, it's shocking to hear coded language—whatever the intention—come from the top. *Atlantic.* Retrieved 14 December 2019 from https://www.theatlantic.com/ideas/archive/2018/10/ americas-long-history-anti-semitism/574234/

THE AMERICAN CONTEXT

3

Looking for Wakanda in the 21st Century

News, Entertainment, and the Politics of Austerity

Lee Artz, Purdue University Northwest

THE TRUMP EFFECT

Since the 2016 presidential elections in the United States, national media have noted increasingly strident political debate. Fox News, the *Wall Street Journal*, and online outlets such as Breitbart applaud the firm directness of the president. Trump supporters display similar resoluteness without fully grasping geopolitical realities. For example, Public Policy Polling found that before the election 41% of Trump supporters favored bombing Agrabah, the fictional kingdom of Disney's *Aladdin* (Bitette, 2015). Meanwhile, more liberal commercial media (from the *New York Times* and CNN to the *Huffington Post*) bemoan the loss of more respectful, reasoned discussions, simultaneously editorializing against the rising incivility of public discourse. Nationally and globally, the divisive tone of recent political discourse has often been attributed to the curt, crude, and simplistic attacks by tweet and off-the-cuff remarks by US president Donald Trump. However, even cursory attention to news media reporting reveals that parallel to the hand-wringing over the loss of decorum, the liberal mainstream media, such as the *New York Times* and *Washington Post*, continue to promote US corporate interests on trade, austerity, and US interventions—from Syria and Yemen to Iran and from Nicaragua and Venezuela to Bolivia. Meanwhile, the "Trump Effect" has provided commercial US media with opportunities for increasing revenues through public distraction by the Trump spectacle while still adhering to their stable and consistent market-based, pro-US frames and ideologies.

The brusque language and unrefined remarks by Trump inform most media assessments and interfere with public knowledge and understanding. For supporters, Trump may be crude, but that very behavior expresses their visceral frustration with an unstable and unpredictable social order. Although some working-class citizens voted for Trump, and contrary to many liberal pundits, the majority were and are middle- to upper-income professionals, managers, or business owners. Two-thirds of 2016 Trump voters had some college education, 65%

earning more than $50K annually, and more than one-third earning over $100K annually (Carnes & Lupu, 2017). This upper-middle social class is threatened by loss of income security, rising inequality, attacks on their standard of living, and the fear of being pushed into the working class with a precarious, non-privileged future. People of color and immigrants provide convenient scapegoats and fodder for Trump's xenophobic outbursts. In contrast, many Trump opponents, rightly alarmed by widespread reversals on civil rights, labor rights, environmental protections, and rising inequality from attacks on the public interest have focused on Trump's erratic behavior, his racist and misogynist announcements, and his obvious narcissistic self-interest. Unfortunately, the spectacle of Trump's daily outbursts not only drives media coverage, it distracts citizens from the actual policies and practices of a tepidly supportive Democratic Congress, while overlooking or obscuring the policies and practices of previously more refined administrations, such as Bill Clinton's (1992–2000) and Barack Obama's (2008–2016). All of which contributes to increasing authoritarian-laced executive power—without the same commercial media attention that Trump has aroused.

TRUMPISM

For the future of democracy and humanity, Trump must be understood and explained beyond his personality and style. Trump represents, indeed epitomizes, contemporary political authoritarianism, cloaked with extreme nationalism. From Hungary to Brazil, authoritarian nationalism characterizes most governments that have extreme right-wing leaders (although some left-leaning governments have adopted authoritarian structures as well). Authoritarianism expresses a prominent late 20th-century trend among many presumably democratic regimes that have devolved to increased executive power. "Top-down and seemingly rudderless, authoritarian governments can exert their control seamlessly . . . streamlining the twin channels of brute force and gentle manipulation" (Matsui, 2019). Given the global expansion of neoliberalism and austerity, the quality of life and security of working classes, women, minorities, and indigenous nations are under attack. Popular resistance to privatization and austerity is growing from France and Spain, from India and China, and from Chile to Lebanon and West Virginia in the United States (Ramonet, 2020); even as right-wing nationalism is on the rise (BBC, 2019). In an attempt to stem the rise of popular social movements, transnational corporations and their representative national governments increasingly rely on coercion, repression, and police action, often centralizing power in extreme nationalist authoritarian leaders.

Authoritarianism may be defined as a political system with a centralized, strong executive that: (1) constrains legislative prerogatives and disregards laws and parliamentary resolutions; (2) expands administrative powers, including enforcing executive orders without legislative or judicial approval; and (3) increases attacks and restrictions on civil liberties, civil rights, press freedom, and the broad public interest. Each of these characteristics appear in authoritarian regimes everywhere, usually accompanied by supportive mass media (such as Fox in the United States and Hürriyet in Turkey). However, given the connection between the Trump administration, the expanding executive power within the United States, and the outsized impact that US economic, political, and military decisions have for the world, 21st-century authoritarianism globally can reasonably be termed "Trumpism"—making a distinction between the individual and the social and political relations that organize and inform a national socioeconomic order—in the historical tradition of Bonapartism that centralized authority in

Napoleon to protect the monarchy (Marx, 1996). Importantly, Trumpism was birthed both within and outside the United States long before Donald.

With the exception of environmental issues, most current US government policies and actions seamlessly continue the policies and actions of previous administrations dating back to the mid-1970s. Significantly, executive power in the United States has been incrementally growing for decades, especially in foreign affairs. Examples include "President Truman's undeclared war against North Korea; President Eisenhower's executive agreements to defend Spain; President Johnson's Gulf of Tonkin Resolution regarding Vietnam; President Nixon's secret bombing of Cambodia and assertions of executive privilege; [President Reagan's illegal contra-war in Nicaragua], President Clinton's undeclared war against Bosnia; and President Bush's countless presidential signing statements, Terrorist Surveillance Program, water-boarding and Iraq war" (Fein, 2012) and, most recently, President Obama's covert drone wars in seven nations. While some media express dismay over fake news claims, partisan social media distortions, and Trump's outrageous tweets, they have uniformly constructed fake contexts and fake history by failing to inform citizens about the actual, empirical evidence of Trump policies that are intimately connected and consistent with the authoritarian policies of previous administrations.

Obama and Executive Decision

References to the Obama administration should suffice to illustrate the continuity across administrations. Trump has authorized drone attacks in Somalia and Yemen without Congressional oversight, although numbers and casualties are unreported. Previously, President Barack Obama (2008–2016) launched 10 times more "covert" air strikes than George W. Bush. In fact, during his first year in office, Obama launched more drone attacks than Bush did during his entire presidency (Purkiss & Serle, 2017), including against six nations not at war with the United States—all as executive-only decisions. In violation of international law and the Organization of American States Charter, Trump imposed brutal sanctions on Venezuela in 2018 leading to 40,000 deaths (Weisbrot & Sachs, 2019)—continuing the illegal sanctions initiated by Obama following his 2015 and 2016 executive decree that claimed Venezuela posed a "national security threat." In 2020, Trump authorized a Pentagon proposal to use cluster bombs and land mines banned by 164 nations; in December 2016, Obama signed the National Defense Authorization Act that continued the use and development of those same anti-civilian weapons, concluding eight years of supplying 80% of the world's weapons. While Trump is blasted in some media for his draconian immigration practices, Obama had cages built for youth and deported more people than the sum of all US presidents in the 20th century (Marshall, 2016). In 2016, 80% were "moms providing for their kids, not gang members" (Young, 2017). In 2019, the Trump US Agriculture Department proposed cutting $4.5 billion from the supplemental nutrition food stamp program (which serves some 38 million) lowering benefits for 700,000 people (Fadula, 2019); in 2014, the Obama administration cut $8.7 billion from the food stamp budget, affecting 850,000 families, including millions of children (Resnikoff, 2014). And although Obama's signature Affordable Care Act (ACA) expanded health insurance to 15 million previously uninsured, the ACA primarily brought record-breaking profits to insurance companies while millions received less medical care due to increased costs (Abelson, 2011). Meanwhile, at the behest of the health industry lobby, commercial media replaced the descriptive phrase "public insurance" with the biased spin to protect "private" citizens from "government-run" insurance (NESRI, 2019). Despite the media's apparent support for Obama-era policies and some consternation with Trump's regular attacks on "fake news," Obama prosecuted more whistleblowers, journalists, and sources—more than double all previous presidents combined (Ackerman & Pilkington, 2015).

Trump tweets racist comments, whereas Obama was more eloquent—yet manifestly unimpressive in addressing racial inequality. According to the *Financial Times*, CNNMoney, and the Pew Research Center, blacks were worse off under Obama: black poverty increased to 27%, household income fell by 9%, the white-black wealth gap increased to eightfold, black unemployment increased, and wages were stagnant (Elder, 2015). This is not to argue that Trump is "better" for African Americans, but media framing contributed to an unfounded perception that Obama was racially progressive. Meanwhile, Obama gave no favors to the wider US middle class and working class: the bank bailout widely reported as $800 billion, actually reached into the trillions according to the US Special Inspector General. A conclusion published in *Forbes*, claimed that Obama's bailout program committed "American taxpayers to permanent, blind support of an ungovernable, unregulatable, hyperconcentrated new financial system that exacerbates the greed and inequality that caused the crash" (Collins, 2015). Even Obama's touted pro-environmental reputation obscures the fact that crude oil production increased by 77% during his presidency (Robertson, 2018) and, using his own executive powers, Obama fast-tracked ecologically damaging oil fracking (Center for Biological Diversity, 2016).

Obama's was only the most recent administration that foreshadowed Trump policies. President Obama "unilaterally commenced war, authorized the assassination of American citizens abroad and denied the writ of habeas corpus to detainees not accused of a crime" (Fein, 2012). Earlier, Bill Clinton (dismantled social welfare and sanctioned Iraq while 500,000 children starved), George W. Bush (unilaterally bombed and occupied Iraq, curtailed environmental regulations), Jimmy Carter (supported and financed dictators in Zaire, Guatemala, El Salvador, Nicaragua, and Indonesia), and other previous presidents constructed very similar track records regarding economic, foreign policy, immigration, health care, and other policies.

Since the 1970s, US corporations, along with most international capitalists, have advocated the privatization and commercialization of public resources and social services. Corporate influence over the elections and Congress assures government actions benefit shareholders and investors, not democracy (Gilens & Page, 2014). Since Reagan, *every* US president has advanced neoliberal policies, including austerity at home—reducing public spending on education, health care, welfare, and general social security. Trump may be distinguished by his bombast and narcissism, but his policies do not veer much from the neoliberal trajectory. Most notably his rhetoric has tapped into a general public dissatisfaction with the results of free market globalization, but his tax and trade policies leave most transnational operations unscathed. A much longer accounting would be necessary to fully contextualize the Trump years within the trajectory of recent US administrations. Significantly, Trumpism—nationalist authoritarianism—has dramatically grown internationally as pro-market governments scurry to coerce citizens resistant to austerity.

Global Trumpism

Suggestions that Trump is the inspiration for the surge of authoritarian nationalist leaders around the world also misrepresents that actual historic record. Even a cursory review of some of the most egregious reductions in democracy reveal that Trump is only the most recent instance, and certainly not the causal link. In fact, the rise of right-wing populism and authoritarian leaders indicates more about responses to the inequality of transnational capitalism than it does about the influence of one Donald Trump.

More than 20 years before Trump, Victor Orbân personified the right-wing hypernationalist rise in Hungary. Later elected prime minister in 2010, Orbân publicly promoted what he called an "illiberal state," replete with calls that fomented anti-Semitic violence, executive actions to undermine the constitution, and organized opposition to refugee immigration in Europe. Since 2012, Russian president Vladimir Putin has modeled authoritarianism for the world, regularly jailing political opponents—giving heft to Trumpist calls to "lock 'em up!" In 2013, an authoritarian outlier, military intelligence director, and coup-leader, Abdel el-Sisi abolished the constitution, tortured and jailed democratically elected parliamentary members of the Muslim Brotherhood, and now fully restricts press freedom in Egypt. (Obama provided $1.5 million in military and economic aid to Egypt in 2015; while Trump referred to Sisi as his "favorite" dictator.) After a decade as prime minister, Recep Erdoğan was elected president of Turkey in 2014. Following his election, Erdoğan, with his Justice and Development Party, moved Turkey from a parliamentary democracy to an "executive presidency," giving him broad authoritarian powers over education, infrastructure, foreign policy, media censorship, and most domestic policies. Also in 2014, Narenda Modi became prime minister of India, centralizing power in his administration, cutting health and welfare programs while inviting foreign direct investment, and promoting an extreme Hindi-nationalism, including restricting citizenship for Indian Muslims. In 2015, Andrzej Duda was elected president of Poland and proceeded to violate the constitution, veto and ignore the democratically elected parliament, and organize anti-immigration rallies and physical attacks on refugees. Six months before Trump was elected, Rodrigo Duterte became president of the Philippines in May 2016, quickly launching right-wing nationalist extrajudicial killings and declaring martial law in Mindanao province, protecting and enriching himself and allies behind unlimited "presidential immunity." These are a few precursors to Trump; none are emulators. Admittedly, given the economic and political power of the United States, as "Trumpists" each of these authoritarian, nationalist, right-wing rulers have been emboldened by the Trump presidency.

NEWS AND ENTERTAINMENT

What is the cultural ground nationally and globally that gives birth to xenophobia? Granted austerity spurs anxiety, social unrest, and resistance to neoliberal globalization, but how does such an anticipated social contradiction foment authoritarianism and polarization? Absent consent for their own inequality, masses of working-class and middle-class people must be coerced into accepting capitalist "accumulation by dispossession" (Harvey, 2004). The preferred method of social control by transnational capitalism is to win public consent, or at least acquiescence through cultural hegemony: winning the hearts and minds, so to speak. Providing reinforcing ideological norms, values, and behaviors facilitates social power. The commercial media industry is essential to that transnational political project (Artz, 2015).

A short comparison of news and entertainment tropes and themes suggests that while commercial news media framing adversely affects public understandings about contemporary authoritarianism and executive power, predominant conventions and themes of entertainment media contribute complementary narratives that help normalize those news frames. Public media literacy, such as it is, moves easily between those familiar forms and codes. Comparing news framing to mass entertainment illustrates the themes and frames that appear in both. Although many have written about infotainment (e.g., Thussu, 2008)—the prevalence of soft news emphasizing style, music, and sensational images in news reporting—the comparison offered here attends to the essential components of constructing both news and entertainment as separate processes that share techniques, components, and ideologies. This chapter undertakes to understand and explain public support for Trumpism—defined as the structures and practices of authoritarian leaders who undermine democracy while winning significant popular consent.

Framing Techniques

Media support for US foreign intervention and expanded executive authority and presidential privilege is not always blatant. Effective media framing that reinforces power relations rests more on subtlety and normative techniques (Entman, 1993, 2007). In a most recent consequential case of global conflict, the US assassination of Iranian general Qassim Suleimani (*New York Times*' spelling is used throughout) provides a representative instance of media framing that facilitates "Trumpism"—the slide to executive power absent congressional and public participation in decision-making. In one assessment, the critical media group Fairness and Accuracy in Reporting (FAIR) analyzed all the editorials in the *Washington Post* and *New York Times* from the assassination January 3 through January 7, about three dozen articles. FAIR found that these two leading "liberal" newspapers were "distinctly limited" in their opposition to the US executive killing of Suleimani (Macleod, 2020).

Commercial US media across the political spectrum united in their representations of Suleimani as evil, a terrorist, a blood-soaked monster comparable to Nazis, and other sinister features. While all gave at least muted applause to the Suleimani killing, the *New York Times* offered an especially well-crafted presentation, maintaining opposition to Trump, while accepting (and thereby legitimizing) executive privilege and increased authoritarianism. After establishing their bona fides as supporters of US military prerogatives, and executive privilege, the *New York Times* editorial board wrote that the real question is "not whether it was justified, but whether it was wise" (Editorial, 2020a). The same editorial wrote that Suleimani was "indisputably an enemy of the American people . . . responsible for the deaths of hundreds of Americans"—an assertion also repeated across all commercial media—based on a questionable Pentagon claim that the Improvised Explosive Devices (IED) were too sophisticated to be made in Iraq. Note that the *New York Times* further obscured the facts by referencing American "people," not troops. Following the 2003 US invasion and occupation of Iraq, many Iraqi Shia resisted. Likewise, after the US-trained and armed Iraqi army collapsed in 2014 and when ISIS was about to take Erbil and Baghdad, it was organized Iraqi Shia and Kurdish Peshmerga militias that saved the country. But to report that Suleimani "provided effective military resistance to foreign occupying forces, including ISIS" evokes a much different evaluation than he "killed hundreds of Americans."

MEDIA FRAMING TRUMPISM AND THE *NEW YORK TIMES*

Media framing, as described by Robert Entman (1993), allows media to define the event, diagnose the causes, provide evaluations, and determine appropriate, selected actions to resolve the situation as defined. Entman's outline is apparent in US commercial media framing of the assassination of Suleimani. The commercial media (including the presumed "liberal" media) defined the assassination as the US response to a pending threat, diagnosed the action as a justified attack on an enemy, evaluating the United States as moral and Suleimani/Iran as villainous, concluding that the assassination was justified, ethical, and legal, although perhaps untimely. To assure this frame, commercial media employed several primary techniques, including (1) emphasizing threats and justifications to legitimate authority and coercion against individualized or generalized evil; (2) relying on government and other privileged "expert" sources, while marginalizing citizen and alternative voices; (3) presenting evaluative descriptors and representations that identify heroes and irrational villains; and finally, (4) normalizing dominant relations without ample historical or geopolitical context.

These observations are based on a review of all the *New York Times* daily print stories directly related to the Suleimani killing for two weeks, from December 27, 2019, through January 11, 2020. From December 30, 2019, through January 11, 2020, the *New York Times* published more than 30 news articles, videos, and podcasts directly related to the January 2 drone missile killing of Suleimani. Additional articles and editorials included responses by US politicians, military experts, political scientists, and world leaders. Five representative news reports were selected for this discussion: the December 30 account of the US airstrikes on Iraqi militias (Barnes, 2019), which established the frame presented over the next two weeks; the January 2 article on the drone strike in Baghdad killing Suleimani (Crowley, Hassan, & Schmitt, 2020); the January 3 opinion piece by the *New York Times* editorial board, laying out the official position of the paper; the transcript of the January 6 "The Daily" *New York Times*' podcast of an interview with its Pentagon correspondent Helene Cooper; and a final closing summary overview by five *New York Times* correspondents evaluating the events of the week (Baker et al., 2020).

The *New York Times* was selected because it is the largest circulating press in the United States (more than five million subscribers, including digital readers), has worldwide influence, and is generally considered the "newspaper of record." Additionally, since the 2016 election, the *New York Times* has also been consistently critical of Donald Trump—although carefully avoiding criticism of "Trumpism" writ large and the expanding US administration power and executive privilege. The *New York Times* has lined up with Trumpism on foreign affairs (Stephens, 2018—Trump made "courageous decision to withdraw from nuclear deal" with Iran), on trade policies targeting China (Editorial, 2018), and on major public policies such as health care (Rosenthal & Luthra, 2018—Medicare is too costly). In other words, the *New York Times*, like other liberal commercial media, challenge Trump even while accepting Trumpism—understood as authoritarian, expanded executive power, which marginalizes Congress, the public, and public interests.

The *New York Times* coverage of the Suleimani assassination (arguably representative of US commercial media framing of global conflict) indicates credible parallels with contemporary entertainment media themes that appear in action-adventure, superhero, and fantasy films. Global action and superhero movies feature at four predominant themes: (1) danger and evil are everywhere; (2) citizens are powerless; heroes must defend them; (3) heroes are just and their violence is necessary and good; and (4) the status quo of existing power and authority are best (Artz, 2015). These themes appear in all major global blockbusters from Disney's *Star Wars* and Marvel superhero movies to Warner Bros. DC Comics franchise, as well as China Film Group's *Wolf Warriors* (2015, 2017) and Canal +/Europa Group's *Taken* (2008, 2012, 2014, and 2017 television) among others. Viewed by millions over several decades, these films seamlessly underwrite commercial media framing of global conflict based on similar themes and techniques—offering some insight into how citizens might be prompted to accept commercial media accounts favorable to Trumpism's claim of legitimate authority to justify military actions. A media entertainment culture of danger requiring heroic violence without regard to the law or civil rights in order to defend the status quo comports well with news media coverage normalizing military actions by executive-dominant regimes without legislative or public support.

Space does not permit a full appraisal, so for illustration, Disney's *Black Panther* was selected as a representative template of action-adventure, animation, and superhero blockbuster movies, including Disney's Marvel franchise. Comparing the texts of the four selected *New York Times* stories surrounding the Suleimani killing to the visual text and dialogue of Disney's *Black Panther* reveals remarkable similarities (see Table 3.1).

Table 3.1.   Comparison of Media Framing Techniques and Superhero Action Themes

Commercial Media Framing Techniques	*Global Action Adventure Themes*

1. threats and justifications
  individual, general evil threats
  legitimize coercion (attacks, invasion)
	1. danger, evil is everywhere
	  irrational villains arise repeatedly, so extreme
	    measures are needed

2. privileged and absent sources
  preferences for government, allies
  marginalize citizens and other perspective
	2. citizens are powerless, silent
	  powerful authority, hero saviors
	  citizens inept, opponents crazed

3. descriptors and representations
  identify heroes and villains
	3. narrative, visuals identify
	  just heroes, irrational villains

4. dominant social relations normalized technology and weapons glamorized	4. status quo power best for all

THE *BLACK PANTHER* AND THE WHITE HOUSE

Disney's *Black Panther*, which grossed almost $1.5 billion in global revenue, followed the standard action-adventure superhero template that has been used by Sony, Columbia, Warner, Disney, Wanda/TenCent, and Europa films such as *Spider-Man, Batman, Superman, Wonder Woman, Iron Man*, the Avengers, and X-Men, as well as more human-level narratives such as *Taken, John Wick,* or *Wolf Warriors,* among others (Artz, 2015). Established order comes under attack by irrational evil, average citizens are unable to repel or withstand the terror, specially trained operatives or superheroes respond with extra-judicial violence, evil is defeated temporarily, the status quo power is reestablished. This narrative and these themes clearly appear in *Black Panther* (2018)—previewing and corresponding to the *New York Times* news media framing of the Suleimani killing in 2020. Courtesy of the *New York Times*, and other commercial media, Disney's *Black Panther* themes complement the White House tropes. *Dangerous threats justify violent response*

The *Black Panther* (2018) movie is based on a 1966 Marvel Comic of the same title by Stan Lee. After black-market arms dealers steal vibranium, a vital technological resource of the fictional nation Wakanda, King T'Chaka is killed in a terrorist attack. His son, T'Challa returns to Wakanda and competes in ritual combat to assume the throne. Wakanda's vital resource is under threat by nefarious forces intending to wreak havoc on the world. Only Wakanda's technology and T'Challa/Black Panther's power and judicious wrath save the nation and usher in a new peaceful world order. Fight scenes between good and evil consume many minutes of the movie, reminiscent of battles against evil by Batman, Wonder Woman, Iron Man and others—even if their actions are against the law. Superhero extrajudicial actions are justified and necessary given the existential threats posed by villains. In the case of *Black Panther*, however, as royalty, T'Challa is the law—portending Donald Trump's announcement: "I am the chief law enforcement officer of the country" (Olorunnipa & Reinhart, 2020). As the *New York Times* notes: "An air of monarchical impunity has colored many of the president's actions" (Editorial, 2020b), again echoing the themes and tropes of superhero action movies.

(Note: Rather than a full description of the movie here, additional references and analyses of *Black Panther* open each of following sections on themes and framing.)

The *New York Times* offers a similar superhero action narrative of a dangerous threat justifying violent response in reporting the US assassination of Suleimani. Beginning with a recounting of the US attacks on Kataib Hezbollah in Iraq and Syria in December 2019, the *Times* framed all US actions as normal responses to unprovoked attacks. Under a headline claiming United States launched "retaliatory" strikes, Julian Barnes (2019) reiterates that the US missile attacks on five sites in Iraq and Syria was a "reprisal," "response," "retaliation," "counterattack," and "not unusual" for the United States. US airstrikes are justified by threats against US occupying forces. Barnes reports that, according to US officials and experts, dangerous Iranian proxy forces carried out 11 attacks over the previous two months, and "low-level escalation" by "unfettered proxies" have put American lives at risk. American commanders warned of a growing risk of attacks on American interests, had given "diplomatic warnings" to Iraq, but after "Iranian-proxy" Kataib Hezbollah launched rockets and killed an American contractor, the United States acted in self-defense and fired on "facilities and command posts that were used to attack American and partner forces."

The same framing justification for the US assassination of Suleimani reappears in the *New York Times* news story on January 2 (Crowley, Hassan, & Schmitt, 2020). Based solely on US official claims, the *Times* accepted that Suleimani was a dangerous threat "actively developing plans to attack American diplomats and service members . . . responsible for the deaths of hundreds of American coalition service members . . . and approved the attacks on the US Embassy in Baghdad" (Crowley, Hassan, & Schmitt, 2020). In January, the White House asserted the assassination was justified because Iranian attacks were "imminent," but its legally mandated report to Congress in mid-February directly contradicted the threat claim (Edmondson, 2020). At the time, the official pronouncement by the *New York Times* editorial board unequivocally concluded that killing Suleimani "was justified" (Editorial, 2020a)—with or without any imminent threat. Even the dislike of evil justified action by good.

In "The Daily" podcast (Young & Quester, 2020) and its summary review of "Seven Days in January" (Baker et al., 2020), the *New York Times* trumpeted the same action-adventure theme/news-framing trope: dangerous threat justified extreme violent response. Pentagon correspondent Helene Cooper asserted that "an Iranian-backed Shiite militia group killing an American contractor" prompted a US attack on the perpetrators—a "pretty measured kind of tit-for-tat response," said podcast host, Michael Barbaro. "Exactly," replied Cooper, "and we'll attack who attacked us"—the justification for airstrikes in Syria and Iraq reinforced. Later Cooper explained: Suleimani is "a very bad guy, and there's no denying that . . . he's responsible for the deaths of hundreds of American troops. That is true as well." Although Cooper considers the assassination "not something that is normally often done in broad daylight," she remembered that "Trump authorized the killing of Baghdadi that ISIS had, and he got a lot of very good and deserved credit for that." In short, threats and attacks justified a "measured"

US military response. Barbaro made it clearer for listeners: "After months of provocation and response between the United States and Iran, President Trump felt it was time for the United States to remind Iran that, at the end of the day, we are the military superpower . . . taking out a person like Suleimani is a reasonable option, given our superiority." The news summary printed January 11 presents similar justifications for the assassination, a tad more subtle, but perhaps more effectively defending executive privilege and authority. Baker et al. (2020) describe the assassination as an "audacious strike on Iran" following a "confrontation that may have actually begun by accident" when proxy forces launched rockets at Iraqi bases inadvertently killing the American contractor. Following the US airstrike that killed 25, US intelligence officials (inaccurately) reported "a worrying pattern" of proxy activity in Iraq, possibly working on "a large-scale attack" intended to drive American forces out of the Middle East—a clear danger to US corporate interests. Perhaps most telling in the *New York Times* summary is a comment by Democratic congressman Gerald Connolly, "what really came across was a sense of disdain and contempt for the legislative branch."

The "Trump Effect" appeared in the *New York Times* framing which echoed the administration assertions of threats and justifications, noting: "In the months to come, [the security establishment] expects Iran to regroup and find ways to strike back"—providing another action-adventure sequel justification for US "retaliation" in defense of goodness against villainy. And like all good superhero franchises, a return of the villain is expected: Suleimani was a "very small part of a very large organization," concluded Ali Alfoneh, from the Arab Gulf States Institute, so "few consider the crisis to be over" (Crowley et al., 2020). Like a good action-adventure movie, danger is everywhere.

Privileged Sources and Silenced Voices

In action-adventure superhero movies, kings, sultans, princesses, mayors, emperors, and other elites hold hierarchical authority. Even team superhero franchises have established authorities, like Disney/Marvel's SHIELD (Strategic Hazard Intervention Espionage Logistics Directorate) organizes the Avengers (Iron Man, Hulk, Captain America, Spiderman, others), Professor Xavier creates and organizes the X-Men, who defer to his authority. The Justice League of Superman, Batman, Wonder Woman, Flash, and others have their own collaborative league of superheroes that mostly uphold the status quo. Although some recent edgier narratives have superheroes challenging existing authorities, more often the protagonist works with legitimate government figures. In Christopher Nolan's (DC/Warner Bros.) Dark Knight *Batman* trilogy (2004, 2008, 2012), Batman works with Gotham's police commissioner to protect elite city leaders. Iron Man accepts US law and dominance. In the television show *Arrow*, Green Arrow even becomes mayor. Average citizens are largely unimportant, appear as inept in their feeble attempts to combat villains, or provide mass fodder for villainous assaults.

In the case of *Black Panther*, celebrated for featuring African American actors in lead roles, most actors are stock characters, dressed in faux-African robes and sandals, unnamed, cheering or fighting without much dialogue. The Queen, Princess, and Black Panther King are primary, along with the Killmonger antagonist, while actors playing royal guards, rival tribal leaders, and a CIA ally have ancillary roles to the royalty. The hierarchy is central to the story. Apparently, Saudi Arabian Prince Muhammed Bin Saud recognized that the *Black Panther* models Trumpism, authoritarianism, and monarchy. The Crown Prince selected *Black Panther* as the first ever movie shown in a public cinema in Riyadh. Unconstrained hierarchy as entertainment was palatable to the feudal house of Saud.

Table 3.2.   Account of Quoted Sources by National Identification Referenced by *New York Times*, in the Four News Stories Considered

		Nationalities of Quoted Source					
		US	EU	Iraqi	Irani	Saudi	Israeli
New York Times	Barnes	23		3			
Article Authors	Crowley et al.	31		3	2		
	Young and Quester	28		4	2		
	Baker et al.	50	8	6	1	4	2
Totals		**132**	**8**	**16**	**5**	**4**	**2**

Whereas the elite command the bulk of camera time in action-adventure movies, government officials and experts from elite think tanks took primary place in the *New York Times*. In the four representative news stories of the *New York Times* selected for review, Trump, his administration, Pentagon officials, and US think tanks had 80% of all quotes (see Table 3.2). The *New York Times* vaunted objectivity and balance appeared as a total of five direct quotes from Iranian sources.

In these *New York Times* accounts, which relied on US administration and military authorities, assertions appeared as fact, without any independent verification. Inconvenient evidence, like the testimony of Iraq's prime minister Adel Mahdi that Suleimani was on a diplomatic mission, was reduced to a "theory" by the *New York Times* (Baker et al., 2020). Iraqi military observations that the Shiite Kataib Hezbollah was not in the Kirkuk Sunni region were not reported by the *New York Times* until more than a month later—and then with skepticism—effectively marginalizing conflicting facts while validating specious US government claims. The *Times'* podcast host, Michael Barbaro, channeled US government justifications for the assassination with the patriotic-nationalist-journalist trope of "we," and parroted, "*we* were attacked by missiles, so *we* will attack with missiles"—legitimizing and normalizing US government sources as the most valid (Young & Quester, 2020).

The authors of the January 11, 2020, *New York Times* summary report acknowledged that their account was "based on interviews with dozens of Trump administration officials, military officers, diplomats, intelligence analysts and others in the United States, Europe, and the Middle East" (Baker et al., 2020). Apparently, few interviews were requested from Iraqi or Irani sources. Given their preference for US government sources—like entertainment media's emphasis on elites—the reporters found few voices of opposition to US actions. One bit slipped through in the podcast and news roundup article. The vote by the Iraqi Parliament to expel US troops was noted almost in passing, without comment. The Iraqi Parliament's vote to expel US troops belied the *Times'* account that Iraqi protests were Iranian-led. Additionally, despite the easy availability of news from the Iraqi Parliament, the *New York Times* did not see fit to share Prime Minister Mahdi's January 5, 2020, speech. Mahdi called the US strike "a political assassination" and said Suleimani was in Iraq to "discuss de-escalating tensions between Iran and Saudis"—and according to National Public Radio, Trump had requested Iraq's help with Iran mediation—even while the United States was planning the killing (Zilber, 2020). Although many commercial media sounded the alarm about escalating tensions and wider war in the Middle East, the *New York Times* failed to report that US actions violated Iraqi sovereignty, international law (United Nations resolutions and International Criminal Court statutes), and US law (including cumulative executive orders from Reagan to Bush banning assassination). Although journalists have the reach and resources to contact Iranian politicians, scholars, and citizens, in the *New York Times*, voices of Iranians were confined to a few clips of the millions of mourners at the Suleimani funeral. Clearly, the important sources for *Times*' reporters were dozens of US officials, not Iranians, not Iraqis, nor Kurdish, Syrian, Iraqi, or Iranian citizens that didn't believe Suleimani was a "bad guy." The *New York Times* narrative marginalization of the millions of Arabs, Persians, and other Middle East peoples parallels entertainment media's marginalization of masses of citizens in favor of hierarchies—from Warner/DC's Gotham City to Disney's China and Wakanda.

Identifying Heroes and Villains

Fictional stories, especially cinematic versions, rely heavily on visuals, culturally symbolic codes, and technical framing, including camera angle, sound, visual effects, and even dialogue. A well-produced film offers clear representations of character identities and rewarded, preferred behaviors. Disney's *Black Panther* presents the hero as sleek, handsome, articulate, well-mannered, good-humored, undertaking powerful yet sympathetic actions. T'Challa loves his mother, respects women, spares the lives of foes, and commiserates about his people and global conflict. In contrast, Marvel/Disney's villain is named Killmonger, so there is no confusion about his character. Killmonger sports hair in dreadlocks—a symbol of urban toughness. He mostly scowls, speaks roughly, with distinct black urban pronunciation and vocabulary. He walks with a menace and stands with disdain. His body scars explicitly mark his killing past and he remains prone to violence, including against Wakanda women and the environment—setting fire to treasured flowers. Killmonger is the primary voice against global inequality, but because he aspires to spread violence and establish a different racial hierarchy, his outrage appears as illegitimate and dangerous. Killmonger represents what US white supremacists claim about black politics—black power is dangerous and threatens whites and democratic freedoms.

Each character's importance in the *Black Panther* narrative can be gauged by their screen time, amount of dialogue, and location in the fictional hierarchy. T'Challa, the Black Panther king, and his scientific-technology-genius princess sister, Shuri, have most of the lines and are central to the action. Shuri creates Black Panther's invincible suit and manipulates and invents other technology. Other Wakanda royalty, tribal leaders, and royal soldiers (mostly women) as well as henchmen for the arms dealer and tribal challengers have a secondary presence to reinforce the film's hierarchy and its narrative conflict between the ethical monarchy and the villains attempting to usurp traditional power and mores. Everett Ross, the CIA agent, is small, mild, and meek—a non-threatening US friend of T'Challa and Wakanda. The African American creator of Marvel's Ross, Christopher Priest, said, for the comic (and the film) to succeed, "it needed a white male at the center, and that white male had to give voice to the audience's misgivings or apprehensions or assumptions. . ." (Smith, 2018). Ross also serves to subtly position the CIA as a non-threatening force for good: fiction at its finest underwriting real-life public diplomacy.

While the *New York Times* now has video news on its website, its print version relies largely on text with complementary photos and captions to reinforce its news accounts. Headlines alert readers to the villains to be described. On December 29, 2019, Julian Barnes reports that US airstrikes "retaliated" against "Iranian-backed" forces, identified as Kataib Hezbollah in the article. Barnes (2019) reports (based solely on US pronouncements) that 11 "rocket attacks over the last two months by Iranian proxies threatened the uneasy peace" and the buildings struck by US missiles housed rockets and drones and "had been used by the group to plot attacks" (Barnes, 2019). Iran has provided weapons and other lethal aid and Hezbollah has tight ties with the Quds Force [an Iranian military division]. . . labeled a terrorist organization" by the United States, wrote Barnes. According to Barnes, Hezbollah "has also facilitated the movement of Iranian arms and logistical support across the border to Syria."

All other *New York Times* reports echoed the same assessment about the villain. In the sub-head to the lead story about the assassination Crowley et al. (2020) reported that Suleimani was the "architect of nearly every operation" by Iran, "causing the death of 100s of soldiers," the "mastermind" of destabilization in the Middle East, and was "openly mocking" President Trump while "planning attacks." In reporting that pro-Iranian militias marched on the US Embassy, the *Times'* wrote that they were "effectively imprisoning diplomats," while thousands of militia "thronged" outside, "burned the reception area, planted militia flags and scrawled graffiti on the walls" (Crowley et al., 2020). US defense secretary Mark Esper bravely stepped forward to assure citizens that Trump will take "pre-emptive action to protect American forces and American lives"—channeling Superman's "truth, justice, and the American way." Affirming these frames, the *New York Times* editorial board asserted that Suleimani was villain *par excellence*: an "architect of international terrorism . . . responsible for the deaths of hundreds of Americans" and was likely in Iraq to "plot the next move against US military and civilians" (Editorial, 2020a). "The Daily" podcast agreed that an "Iranian-backed Shiite militia group launched an attack" that killed an American contractor and Suleimani was responsible for the deaths of hundreds of Americans—a refrain (with no confirming evidence) appearing in the *New York Times* and most other media reports. Alternatively, Trump (heroically?) deserved much credit for the assassination of ISIS leader Baghdadi, according to the *Time'*s Pentagon correspondent, Helene Cooper. And "The Daily" host, Michael Barbaro almost proudly claimed that "taking out Suleimani is a reasonable option" and Trump (heroically?) "just called Iran's bluff."

Capping the crisis reporting, the *New York Times* wrap-up found that Trump's "audacious attack" will "reestablish deterrence" (Baker et al., 2020). Inserted within the multi-page assessment is a link to "Americans who lost limbs and loved ones see justice in Suleimani death." This final *Times'* account finds Trump's decision justifiable, but perhaps tactically questionable (as the Editorial Board wrote earlier). So, no standing ovation for Trump the superhero to the rescue. Yet, readers may find comfort in the hero-like confidence of CIA director Gina Haspel. Convinced that Suleimani was planning attacks, she "reassured" colleagues (and the *New York Times*) that the Iranian response would be "measured," likely an "ineffectual missile attack" (Baker et al., 2020). Like Agent Ross in *Black Panther*, Haspel's role in the *New York Times'* script is to calmly assure citizens that all will be well because legitimate authorities took action.

Normalizing the Status Quo and Executive Authority

Like Warner's DC superhero franchise, the Marvel franchise from the Avengers to X-Men, as well as most Disney animation features from *Lion King* and *Aladdin* to *Mulan*, the *Black Panther* storyline ends when the hierarchical tradition and the rightful authority is firmly in control of the status quo. Following the entertainment media norm, *Black Panther*'s Wakanda elite heroes are successful, villains vanquished, all is good and right. All is right when *Batman*'s Gotham is saved; when the lion King, *Aladdin*'s Sultan, *Mulan*'s Chinese Emperor, and *Black Panther*'s Wakanda King are returned to the throne. T'Challa defeats Killmonger and recovers his kingship. Tradition triumphs. Killmonger dies. Wakanda reaches a global agreement to share its resources for peace. The Black Panther builds a new recreation center in Oakland, California, leaving US racial inequality intact.

The *New York Times* narrative normalizes a similar real-world result. Even after asserting the Suleimani killing was justified, the *Times'* editors insisted that Trump's explanation "had better be good" (Editorial, 2020a). Or what? The editors said Congress and the American public needed the facts, but offered none of their own, despite available and ample information from multiple sources in Iraq and Iran, *Times'* reporters instead favorably framed the US government's explanation.

The *New York Times'* summary account had all the features of status quo defense, replete with supporting photos, maps, and graphics which helped normalize the military action—shifting reader's attention to the "objective" details of time, place, strategy, and technology, away from historical context, ethics, legality, democracy, and humanity. After "Trump pushed the United States and Iran to the brink of war" in an operation that "took out" Suleimani (in action movie terminology) and "led to the most perilous chapter" of the Trump regime, he was able to "keep the ensuing crisis from mushrooming out of control" (Baker et al., 2020). Ultimately, the United States returned to full control, having called Iran's "bluff" (Young & Quester, 2020). As CIA director Gina Haspel predicted, Iran fired an "ineffectual missile strike" on a US base in Iraq. In fact, Iran alerted the United States (through Swiss diplomacy) of the impending strike, troops took to shelter, no one was killed, and "that was it. That was their retribution," concluded Peter Baker and *Times'* colleagues (Baker et al., 2020).

And all returned to normal. The faux Republican-Democratic divide returned. Many Democrats excoriated US national intelligence officials for lack of transparency and deceit (the same information that the *New York Times* and other commercial media accepted as valid), while most Republicans defended executive actions as good for American safety. Subsequently, Congress passed a bill limiting executive war powers—vetoed by Trump in keeping with his executive authority under the US Constitution. As Trump tweeted on January 7, 2020: "All is well."

An authoritarian nationalist sits in the executive suite. Congress, the media, US citizens, and the world are either unaware or coerced. If we're looking for a Wakanda that normalizes inequality without citizen decision-making, this episode further exposes the intimate relations among commercial news, entertainment, and the politics of austerity.

FINDING WAKANDA IN THE POLITICS OF AUSTERITY

Commercial media accounts and dominant political communication read like a Disney movie: all is good when Wakanda returns to normal and the elite are in power. The pre-Trump "Trump Effect" in nations around the world represents the move to austerity, coercion, executive power—all of which portend the rise of authoritarian states. The "Trump Effect" also channels the consistent entertainment media conventions and concerted commercial news practices of media framing; both of which affect public discourse and political partisanship (Klein, 2020).

The parallels between news and entertainment are remarkable in their transparent underwriting of neoliberal market practices and ideology. It's almost predictable that a media culture of superhero action tropes regularly accepts favorable media framings of government military actions. While not the cause, entertainment media and commercial media framing certainly contributed to 53% US public approval of the US assassination of Suleimani (Clement &

Guskin, 2020). Commercial news media demonize enemies, justify government actions, legitimate existing government authority, and promote market socioeconomic relations. Entertainment media, especially superhero movies and action-adventure films, feature elite authority, evil protagonists, and heroic coercion in narratives that legitimate the fictional and hierarchical status quo. Both news and entertainment marginalize citizens and the public—underwriting the "Trump Effect" on civic discourse and democracy.

Increasingly news media have taken on Trump-like entertainment techniques, including spectacle, personalized drama, technological (or magical) fixes, and ahistorical contexts for good and evil. In the mix, privatization of public resources, reliance on spectacular violence, and the loss of citizen participation appear as normal and necessary for the safety and security of fictional and actual societies—politically translated as a defense of necessary austerity, market values, and social hierarchy. In short, news media accounts of dominant political communication appear like a Disney movie: all is good when Wakanda returns to normal and the transnational elite are on their thrones of wealth.

For several decades US administrations and authoritarian nationalist leaders around the world have prepared the political and cultural ground for Trump—instituting neoliberal policies of austerity by privatizing and commercializing public resources and expanding executive power and control over national and foreign policy. Entertainment media narratives fictionalized these same social relations and a status quo attached to Trumpism as normal, preferred, and reassuring. Superhero moves and action-adventure films preview and complement similar commercial news media framing of extreme, internationally illegal actions as usual, beneficial, and necessary for citizen safety. It's quite clear that Russian, Turkish, Egyptian, Filipino, Hungarian, Brazilian, (US) American, and numerous other "elected" authoritarian nationalist leaders have nurtured Trumpism, expecting the acquiescence of their cooperating liberal opponents and relying on their own national commercial media to frame authoritarian power as in the best interests of citizens.

Trumpism—the political trajectory that enables executive power to ignore, create, and enforce selected laws and policies with little or no legislative and citizen decision-making, while constraining civil liberties, including freedom of speech and press—was rising before Donald Trump. The "Trump Effect" is best understood as the nationalist populist upsurge within the United States and internationally that followed the 2016 US election of Trump as president. The "Trump Effect" can also be seen in profit-driven commercial media sensationalist coverage of "Twitter Trump" the person—with little news or information in the context of neoliberal globalization and the global tendency to authoritarian states. Focusing on Trump—as commercial media and the liberal opposition do—distracts from the larger structural constraints and tendencies, including the social and cultural consequences of transnational capitalist class activities. Major transnational corporations and their national governments support authoritarian nationalism when needed as a coercive preparation for enforcing austerity. The ongoing neoliberal attacks on public services, public resources, and democratic rights will prompt resistance and social movement protests. "In countries as diverse as Chile, Puerto Rico, Spain, France, extremely important social protests are taking place, almost all of them with the same characteristics: great participation of youth and women, and many violently repressed, as a result of the awakening of humanity" (Ramonet, 2020). Confrontations are coming.

Confrontations are coming; yet, democratic public communication and the public space for democratic consideration and debate by citizens are shrinking. Simultaneously, as part of the transnational consolidation of all industries, global entertainment media and commercial news media include themes, narratives, and actors ridiculing democracy and undermining the interests of humanity on behalf of transnational capitalists and their authoritarian nationalist governments. Four billion people worldwide have fewer assets than 26 capitalists—in a world of increasing inequality. Looking for the kingdom of Wakanda only benefits economic and social hierarchies. There is no Wakanda for democracy or civil rights.

In their aggregate, government and military officials, commercial news media, and global entertainment media present moving stories of elites against democracy. Only an informed, concerted effort of citizens organized against capitalist austerity and authoritarianism can construct a world without hierarchy and undemocratic authority. Only citizen protagonists, drawing on their own life experiences, can build a more participatory, human-centered, and non-dystopian world.

REFERENCES

Abelson, R. (2011, May 13). Health insurers making record profits as many postpone care. *New York Times.* https://www.nytimes.com/2011/05/14/business/14health.html

Ackerman, S., & Pilkington, E. (2015, March 16). Obama's war on whistleblowers leaves administration insiders unscathed. *The Guardian.* https://www.theguardian.com/us-news/2015/mar/16/whistleblowers-double-standard-obama-david-petraeus-chelsea-manning.

Artz, L. (2015). *Global entertainment: A critical introduction.* Malden, MA: Wiley-Blackwell.

Baker, P., Bergman, R., Kirkpatrick, D. D., Barnes, J. E., & Rubin, A. (2020, January 11). Seven days in January: How Trump pushed US and Iran to the brink of war. *New York Times.* https://www.nytimes.com/2020/01/11/us/politics/iran-trump.html

Barnes, J. (2019, December 30). United States attacks Iranian-backed forces in Iraq and Syria in retaliatory strikes. *New York Times.* A5.

BBC. (2019, November 13), Europe and right-wing nationalism: A country-by-country guide. *BBC News.* https://www.bbc.com/news/world-europe-36130006

Bitette, N. (2015, December 18). The Return of Jafar: Poll finds 41% of likely Trump voters want to bomb Agrabah—the fictional city from Aladdin. *New York Daily News.* https://www.nydailynews.com/news/politics/poll-finds-41-trump-voters-bomb-aladdin-city-article-1.2470693

Carnes, N., & Lupu, N. (2017, June 5). It's time to bust the myth: Most Trump voters were not working class. Washington Post. https://www.washingtonpost.com/news/monkey-cage/wp/2017/06/05/its-time-to-bust-the-myth-most-trump-voters-were-not-working-class/

Center for Biological Diversity. (2016, June 28). Obama administration permitted 1200 offshore fracks in the Gulf of Mexico. Press Release. https://www.biologicaldiversity.org/news/press_releases/2016/offshore-fracking-06-28-2016.html

Clement, S., & Guskin, E. (2020, January 28). A slim majority of American's approve of Trump's Soleimani strike. *Washington Post.* https://www.washingtonpost.com/politics/2020/01/28/trumps-strike-soleimani-garners-approval-well-concerns-about-escalation-with-iran-post-abc-poll-finds/

Collins, C. (2015, July 14). The big bank bailout. *Forbes.* https://www.forbes.com/sites/mikecollins/2015/07/14/the-big-bank-bailout/#425ab3bb2d83

Crowley, M., Hassan, F., & Schmitt. E. (2020, January 2). United States Strike in Iraq kills Qassim Suleimani, commander of Iranian Forces. *New York Times.* https://www.nytimes.com/2020/01/02/world/middleeast/qassem-soleimani-iraq-iran-attack.html

Editorial Board. (2018, December 4). You don't understand tariffs, man. *New York Times.* https://www.nytimes.com/2018/12/04/opinion/tariffs-trump-china-trade-xi.html

Editorial Board. (2020a, January 3). The game has changed. *New York Times.* https://www.nytimes.com/2020/01/03/opinion/iran-trump-suleimani.html

Editorial Board. (2020b, February 20). When Donald Trump is the law. *New York* Times: A26.

Elder, L. (2015, July 25), Under Obama, Blacks were worse off—far worse. *Black Community News*. https://blackcommunitynews.com/under-obama-blacks-are-worse-off-far-worse/

Emondson, C. (2020, February 15). Soleimani strike report cites no imminent threat. *New York Times*: A17.

Entman, R. (1993). Framing: Toward clarification of a fractured paradigm. *Journal of Communication, 43*(4): 51–58.

Entman, R. (2007). Framing bias: Media in the distribution of power. *Journal of Communication, 57*: 163–173.

Fadula, L. (2019, October 4.) Trump administration unveils more cuts to the food stamp program. *New York Times*. https://www.nytimes.com/2019/10/04/us/politics/trump-food-stamp-cuts.html

Fein, B. (2012, April 27). A history of the expansion of presidential power. *New York Times*. https://www.nytimes.com/2012/04/28/opinion/a-history-of-the-expansion-of-presidential-power.html

Gilens, M., & Page, B.I. (2014). Testing theories of American politics: Elites, interest groups, and average citizens. *Perspectives on Politics (12)*3: 564–581.

Harvey, D. (2004). The "new" imperialism: Accumulation by dispossession. *Socialist Register, 40*: 63–87.

Klein, E. (2020). *Why we're polarized*. Simon & Schuster.

Macleod, A. (2020, January 9). From resistance to assistance: Little pushback to Trump's Iran assassination. *Fairness and Accuracy in Reporting*. https://fair.org/home/from-resistance-to-assistance-little-pushback-to-trumps-iran-assassination/

Marshall, S. (2016, August 29). Obama has deported more people than any other president. *ABC News*. https://abcnews.go.com/Politics/obamas-deportation-policy-numbers/story?id=41715661

Marx, K. (1996). *The eighteenth Brumaire of Louis Napoleon*. International Publishers.

Matsui, J. (2019). Liberal derangement. *Counterpunch, 26*(5): 9.

NESRI (National Economic and Social Rights Initiative). (2019). Parroting the right: How media and polling company adoption of insurance industry spin warps democracy. NESRI. https://parrotingtheright.org/

Olorunnipa, T., & Reinhart, B. (2020, February 19). Post-impeachment, Trump declares himself "chief law enforcement officer" of America. *Washington Post*. https://www.washingtonpost.com/politics/post-impeachment-trump-declares-himself-the-chief-law-enforcement-officer-of-america/2020/02/18/b8ff49c0-5290-11ea-b119-4faabac6674f_story.html

Purkiss, J., & Serle, J. (2017, January 17). Obama's covert drone war in numbers: Ten times more strikes than Bush. *Bureau of Investigative Journalism* https://www.thebureauinvestigates.com/stories/2017-01-17/obamas-covert-drone-war-in-numbers-ten-times-more-strikes-than-bush

Ramonet, I. (2020, February 14). ACN: Ignacio Ramonet warns of inequality's impact on modern societies. *CubaNews*. https://groups.io/g/cubanews/topic/acn_ignacio_ramonet_warns_of/71324086?p=,,,20,0,0,0::recentpostdate%2Fsticky,,,20,2,0,71324086

Resnikoff, N. (2014, February 7). President Obama signs $8.7 billion food stamp cut into law. *MSNBC*. http://www.msnbc.com/msnbc/obama-signs-food-stamp-cut

Robertson, L. (2018, November 30). Obama's misleading oil boast. *FactCheck.org*. https://www.factcheck.org/2018/11/obamas-misleading-oil-boast/

Rosenthal, E., & Luthra, S. (2018, October 19). Don't get too excited about Medicare for all. *New York Times*. https://www.nytimes.com/2018/10/19/opinion/sunday/medicare-single-payer-health-care.html

Rubin, A. J. (2020, February 7). Iraqis say ISIS, not a Tehran-backed militia, may have attacked base. *New York Times*. A11.

Smith, Z. (2018, February 16). Priest on Black Panther, Pt. 2: It's Not Arrogance, it's Competence. *Newsarama.com*. https://www.newsarama.com/25506-priest-on-black-panther-pt-2.html

Stephens, B. (2018, May 8). A courageous Trump call on lousy Iran deal. *New York Times*. https://www.nytimes.com/2018/05/08/opinion/trump-courageous-iran-decision.html

Thussu, D. K. (2008). *News as entertainment: The rise of global infotainment*. Sage.

Weisbrot, M., & Sachs, J. (2019, April) Economic sanctions as collective punishment: The case of Venezuela. *Center for Economic and Policy Research.* http://cepr.net/images/stories/reports/venezuela -sanctions-2019-04.pdf

Young, A. L., & Quester, R. (Producers). (2020, January 6). The killing of General Qassim Suleimani. Transcript of "The Daily" podcast. *New York Times.* https://www.nytimes.com/2020/01/06/podcasts/ the-daily/trump-iran-soleimani.html?searchResultPosition=6&showTranscript=1

Young, E. (2017, February 7). The hard truths about Obama's deportation priorities. *Huffington Post.* https://www.huffpost.com/entry/hard-truths-about-obamas-deportation-priorities_b_58b3c9e7e4b0 658fc20f979e

Zilber, A. (2020, January 6). Iraqi prime minister says Qassem Soleimani was in Iraq to discuss "de-escalating tensions between Iran and Saudis" when he was killed. *Daily Mail Online.* https://www .dailymail.co.uk/news/article-7854971/Soleimani-Iraq-discuss-escalating-tensions-Saudis-killed-PM -says.html

AUSTRALIA

4

What's He Done Now?

Seeing the United States and Trump Through the Australian Media

Hart Cohen, Western Sydney University, Sydney
Myra Gurney, Western Sydney University, Sydney
Antonio Castillo, Western Sydney University, Sydney

INTRODUCTION

Since the 2016 US election, as across much of the world, Australian media has been fixated on the ongoing political dramas of President Donald Trump. Historically, Australia and the United States have a close relationship, forged over many years. The nations share a similar cultural heritage as former British colonies but with significant differences nuanced by Australia's long-standing links to the UK. National security has effectively been underwritten by the United States since 1942 when the Australia, New Zealand, and United States Security Treaty, or ANZUS, defense alliance was established.[1] Our central interest is in how the Australian fixation with the US president is being played out in Australian mainstream media.

Historically, Australian prime ministers have sought to cultivate favor with successive US administrations.[2] Despite these close historical, cultural, and strategic ties, a recent study by the US Studies Centre[3] noted a number of striking differences in terms of general attitudes

Acknowledgments: Our thanks to the following people who provided background for this research: Gaven Morris, Head of News ABC, journalists John Barron and Chas Licciardello, Matt Bevan and Richard Glover who all provided detailed email responses to our interview questions; our colleague Tim Dwyer from University of Sydney provided up-to-date information on the current state of the Australian media environment; and Howard Bell who kindly read over a draft of this chapter.

1. The ANZUS Treaty was formally signed in 1951 to provide security to the Pacific. The pivot toward the USA by Australia at that point in time suggests a point where Australia's traditional patron, the UK, was not focused on the Pacific.

2. Harold Holt (1966–1967) declared "all the way with LBJ" in support for Australia's deployment of troops to Vietnam and for the establishment of intelligence bases at Pine Gap and Tidbinbilla. John Howard (1996–2007) committed Australian troops to George W. Bush's Coalition of the Willing despite questions over the existence of Iraq's so-called weapons of mass destruction. In 2003, Bush dubbed Howard as a "man of steel."

3. The US Studies Centre is a research centre at the University of Sydney dedicated to analysis of American foreign policy, economics, politics, and culture. It regularly publishes reports and provides experts to media.

toward the role of government broadly and particularly in relation to social issues such as abortion, welfare, health care, and religion. Notably, the study concluded that while most Australians hold positive attitudes toward the United States generally, President Trump is remarkably unpopular (only 20% indicating they support Trump winning a second term), and in fact Australian conservative voters have more in common with Hillary Clinton than with Donald Trump (Jackman et al., 2019).

While Australian TV screens and music playlists are dominated by American culture, some aspects (such as the US obsession with gun ownership) are found to be repugnant. This ambiguity has long been a part of Australians' love-hate view of the United States. The election of Trump, however, has taken this to another level. For example, a database search of comparative numbers of Australian news articles mentioning "Trump" and "US" during the periods of 2016–2017 and 2018–2019 with articles mentioning "Obama" and "US" during the same periods in Obama's first term, indicated more than double the number of results in all categories of news publications. Media monitoring company Isentia reported that "Australian broadcast media gave roughly twice as much coverage to the US election as it did to the country's own election" (Clark, 2016). Since 2016, therefore, Australian media could be said to have developed what Sky News (Australia's version of Fox News, owned by Rupert Murdoch's News Corp) labeled a "Trump derangement syndrome" (Kenny, 2019).[4]

Similarly, Australian Broadcasting Corporation (ABC)[5] news director Gaven Morris[6] noted the tendency for Washington correspondents (not just from the ABC) to rely on Trump as a focus of their reporting. He echoed concerns (e.g., O'Neill, 2019; Glover, 2019) that "over-exhaustion" of media focus on the minutiae of US politics and on Trump in particular, tended to suck the oxygen from other significant US and international political stories, adding that he encouraged his producers to look for angles beyond the daily soap opera of the president's tweets. Reflecting on her time as ABC Washington bureau chief, Zoe Daniel (2019) observed that this is easier said than done given the unparalleled disruption of Trump via his "chaos theory approach" to policy making and politics.

The manner in which Trump's "showbiz sensibility"[7] has merged, divided, and conquered the media is also worthy of comment. Tiffen (2017) notes that "it is easy to underestimate Trump's media manipulation skills. . . . He is a practiced television performer." Trump's early engagement with American television, in the words of TV critic James Poniewozik, author of *Audience of One: Donald Trump, Television and the Fracturing of America* (2019): "has everything to do with the formation of Trump's character—his manners, his place in the commercial culture, his ability to track and manipulate popular sentiment and opinion" (cited in Bromwich, 2019).

More worrying, however, has been the emergence of Trump himself as a "species" of media (Manovich, 2007, p. 4), and from an Australian point of view, how this impacts on the discourse of our own politicians. Trump's media manipulation skills are clearly reflected in his Twitter feed, which bypasses conventional channels to speak directly to his millions of followers and in so doing establishes the age of "post-truth" in media reportage. His "alternative facts"

---

4. The Urban Dictionary defines "'Trump derangement syndrome' [as] a mental condition in which a person has been driven effectively insane due to their dislike of Donald Trump, to the point at which they will abandon all logic and reason."

5. The Australian Broadcasting Corporation (ABC) is Australia's national broadcaster, founded in 1929. It is principally funded by direct grants from the Australian government but is expressly independent of government and partisan politics. It is not to be confused with the US ABC.

6. Gaven Morris, personal communication (December 2, 2019).

7. Phrase borrowed from MSNBC's *AMJoy* program (February 10, 2020).

and declarations of news outlets who criticize him as "enemies of the people" have seriously undermined faith in both the traditional institutions of government as well as the fourth estate in the United States—a trend that can be seen to be happening in Australia (Farhall et al., 2019).

But for the purposes of this chapter, we are focused on how Trump's actions are viewed and presented through the various ideological prisms and platforms of Australian media, how they reflect Australia's relationship with the United States and impact our domestic political landscape. This chapter will provide an overview of Trump media coverage across a variety of Australian news platforms. Australian media have had to react to the many Trump/US scenarios from the Mueller investigation to the impeachment process.

Given the divisions these have generated in the United States, it is not surprising to find similar divisions in both the political classes and the media of Australia. For example, our interest was especially piqued by the pivotal parts played by two prominent Australians—former Liberal government minister Alexander Downer[8] and Wikileaks founder Julian Assange[9]—in the ongoing controversy over Russian interference in the 2016 election. Perhaps this suggests that Australian media interest in Trump and the United States peaks when either Australians themselves are caught up in the various imbroglios or if the Australian national interest is at stake. Either way, Trump has been a boon to media outlets of all political stripes in Australia as he has been in the United States and globally—another irony in the saga of the Trump presidency.

TRUMP COVERAGE IN MAINSTREAM AUSTRALIAN NEWS OUTLETS

It is important to note that Australia has an extremely concentrated media landscape, made more so by the 2018 repeal of anti-competitive laws, further reducing media ownership and diversity: *Nine Entertainment*, "a company known more for its tabloid style than independent journalism" (Dwyer & Koskie, 2019), and Rupert Murdoch's *News Corp*, now control roughly 70% of daily circulation, and *Fairfax Media*, Australia's second largest newspaper company, owned now by *Nine Entertainment*, roughly 20%.

As elsewhere, Australians are increasingly sourcing their news online, with research indicating that online (including social) news consumption sits at 82% (Dwyer & Koskie, 2019). Further, the Reuters Digital News Survey (2018) reported that *ABC News Online* along with *News.com.au* were the highest sources of online news (26%) further noting that in 2018, 58% of news consumers were using their smartphones to access news. This platform shift has significantly impacted the revenue streams of traditional news organizations as well as the style, formats, and approach taken by these outlets.

Despite these challenges, the major news outlets in Australia remain powerful agenda setters and "for all their cutbacks in journalistic capacity, it is still the newspapers that inject the [newest] material into the 24/7 news cycle" (Muller, 2017). What follows is an overview of news coverage in a sample of these outlets with a view to identifying their focus, approach, and stance on the president since 2016.

---

8. Alexander Downer was a former minister for foreign affairs and high commissioner to the UK. His report to the Australian Department of Foreign Affairs (DFAT) on a meeting with Trump aid George Papadopoulos in May 2016 initiated what became the Mueller inquiry into Russian interference in the 2016 election (LaFraniere, Mazzetti, & Apuzzo, 2017).

9. Julian Assange (currently in jail in the Britain awaiting possible extradition to the United States) has been accused of acting as a conduit between Russia and the Trump campaign to undermine Hillary Clinton by publishing hacked emails from the DNP server (Mazzetti & Barnes, 2019).

News Corp: *The Australian*

The Australian is Australia's only remaining nationally distributed newspaper and is owned by Rupert Murdoch's News Corp, a conservative right-wing news organization with a significant political, economic, and cultural influence in Australia. It is home of some of the most influential right-wing journalists and commentators, and according to the *New York Times* (Chozick, 2017), Murdoch and Trump have been in regular contact since Trump's inauguration, Fox News being the president's preferred cable news outlet.

Traditionally Murdoch publications have had conservative or center-right leanings but in recent years they have been accused by various commentators (Muller, 2017; Simons, 2014), as well as by former employees (Alcorn, 2019; Meade, 2019), of deliberately fomenting political partisanship and a right-wing agenda on issues such as climate change and immigration. It has been suggested that this has impacted on a decline in readership (and profit) in comparison with the more balanced approach by media competitors (Meyer, 2020).

Generally speaking, the *Australian* reports Trump favorably. Influential opinion writers including Greg Sheridan, Dennis Shanahan, and Cameron Stewart in particular construct Trump as positive to the interests of Australia. Sheridan, who is foreign editor, described himself as initially a "never-Trumper"[10] and no fan of the way Trump conducts himself. In terms of foreign policy, he noted early on that Trump "seems absolutely allergic to complexity."[11] More recently, however, he has "made his peace" with the president[12] and now is arguably a vocal Trump booster, describing him as "a master of political strategic communication."[13] The 2019 assassination of ISIS leader Abu Bakr Al-Baghdadi for instance, Sheridan described as a political victory for the US president.[14] Sheridan believes that Trump is almost unbeatable at the 2020 election due to his strong economic credentials and his moves to control immigration.[15] Always the ideological warrior, writing about the Trump impeachment, Sheridan (October 31, 2019) railed against the Democrats, accusing them of cynically "trashing the Constitution": "This impeachment is one of the most contemptible acts in modern American politics and illustrates the growing determination among parties of the left around the western world to try to outflank, frustrate and deny democracy."

Dennis Shanahan is Canberra bureau chief and his pieces focus on Trump through the prism of Australian politics. Trump, he argues, is good for Australian business in particular and the US stand on China is overdue.[16] During the Australian prime minister's September 2019 state visit, Scott Morrison's obsequiousness was celebrated as "victorious" and a "triumph"[17] while his local political critics were derided as "desperate." This was in contrast with pundits elsewhere who warned Morrison of the danger of being "sucked into Trump's orbit."[18]

Finally, Washington correspondent Cameron Stewart is more measured in his reporting. While he is not uncritical of Trump, labeling him a populist and nationalist and a danger to

---

10. ABC Q&A panel discussion (November 27, 2019).
11. "Trump's Mid-East retreat raises the threat of war" (October 31, 2019).
12. ABC Q&A panel discussion.
13. "Trump's Mid-East retreat raises the threat of war" (October 31, 2019).
14. "Death of ISIS leader a triumph, but savage ideology outlasts him" (October 29, 2019).
15. "All hail the chief" (February 8, 2020).
16. "New world order needed for China, Morrison warns" (September 24, 2019)
17. "Bid to undermine Morrison's US triumph shows leader's desperation" (September 25, 2019).
18. "Scott Morrison sucked into Donald Trump's orbit as the president takes the prime minister hostage" (September 29, 2019).

global liberalism,[19] his reports are notable for their framing of Trump's narratives via the use of strong adjectives and adverbs ("forceful," "savage criticism," "powerful warning").[20]

Nine Entertainment Newspapers

The former Fairfax Media mastheads make up the bulk of those now owned by Nine Entertainment and constitute News Corp's most serious traditional competitor in terms of coverage and ability to influence the daily news agenda. Unlike the News Corp publications, which are more unapologetically right leaning, the Nine Entertainment newspapers, the *Sydney Morning Herald*, the *Age, and* the *Australian Financial Review (AFR)* are more balanced and tend to publish a wider range of views.

Reviewing their extensive Trump coverage, several consistent themes emerge. Recurring narrative motifs include "chaos," "erratic," and "norm shattering" even among those correspondents with conservative leanings such as former ABC and now Nine News political correspondent Chris Uhlmann and former Liberal Party leader John Hewson. Both are consistently critical of Trump's style and approach and express concern about the longer-term impact on Australia, on conservative politics, and on geopolitics in general.[21] From this perspective, political and international editor Peter Hartcher noted that "the conservative movement more broadly . . . has moved to a new rejectionism"[22] with a president whose aggressive tweeting is indication of his willingness to "throw tradition to the wind."[23]

This is particularly relevant to both US foreign and economic policy and the manner in which the president has sidestepped diplomatic convention in dealing with foreign leaders and traditional allies. Trump made headlines early in his term when his 2017 "combative" phone call with then Australian prime minister Malcolm Turnbull was leaked by the *Washington Post*.[24] In response, national affairs editor Mark Kenny described the president as "the Mad King: volatile, vainglorious, and untrustworthy," warning other world leaders that "Trump's conversations are not private and his word, unreliable."[25] Since then, the theme has continued with respect to Australia's close strategic ties with the United States and in particular the impact on China, our largest trading partner, with many calling for a more nuanced approach to defense and foreign policy. After the US/North Korea summit, prominent Fairfax journalist Peter Hartcher warned that "US allies cannot leave their futures in America's hands. That includes Australia."[26] In the wake of the US withdrawal of troops from Syria in October 2019, the headline in a piece by the *Australian Financial Review*'s Phillip Coorey warned "Careful, Trump may betray you too."[27] Even Joe Hockey, former federal treasurer, US ambassador, and purported "Trump whisperer" and golfing buddy, commented on his time in Washington observing that "the diplomatic rule book was thrown on the funeral pyre the day of the 2016

---

19. "Trudeau's second chance" (October 24, 2019).
20. "Era of globalism doomed, says Trump" (September 26, 2019).
21. "Time for a dose of Vladimir Putin's realism in Australia" (July 3, 2019).
22. "How conservatives stole the Liberal Party" (February 2, 2019).
23. "Emergency declaration a shattering step, even for Trump" (February 15, 2019).
24. *Washington Post* (February 22, 2018) published a leaked transcript of the phone call writing that "On his eighth day in office, President Trump blasted and badgered Australia's leader over an immigration dispute, telling Prime Minister Malcolm Turnbull, 'this is the most unpleasant call,' before abruptly hanging up on the head of one of America's staunchest allies."
25. "Malcolm Turnbull's approach vindicated by President Trump's madness" (February 2, 2017).
26. "Australia forced to confront a scary subject—its military vulnerability" (July 2, 2019).
27. October 10, 2019.

election."[28] While mostly positive about Trump, he warned that "values that made America great are under pressure and no-one should take the US alliance for granted."[29]

The financial press has also devoted considerable column inches to Trump's economic policies, in particular his isolationist trade approach, his obsessions with "America first" and trade surpluses, and his trade war with China. Senior business columnist at Fairfax Media Stephen Bartholomeusz regularly critiques the president's economic strategies, commenting on the erratic nature of Trump's policies and his illogical take on issues like tariffs and rate cuts and his interference in the actions of the Federal Reserve.[30] He notes the volatility created by Trump's Twitter feed and the resulting "impact on global growth, economic uncertainty and market volatility,"[31] on Australia in particular and on world trade broadly.

Finally, another regular theme of reporting relates to the impact of what is labeled "Trumpism" and the importing of "Trump style" on Australian politics and political discourse. Since the May 2019 reelection of prime minister Scott Morrison, his actions and rhetoric have been regularly derided as "Trump-lite"[32] with attacks on Australian media, his populist and obfuscating rhetoric, and general resistance to government accountability. Others have warned of the impact of importing Trump-style ideological belligerence, racist dog whistling, and denigration of bureaucrats and bureaucratic processes if they disagree or push back.[33]

Australian Broadcasting Corporation (ABC)

The third major source of mainstream media coverage of Trump is the national broadcaster, the Australian Broadcasting Corporation, or ABC. Since its founding in 1929, the ABC has been a trusted source of quality entertainment, news, and information and its Annual Report (2019, p .18) noted that it "is the market leader on third party news platforms . . . [with] No. 2 ranking among Australian online news brands." Further, an Australia Institute study concluded that the ABC is regarded as increasingly important in an age of "fake news" and social media despite regular attacks by conservative critics (Denniss, 2018).

Today, ABC journalists report across multiple platforms, and compared to other online and commercial television outlets, the national broadcaster provides the most comprehensive coverage of US politics, its varying approaches designed to appeal to a diverse range of audiences from those with a passing interest to the politics nerds. The Washington bureau provides regular updates on the nightly news of Trump rallies and election events, adding color and movement to the Trump story. Complementary pieces are posted on the ABC news website, which tellingly now corrals US political news stories separately on a page titled "Trump's America," such has been the sheer volume and extraordinary nature of Trump news since 2016. While DC bureau chief, Zoe Daniel also posted a weekly blog that provided a quirky personal perspective from Washington "ground zero" of the Trump experience.

Further, the ABC's flagship current affairs and investigative journalism program, *Four Corners* created headlines with its three-part investigative series titled *Trump/Russia: Follow the Money* (2018). Filmed across the United States, Britain, and Russia over six months by award-

---

28. "How Joe Hockey made himself into Australia's Trump-whisperer" (January 17, 2020).
29. "'Americans need to chill': Joe Hockey on what the US can learn from Australia" (October 30, 2019).
30. "Confusion reigns as the Fed cuts rates for the first time in a decade" (August 1, 2019).
31. "Trump is threatening to blow up the WTO—and potentially cause anarchy" (November 20, 2019).
32. "GetUp gets stuck in to 'populist' Morrison government" (October 16, 2019).
33. "US right-wing ideas do not all translate to Australia" (August 7, 2019).

winning journalist Sarah Ferguson, it charted the allegations, evidence, and central characters of the unfolding story of what became the Mueller inquiry.

SPECIALTY TRUMP PROGRAMS

In addition to more traditional news coverage, the Trump era has also spawned a range of niche programs. Three examples that we will discuss are produced by the ABC and aim to provide their audiences with timely and varied levels of focus and analysis into unfolding political events. *Planet America* (television), *Trump Tuesday* (radio), and *Russia, If You're Listening* (podcast) are all meticulously researched and fact-checked (as required by the ABC charter), and while their formats could be described as being couched in an entertainment trope where news and comedy intersect, they are nonetheless serious news programs. The genesis of each of these programs grew from ideas pitched by individual journalists, rather than as a result of specific ABC programming strategy.[34] Staff are provided with small budgets and freedom to experiment with format as long as they adhere to the ABC editorial guidelines of balance and impartiality. These program formats expand the reach of the national broadcaster by tapping into the various digital and social media platforms such as *Facebook*, *Twitter*, the *ABC Listen* app, and *ABC iView* streaming service.

In each case, interest has far exceeded initial expectations, particularly among younger Australians who are not the mainstream ABC audience demographic. Just as the historic nature of Obama's presidency and Hillary Clinton's candidacy stimulated interest, the convention-smashing presidency of Donald Trump has created many slightly alarmed people who tune in to find out what he's done this week. As ABC radio host Richard Glover (2019) noted with regard to his own 20-something son's sudden obsession with US politics, "America . . . has always been the most compelling miniseries in the world. But it's now Season 9."

TV Shows: *Planet America*

Planet America is a weekly TV news program that first aired in the lead up to the 2012 US elections and has grown to become one of the ABC's most watched news and current affairs shows.[35] The program title encapsulates Australia's fascination with American politics: something from another planet. What began as a live half-hour program, is now, thanks to Donald Trump, focused beyond the US election season, and in 2020 is airing two episodes per week.

The show is hosted by journalist John Barron[36] and writer and satirist Chas Licciardello, both of whom have a long interest in US politics. The format of *Planet America* could be described as a news program couched within an entertainment frame. The sophistication of production values has evolved significantly since 2012 when the hosts sat in front of a couple of American flags while today they present from behind a desk in "the Fauxval Office," a set designed to mimic the real thing.

---

34. Gaven Morris, personal communication (December 2, 2019).
35. Gaven Morris, personal communication (December 2, 2019).
36. Barron has covered US politics since 1992, published a book on the history of US primary campaigns, *Vote for Me: The Long Road to the White House* (2008), produced two documentaries on US politics, and also taught media and campaign politics at the US Studies Centre.

The show is pacey, somewhat casual in presentation style, yet in-depth.[37] The presenters are framed in contrasting styles: Barron wears a traditional suit while Licciardello dons his obligatory US campaign T-shirt.[38] There is a mix of tightly scripted analysis and commentary interspersed with lighthearted banter. There is also the "voice of Trump," John Di Domenico, who punctuates the show reading the latest Trump tweets.

The program aims to provide detail not presented elsewhere in Australia or on US cable networks. The hosts prefer to interview guests who have been personally involved in campaigns or on Capitol Hill—people who are able to offer their experiences, not just their opinions.[39] Notable interviewees have included Michael Dukakis, Howard Dean, Newt Gingrich, and Robert Shrum, while recently many of the key players from both sides of the political divide have appeared—Roger Stone, John Podesta, Sebastian Gorka, Anthony Scaramucci, Neera Tanden, and recently, Wikileaks editor-in-chief Kristinn Hrafnsson. Finally, it should be noted that compared to equivalent US shows, there is considerable effort to report and analyze contradictory facts and to interview guests from both sides: that is, it is not all "anti-Trump."

Podcast: *Russia, If You're Listening*

In recent years, Australian audiences, as elsewhere, have developed a huge appetite for podcasts, the most popular being those based on true crime stories. Podcasts allow on-demand listening through a range of digital devices and lend themselves to audiences who are increasingly consuming their media in transit and who wish to be freed from the "tyranny of live radio" (Berry, 2015). In many ways, podcasts mimic the appeal of the classic radio serials of the past.

From this perspective, it is ironic that one of the most successful recent Australian political podcasts has been *Russia, If You're Listening*, written and produced by ABC Radio National (RN) journalists Matt Bevan, Will Ockenden, and Ruby Jones. Seasons 1 and 2 (2018) focused on the characters featured in the Mueller inquiry. Season 3 (2019) explored Vladimir Putin's interest in disrupting the 2016 US election in favor of Donald Trump—the broadcast presciently preceded the publication of the whistleblower complaint central to Trump's impeachment for attempted coercion of Ukraine.[40] Episodes are relatively short (around 15–20 minutes) and have a pacey narration, quirky music, and a narrative style reminiscent of a John Le Carré spy novel. Individual episodes focus on a separate theme or character, and across the seasons, the complex backstory of Russian and UK spies, murky backroom deals, shady underworld figures, and political intrigue are unraveled in an accessible, informative, and entertaining way.

As the esoteric nature of the Trump phenomenon unfolded during 2016, and then as news related to the Mueller inquiry kept breaking in 2017, writer and narrator Matt Bevan[41] noted

37. The show is produced on a relatively small budget, with the presenters doing their own weekly research. Licciardello estimates that he can spend up to 16 hours a day ahead of the recording reading blogs, stats, and polls while Barron prefers the more traditional news outlets such as the *Washington Post* and *New York Times* (Knox, 2017). Fact checking and alternative views are an essential part of the balance of the show.

38. Licciardello never wears a T-shirt from a current campaign: he waits until the candidate drops out, so it doesn't look like he's supporting anyone. There are strict rules around foreign campaign contributions and an Australian can't buy an official Biden or Bernie shirt—so Chas gets knockoffs. Email interview (December 9, 2019).

39. Email interview (December 9, 2019).

40. The Trump-Ukraine scandal revolved around efforts by President Trump to coerce Ukraine into announcing an investigation into the son of potential 2020 Democratic Party candidate and former vice president Joe Biden.

41. Matt Bevan, email interview (December 20, 2019).

that it became increasingly difficult to fit the required background context into his allocated RN news segments. The idea of a podcast where the characters mostly speak for themselves fitted the nature of the Russia story perfectly and "hearing the actual voices of the people involved is often more powerful than just reading a transcribed quote."[42] Such has been Bevan's skill at finding audio sound bites that he has been accused several times of being a Five Eyes intelligence operative or CIA stooge.[43]

Written to provide an entry point for listeners into the Russia investigation as it unfolded, each episode is evocatively titled (e.g., S01#1 "Donald Trump: A Russian Love Affair"; S01#6 "Christopher Steele: The Spy and the Pee Tape") and focuses on key people and incidents: Carter Page, James Comey, Roger Stone, Paul Manafort, Michael Cohen, Donald Trump Jr., and Jared Kushner, to name some of the extensive cast. "Trumpdates" punctuated each season and provided just-in-time updates from the Mueller inquiry as it unfolded. Season 3 focused on Vladimir Putin and the background to Russia's spread of misinformation, of which the 2016 hacking of the DNC server was only the beginning.

A major coup of Season 2 was an interview with two of the chief protagonists in the Russia Inquiry: George Papadopoulos[44] and former high commissioner to the UK, Alexander Downer (S02 #8 "The Night at the Wine Rooms"). This became the most popular episode of this series and their contrasting accounts of the same meeting is instructive. Both have referred to this interview with Papadopoulos accusing Downer of being a "Clinton errand boy and wannabe spy" (Burke, 2019), a claim both Downer and the Australian government vehemently deny (Stewart, 2019). The series has received a number of plaudits both in Australia and overseas and has been listed as one of the best podcasts of 2018–2019 (Wells, 2019).

Radio Segment: *Trump Tuesday*

The third example of the unique Trump effect on mainstream Australian media is a dedicated weekly segment titled *Trump Tuesday*, broadcast on ABC radio Sydney's *Drive* show, hosted by veteran journalist, writer, and broadcaster, Richard Glover.[45] The segment, which lasts about eight minutes each week, updates listeners on the latest Trump news with Glover interviewing resident expert Dr. David Smith from the US Studies Centre. Post-2016 election, producers decided to expand Smith's appearances into a regular segment, which is introduced with an audio collage of Trump soundbites and the regular refrain of "What's he done now?"

In a piece for the *Washington Post*, Glover (2019) explains that his audience's ongoing fascination with Trump has far exceeded the expected use-by date of the segment. He recounts that: "[e]ach week has been more newsworthy, more attention-grabbing, more eye-widening than the last. . . . The Tuesday session is by way of a catch-up: just in case a listener was away from the radio for a moment and missed some new, outrageous plot development."

---

42. Matt Bevan, email interview (December 20, 2019).
43. The Five Eyes (FVEY) is an intelligence alliance comprising Australia, Canada, New Zealand, the United Kingdom, and the United States.
44. George Papadopoulos is a former member of the foreign policy advisory panel to Donald Trump's 2016 presidential campaign and is the first known link between the Trump campaign and Russia. In 2017, he pleaded guilty to making false statements to FBI agents about the timing and the possible significance of his contacts in 2016 in relation to Trump's presidential campaign. He has served 12 days in federal prison and at the time of writing is on supervised release. His story initially appeared in S01#4 "The Coffee Boy," a title given to him by Trump aides who dismissed his significance to the campaign.
45. Richard Glover is a popular long-term ABC broadcaster and author of numerous best-selling books. He also writes a weekly column for the *Sydney Morning Herald* as well as occasional columns explaining Australian perspectives for the *Washington Post*.

Glover's style is whimsical, quirky, and entertaining while at the same time well informed, and *Trump Tuesday* complements coverage elsewhere in the show. Glover opines to his American readers, "Explaining America to the rest of the world is now a boom industry" and that "your new president is a genius, he has single-handedly rescued American journalism." The segment is not without its critics, especially from the conservative commentariat,[46] who regularly lambast the ABC and Glover for anti-Trump bias, a criticism he rejects.[47]

CONCLUSION

As he has done in other spheres, Donald Trump has had a disruptive and polarizing effect on media broadly. Our exploration of the Australian media experience of Trump is illustrative of this polarization, as well as of the differences in perspectives that can be traced to Australia's unique history, geography, and culture. As the US Studies Centre report (Jackman et al., 2019) noted, there are many similarities as well as striking differences between the two nations, which may well give insight into the nature of Australia's media coverage:

> Australians can clearly differentiate between a president and a country. As much as Australians may dislike the current US president, most Australians hold positive evaluations of the United States and of Australia's relationship with the United States. Second, while the United States seems so familiar to many Australians, there is clearly much . . . that Australians don't appreciate. (p. 9)

The Trump story, as told through the various platforms outlined above, speaks both to the nature of his unique impact as well as to the current state of politics, political communication, and the "mediasphere" in Australia. If there is a concern to be expressed by the way the Australian media have represented Trump, it may be more because it is an epiphenomenon of a larger global trend in media reportage. It has often been said that democracy is the product of an embedded dynamic of communication and exchange. Questions arise, however, as to how this particular form of polarizing exchange, in which contemporary technology drives public discourse into permanent conflict, serves to promote or undermine democratic dialogue. In her essay "On Disruption" (2018), *Guardian* journalist Katherine Murphy observed "conflict has become the pulse and the respiration of our harried and hyperconnected lives," a commodity harnessed by cynical political actors to fire up a partisan "base" with the objective of maintaining short-term attention rather than achieving genuine long-term solutions.

We have also noted how, in reaction to the Trump phenomenon, unique forms of radio, television news, and current affairs have emerged, frequently in the form of political satire. Freud (1905/1960) sorted humor into three categories: jokes, comic, and mimetic. The idea of mimetic humor is most relevant in relation to the ABC's approach because it suggests the use of humor is in the service of a representation of the *real* and results in a de-escalation of (emotional) tension. Like other forms of humor identified by Freud, jokes tend to disguise underlying anxieties and are a form of release or escape from the pressures exerted by those anxieties. The effect is one of a *distancing*—of providing a new perspective on things. These programs remain however—as one of our sources told us—"news programs first and foremost."[48]

---

46. Conservative commentators Andrew Bolt and Gerard Henderson regularly lambast Glover, *Planet America*, and the ABC in general for what they see as an anti-Trump bias (e.g., Henderson, 2019; Bolt, 2018).
    47. Richard Glover, email interview (January 24, 2020).
    48. Gaven Morris, personal communication (December 2, 2019).

However, the other dominant form of media/reportage in Australia is the polar opposite of humor. The Murdoch press in Australia (e.g., the nationally circulated *The Australian*), for example, rarely if ever uses humor, and Freud (1905/1960) noting that not everyone was capable of formulating humor, suggests that this may be a form of maintaining and reinforcing the status quo whether that be political or emotional. The right-wing media in Australia could be seen as a harsh superego denying humor and the pleasure it elicits altogether. It may wish to reinforce a sense of foreboding or anxiety with the objective of maintaining the political status quo.

If there is anxiety in Australia relating to the long-standing defense alliance between Australia and the United States, this is one of many foreign policies influenced by Trump to have disrupted old relationships. The European Union, UK, Mexico, Canada to name a few, have also come under the Trump effect. In what now is considered "normal," these relationships would have been seen as in *crisis* in the early days of the Trump administration.

Similarly, Australian politics and Australian society have a long history of division along the lines of left and right. With a sharpening of conflict in public discourse, the retreat of media organizations to their expected tribal affiliations and the constant presence of social media interventions make polarization central to media effects and impact. Add to this, that, at any moment in the news cycle we can have available a re-tweet from DJ Trump of a deep fake representation of one of his main Democratic rivals for the upcoming election.[49] To make sense of this intervention as determinate meaning will have no purchase except as it reinforces the political views of one side or the other and in this way, simply underpins conflicting views that already exist.

The Australian media experience of Trump, therefore, is a deeply divided one. The media provides radically different coverage and the audiences experience that difference acutely. We could say the Australian media is polarizing in the way that contemporary researchers and commentators have recently indicated.[50] In this regard, the view of Australian media as mimicking US media has come full circle. The key point of this discussion that relates to our survey of Australian media's treatment of Trump and the United States is that it demonstrates an unrelenting division in Australian society. But rather than placing the media in a determinative relationship to these divisions, it may be that media *refracts* the social and political divisions already in place.

As a potential alternative media trope, the Australian public media approach in the form of the ABC does offer a somewhat different option when it provides evidence-based insights into the US political situation. It also allows for a sense of a greater perspective through its use of humor, because these insights are something that we can see from a *distance*. Though a famous Australian cliché, "the tyranny of distance" (Blainey, 1966), was meant to imply a constraint for Australia in its dealings with the world, distance may now seem like both a viable communicative strategy and a blessing when confronted with the current machinations of US politics in the world at large.

---

49. https://twitter.com/realDonaldTrump/status/1229898049746427904?cn=ZmxleGlibGVfcmVVjc18y&refsrc=email

50. In Australia and elsewhere, there are concerns that a rapid growth in polarization and populist agitation is undermining public debate and threatening previously stable societal consensus structures. This crucial new empirical evidence assesses the scale of the problem of contemporary political polarisation, and provides the basis for formulating workable approaches to addressing it. Personal communication, Axel Bruns (2019).

REFERENCES

ABC (Australian Broadcasting Corporation) (2019). *Annual report.* ABC.

Alcorn, G. (2019, May 11). Australia's Murdoch moment: Has News Corp finally gone too far? *The Guardian.* https://www.theguardian.com/media/2019/may/10/australias-murdoch-moment-has-news-corp-finally-gone-too-far

Barron, J., & Licciardello, C. (Presenters) (2019). *Planet America* [television program]. Australian Broadcasting Corporation.

Berry, R. (2015). A golden age of podcasting? Evaluating *Serial* in the context of podcast histories. *Journal of Radio & Audio Media, 22*(2), 170–178.

Bevan, M. (Presenter). (2019). *Russia, if you're listening* [audio podcast]. ABC. https://www.abc.net.au/radio/programs/russia-if-youre-listening/

Blainey, G. (1966). The tyranny of distance: How distance shaped Australian history. Sun Books.

Bolt, A. (2018, June 16). How much Trump-hate can the ABC spit out? *Andrew Bolt Blog* . https://www.heraldsun.com.au/blogs/andrew-bolt/how-much-trumphatred-can-the-abc-spit-out/news-story/e285bd695aa0de5f6b6abc2bbfb62d6a

Bromwich, D. (2019, December 5). The medium is the mistake. *New York Review of Books.* https://www.nybooks.com/articles/2019/12/05/trump-television-medium-is-the-mistake/?printpage=true

Burke, K. (2019, July 25). Alexander Downer accused of spying by US Republicans in Mueller probe. *7 News.* https://7news.com.au/politics/world-politics/alexander-downer-accused-of-spying-by-us-republicans-in-mueller-probe-c-365172

Chozick, A. (2017, December 23). Rupert Murdoch and President Trump: A friendship of convenience. *New York Times.* https://www.nytimes.com/2017/12/23/business/media/murdoch-trump-relationship.html

Clark, H. (2016, November 9). Australians' view of President Trump: Depends when you ask. *South China Morning Post.* https://www.scmp.com/week-asia/politics/article/2044437/australians-view-president-trump-depends-when-you-ask

Daniel, Z. (2019, December 13). In four years as the Washington bureau chief, I watched Donald Trump explode the limits of what a politician can get away with. *ABC News.* https://www.abc.net.au/news/2019-12-13/donald-trump-zoe-daniel-on-four-years-of-covering-us-presidency/11795688

Denniss, R. (2018, July 24). The ABC needs fixing, not "saving." The Australia Institute. https://www.tai.org.au/content/abc-needs-fixing-not-saving

Dwyer, T., & Koskie, T. (2019). Press platforms and power: Mapping out a stronger Australian media landscape. *Global Media Journal—Australia 13*(1). https://www.hca.westernsydney.edu.au/gmjau/?page_id=2

Farhall, K., Carson, A., Wright, S., Gibbons, A., & Lukamto, W. (2019). Political elites' use of fake news discourse across communications platforms. *International Journal of Communication, 13,* 23.

Ferguson, S. (Presenter). (2018). *Trump/Russia: Follow the money* [three-part series]. *ABC Four Corners.* https://www.abc.net.au/4corners/trumprussia:-follow-the-money/9840958

Freud, S. (1960). *Jokes and their relation to the unconscious.* Translated by J. Strachey. W.W. Norton. (Originally published 1905)

Glover, R. (2019, September 30). All Trump, all the time—in Australia. *Washington Post.* https://www.washingtonpost.com

Henderson, G. (2019). The US[eless] Studies Centre's Trump hater-in-chief David Smith rants again. *Media Watch Dog* (issue 463). https://thesydneyinstitute.com.au/blog/issue-463/

Jackman, S., Meers, Z., Ratcliff, S., Mondschein, J., & Brennan, E. (2019). *Public opinion in the age of Trump: The United States and Australia compared.* United States Studies Centre. https://www.ussc.edu.au/analysis/public-opinion-in-the-united-states-and-australia-compared

Kenny, C. (2019, October 1). Media is suffering from "Trump derangement syndrome." *Sky News.* https://www.skynews.com.au/details/_6090822171001

Knox, D. (2017, September 5). Chas Licciardello making *"Planet America"* great again. *TV Tonight.* https://tvtonight.com.au/2017/09/chas-licciardello-making-planet-america-great-again.html

LaFraniere, S., Mazzetti, M., & Apuzzo, M. (2017, December 30). How the Russia inquiry began: A campaign aide, drinks and talk of political dirt. *New York Times.* https://www.nytimes.com/2017/12/30/us/politics/how-fbi-russia-investigation-began-george-papadopoulos.html

Manovich, L. (2007). *Understanding hybrid media.* http://manovich.net/index.php/projects/understanding-hybrid-media/

Mazzetti, M., & Barnes, J. (2019, April 11). After arrest of Julian Assange, the Russian mysteries remain. *New York Times.* https://www.nytimes.com/2019/04/11/us/politics/julian-assange-wikileaks-russia.html

Meade, A. (2019, May 10). "Craziness has been dialled up": News Corp journalist unloads on his own paper. *The Guardian.* https://www.theguardian.com/media/2019/may/10/news-corp-rick-morton-australian

Meyer, R. (2020, February 7). News Corp hits dangerous times as profits slump. *The New Daily.* https://thenewdaily.com.au/finance/finance-news/2020/02/07/news-corp-rupert-murdoch/

Muller, D. (2017, June 19). Mixed media: How Australia's newspapers became locked in a war of left versus right. *The Conversation.* https://theconversation.com/mixed-media-how-australias-newspapers-became-locked-in-a-war-of-left-versus-right-79001

Murphy, K. (2018). *On Disruption.* Melbourne University Publishing.

O'Neill, M. (2019, January 23). How the media's fixation with Trump was exported. *The Interpreter.* https://www.lowyinstitute.org/the-interpreter/how-media-s-fixation-trump-was-exported

Poniewozik, J. (2019). Audience of one: Donald Trump, television, and the fracturing of America. Liveright Publishing Corporation.

Reuters Institute for the Study of Journalism. (2018). *Digital news report 2019.* http://www.digitalnewsreport.org/survey/2018/australia-2018/

Sheridan, G. (2019, December 19). Pelosi and co defile founding document. *The Australian.*

Simons, M. (2014, July). The decline of "The Australian." *The Monthly.* https://www.themonthly.com.au/issue/2014/june/1403486074/margaret-simons/daily-narcissist

Stewart, C. (2019, November 12). I didn't try to foil Donald Trump, says Alexander Downer. *The Australian.*

Tiffen, R. (2017, February 24). Journalism in the Trump era. *Inside Story.* https://insidestory.org.au/journalism-in-the-trump-era/

Wells, P. (2019, October 17). Dark material makes for a riveting podcast. *Sydney Morning Herald.* https://www.smh.com.au/culture/tv-and-radio/dark-material-makes-for-a-riveting-podcast-20191014-p530hp.html

CHINA

5

Comprehensive and Balanced

Unveiling the Portrayal of the United States and Trump Through the Chinese Media 2017–2019

Lizhou Sun, Southwestern University of Political Science and Law
Fei Song, Henan University of Technology

A BRIEF INTRODUCTION OF *PEOPLE'S DAILY* IN CHINA

People's Daily is the only official newspaper of China's ruling party, the Communist Party of China (CPC). It started in 1946, three years before the birth of People's Republic of China (PRC). *People's Daily* writes in simplified Chinese characters. Most CPC organizations, government offices at different levels, public universities and schools, and state-owned enterprises, are required to subscribe to *People's Daily*. It can also be found in almost all the libraries in China.

People's Daily always puts the reports on top national leaders on the front page. Therefore, Trump appears on the front page of *People's Daily* whenever he meets Chinese president Xi Jinpin or makes a phone call with him. CPC members are often required to learn the facts and views in *People's Daily*. CPC members sometimes discuss the feedback in the "political study" activities organized by their grassroots party organizations. Foreign scholars and analysts often study the articles in *People's Daily* to understand continuities and changes in China's domestic and foreign policies.

People's Daily has an online English version. However, the contents are quite different from the print version of *People's Daily* in the Chinese language (*Ren Min Ri Bao*). In the Chinese-language print version, articles about Trump are much fewer than in the online English version. For example, from Trump's inauguration day (January 20, 2017) to December 31, 2017, there were 978 articles mentioning Trump in the online version, while there were only 974 articles in total in the print Chinese-language *People's Daily*. (One article extending to two pages in *People's Daily* is counted as two articles in the *People's Daily* images and articles database, so the actual number of articles mentioning Trump is a little smaller.) Some articles are only slightly different between the Chinese-language print version and the English language online version. For example, On December 29, 2017, both the Chinese-language print version and

69

the English-language online version published the same article "Top 10 International News Stories of 2017 Selected by *People's Daily.*" In both the Chinese print and online versions, the title of the number two news story was "U.S. Withdraws from International Groups Reflects Unilateralism, while 'America First' Impacts Global Governance" (Wang & Yang, 2017). In the English online version, the title of this story was "U.S. Withdraws from Multiple International Mechanisms in Shift toward Unilateralism" (Anonymous, 2017).

In addition, *People's Daily* has an overseas Chinese language version (*Ren Min Ri Bao Hai Wai Ban*), which has different articles and mainly targets the overseas Chinese population.

One fact needs attention from readers around the world. *Global Times* is *People's Daily's* sister newspaper, which focus on international news. However, many people say that *Global Times* (both Chinese and English versions) is more nationalistic than *People's Daily*.

THE FREQUENCY OF PRESIDENT TRUMP'S APPEARANCE IN *PEOPLE'S DAILY*

The Belt and Road Initiative is one of China's most important foreign policy initiatives. "The Belt and Road Initiative has endowed the ancient Silk Road with a new meaning of the times, and is aimed to build an economic cooperation belt of peace and win-win development by means of "policy coordination, facilities connectivity, unimpeded trade, financial integration and people-to-people bond" (Wang & Wang, 2017). This ambitious initiative has already involved more than 120 countries in six continents. The success of this initiative needs the United States' cooperation in both Sino-US relations and US policies toward other countries. Therefore, *People' Daily* closely follows Trump's activities and statements.

We will look at the following period for *People's Daily's* reports and comments on Trump. There are 985 days from January 20, 2017, to October 1, 2019. The PRC had the biggest-ever military parade on October 1, 2019 (China's 70th National Day). Trump congratulated China's 70th National Day despite uneasy US-China relations in the second half of 2019.

In the 560 days from January 20, 2017 (Trump's Inauguration Day) to October 1, 2019 (the PRC's 70th birthday), there were 734 articles in the Chinese-language print version of *People's Daily* that mentioned "Trump." Therefore, the word "Trump" was mentioned in *People's Daily* an average of 1.31 times a day during this period. Among these 734 articles, "Xi Jinpin" (the name of China's current president) was mentioned in 242 articles. It shows the close personal relations between the two leaders. The number of articles with Trump in the headline is 47 from January 20, 2017, to October 1, 2019.

The key words are written with each article in the *People's Daily* Photos and Articles Database (*Ren min ri bao tu wen shu ju ku*). In this database, each *People's Daily* article has three key words. The number of articles with Trump in the key words is 71 in the same period.

We counted the numbers of articles mentioning "Trump" in each month from January 20, 2017, to October 1, 2019, as shown in Table 5.1. The highest number is 66 in the 15th month (March 20 to April 19, 2018), when Trump's trade war against China was very intensive. The lowest number is 0 in the 28th month (April 20 to May 19, 2019).

Table 5.1. Frequency of the Word "Trump" in *People's Daily*

Serial Number of the Month	Time Span	Number of Articles Mentioning Trump	Number of Articles with Trump in the Title and the Percentage	Number of Articles with Trump in the Key Words and the Percentage
1	Jan 20 to Feb 19, 2017	59	3 (5.1%)	6 (10.2%)
2	Feb 20 to March 19, 2017	34	1 (2.9%)	2 (5.9%)
3	March 20 to April 19, 2017	48	4 (8.3%)	3 (6.3%)
4	April 20 to May 19, 2017	25	1 (4.0%)	3 (12.0%)
5	May 20 to June 19, 2017	20	0 (0.0%)	2 (10.0%)
6	June 20 to July 19, 2017	32	3 (9.4%)	5 (15.6%)
7	July 20, 2017 to Aug 19, 2017	37	1 (2.7%)	5 (13.5%)
8	Aug 20 to Sep 19, 2017	20	2 (10.0%)	3 (15.0%)
9	Sep 20 to Oct 19, 2017	31	2 (6.5%)	2 (6.5%)
10	Oct 20 to Nov 19, 2017	40	11 (27.5%)	10 (25.0%)
11	Nov 20 to Dec 19, 2017	26	1 (3.9%)	1 (3.9%)
12	Dec 20, 2017 to Jan 19, 2018	35	2 (5.7%)	4 (11.4%)
13	Jan 20 to Feb 19, 2018	38	1 (2.6%)	1 (2.6%)
14	Feb 20 to March 19, 2018	23	2 (8.7%)	4 (17.4%)
15	March 20 to April 19, 2018	66	1 (1.5%)	3 (4.5%)
16	April 20 to May 19, 2018	30	2 (6.7%)	4 (13.3%)
17	May 20 to June 19, 2018	25	1 (4.0%)	2 (8.0%)
18	June 20 to July 19, 2018	24	0 (0.0%)	1 (4.2%)
19	July 20 to Aug 19, 2018	21	0 (0.0%)	0 (0.0%)
20	Aug 20 to Sept 19, 2018	5	1 (20.0%)	0 (0.0%)
21	Sept 20 to Oct 19, 2018	9	0 (0.0%)	0 (0.0%)
22	Oct 20 to Nov 19, 2018	12	2 (16.7%)	2 (16.7%)
23	Nov 20 to Dec 19, 2018	12	2 (16.7%)	1 (8.3%)

(*continued*)

Table 5.1. *Continued*

Serial Number of the Month	Time Span	Number of Articles Mentioning Trump	Number of Articles with Trump in the Title and the Percentage	Number of Articles with Trump in the Key Words and the Percentage
24	Dec 20, 2018 to Jan 19, 2019	16	1 (6.25%)	2 (12.5%)
25	Jan 20 to Feb 19, 2019	9	0 (0.0%)	0 (0.0%)
26	Feb 20 to Mar 19, 2019	3	0 (0.0%)	2 (66.7%)
27	Mar 20 to Apr 19, 2019	7	0 (0.0%)	1 (14.3%)
28	Apr 20 to May 19, 2019	0	0	0
29	May 20 to Jun 19, 2019	9	1 (11.1%)	1 (11.1%)
30	Jun 20 to July 19, 2019	9	2 (22.2%)	1 (11.1%)
31	July 20 to Aug 19, 2019	5	0 (0.0%)	0 (0.0%)
32	Aug 20 to Sep 19, 2019	5	0 (0.0%)	0 (0.0%)

In the 10th month, both the number of articles with "Trump" in the titles and the number of articles with "Trump" in the key words reached the peak. Trump and his wife paid an official visit to China in that month.

People's Daily's Comprehensive Reports on President Trump

From January 20, 2017, to October 1, 2019, *People's Daily*'s reports on Trump covered almost all the aspects and themes, as shown in Table 5.2 and Table 5.3.

Xi visited Florida in the United States and met Trump from April 6 to April 7, 2017. Therefore, there were 31 articles mentioning "Trump" from March 20 to April 19 that can be categorized as Sino-American relations, reaching the peak (Anonymous, 2017).

We divide the articles into different categories according to the main topic of each article. For example, if an article reported that the Chinese foreign ministry made a comment on Trump's Iranian policy or the European Union expressed concerns on Trump's international trade measures, that article would be categorized as US foreign policy issues. The word "Trump" also appeared in the category "Issues in other countries or regions," which has 20 articles. This phenomenon shows the United States' global influence.

The total number of articles with US domestic issues as the topic is 120, accounting for around 16.3% of all the articles mentioning "Trump" in this period. The total number of articles with US foreign policy issues (excluding U.S.-China relations) as the topic is 123, accounting for around 32.0% of all the articles mentioning "Trump" in this period. The total number of articles with Sino-American relations as the topic is 227, accounting for around

Table 5.2. Classification of Articles Mentioning Trump in *People's Daily* according to the Geographic Areas (Time span is same as Table 5.1.)

Serial Number of the Month	US Domestic Issues and Percentage	US Foreign Policy Issues (Excluding US-China Relations) and Percentage	Sino-American Relations and Percentage	Issues in Other Countries or Regions (Excluding US and China) and Percentage	China's Foreign Policy (Excluding China-US Relations), Domestic Issues and Percentage	Global Issues and Percentage
1	18 (31.6%)	13 (22.8%)	6 (10.5%)	12 (21.1%)	1 (1.8%)	7 (12.3%)
2	5 (14.7%)	8 (23.5%)	8 (23.5%)	5 (14.7%)	6 (17.6%)	2 (5.9%)
3	3 (6.4%)	6 (12.8%)	31 (66.0%)	4 (8.5%)	2 (4.3%)	1 (2.1%)
4	9 (37.5%)	5 (20.8%)	3 (20.8%)	4 (16.7%)	3 (12.5%)	0 (0.0%)
5	6 (30.0%)	6 (30.0%)	4 (20.0%)	2 (10.0%)	2 (10.0%)	0 (0.0%)
6	7 (22.6%)	4 (12.9%)	10 32.3%	6 (19.4%)	4 (12.9%)	0 (0.0%)
7	9 (24.3%)	15 (40.5%)	7 (18.9%)	4 (10.8%)	2 (5.4%)	0 (0.0%)
8	6 (30%)	4 (20%)	6 (30%)	1 (5.0%)	3 (15%)	0 (0.0%)
9	4 (12.9%)	6 (19.4%)	17 (54.8%)	1 (3.2%)	2 (6.5%)	1 (3.2%)
10	3 (7.5%)	0 (0.0%)	28 (70.0%)	2 (5.0%)	6 (15.0%)	1 (2.5%)
11	4 (15.4%)	7 (26.9%)	8 (30.8%)	1 (3.8%)	6 (23.1%)	0 (0.0%)
12	5 (14.3%)	14 40.0%	2 (5.7%)	4 (11.4%)	6 (17.1%)	4 (11.4%)
13	12 (31.6%)	11 (28.9%)	4 (10.5%)	6 (15.8%)	5 (13.2%)	0 (0.0%)
14	10 (43.4%)	4 (17.4%)	5 (21.7%)	0 (0.0%)	4 (17.4%)	0 (0.0%)
15	3 (4.5%)	31 (47.0%)	22 (33.3%)	5 (7.6%)	4 (6.1%)	1 (1.5%)
16	2 (6.7%)	14 (46.7%)	7 (23.3%)	5 (16.7%)	1 (3.3%)	1 (3.3%)
17	2 (8.0%)	14 (56.0%)	5 (20.0%)	2 (8.0%)	2 (8.0%)	0 (0.0%)
18	3 (12.5%)	12 (50%)	3 (12.5%)	3 (12.5%)	3 (12.5%)	0 (0.0%)
19	3 (14.3%)	11 (52.4%)	6 (28.6%)	1 (4.8%)	0 (0.0%)	0 (0.0%)
20	1 (20.0%)	3 (60.0%)	0 (0.0%)	0 (0.0%)	1 (20.0%)	0 (0.0%)
21	0 (0.0%)	4 (44.4%)	5 (55.5%)	0 (0.0%)	0 (0.0%)	0 (0.0%)
22	0 (0.0%)	5 (41.7%)	7 (58.3%)	0 (0.0%)	0 (0.0%)	0 (0.0%)
23	1 (8.3%)	1 (8.3%)	7 (58.3%)	0 (0.0%)	3 (25.0%)	0 (0.0%)
24	3 (18.8%)	3 (18.8%)	6 (37.5%)	0 (0.0%)	2 (12.5%)	2 (12.5%)
25	0 (0.0%)	3 (33.3%)	3 (33.3%)	3 (33.3%)	0 (0.0%)	0 (0.0%)
26	0 (0.0%)	1 (33.3%)	1 (33.3%)	0 (0.0%)	1 (33.3%)	0 (0.0%)
27	0 (0.0%)	3 (42.9%)	3 (42.9%)	0 (0.0%)	1 (14.3%)	0 (0.0%)
28	0	0	0	0	0	0
29	0 (0.0%)	4 (44.4%)	4 (44.4%)	0 (0.0%)	1 (11.1%)	0 (0.0%)
30	0 (0.0%)	3 (33.3%)	5 (55.6%)	1 (11.1%)	0 (0.0%)	0 (0.0%)
31	0 (0.0%)	1 (20.0%)	3 (60.0%)	0 (0.0%)	1 (20.0%)	0 (0.0%)
32	1 (20.0%)	0 (0.0%)	4 (80.0%)	0 (0.0%)	0 (0.0%)	0 (0.0%)

Table 5.3.   Classifications of Articles Mentioning Trump according to the Themes. (Time span is the same with Table 5.1 and Table 5.2.)

Serial Number of Months	Total Number of Articles	Politics, Diplomacy, or Law and Percentage	Economics, Trade or Finance and Percentage	War, Military, or Security and Percentage	Culture or Society and Percentage	Environment, Science or Climate and Percentage
1	59	31 (52.5%)	18 (30.5%)	8 (13.6%)	2 (33.0%)	0 (0.0%)
2	34	14 (41.2%)	13 (38.3%)	2 (5.9%)	4 (11.8%)	1 (2.9%)
3	48	32 (66.7%)	7 (14.6%)	5 (10.4%)	2 (4.2%)	2 (4.2%)
4	25	10 (40.0%)	7 (28.0%)	3 (12.0%)	4 (16.0%)	1 (4.0%)
5	20	9 (45.0%)	5 (25.0%)	1 (5.0%)	3 (15.0%)	2 (10.0%)
6	31	19 (61.3%)	6 (19.4%)	3 (9.7%)	3 (9.7%)	0 (0.0%)
7	37	15 (40.5%)	10 (27.0%)	2 (5.4%)	5 (13.5%)	5 (13.5%)
8	20	9 (45%)	4 (20%)	2 (10.0%)	3 (15.0%)	2 (10.0%)
9	31	14 (45.2%)	3 (9.7%)	6 (19.4%)	6 (19.4%)	2 (6.5%)
10	40	22 (55.0%)	9 (22.5%)	4 (10.0%)	4 (10.0%)	1 (2.5%)
11	26	13 (50.0%)	5 (19.2%)	3 (11.5%)	3 (11.5%)	2 (7.7%)
12	35	17 (48.6%)	6 (17.1%)	9 (25.7%)	1 (2.9%)	2 (5.7%)
13	38	21 (55.3%)	5 (13.2%)	9 (23.7%)	2 (5.3%)	1 (2.6%)
14	23	15 (65.2%)	2 (8.7%)	5 (21.7%)	1 (4.3%)	0 (0.0%)
15	66	8 (12.1%)	45 (68.2%)	10 (15.1%)	3 (4.5%)	0 (0.0%)
16	30	10 (33.3%)	6 (20%)	9 (30%)	5 (16.7%)	0 (0.0%)
17	25	14 (56.0%)	6 (24.0%)	4 (16.0%)	0 (0.0%)	1 (4.0%)
18	24	9 (37.5%)	4 (16.7%)	8 (33.3%)	3 (12.5%)	0 (0.0%)
19	21	5 (23.8%)	8 (38.1%)	7 (33.3%)	0 (0.0%)	1 (4.8%)
20	5	2 (40.0%)	2 (40.0%)	0 (0.0%)	0 (0.0%)	1 (20.0%)
21	9	2 (22.2%)	4 (44.4%)	3 (33.3%)	0 (0.0%)	0 (0.0%)
22	12	2 (16.7%)	1 (8.3%)	8 (66.7%)	1 (16.7%)	0 (0.0%)
23	12	9 (75.0%)	2 (16.7%)	0 (0.0%)	0 (0.0%)	1 (8.3%)
24	16	15 (93.8%)	0 (0.0%)	1 (6.3%)	0 (0.0%)	0 (0.0%)
25	9	1 (11.1%)	4 (44.4%)	4 (44.4%)	2 (22.2%)	0 (0.0%)
26	3	2 (66.6%)	1 (33.3%)	0 (0.0%)	0 (0.0%)	0 (0.0%)
27	7	1 (14.3%)	1 (14.3%)	3 (42.9%)	2 (28.6%)	0 (0.0%)
28	0	0	0	0	0	0
29	9	2 (22.2%)	4 (44.4%)	2 (22.2%)	1 (11.1%)	0 (0.0%)
30	9	5 (55.5%)	3 (33.3%)	1 (11.1%)	0 (0.0%)	0 (0.0%)
31	5	4 (80.0%)	1 (20.0%)	0 (0.0%)	0 (0.0%)	0 (0.0%)
32	5	3 (60.0%)	1 (20.0%)	1 (20.0%)	0 (0.0%)	0 (0.0%)

30.1% of all the articles mentioning "Trump" in this period. The total number of articles with issues in other countries or regions (excluding United States and China) as the topic is 70, accounting for around 9.5% of all the articles mentioning "Trump" in this period. The total number of articles with issues of China's foreign (excluding China-US relations) and domestic policy issues as the topic is also 70, accounting for around 9.5% of all the articles mentioning "Trump" in this period. The total number of articles with global issues as the topic is 20, accounting for around 2.7% in the same period.

As Table 5.3 shows, according to the themes, 337 articles are about politics, diplomacy, or law. The percentage is around 45.9%. There were 193 articles about economics, trade, or finance. The percentage is around 26.3%. Articles on war, military, or security numbered 120. The percentage is around 16.3%. There were 60 articles about culture or society. The percentage is around 8.2%. And 25 articles were about environment, science, or climate. The percentage is around 3.4%.

If development is compared to climbing a hill, China's economic development has been at the halfway point after rapid growth over the past few decades (Liang, 2017). Before our study on *People's Daily*'s reports on Trump, we assumed that the bilateral trade and investment issue between the United States and China was the major topic concerning Trump. However, the articles discussing economics, trade, or finance were only a little more than a quarter of all the articles mentioning Trump. Our strong impressions on China-US trade issues might be caused by the hot discussions and debates on these issues in China's social media, especially Weibo (similar to Facebook) and WeChat (similar to twitter).

Among the articles discussing security, some were about online or cyberspace security. When Chinese state councilor Guo Shengkun visited the United States, he had meetings with US Attorney General Jeff Sessions and Acting Secretary for Homeland Security Elaine Duke. The two sides would continue to push forward pragmatic cooperation, guaranteeing mutual benefit and promote a peaceful, safe, open, cooperative, and orderly cyberspace, Guo said (Xinhua, 2017).

The bilateral talks on cyberspace are in line with President Xi's idea (2017): "Inspired by a sense of duty to society and the people, we must step up our law-based governance of cyberspace, develop better online content, strengthen positive publicity, and work to foster a positive, healthy, upright online culture."

People's Daily's Balanced Reports and Comments on President Trump

Contrary to the common perception, in general, *People's Daily*'s reports and comments on Trump are not one-sided, but quite balanced.

Despite Trump's large-scale trade war against China and his administration's close relations with Taiwan, *People's Daily* maintains a balanced view. This position is related to the general perception of Sino-America relations of the Chinese leadership. In 2013, when President Xi met the press with President Obama, Xi said:

> Both the Chinese and American nations are great nations, and both peoples are great peoples. I believe that, with determination, confidence, patience and wisdom, the two sides will accomplish our goals as long as we keep the overall situation in mind while starting with the daily routine and making constant progress. (Xi, 2014)

As Table 5.4 demonstrates, among the 734 articles in total, 253 are positive (34.5%), 207 are neutral (28.2%), 274 are negative (37.3%). The highest percentage of positive articles is 85.0% in the 10th month (October 20 to November 19, 2017), when Xi met Trump in Florida. The highest percentage of negative articles is 83.3% in the 15th month (March 20 to April 19, 2018), when Trump announced that a massive tariff increase would be on imposed on imports from China. In addition, Chinese investments, mergers, and acquisitions would be limited. Trump made these decisions according to the 301 investigation reports released by the office of the US Trade Representative. Among the 32 months, in 14 months positive articles are more than negative articles, while in 17 months, positive articles are less than negative articles. In 6 months, neutral articles are more than either positive or negative articles.

Table 5.4. Classifications of Articles Mentioning Trump according to the Emotional Tendency. (Time span is the same with Tables 5.1–5.3.)

Serial Number of Month	Total Number of Articles	Positive Percentage	Neutral Percentage	Negative Percentage
1	59	8 (13.6%)	34 (57.6%)	17 (28.8%)
2	34	9 (26.5%)	14 (41.2%)	11 (32.3%)
3	48	37 (77.1%)	6 (12.5%)	5 (10.4%)
4	25	7 (28.0%)	13 (52.0%)	5 (20.0%)
5	20	6 (30.0%)	6 (30.0%)	8 (40.0%)
6	31	14 (45.2%)	9 (29.0%)	8 (25.8%)
7	37	6 (16.2%)	13 (35.1%)	18 (48.6%)
8	20	8 (40.0%)	3 (15.0%)	9 (45.0%)
9	31	17 (54.8%)	6 (19.4%)	8 (25.8%)
10	40	34 (85.0%)	4 (10.0%)	2 (5.0%)
11	26	12 (46.2%)	6 (23.1%)	8 (30.8%)
12	35	5 (14.3%)	9 (25.7%)	21 (60.0%)
13	38	12 (32.6%)	4 (10.5%)	22 (57.9%)
14	23	8 (34.8%)	11 (47.8%)	4 (17.4%)
15	66	3 (4.5%)	8 (12.1%)	55 (83.3%)
16	30	8 (26.7%)	6 (20.0%)	16 (53.3%)
17	25	9 (36.0%)	4 (16.0%)	12 (48.0%)
18	24	5 (20.8%)	7 (29.2%)	12 (50.0%)
19	21	0 (0.0%)	8 (29.6%)	13 (61.9%)
20	5	0 (0.0%)	2 (40.0%)	3 (60.0%)
21	9	1 (11.1%)	3 (33.3%)	5 (55.6%)
22	12	7 (58.3%)	2 (16.7%)	3 (25.0%)
23	12	9 (75.0%)	2 (16.7%)	1 (8.3%)
24	16	10 (62.5%)	4 (25.0%)	2 (12.5%)
25	9	3 (33.3%)	6 (66.7%)	0 (0.0%)
26	3	2 (66.7%)	1 (33.3%)	0 (0.0%)
27	7	4 (57.1%)	1 (14.3%)	2 (28.6%)
28	0	0	0	0
29	9	2 (22.2%)	1 (11.1%)	6 (66.7%)
30	9	2 (22.2%)	6 (66.7%)	1 (11.1%)
31	5	1 (20.0%)	2 (40.0%)	2 (40.0%)
32	5	2 (40.0%)	0 (0.0%)	3 (60.0%)

EXPLANATIONS OF "POSITIVE," "NEUTRAL," AND "NEGATIVE"

We decide that if an article uses positive words to praise Trump's decision, behavior, or talks, it is positive. For example, in the 10 important news stories in 2017, selected by *People's Daily*, Trump's meeting with Xi is ranked number five. The title of this news story is "Meeting between the Presidents of China and the United States." *People's Daily* commented that "The two countries reached multiple agreements on the development of bilateral ties during Trump's visit to China in November. The stable and healthy development of relations between the two major powers has become a wide aspiration for international society. The words "stable and healthy" are obviously positive in meaning.

If an article does not include any words to praise or blame Trump, we say it is a neutral one. For instance, the article "U.S. President Trump Announces the Change of Secretary of State" on March 14, 2018, is a neutral report (Guo, 2018). It did not make any comments on the change of personnel in this important government post.

In *People's Daily*, some articles are obviously commentary articles, which welcome or criticize Trump's actions or statements. Furthermore, in many reports, the writers showed their feelings toward Trump's actions or statements by using words that have positive or negative connotations in the contexts of China's political language. Therefore, it is not necessary to divide the articles mentioning Trump into reports and commentaries.

Since the 18th CPC Congress in November 2012, President Xi has shown clear "opposition to 'Cold War era' adversarial, zero-sum thinking and policies, 'expansionism,' 'hegemonism,' and power politics" in his speeches and writings (Swaine, 2015).

In official Chinese usage, the term *trade protectionism* is quite negative. International comments sometimes say that China is the number one driving force of free trade and globalization. China also encourages multilateralism in international cooperation and opposes unilateralism in all forms and areas. For example, in the article "Multilateralism Needed in Governance of Middle East," Zhong Sheng (a pen name representing *People's Daily*'s own voice) commented that "the US has injected huge instabilities into the complicated situation of the region with its selfish and unilateral Middle East policies" (Zhong, 2019).[1] In the article "Trade Uncertainties, Economic Recession Fears Drag Down U.S. Equities," China's Customs Tariff Commission said that "China's imposition of additional tariffs is a forced response to U.S. unilateralism and trade protectionism" (Guo, 2019).

In the recent 30-plus years, China often uses the word "hegemony" or "hegemonism" (*ba quan zhu yi*) to criticize American foreign policy. Thirty-nine articles used the word "hegemony." For example, on June 14, 2019, an article in *People's Daily* said "Regrettably, the US 'digital hegemony' is not followed by other countries" (Shi, 2019).

Therefore, in the 117 articles that include both "Trump" and "protectionism," 41 articles include both "Trump" and "unilateralism," 85 articles include both "Trump" and "trade war," and 8 articles include both "Trump" and "bully," and all are negative articles. The word "bully" has a Chinese transliteration *ba ling*. In these articles, *People's Daily* used the word "bully" to describe US policy and statements under the Trump administration. For instance, on August 6, 2018, a *People's Daily*'s editorial, "China Will Not Surrender to U.S. Threatening Tactic," stated that "The mainstream opinion is that the United States wants to use carrot-and-stick diplomacy to bully China into unilateral trade concessions, while some others hold that the hardliners in the White House overwhelm those calling for talks" (Anonymous, 2018).

In addition to the above political words, *People's Daily* also used words in conversational language, such as "selfish," "selfishness," "arrogant," and "reckless" to describe and criticize Trump. In the article "United States, Don't Underestimate China's Ability to Strike Back," by Wu Yuehe in *People's Daily*, "Some decision-makers in the United States" are criticized as "selfish and arrogant" (Wu, 2019).

In the article "PD Commentary: Bullying Mindset behind US Trade War against China" in *People's Daily* Online, the author Zhang Hong said, "It seems that the United States is ignoring its own tremendous advancements due to globalization, attempting to gain greater profits by launching deglobalization, which indicates its selfish mindset of hegemony that leaves the interests of other countries behind."

However, according to *People's Daily*'s English online edition, Trump also used the word "selfish" in the domestic political struggle. He sent a six-page letter to House Speaker Nancy

---

1. Sixty-six articles used the word *unilateralism*.

Pelosi on December 17, 2019. In this letter, Trump wrote to Pelosi, "You are the ones bringing pain and suffering to our Republic for your own selfish personal, political, and partisan gain" (Xinhua, 2019). We have read all the _People's Daily_ articles in our research period carefully in order not to include this kind of article in the category "negative."

In _China Daily_'s online English edition, 15 articles used the word "selfish" and 7 articles used the word "selfishness" to describe Trump's actions and his motivations. For example, a scholar in China Institutes of Contemporary International Relations wrote in _People's Daily_ on August 3, 2018: "The selfishness in the ongoing US policies on economy and trade, global governance and collective security reflects the public opinion and demands of the American people" (Sun, 2018).

In _China Daily_'s online English edition, 43 articles used the word "reckless" to describe President Trump. Among those articles, 32 are in the time span from January 20, 2017, to October 1, 2019. For example, an article in _People's Daily_ online also stated that "The most recent entry shows Trump's decision to take the US out of the global fight against climate change, a selfish and reckless decision that carries huge human rights implications for the entire world" (Stone, 2017).

In addition, on December 19, 2019, _People's Daily_'s English online edition reported that Speaker of the House Nancy Pelosi said "It is tragic that the president's reckless actions make impeachment necessary. He gave us no choice," before the House passed the vote to impeach Trump (Xinhua, 2019). These articles which displayed other US politicians' attitudes toward Trump are included in our research.

Fourteen articles use the word arrogant to describe Trump's policy. The editorial on August 6, 2018, said, "the eye-catching economic figure released recently boosted Washington's confidence, making the arrogant Uncle Sam unaware of where it really is before having rounds of clash with China" (Anonymous, 2018).

Despite the criticism displayed above, in general, _People's Daily_ showed a pretty balanced attitude toward Trump. Among the 32 months in the period, positive articles exceeded 50% in 8 months, neutral articles exceeded 50% in 4 months, negative articles exceeded 50% in 8 months. In the remaining 12 months, none of positive, negative, or neutral articles exceeded 50%.

CONCLUSION

Through this research, we find that as a mouthpiece of the Chinese government under the leadership of the CPC, during more than two and half years, _People's Daily_ tried to give comprehensive coverage of President Trump and the United States under his leadership. In these articles mentioning Trump, _People's Daily_ rarely used ideological terms such as "monopoly capitalist" or "American imperialism" to describe the United States.

Sino-American relations, especially the trade war between China and the United States, which attracted wide attentions in both countries as well as the whole world, are not the sole focus of _People's Daily_'s reports and commentaries on Trump and the United States.

As a great power, or emerging super power, China's most important newspaper aims to give the readers a comprehensive and balanced impression on US president Donald Trump. _People's Daily_ reported Xi's and other Chinese leaders' contacts and communications with Trump in detail, in order to show China's goodwill on Sino-US relations. When criticizing Trump, _People's Daily_ sometimes quotes the comments from American media or media in Russia, Iran,

Cuba, or Democratic People's Republic of Korea, which has troublesome relations with the United States. Only on some occasions when Trump's decisions directly hurt China's national interests or national prestige did *People's Daily* use its own harsh words to criticize him.

Therefore, it is not surprising to find that Trump's image in *People's Daily* in China is much better than his image in the American mainstream media such as Cable News Network (CNN) or *New York Times*. Trump never personally criticizes *People's Daily*'s reports or comments on him.

Our research depends on the classification of *People's Daily*'s articles mentioning Trump, which has the following limitations: first, because we do not have enough time to read all the contents of the 734 *People's Daily* articles mentioning Trump in detail, our classification might be inaccurate in a few articles; second, in the modern world, the fields of politics, economics, culture, and security are often overlapping and intertwining, so dividing the articles into these categories may miss the larger picture; third, emotional feelings in an article about a particular person are quite subjective. In some articles, the feelings may be mixed and can't be described in the simple words such as positive, negative, or neutral.

When we wrote this chapter, the US presidential election was getting near. It seemed that the Democrats were so ideologically divided that they might not select a candidate who could unite the party supporters and compete strongly with Trump. We will continually follow *People's Daily*'s reports and comments on President Trump, especially his efforts to be reelected.

REFERENCES

Anonymous (2017, December 29). Top 10 international news stories of 2017 selected by *People's Daily*. People's Daily Online. Retrieved from http://en.people.cn/n3/2017/1229/c90000-9310121.html, February 21, 2020.

Anonymous (2018, August 6). Editorial: China will not surrender to US threatening tactic. People's Daily Online. Retrieved from http://en.people.cn/n3/2018/0806/c90000-9488193.html, Feb 28, 2020.

Guo, P. R. (2019, August 24). Trade uncertainties, economic recession fears drag down U.S. equities. People's Daily Online. http://en.people.cn/n3/2019/0824/c90000-9608904.html.

Liang, G. Y. (2017). *Chinese economy 2040: The changing landscape of globalization and a new path for development*. Beijing: Renmin University.

Shi, W. S. (2019, June 14). Global communication shall not be subject to US "digital hegemony." People's Daily Online. http://en.people.cn/n3/2019/0614/c90000-9587888.html.

Stone, C. (2017, June 20). Voice of China: US should look in the mirror before lecturing the world on human rights. People's Daily Online. http://en.people.cn/n3/2017/0620/c90000-9230827.html.

Sun, C. H. (2018, August 3). Commentary: Trump goes further along strategic contraction. People's Daily Online. http://en.people.cn/n3/2018/0803/c90000-9487513.html.

Swaine, M. D. (2015). Xi Jinping on Chinese foreign relations: The governance of China and Chinese commentary. *China Leadership Monitor*, 48, 1–14.

Wang, L., and Wang L. Q. (2017). *The belt and road towards win-win cooperation*. Beijing: Social Science Academic Press.

Wang, R. H., and Yang, M. (2017, December 29). 国际十大新闻 (十大新闻·寰宇)[Top 10 international news in 2017(10 top global news)]. *People's Daily*. Retrieved from http://world.people.com.cn/n1/2017/1229/c1002-29734872.html.

Wu, Y. H. (2019, May 31). United States, don't underestimate China's ability to strike back. People's Daily Online. http://en.people.cn/n3/2019/0531/c202936-9583292.html.

Xi, J. P. (2014). *The governance of China I*. Beijing: Foreign Language Press.

Xi, J. P. (2017). *The governance of China II*. Beijing: Foreign Language Press.

Xinhua (2017, October 7). Spotlight: Law enforcement, cybersecurity dialogue strengthens China-U.S. cooperation. People's Daily Online. http://en.people.cn/n3/2017/1007/c90000-9276990.html.

Xinhua (2019, December 18). Trump sends letter to Pelosi, slamming impeachment ahead of full House vote. People's Daily Online. http://en.people.cn/n3/2019/1218/c90000-9641429.html.

Zhong, S. (2019, December 3). Multilateralism needed in governance of Middle East. People's Daily Online. Retrieved from http://en.people.cn/n3/2019/1203/c90000-9637570.html.

COLOMBIA

6

The Magnate Became President

How the Colombian Media and Citizens Perceive the United States and Trump

Jesus Arroyave, Universidad del Norte

INTRODUCTION

There is little doubt that over the past five years the way in which the United States of America is perceived has changed. The new generations no longer view the United States as a desirable destination for immigration. For some, the country's position of leadership, both internationally and in Latin America, has dissolved completely. For others, the first amendment of the US Constitution encouraging and guaranteeing freedom of expression and freedom of the press has been seriously undermined. The North American territory once seen as the melting pot of different cultures, ethnic groups, nationalities, beliefs, and traditions is no longer perceived as a pluriethnic safe haven. It is inconceivable that in such a short period of time a leader with a particular style has contributed to changing the image of a once highly admired country.

These are some of the initial conclusions reached after exploring the ways in which the media have perceived the government of the United States. National and regional media were examined for the period prior and after the 2016 elections. Alongside this analysis, the opinions of Colombians of different ages, social status, and education were canvassed.

Similar conclusions that reflect concrete opinions about the US government, but in particular about its most characteristic leader, President Donald Trump, emerged from different discussion groups.

Ever since Donald Trump began his campaign as the possible Republican candidate for the White House, the national press demonstrated signs of skepticism toward his candidacy and subsequent election. Similarly, participants in the discussion groups saw the real estate magnate's candidacy more as a whim than a real bid. For this reason, many assumed that the candidacy had no future.

At the time, a climate of doubt about his nomination dominated. He was known as a somewhat crooked multimillionaire who had used his economic power for occasional incursions in the media. He was known for this and not for his leadership style or statesmanship or his political thought. Against all prognostics Donald Trump won the 2016 elections and became president in January 2017. Since then, no other leader of the Western developed world has been more questioned, criticized, and ridiculed as Trump. Thousands of media outlets have presented serious criticism of the actions, declarations, and positions held by the magnate president. Others have denounced his lies and lack of accuracy in his role as a political leader; his constant inaccuracies would be unacceptable in other leaders in his position. This constant media attention has, however, guaranteed that he remains a constant in the lives of the many who are connected to media outlets. Donald Trump is always present through social media, newspapers, TV news shows, radio, and Twitter, which are constantly transmitting what he says.

The objective of this chapter is to explore how the national press and regular citizens perceive Donald Trump's government. Our analysis has focused on opinion and editorial pieces because they reflect a critical view of the most important national and international events. As they tend to transcend the act of informing about an event, they allow us to better identify which issues are of greater concern and the very specific assumptions made about them. To collect the opinions and perceptions of the common citizen, several focus groups of all ages and educational levels were organized. This allowed us to compare editors' and journalists' opinions with the perceptions of the common citizen. Therefore, the results derive from a qualitative content analysis of digital media output over a four-year period (2016–2019) at the national and regional level. It is also the product of textual analysis of several news stories and editorials as well as an analysis of the opinions gleaned from the focus groups. What emerges is a complex picture of a multifaceted person who has inaugurated a new form of politics. At its core, this study is an inductive research project aimed at investigating what conclusions can be reached both from media articles and the perceptions of the common citizen who reads them.

PERCEPTIONS ABOUT THE UNITED STATES OF AMERICA

For a long time, the perception of the United States among many Colombians has been contradictory and complex, filled with both disenchantment and positive surprises. On the one hand, generations of Colombians have grown up with a flood of media output that has familiarized them with different aspects of US culture. Many TV series, from children's programs, comedies, action films through to police series have been a constant in standard Colombian imagery. Movies are another great factor that has encouraged a feeling of closeness with the US context that is unknown in any other geographic area. Movie theaters in Colombia are dominated by Hollywood films. It is true that European, Latin American, and Asian films are sometimes shown, usually in places that tend to focus on screening indie or alternative movies. We can confirm that these then to be more the exception than the rule. An exercise exploring the number of films originating in the United States would surprise many as to the high level of exposure to US movie productions.

Similarly, new platforms that show series, documentaries, and reality TV have content that is predominantly produced in the United States. There is no doubt that those with the power to tell a story can choose a discourse that is favorable to them as well as impose a narrative that encourages their own worldview. Using the theory of cultivation as a framework, we can argue that several generations of Colombians have cultivated a feeling of closeness with the American context as a result of high exposure to its popular culture (music, videos, artists, etc.). In the same way, the physical appearance, the ways in which stories are narrated, the structure, and the plot are narratives imposed by the North. From the political and ideological perspective, unwanted American intervention in Colombia's internal affairs has periodically arisen. Many have questioned the strong influx of neoliberal ideas from the North that have not only affected politics but also the economy of the country. Sectors of the political left have questioned the imperialism inherent in trying to dominate the market. There is a questioning of the consumption of products and merchandise with the tag "made in United States," which have always been present despite the fact that nowadays many of these goods are not actually US products.

A common familiar discourse was that of family stories that involved a relative who had migrated to the United States. They became very successful and lived in very comfortable circumstances. The idea of the American dream and the possibility of economic prosperity once someone had emigrated north were in no way foreign to the young. Many had consumed similar stories in media products that used to celebrate the triumph of individualism.

Much of this perception has begun to change. In many ways the North American president Donald Trump in less than four years has managed to change perceptions in a way that neither the left with its criticism of imperialism or savage capitalism had ever managed. Many young people no longer see in the United States a safe destiny for immigration. In terms of foreign policy, many leaders no longer know what to expect from a White House that has such a volatile and unstable leader. Any decision is possible, even those that may negatively affect national interests. All the efforts previously made in the fight against drug cartels and their death tolls have been discredited because of statements made by President Trump.

The image of an arrogant, misogynistic, discriminating, racist, uneducated, ignorant, and untouchable leader who is predominantly interested in protecting the interests of the financial and business elites to the detriment of everyone else has gained considerable traction in the media. This same perception was present in the minds of the focus group participants. The United States is no longer the country of hope where many could change their status because it allowed for social mobility. It is no longer the country that will allow you to financially help your relatives that have stayed behind in your home country. It is also no longer the great country that could intervene in any international conflict. All these ideas have been drawn from the analysis conducted on the different media outputs and on the focus groups.

The analysis allowed us to identify four categories that grouped ideas about the US government but especially about its president. These categories were: (1) the mood of Trump, (2) the most anti-immigrant president, (3) why Donald Trump was elected, (4) the most mediatic president. In the following sections each of these categories will be explained.

1. The Mood of Trump: The Candidate Who Would Never Be President

From the beginning of his campaign, Donald Trump generated a great level of skepticism among national media analysts. Editors and columnists demonstrated in their writings that they did not believe the Trump campaign or predicted a disastrous failure to his presidential aspirations. Epithets such as *clown*, *ignorant*, *ridiculous* were associated with his political aspirations.

This was the style of columnist Pablo Ochoa (2016) in the newspaper *El Tiempo*, where Ochoa described him thus:

> Trump is a misogynistic, xenophobic, racist, ignorant, and vulgar clown who has become president of the United States to put an end to what is left of the world. A jester who will be able to undo all that his predecessor achieved. . . . A bastard who will be able to elect up to three

Supreme Court judges with serious consequences for all future generations on fundamental rights issues in North America.

Columns that frequently used negative adjectives were very common. In a way, this was a new style of journalism that negatively qualified the presidential candidate of a developed country such as the United States. A recurring idea that emerged was that only a very naive audience would believe in Donald Trump's harebrained proposals.

Juan Manuel Ramírez Moreno (2016), of *El Tiempo*, suggested:

> Trump is a candidate without proposals or arguments. He is a selfish, unfocused fabrication of Hollywood that is superficial, materialistic, and what's worse, without public service experience. His candidacy has conquered those naive viewers of reality TV and donut eaters that still confuse Colombia with Columbia.

As his campaign progressed, many national columnist and editors were perplexed at Trump's way of doing politics. The adjectives describing the magnate only increased. Cecilia Rodriguez (2016), columnist of *El Tiempo*, did not just describe Trump but also proposed something radical. If Trump were elected president this would have negative consequences for global democracy.

Trump has been cited lying about many things in so many ways and so often, like no other presidential candidate in history. The fact that a man as erratic, empty, cruel, intolerant, corrupt, and untruthful as Trump could possibly win the election should be a warning for the world's democracies. In a similar way, a series of very concrete ideas emerged from the focus groups that associated the US government with the particular style of its president rather than state policy of government in a broader sense. In other words, for them to speak of the form of government was to speak of the president and his particular style of politics. A number of adjectives were used to describe Donald Trump, including: *despot, abuser, arrogant, xenophobe, misogynist, bad mannered, temperamental, racist*, and *ignorant*. This first finding was in itself overwhelming. The participants did not spare the negative adjectives to describe what can be considered the most well-known leader of the Western world.

Digging deeper into these perceptions, interesting explanations emerged. Some of them were connected with capitalism in its latter stages. For many, the magnate president Trump represented the worst form of capitalist system, the exacerbated arrogance of the magnate who thinks he can do anything he wishes because he has the money to do it. One participant mentioned: "It seems that in the capitalist culture of the country money can buy anything. If you are a magnate you can even buy the country's presidency even if you are unprepared for it or for the managing of its diplomacy." For another participant, the magnate candidacy was merely a whim: "For Trump, the presidency is nothing more than one more whim. In the end, the whim ended up being more expensive than he had anticipated. Now he is in the thick of it, but because of his ego he is unable to recognize that the job is too much for him."

Another aspect that was discussed in the focus groups had to do with Trump's approach to gender. Many of the images that have been presented in the media about his dealings with opposing candidate Hillary Clinton were still fresh in the minds of the participants.

> I have never seen such a jerk for a politician. It is inconceivable that he should deal with his opponent in such a lewd way as Trump did during the presidential campaign. The worst thing is that the audience did not punish his behavior. I think the silence and support for this type of behavior is the worst of it all.

Some argued that this way of doing politics was destroying all that had been achieved in terms of gender equality and the rights of women over the past century. With his style of doing politics, Trump has destroyed all that has been built in terms of gender equality and the rights of women. No other candidate has ever been so disrespectful and offensive toward his opponent. His presidency will be marked by this way of treating women.

Another idea that persistently emerged made reference to his manners. His facial expressions, his mannerisms, and his rudeness were fresh in the memory of many of the participants: "I remember that on many occasions he did not shake hands with people he did not particularly like. This happened with Hillary Clinton, with Nancy Pelosi."

Another participant mentioned: "There is an image that no one forgets from when Trump went to visit the Obamas in the White House. While Barack Obama was shaking his wife's hand and let her walk into the White House first, Trump ignored his wife, leaving her alone. That is the behavior of a jerk."

For this reason, many female journalists made evident the misogynistic and discriminating discourse that characterized the Trump campaign. Interestingly, what many of these columnists emphasized of the discourse was that it went against the principles that had characterized the North American government and were a part of its constitution. In this way, Tatiana Dangond (2016), from the regional newspaper *El Heraldo*, made the following reflection:

> Trump used a misogynistic strategy that was radically chauvinistic and disrespectful of Hillary Clinton. His speeches were filled with hate toward women and trivialized the female sex. Trump is an example of a country that speaks of principles of equality and democracy but which still has difficulties maintaining these values when making weighty political decisions.

In regard to Trump's education, another focus group participant proposed an idea that was constantly present in several of the discussion groups: "Trump's ignorance is the most scandalous thing I have seen in politics in recent times."

The flat, underdeveloped discourse that used the famous phrase "Make America great again" felt superficial to many commentators and columnists. This was especially true in a country such as Colombia where presidents and public figures have put themselves forward as intellectuals. Colombia's national history counts with poets, authors, journalists, and generally, writers that have held high political office, among them presidents of the Republic.

It is mentioned that of the 28 presidents that Colombia had between 1886 and 1994, 22 were newspaper directors or columnists or owners of newspapers (Herrán, 1991). As president, Alberto Lleras Camargo (1966–1970) was considered an author that had taken a detour into politics. The rhetoric of Jorge Eliecer Gaitán, one of the most remembered founders of Colombia, displayed ample knowledge of ancient Roman-Greek culture. President Alfonso López Michelsen (1974–1978) wrote the highly acclaimed novel *Los Elegidos*. The president Belisario Betancourt (1982–1986) published approximately 20 books. When Cesar Gaviria (1990–1994) left the Colombian presidency, he gave an interview in which he lamented that what he missed the most was having time to read books of poetry. In this context, the Trump candidacy can come as a shock to a country whose public life was marked by a high level of intellectual and literary activity among those that aspired to the presidential seat.

In this way, the first analysis about the perception of the government of the United States in Colombia brought us to a meditation on its current president. From the first moment of his primary candidacy, the editorials as well as the focus group discussions that were analyzed have been extremely negative. No other candidate has received such negative adjectives or criticism in recent political history as Donald Trump. Particularly salient has been the perception that

Donald Trump is the incarnation of the worst type of late savage capitalism where the market and the self-interest but not the people are what matter.

2. "The Most Anti-Immigrant President" or Why He Hates All Non-Whites

One of the strongest lines of Donald Trump's discourse has been his anti-immigrant policy. Nothing could be furthest from the United States' reality as a country forged through immigration. The Native American Sioux, Navajos, Seminoles, Creeks Choctaws, Chickasaws, and Cherokees were successively invaded and pushed out of their territories by different groups of European immigrants, among them English, Dutch, German, Italian, and Irish. This process helped form the nation that exists today. Trump's own family descends from a family of immigrant Germans that arrived fleeing from World War I.

Stories of having a relative that immigrated to the United States are common in Colombia. It is in its way the story of the person who somehow managed the American dream. That uncle or aunt would regularly return carrying gifts and spectacular stories of the reality they were living in the North. These stories were fed by content in TV and films that was being consumed by Colombians. These individualist stories filled with examples of rapid success through hard work or illegal activities were set in the content of the opulence that had made the American dream famous. Several generations grew up with a desire to emigrate searching for better economic opportunities, although in many cases it was also emigration away from the problems and tragedies of war. The country was living in a period of great uncertainty as the armed conflict in Colombia worsened.

Trump managed to quickly turn the American dream into a nightmare. Many of the columnists and discussion group participants mentioned that Trump had eliminated any interest in immigrating to his country. His exacerbated racism, his obvious disdain for Latin Americans made evident in his continued criticism of Mexicans, has made many rethink their preferred immigration destination.

Publications in opinion pieces made a series of ideas evident. The analyst Jorge Castañeda (2016) in his column of *El Tiempo* stated that no other president from an advanced democracy had shown so much hate for one of its neighbors. What made matters worse was that this hate-filled speech had gained traction and been accepted by voters. It is surprising to see that in a developed democracy such an openly hostile leader should be elected. Over the past 18 months Trump has demonstrated vulgar behavior, insulting rhetoric, and violent incitement.

Columnist Jorge Ramos (2016) warned with some concern that while the discourse of hate was not taken seriously by news outlets it was being normalized in the United States and believed by his followers. Though Trump defends his speeches under the flag of freedom of speech, the language used offends, threatens, and insults different groups because of their race, color, religion, national origin, sexual orientation, or disability. It is furthermore an affront to the rules of civilized coexistence, as it encourages prejudice and persecution. As a matter of fact, the same journalist Jorge Ramos (2017) remembered, in this column for *El Colombiano*, the regional Antioquia's newspaper, that from the very beginning Trump's campaign has been characterized by racism and offensive language.

Many thought that the voters of the United States would never elect a presidential candidate with racist, sexist, xenophobic, and anti-ecological ideas. By electing Donald Trump, they have repeatedly shown us that our assumption was wrong. Everything began two years ago when on June 16, 2015, his presidential bid was launched from his golden tower in New York. In it he said that Latin American immigrants "brought drugs, brought crime, were rapists, and some, I guess, are good people. . . . This all comes from beyond the Mexican borders. It comes from the south and from Latin America."

In another column the same journalist suggested that there existed a sort of ranking among immigrants to the United States. "Through his speech and vision of the world it has become clear that for Trump ideal immigrants are those that speak English and are from the European context. This discourse makes evident his denial of the entire reason for emigrating. If Trump could, he would change the immigration law . . . giving preference to migrants from rich countries, preferably English speakers with a high level of education."

The idea that the "American dream" has become a "nightmare" was also made evident in the focus groups. The United States has ceased to be an ideal destination, and other geographic spaces have begun to emerge as more welcoming to immigration:

> People no longer want to immigrate to the US. Since Trump became president, we look to other destinations because his country no longer feels safe. Now it is better to go to Europe rather than the US. Trump has awakened racism and it is no longer safe. Plus, there is always the "ghost" that they will want to deport. Now what exists is the European dream. Trump made us hate the US. It may be farther away but it is safer for Colombians.

Concern was not only focused on the possible illegal status that an immigrant might have. As one participant said: "It is not just about being illegal. You may have the right documents but for the racist groups fed by Trump's rhetoric you are an unwanted immigrant. So even if you are legally there you are not actually safe."

Aside, however, from considering other destinations when thinking of emigration, a second possibility began to arise as a result of Trump's racist and xenophobic rhetoric. Staying and innovating has become a real possibility, which could have a positive effect not just on those that stay but as a way to avoid brain drain.

> Young people are now thinking of start-ups in their own country. As things become harder abroad succeeding at home looks more appealing. I think that is marvelous, as it reduces the amount of brain or talent drain. Now people are investing here. . . . Deep down Trump may have done us a favor.

During the discussion, both Trump's rhetoric with regard to the wall he intended to build on the border and his radical position with reference to the caravans from Central America came up. Trump showed he lacked any compassion or human feeling. In the face of the wave of immigrants he could have been more indulgent and offered some alternative. Instead he continued to be the bully that threatens the weakest. His radical discourse has prompted certain Colombian opinion journalists to equate him with some of the darkest figures of history, going as far as radicalizing further his discourse on racist or xenophobic topics.

In this way journalist José Miguel Alzate (2016) of *El Tiempo* wrote:

> Trump was the least prepared for the election campaign. He showed his xenophobia by accusing all Mexicans of being drug dealers and rapists, and then generalizing it to the rest of Latinos. He does not accept the mixing of cultures, especially the Latino culture. This aversion is similar to that expressed by Hitler about the Jews.

In a similar vein, Cristo García Tapias (2018) in his column for *El Espectador* compared Trump and his dealings with Latino immigrants to the concentration camps of Hitler's Germany:

Hitler's new concentration camps are in 21st-century North America. In the same North America that in solidarity and compassion once liberated Auschwitz from the darkness of Nazi extermination during World War II. The methods and practices applied against children by incarcerating them are Trump's version of those detained by Hitler in Nazi Germany for the same reasons of race, ethnicity, religion, politics, and culture.

Following this same line of thought, journalist Sergio Múñoz (2018) used the well-documented parallel suggested by Madeleine Albright between Mussolini and Trump. Like a good academic, Albright uses histories in which the parallelism between Trump and Mussolini is shockingly similar. "A fascist—she writes—is someone who claims to speak for a nation, does not worry about the rights of others, and is open to using violence." She adds: "Trump is the first antidemocratic president of the modern era and if it weren't for the strength of the country's institutions he would be its first dictator."

Finally, Alfonso Cuellar (2018), in his article titled "The World's Most Dangerous Man?" used another historical figure to offer a parallel with the North American president. While this was not a direct comparison there was strength in the metaphor:

> While Trump is not Saddam Hussein, his impact on global stability is high. He is like an elephant in a porcelain shop destroying everything in his way. For him, the problem of the commercial wars is that their consequences are unpredictable. As unpredictable as the current occupant of the White House.

This is another important discovery from the analyzed data. The extent to which Trump has radicalized his discourse against immigrants, Mexicans, and other Latin Americans has been compared with some of the darkest figures in history: Hitler, Mussolini, and to an extent Saddam Hussein. For new generations of Colombians, immigration to the United States is no longer an attractive option. Europe has emerged as a safer and more desirable destination. The situation may have even encouraged many Colombians to stay home and invest in their own country. This is considerable change in such a short period of time as to how the United States is perceived.

3. How Was It Possible for Him to Be Elected President?

Many journalists could not believe what was happening. Against all predictions and expectations Donald Trump had conquered the presidency of the United States. This historic event requires some explanation. Several theories emerged about this election. First of all, radical voices emerged in the editorials that predicted the worst happening to Latin Americans and Colombia.

"Trump's election is a total disaster for the region," wrote Jorge Castañeda (2016) in his column: "We could be optimistic and think that Trump will be unable to proceed with his agenda and that his speeches were not serious but these expectations would be naive. Trump's mandate will be a difficult road for Americans and Latin Americans. It will be especially negative for business and foreign affairs."

A recurring idea that was consistent in the different opinion columns analyzed was the thought that Trump's election was a sign of our times. A time in which populism, whether of the right or left, has become deeply engrained in today's society.

It was in these terms Adriana La Rotta (2016) wrote in her column for *El Tiempo*:

> Trump's election would be an extraordinary thing, but it would be consisted with a change in global politics. Traditional politicians—both good and bad ones—are being rejected, the political centre is

being diluted, and societies are being torn apart drawn by populisms of the political right and left. Populism is the reason that not even the accusations against Trump hindered his campaign.

Some associated the rise in populism to a discontent with traditional institutions and the political class more generally. This was the argument posed by the editorial of *El Tiempo* (2016):

> It is noteworthy that the United States is not free of the type of populist or anti-establishment phenomena that is no longer about a struggle between rich and poor or about paradigmatic ideologies of the right or left. It reflects a profound discontent in society with the political class and the traditional institutions.

Other possible explanations pointed to the actual institutional crises that have led many in search of a messiah or savior. With a different discourse they offer something new to the citizenry. Sergio Ocampo (2016, November 11) suggested: "The only thing that explains the absurdity of Trump's triumph in a country that we thought had strong institutions is that these institutions are no longer perceived as strong, trustworthy or efficient. They have entered into a crisis and it is there that messiahs and savior find their role."

It is interesting to see how the journalist saw in Trump's election a phenomenon that had spread like a virus from the South of the Americas to the North. Sergio Ocampo also stated: "Latin America has managed to export its populism and demagogy to the United States, which is what caused the arrival of Trump at the White House."

Tatiana Dangond (2016) similarly wrote that institutions were no longer that important and now what dominated was a leader that rose above them, but this would eventually affect democracy.

Donald Trump, like Hugo Chavez and Alvaro Uribe Velez, is proof that political parties are experiencing a considerable loss in popular appeal. Their institutions no longer represent the main interests of society. Now they are focused on one person that ends up threatening the very idea that democracy is built on a political spectrum.

Catalina Ruiz (2016) in *El Espectador* suggests that it was a feeling of victimhood that had led the electorate to vote for Trump. Nussbaum argues that one of our difficulties with politics is that we, as humans, feel unprotected. For this reason, populisms function by feeding people with fantasies of invulnerability. That is exactly what just happened with Trump. For the author Piedad Bonnet (2016) in her *El Espectador* column, it was Trump's eccentricities that served him well in the media. It led to them being always in the spotlight feeding his popularity.

His idiotic comments were effective for two reasons: his silly comedian tone was celebrated by the sector in society that is as racist, chauvinistic, and ultraconservative as him, and since the media focused so much on every single one of his statements, they allowed him to reach an ever-larger group of audiences. Participants in the focus groups suggested that was the disenchantment with the political class and the traditional institutions that have made it possible for Trump to be elected. One participant said: "People were bored with the same politicians and they saw in Trump someone who was not a career politician and offered something new."

Other comments emerged that were less positive about the change that had allowed his election: "People were tired of the same thing, so they decided to experiment with a different type of candidate. The problem was that the change was for the worst."

The geopolitical explanation offered by another participant was more interesting as it suggested that Trump was the type of leader that demanded an "empire" to continue to guarantee global economic hegemony:

Trump is the product of a later capitalism that tries to maintain the United States' hegemony in the world. His eccentric and in appearance impulsive behavior is preventing China's great advance into the world economy. A coherent president respectful of international law would not be able to do this. The empire continues to renew itself through actors that fulfill this role. . . . That is what most people don't understand.

Another interesting explanation focused on a certain degree of punishment enacted by the public on the political class: Choosing Trump signified an extremely radical rejection of the political institutions.

Sergio Ocampo (2016, December 2), one of the opinion columnists that has most written about Trump pointed out:

The results of the elections in the United States demonstrate that the Americans continued to be segregationists, ignorant provincials, that the US is a country of immigrants but that there is a hierarchy among them. An Irishman is seen as more worthy than a Hispanic. The United States hides a conservative spirit under all the guarantees of absolute individualism, that the patriarchy is still strong, and that there is a reversal of the integration of the African American community. For this reason, populism has reached the United States.

Another fascinating discovery was the idea, circulating in many of the opinion columns, according to which Trump's election meant the United States was more similar to Latin America than previously thought. Latin America's history of populist and messianic leaders that have written many pages of its dark history has moved north with Trump's election: "In electing Trump the United States has lost its moral capacity to judge the decision and actions of other countries. The Latin American nations can now feel less embarrassed about their own mistakes."

It becomes evident that many of the columnists and focus group participants attributed Trump's win not to his qualities as a political leader or as a statesman but to disenchantment with the political institutions. Trump was a "type of punishment of the political institutions," as one of the focus group participants mentioned. This signified a fatigue with the political class and a desire for something new.

His election, however, has also signified that populism, whether of the right or left, has extended itself across the entire continent. It has placed itself as a different and hopeful alternative for those that see in a messianic figure the solution for correcting the mistakes of the traditional political class.

Without a doubt, the explanation that Trump is a kind of "character" needed by the "empire" is fascinating. He is viewed as a figure necessary for maintaining economic hegemony in the face of an ever-stronger China. From this perspective, his way of acting is something well calculated in order to maintain the interests of the empire.

4. The Most Mediatic President: Trump and Social Media

Another subject that has frequently emerged in the different columns over the past four years has been Trump's management of the media. This also came up in the focus group discussions. For many, Trump is the first president of the developed world that has found in Twitter his main communication outlet.

In this sense, many feel that there is a similarity between the concise nature of tweets and the superficial style of the president. Several participants said: "Twitter is a superficial means for a superficial person. . . . There is no political doctrine that can be explained in so few characters. I think Twitter adapts itself well to an impulsive character. He just throws ideas about in the heat of the moment without measuring the consequences."

This same idea was repeated in the focus groups. Another participant said: "Twitter would be the ideal media outlet for someone like Trump. It is instantaneous and forces you to say things without much depth. . . . He just reacts, he does not offer profound ideas that explain his decision or develop themes at greater length."

This type of remark also came up in opinion columns. For the analyst Benito Lázaro (2017), Trump spent more time tweeting than reflecting: "Because of this, Trump's style of governing has been more reactive than effective, more confrontational than characterized by dialogue, and more divisive than unifying. Trump feels more comfortable signing presidential decrees, watching Fox News, and tweeting than truly governing and solving problems."

Lázaro (2017) also wrote in similar terms of this idea of a *showman* without a political education who was unable to explain his political agenda beyond the 140-character limit: Trump's government has been characterized by the traits of Trump the *showman* and candidate. Since the presidential campaign Trump's total lack of knowledge about the mechanisms of government has been evident. This has seriously impeded the development of a political agenda. As candidate, Trump never quite specified his agenda; rather, he focused on presenting general information with a strong post-truth dose. As president, Trump rarely goes beyond the 140-character tweet.

What did, however, emerge from the focus groups was his expertise in managing his image through the different media outlets. All of his eccentricities, apparent mistakes, and his colorful behavior deep down achieved what he wanted: to become the media center of attention.

Such was the statement made by one of the participants: "Everyone thinks Trump is stupid enough to make any sort of inappropriate mistake. What they don't realize is that his behavior is calculated and aimed at achieving constant media coverage. . . . Everyone is always talking about him, what he says doesn't matter."

Another participant put it slightly differently: "Trump has had the type of free advertising that no other candidate has enjoyed." Social media platforms have been largely responsible for making newsworthy superficial events that have subsequently become very popular. This situation has played out in favor of the president magnate. Such was the analysis presented by journalist Héctor Abad Faciolince (2016): "This craziness is largely due to Facebook. And it wasn't done intentionally by Facebook, but rather by its hypocrisy and omissions. The blind algorithm, which highlights the news bytes that are most popular, is indifferent to their accuracy or lack thereof."

And the Enemy of the Press Gained Power

Donald Trump's relationship with the press has been another subject that came up in both the editorials and the focus groups over the past four years. One of the more curious ideas to emerge was that Trump's opinions made it possible to compare him with a political figure that was opposed to the North American president. For some of the columnists, Trump was positioning himself quite closely with Chavez in trying to censure the press. This comparison was done by the analyst Oppenhaimer (2017):

It was likely a ploy by President Trump to deflect attention from the fact that more and more people had begun seeing him as an incompetent president. Trump's message of the 11 of October where he threatened not to renew NBC's license for spreading fake news was the same as that which was used by Chavez to close down the RCTV TV network in 2007 in Venezuela.

Another phenomenon commented on through opinion pieces has been that since the Trump era began, truth no longer makes any sense. Several editors and columnists did not previously think it possible that a high-ranking political figure could lie so systematically and persistently without it having dire consequences. It was not just that he openly lied, but also that events and facts were altered, twisted, and changed in favor of a false rhetoric. One columnist wrote: "Trump and his campaign have spread so many false facts that at a certain point reality no longer counts."

The consistent analysis and researching of facts in the press releases and speeches given by Trump have scandalized many Colombians. They fail to understand how someone like that could remain in power. One of the participants stated: "It makes no sense that Trump continues in power after one of the most important newspapers in the world, the *New York Times*, has pointed out the many lies publicly uttered by Trump."

We are all susceptible to making inaccurate statements, but it is unacceptable in the president of the United States. Another participant transmitted a more apocalyptic vision of Trump's lies: "Trump has inaugurated an era in which the truth is no longer important. It is the end of times." Another participant in the focus groups used words that brought back the apocalyptic vision: "Now lies and manipulation are the new style of doing politics that is dominating the Western world."

Lies, however, were not only expressed by Trump in his speeches. They were also created by third parties that supported Trump, with the idea of discrediting his opponents. The columnist Juan Manuel Hoyos (2017) wrote in *El Colombiano* suggesting that fake news items circulating in social media were instrumental in Trump's election. Some of these were:

- that Hillary Clinton had sold arms to the Islamic State
- that she ran a satanic sect that murdered children
- that Pope Francis supported Trump's candidacy
- that Barack Obama was born in Kenya and falsified his documents in order to become president

Many of these fake news reports were fabricated in Macedonia, wrote one of the columnists: "After the campaign there was a sort of 'digital gold fever' in Macedonia. Its streets filled with new cars and bars filled with youth dressed in expensive cloths and drinking sophisticated cocktails." One teenager said that he worked creating fake news for one month and managed to make approximately $1,900. Minimum wage in Macedonia is $380 per month.

CONCLUSION

This chapter discusses the perception of the United States government and especially of its president in different media outlets and regular citizens across Colombia. The opinions of regular citizens were collected through focused discussions groups. What emerged was that popular opinion and what was being written by news outlets was similar and intertwined. What was varied and fascinating were the different explanations given for Trump's behavior.

Though there were quite a few conspiracy theories, they were grounded in facts and demonstrated the analysis of those that suffer from the decisions made in high political positions.

One of the first themes to arise from the analysis of both the media and the focus groups was the highly negative opinion of Trump before, during, and after the election. That is without a doubt a new phenomenon. Never before has a leader of the Western world been so criticized and yet gotten elected.

Both columnists and participants were very surprised when the candidate magnate was elected. Skepticism arose because the events seemed unreal. A leader that had been labeled misogynist, arrogant, liar, ignorant, racist, temperamental, and many other negative adjectives had been elected in what was viewed as one of the most respected democracies of the Western world.

The way in which participants and columnists explained Trump's election shed light on how events were perceived by many. The most repeated explanation was that populism had reached the United States as an export from Latin America. Institutions had opened up to the image of a "redeeming messiah" who promised to fix things. Burnout from traditional politics was forcing people to seek out new figures from outside of the traditional sphere. These new figures captured the imagination of a disillusioned electorate with speeches that were at times grating but which went against the establishment.

Maybe the most original of explanations connected the president magnate and the mode of late capitalist production. For many, Trump embodies the worst of the late capitalist system. For others, he was the necessary figure needed to perpetuate the "empire" in the face of an ever-stronger China. In other words, a figure such as this was a product of the present time in which the "empire" needed to find a way to maintain its hegemony. All of his histrionic, unpredictable, volatile behavior was what the empire needed at this point in time. One of the most recurrent criticisms found in both the columns and the opinions of focus group participants was his markedly anti-immigrant stance. He often became xenophobic and treated women badly to the point of being misogynist. In the minds of many of the focus group participants, the multiple times he failed to greet a woman or was impolite to his wife or a political opponent were still fresh. In the same way, his negative behavior toward Mexicans had affected the perception of many. The United States under Trump was no longer the ideal place to immigrate to. His speeches had fed white supremacy and had become a barrier that intimidated anyone thinking of immigrating to the great country in the North.

Another recurring theme in both the opinion columns and the focus groups was that he was a vacuous candidate, made important by the media, newspapers, and social media. The attention given by the media had played in his favor in the political sphere. The same screen that had made evident his ridiculousness had at the same time had a multiplying effect that had taken his image to thousands upon thousands of people. With Trump, events lacked any value. The truth lost its meaning. The respected columnist Moises Naim (2018) complained that his followers had a lot to forgive:

> The list of Trump's decisions and behaviors that need to be forgiven by those that follow him is quite long and continues to grow. Evidence that the commercial activities engaged by the Trump Organization frequently broke the law is abundant. The list of his collaborators in business, politics, and government that were on trial or had been condemned has revealed a criminal environment that surrounds the president. His followers, however, forgive even that which makes evident the truth behind Trump's horrible statement in January of 2016: "I could shoot someone on 5th Avenue. And I would not lose a single vote."

What emerges here, although incomplete and subjective, is a testimony of a historical moment that Colombia, and in a certain way Latin America, has experienced with the arrival of right-wing populism embodied by Donald Trump to power. Since the magnate came to the White House the way of doing politics has changed dramatically. Not in vain, has the *Washington Post* placed as its new slogan *Democracy Dies in Darkness*.

REFERENCES

Abad Faciolince, H. (2016, November 12). El día del mal juicio. *El Espectador*. https://www.elespectador.com/opinion/opinion/el-dia-del-mal-juicio-columna-665255

Alzate, J. (2016, November 28). El discurso xenófobo de Donald Trump. *El Tiempo*. https://www.eltiempo.com/opinion/columnistas/jose-miguel-alzate/el-discurso-xenofobo-de-donald-trump-jose-miguel-alzate-columna-el-tiempo-53256

Bonnet, P. (2016). Emociones políticas. *El Espectador*. https://www.elespectador.com/opinion/opinion/emociones-politicas-columna-664645

Castañeda, J. (2016, November 16). La conmoción Trump en América Latina. *El Tiempo*. https://www.eltiempo.com/archivo/documento/CMS-16751779

Cuellar, A. (2018, March 3). ¿El hombre más peligroso del mundo? *Semana*. https://www.semana.com/opinion/articulo/donald-trump-el-hombre-mas-peligroso-del-mundo-por-alfonso-cuellar/558823

Dangond, T. (2016, November 9). Más allá de Trump. *El Heraldo*. https://www.elheraldo.co/columnas-de-opinion/mas-alla-de-trump-300619

El Tiempo. (2016, November 10). El tiempo de Trump. *El Tiempo*. https://www.eltiempo.com/mundo/eeuu-y-canada/el-tiempo-de-trump-editorial-el-tiempo-10-de-noviembre-de-2016-33988

García Tapias, C. (2018, October 25). Los campos de concentracion de Trump. *El Espectador*. https://www.elespectador.com/opinion/los-campos-de-concentracion-de-trump-columna-819903

Herrán, M. T. (1991). *La industria de los medios de comunicación en Colombia* [The mass communication media industry in Colombia]. Bogotá: Fescol.

Hoyos, J. (2017, November 6). Con amor, desde el oficio más bello del mundo. *El Colombiano*. https://www.elcolombiano.com/opinion/columnistas/con-amor-desde-el-oficio-mas-bello-del-mundo-BL7638939

La Rotta, A. (2016, November 4). Una candidatura indestructible. *El Tiempo*. https://www.eltiempo.com/opinion/columnistas/adriana-la-rotta/una-candidatura-indestructible-adriana-la-rotta-columna-el-tiempo-54491

Lázaro, M. (2017, December 17). Donald Trump sigue siendo Donald Trump. *El Espectador*. https://www.elespectador.com/noticias/el-mundo/donald-trump-sigue-siendo-donald-trump-articulo-728746

Múñoz, S. (2018, April 17). ¡Cuidado, resurge el fascismo! *El Tiempo*. https://www.eltiempo.com/opinion/columnistas/sergio-munoz-bata/cuidado-resurge-el-fascismo-205896

Naim, M. (2018, November 3). Perdonando a Trump. *El Tiempo*. https://www.eltiempo.com/opinion/columnistas/moises-naim/perdonando-a-trump-moises-naim-289472

Ocampo, S. (2016, November 11). La "Trumpada" a la inteligencia. *El Tiempo*. https://www.eltiempo.com/archivo/documento/CMS-16748358

Ocampo, S. (2016, December 2). Señor Trump, el muro es urgente. *El Tiempo*. https://www.eltiempo.com/opinion/columnistas/sergio-ocampo-madrid/senor-trump-el-muro-es-urgente-sergio-ocampo-madrid-columna-el-tiempo-52893

Ochoa, P. (2016, November 13). Chibchombia. *El Tiempo*. https://www.eltiempo.com/archivo/documento/CMS-16749776

Oppenheimer, A. (2017, October 18). La nueva embestida de Trump contra los medios. *El Colombiano*. https://www.elcolombiano.com/opinion/columnistas/la-nueva-embestida-de-trump-contra-los-medios-BF7513344

Ramirez, J. M. (2016, March 1). Los latinos ingenuos que votan por Donald Trump. *El Tiempo*. http://blogs.eltiempo.com/egonomista/2016/03/01/los-latinos-ingenuos-que-votan-por-donald-trump/

Ramos, J. (2016, June 22). Dos años de Trump. *El Colombiano*. https://www.elcolombiano.com/opinion/columnistas/dos-anos-de-trump-LE6767814

Ramos, J. (2017, November 16). Trump contra los inmigrantes. *El Colombiano*. https://www.elcolombiano.com/opinion/columnistas/trump-contra-los-inmigrantes-CD7702985

Rodriguez, C. (2016, November 7). Lo cierto es que todos mienten. *El Tiempo*. https://www.eltiempo.com/opinion/columnistas/cecilia-rodriguez/lo-cierto-es-que-todos-mienten-cecilia-rodriguez-columnista-el-tiempo-54637

Ruiz, C. (2016, November 9). Emociones políticas. *El Espectador*. https://www.elespectador.com/opinion/opinion/emociones-politicas-columna-664645

EGYPT

7

The Portrayal of the Trump Administration in the Egyptian Media

Rasha Allam, The American University, Cairo

INTRODUCTION

Egypt has been an important country for the United States based on its geography, demography, and diplomatic posture. The diplomatic ties between the two countries date back to 1922. During the final year of Barack Obama's administration, the ties between the two countries were tense, which led to hindering the US-funded economic assistance programs to Egypt. Donald Trump's administration has tried to normalize the ties with the Abdel Fattah Al-Sisi government that were generally perceived as strained under President Obama. President Trump has praised the Egyptian government's counterterrorism efforts while his administration has worked to restore high-level diplomatic engagement.

The US administration is always given a good amount of coverage in the Egyptian media due to the crucial diplomatic ties. This chapter investigates the portrayal of the Trump administration in the Egyptian newspapers. The chapter uses quantitative method through analyzing the content of two newspapers: *Al-Ahram* and *Al-Masry Al-Youm*. The chapter will analyze the news stories and opinion articles to get a deeper understanding of how the US administration is framed. These two newspapers have the highest distribution and circulation in Egypt and reflect the two main segments in the market: government and private owned.

Egypt has been an important country for US national security interests based on its geography, demography, and diplomatic posture (Piazza, 2019). The United States has provided significant military and economic assistance to Egypt since the late 1970s. Successive US administrations have justified aid to Egypt as an investment in regional stability, built primarily on long-running cooperation with the Egyptian military and on sustaining the 1979 Egyptian-Israeli peace treaty.

All US foreign aid to Egypt (or any recipient) is appropriated and authorized by Congress. Since 1946, the United States has provided Egypt with over $83 billion in bilateral foreign aid (calculated in historical dollars—not adjusted for inflation). There are several conditions that are reviewed annually which govern the release of these funds. All US military aid to Egypt finances the procurement of weapons systems and services from US defense contractors.

Under presidents Al-Sisi and Trump, the tone of US-Egyptian relations has been cordial. The president and secretary of state have each praised President Al-Sisi for combating terrorism, promoting women's rights, and advancing religious freedom.

BACKGROUND

The relationship between Egypt and the United States has gone through different phases with ups and downs, yet Egypt has always remained a major strategic and political cornerstone of American policy in the Middle East. In the period of 1952 to 1967 before the 1967 war, Egypt was receiving intermittent financial aid, so the United States could keep a close eye on Gamal Abdel Nasser and his Egypt at the time, in case he might actually detach from his close ties with the Soviet Union. The Egyptian-US ties at that time were not that strong compared to their later alliance, which would be immensely strengthened (Brownlee, 2012). Moving along to the 1970s, Egypt's foreign policy was revisited. Under the rule of Anwar El-Sadat in the 1970s, the ideas of state socialism started to be uprooted and replaced by a more liberalized, open, free market. Gradually, Sadat managed to strategically make changes and the changes that he had implemented appeared on the domestic and regional levels. During the period of 1974 to 1977, Sadat was able to earn US approval, release the tension in the relationship that used to exist during Nasser's government, and reconcile ties between the two countries. A major step in Sadat's period was his ability to portray Egypt positively when he replaced Nasser's one-party system with one that took the form of "controlled political pluralism," which was one of the main reasons behind US-Egyptian reconciliation (Brownlee, 2012).

While Sadat made sure to keep the Soviet army in check, economic aid from the United States to Egypt reached $900 million in 1979 (Brownlee, 2012; Ottoway, 2011). The United States gave Egypt six C-130 military transport aircraft, but Sadat was yet to be satisfied with the military aid, since he wanted to guarantee the credibility of his army. In the beginning of 1978–1979, the military aid grew astoundingly larger for Egypt. The American military contribution reached $1.3 billion a year. The Egyptian military has always been known for being one of the strongest armed forces in the region, and Sadat made sure to continue his military investment, especially when the strength of the Egyptian military was automatically a translation and reflection of the strength of his reign. The US economic and military aids were dominant objectives for Sadat and at the top of his agenda, in addition to protecting a strong relationship with the United States as well as with other pro-Western Arab governments in the region. Sadat succeeded in his plans with the military aid, which had been a fundamental priority to Egypt throughout this entire time period (Ottoway, 2011).

Later, when President Hosni Mubarak took office in 1981 after Sadat's assassination, his political, economic, and military objectives were parallel to Sadat's plan, and they followed the same political and economic agendas, in addition to other items. Mubarak had a strategic view from day one, which was continuing on the path of Sadat (Tadros & Brown, 2017; Ottoway, 2011).

Thus, Mubarak did care immensely about the Arab world, not just in terms of political and economic reforms, but also in terms of an issue of identity, and the importance of branding the Arab unity. Mubarak as well wanted to implement direct investment, mergers, joint-ventures, and other trade that could occur as inter-Arab cooperation (Piazza, 2019). Maintaining the open-door policy, as well as multiple political parties had kept Egypt as an ally to the United Sates. In addition, Mubarak had taken steps to allow the private sector to operate effectively. However, the relationship with the United States started to be affected by the "succession crisis" (Ottaway, 2011), which stemmed from Mubarak's plan that in the event of his death, his son Gamal would ascend to the presidency.

In 2011, the United States was taken by surprise when the Egyptians took to the streets of Cairo, and in particular Tahrir Square, on January 25, and ousted the 30-year-long presidency in a period of 18 days. By then, Barack Obama's administration was in place. Initially, the United States thought it was time for change and more democratic alterations in the system that would hopefully take place in the hands of Mubarak. Hillary Clinton, then secretary of state, had made a claim at the beginning of the Egyptian revolution that she thought the Egyptian government was stable and just needed to make some alterations and respond to the legitimate interests of the Egyptian people (Ottaway, 2011). The truth was that the United States wanted to ensure Mubarak would stay in office to steer the required change Egyptians were demanding. When Mubarak was ousted on February 11 and the entire country was in an excited celebratory mode, Obama applauded the revolutionary act and was thrilled about the new era of democratic change that the Egyptian people were to see (Cook, 2011). In 2013, All media platforms—state-controlled and private—were no longer discreet about their opposition or distaste for both Morsi and the Muslim Brotherhood (Ottaway, 2011). It was quite obvious that Morsi was trying to impose sharia law in Egypt through the 2012 constitution. In addition, secular politicians refused to cooperate with the Muslim Brothers, as now they were in dire need of intervention and crisis management. Egyptians revolted against the Muslim Brotherhood system and on June 30, 2013, the protests were a much shorter rendition of what happened back in 2011: spectatorship sufficed for the United States, Egyptians once again took to Tahrir Square and elsewhere to demand the ouster of Morsi, requesting the military to step in and take charge in the interim period.

Despite the aid the United States had been giving out over the past three decades, and the hundreds of Egyptian military officers who had received intensive training in the United States for the longest time, the Unites States was not happy with the ousting of Morsi and was stuck in a rough position. In the end they suspended the 30-year-long aid to Egypt.

After President Abdel Fattah Al-Sisi took control and Donald Trump became president, both leaders wanted to reconcile relations. For the first time, an Egyptian president was welcomed in the White House since Obama hosted Mubarak a long while back. This visit was considered to be an essential meeting that aimed mainly to make sure everything was still intact.

While the main idea remained that the countries were considered allies, Trump did not hesitate to express his dissatisfaction with various issues in Egypt including the public instability and the general idea of lack of democracy. On the other side, Egyptians were happy with the end of Obama's presidency term and the takeover of the Trump administration, and the Egyptian media was cheering for the Trump administration.

US MEDIA AND PUBLIC DIPLOMACY

The United States has tried different public policy techniques throughout history to ensure its positive impact generally in many countries all over the world, and in the Arab region specifically. Public diplomacy is defined as ways through which a country tries to reach out to global publics directly, rather than through their governments. This can be executed in several ways, ranging from micro approaches to macro ones that rely on various forms of mass media.

The idea of public diplomacy is based on some principles and strategies primarily encompassing the influence of public attitudes on international relations and on the formation and execution of foreign policies. It mainly aims to influence public opinion in other countries as a way to create cultural bridges between the states in parallel with the formal diplomatic channels (Iskander, 2005).

It all started during the Cold War in the 1970s and 1980s, which brought the greatest attention to public diplomacy and the importance of approaching public opinion in foreign countries. The basic argument was that the spread of American ideas could be an effective weapon in the ideological war between the Western and Soviet camps (Abshire, 1976). This period marks the time as well when scholars noted the relationship between the revolution in mass communication and the rise of a new kind of diplomacy: public diplomacy (Hoffman, 1968).

Academics as well as policy makers have focused on the role of the media in public diplomacy strategies, since many of them believe the media act as vehicles of public diplomacy. The first platform to play this public diplomacy role was Voice of America (VOA) through presenting the American version and view of world events (Fortner, 1994). Some years after its launch, and particularly after 9/11, the VOA changed its program format from a news focus to a music-culture focus to soften the relationship between the United States and the Arab countries, yet it was not able to prove success.

Later on, with the start of *al-Hurra* TV channel, the aim was to reflect the American side of the story, yet although it was assumed that since the American side of the story was being told, Arab public opinion would be more receptive to US policies and be attracted to the American style in the representation of the news. However, a study surveyed a sample of Arab university students in five Arab countries to measure their perceptions regarding the news credibility in the two US-sponsored networks targeting the Arab audience—Radio *Sawa* and Television *al-Hurra*. Results show that there is no correlation between the respondents' frequency of listening to Radio *Sawa* or watching *al-Hurra* and their perception of its credibility. In addition, the study showed that Arab students' attitude toward US policies had worsened since they started to be exposed to Radio *Sawa* or watching *al-Hurra* (El Nawawy, 2006).

A study conducted in 2009 about the image of the United States during the Bush and Obama administrations found that it is declining, especially when US leaders start to declare that the Arab peoples are unable to practice democracy, which results in the loss of American credibility in the Arab world (Ezzat, 2009).

PORTRAYAL OF THE TRUMP ADMINISTRATION IN THE EGYPTIAN PRESS

As mentioned earlier, this chapter investigates the portrayal of the Trump administration in the Egyptian newspapers. Using a quantitative method through analyzing the content of two newspapers: *Al-Ahram* and *Al-Masry Al-Youm*, the chapter analyzes the news stories and opinion articles to get a deeper understanding of how the Trump administration is portrayed. *Al-Ahram* and *Al-Masry Al-Youm* represent the two main newspaper segments in the Egyptian market: government and private owned, and are the highest in terms of distribution and circulation.

The content of the coverage of the two newspapers is analyzed to give a quantitative estimation of the frequency of the issues being discussed, the tone of coverage and the trends they represent. *Al-Ahram* is considered a government-owned newspaper, as it is mainly funded through government subsidy and is keen to reflect the government policies and agenda. As for *Al-Masry Al-Youm*, it is considered the most dominant independent newspaper in the market with the highest in terms of distribution and a very dynamic news website and social media platforms.

The search yielded 154 (64.2%) news stories and 86 (35.8%) opinion columns, all included for analysis. The unit of analysis employed was the news article and opinion articles for the newspaper, and the intercoder reliability was .95 (Wimmer & Dominick, 2014).

The time frame of the study was six months, from January 2019 until June 2019. This time frame was chosen because it is considered a mid-period after Trump's and Al-Sisi's taking power, and not toward the beginning where there could have been over-focus on coverage.

In the area of media and communication studies, media frames or framing is an important branch of media studies undertaken by scholars mainly to identify more deeply the content of media or other communication texts. The framing of an event or an issue is a critical act by which we organize, categorize, and solve situations. Frames are publicly presented definitions of a situation containing three elements: a problem, a protagonist, and a solution (Levin, 2005). Humans subconsciously incorporate framing into nearly every communicative act (Goffman, 1974). Framing analysis makes visible how people define and construct a given issue.

Newspaper news articles and opinion columns provide citizens and political elites with saliency cues regarding key affairs. Research on opinion journalism points to the potential impact that opinion articles have on elite debate, government policy, and public opinion as they provide a platform where readers will be made to think through the presentation of diverse points of view regarding key issues.

Opinion articles provided by newspapers contribute to the enhancement of public discourse due to their presentation of diverse opinions. The opinion section is a platform for issue advocates who are debating a particular issue to ensure pluralism and promote a market place of ideas.

De Vreese (2005) pointed out that framing significance lies in its impact on individuals who can change their attitudes after being exposed to certain frames, and the society where frames can influence behavior such as political socialization or collective actions. Studying media framing is important because audiences depend on media outlets to get informed and make decisions (Entman, 1993). Entman emphasized that the strength of the framing concept lies in the selection of a particular issue and the process of making it more salient than the other (Entman, 1993).

Framing theory emphasizes the ability of any entity, whether media, individuals, or organization to influence or define other people's reality, through highlighting some aspects while de-emphasizing others. Frames act as a guide to different concepts through which individuals rely in making sense of their surrounding environment (McCombs & Ghanem, 2001).

The application of framing analysis to research of opinion journalism is of particular salience, since it allows researchers to identify the central arguments presented by the opinion writer. Shen argues that news media emphasis on certain aspects of issues will make these aspects more accessible or salient to the audiences and more likely to be used in audience decision-making or their subsequent evaluations of publicly salient issues.

Sample Chosen

Al-Ahram newspaper, semi-official, and *Al-Masry Al-Youm*, independent, were chosen to represent the two types of ownership. These two newspapers were selected because they feature high readership and print circulation, and the highest number of unique visitors to their websites (Allam, 2018). *Al-Ahram* represents the semi-official category because of the strong elements of government control (Hamdy & Gomaa, 2012). The search yielded 77 news articles and all were included for analysis. *Al Masry Al-Youm* represented the independent category, as it is branded as the most balanced newspaper compared to its peers in the market (Allam, 2018). Using the same criteria, the search yielded a total of 43 opinion columns, and they were all included for analysis.

Results show that although *Al-Ahram* and *Al-Masry Al-Youm* had almost equal distribution of story placement in the front pages (19.5% and 25%) and in the inside pages (80.5% and 75%), the percentage of news stories and the editorials vary between the two papers.

Al-Ahram newspaper featured more news stories (76.3%) than editorials (23.7), whereas *Al-Masry Al-Youm* dedicated (43.2%) for news stories yet (56.8%) for editorials. Both newspapers focused more on political topics followed by economic and military. More than half of the stories and editorials in both papers framed the relationship with the Trump administration as neutral, while almost one-third showed it as co-operative and only around 10% showed that there is a conflict. Articles that showed a conflict relationship with the Trump administration were mainly covering the US relationship with other countries, such as Syria or China.

The ties with the United States in both newspapers were mainly framed as strong: *Al-Ahram* (75%), and *Al-Masry Al-Youm* (62%), yet it is important to mention that *Al-Masry Al-Youm* was a bit more critical in labeling the Trump administration as unsatisfactory (40%), especially in the editorial pieces, where there is usually more room to express criticism indirectly. This view was clearer during the measurement of the articles' slant, where 53% of the articles in *Al-Masry Al-Youm* appeared as unfavorable for the Trump administration, whereas *Al-Ahram* showed only 17% as unfavorable.

Both newspapers focused almost half of the articles on the US affairs with other countries, and the other 50% was almost equally divided to cover US internal affairs and US affairs with Egypt.

Unexpectedly, only 14% of the stories in both papers were about "fighting terrorism" although President Trump is always showing his support for Egypt in its fight against terrorism. The rest of the articles were tackling a list of other topics. *Al-Masry Al-Youm* talked about: criticism of the Trump administration after the United States struck against Syria, President Abdel Fattah Al-Sisi's visit to the United States and the importance of economic and education cooperation, analyzing the contradicting statements about Trump in regard to Syria and other political issues, and finally possible cooperation in the education, health, and energy fields.

As for *Al-Ahram*, it had a wider range of other topics, such as analyzing the meeting between Trump and China's president, criticism of the US invasion of Syria and comparing it with Iraq's crisis, US conflict with Sweden after Trump's announcement about refugees in Sweden, the positive effect of Trump's administration in trading polices on Egypt, the US investment in Egypt, the praising of US-Egyptian relations in Trump's administration, analyzing Trump's personality and statements, criticizing the suggestion of moving the American embassy to Jerusalem, ISIS as a tool used by the US to pressure Bashar Al-Assad to negotiate with them in Washington, Egypt's relation with the United States and the European countries, the US-Russian dispute about the Syrian crisis, the implications of Trump's visit to Kuwait on Egypt, and the meeting between US, UN, and Russian diplomats to discuss the Syrian crisis.

CONCLUSION

Reading through history, it is apparent that the Egyptian-US relationship is quite strategic and Egypt is a major strategic and political cornerstone of American policy in the Middle East. Since the Trump administration took over, the Egyptian media have changed their tone toward the US administration in general. One can notice that the rigid language that was used against the Obama administration has been smoothed and softened since the Trump administration took over. Although the Trump administration slightly criticized Egypt a few times, this criticism was indirect. At the same time, covering stories about potential cooperation between Egypt and the United States in different fields, the Egyptian newspapers made it clear that a new page of relationship would begin under the Trump administration.

Variance of coverage between the two newspapers was not noticeable except in the opinion columns where *Al-Masry Al-Youm* indirectly criticized the United States in its international affairs with other countries. Although *Al-Masry Al-Youm* was in total supportive and framing a positive image to Trump's administration, it was a warning about over-expectations that Egyptians would put on any US administration. Both newspapers are aware of the strong ties that have to remain strategically between the countries. Both newspapers were keen to highlight the United States as a strategic partner, and this was clear in their reflection on policies, whether in its negative attitude toward Obama's administration or positive attitude toward Trump's.

Finally, the Egyptian newspapers played a major role in portraying the US administration positively and were successful in influencing Egyptians and presetting the new administration as a needed ally. News stories were quite balanced in both papers. *Al-Masry Al-Youm* was more able compared to *Al-Ahram* in using the opinion columns section to offer a more balanced presentation of conflicting stands regarding controversial issues. Several studies indicate that newspapers tend to use the opinion section as an "echo chamber," to reinforce similar issue perspectives. The United States is an important ally to Egypt and vice versa, and the Egyptian newspapers were able to reframe the Trump administration positively and played an influential role in reconciling relations after the negative footprints of Obama.

REFERENCES

Abshire, D (1976). *International broadcasting: A new dimension of Western diplomacy.* SAGE.

Allam, R. (2018). Egyptian media landscape. European Journalism Center. https://medialandscapes.org/country/egypt

Brownlee, J. (2012). *Democracy prevention: The politics of the U.S.–Egyptian alliance.* Cambridge University Press. doi:10.1017/CBO9781139198721

Cook, S. A. (2011). *The struggle for Egypt: From Nasser to Tahrir Square.* Oxford University Press.

De Vreese, C. (2005). News framing: Theory and typology. *Information Design Journal+DocumentDesign, 13*(10), 51–62. http://www.tveiten.net/ futurelearninglab/menu4/1233468300.pdf

El Nawawy, M. (2006). "US public diplomacy in the Arab world: The news credibility of Radio Sawa and Television al-Hurra." *Global Media Communication* 2 (2)http://gmc.sagepub.com/cgi/content/absract/2/2/183.

Entman, R. (1993). "Framing: Toward clarification of a fractured paradigm." *Journal of Communication, 43*(4), 51–58.

Ezzat, I. (2009, February 16). The international image of the United States during Bush and Obama Administration. A research paper on the role of mass media in creating the image of U.S. Faculty of Economics and Political Science. Cairo University.

Fortner, R. (1994). *Public diplomacy and international politics: The symbolic constructs of summits and international radio news.* Praeger.

Goffman, E. (1974). Frame analysis: An essay on the organization of experience. Harper & Row.

Hamdy, N., & Gomaa, E. 2012. Framing the Egyptian uprising in Arabic-language newspapers and social media. *Journal of Communication, 62*(2), 195–211. https://doi.org/10.1111/j.1460-2466.2012.01637.x

Hoffman, A., ed. (1968). *International communication and the new diplomacy.* Indiana University Press.

Iskander, A. (2005). "Speaking to the enemy: US government public diplomacy and discourses of cultural hybridity." Paper presented at the annual meeting of the International Communication Association. http//www.allacademic.com/meta/p15071_index.html. Retrieved: January 10, 2020.

Levin D. 2005. Framing peace policies: The competition for resonant themes. *Political Communication, 22,* 83–108.

McCombs, M., & Ghanem, S. (2001). The convergence of agenda setting and framing. In S. Reese, A. Grant, & O. Gandy (Eds.), *Framing public life* (pp. 67–82). Lawrence Erlbaum Associates.

Ottaway, M. (2011). Between democratic values and state interests: The United States and Egypt after the uprising. European Institute of the Mediterranean. https://www.iemed.org/publicacions/historic-de-publicacions/monografies/sumaris-fotos-monografies/usa-egypt-after-uprising-ottaway-marina.pdf

Piazza, B. A. (2019). The foreign policy of post-Mubarak Egypt and the strengthening of relations with Saudi Arabia: Balancing between economic vulnerability and regional and regime security. *Journal of North African Studies, 24*(3), 401–425. doi:10.1080/13629387.2018.1454650

Tadros, S., & Brown, E. (2017). Renewing the American-Egyptian alliance. *Hudson Institute*, 1–49.

Wimmer, R., & Dominick, J. 2014. *Mass media research: An introduction*, 10th ed. Wadsworth.

ENGLAND

8

Special Relations

Trump, Brexit, and the British Media

Graham Murdock, Loughborough University

ABSTRACT

For many commentators reviewing the events of 2016, the unexpected success of the Leave campaign in the referendum on whether Britain should exit the European Union (Brexit) and the election Donald Trump as president of the United States marked a decisive break with the past conduct of politics in mature democracies, prompting a search for novel factors that might offer an explanation. They have pointed to both campaigns' staging of news events that deliberately violate the accepted conventions of political communication and their extensive use of digital media to connect directly with their supporters. These are important and relevant, but a full analysis of Trump and Brexit needs to look beyond these immediate factors and examine their roots in two embedded features of the world's two oldest mass democracies: the periodic eruption of authoritarian populist movements that exploit the perceived failures of established institutions of representation, and persistent anxieties over the future of national position and power in a globalized world order. For the United States at the turn of the twentieth century concern crystalized around the idea of America First. For Britain it centered on future relations with Europe and the imagined "special relationship" with the United States rooted in a shared language and culture. Retrieving these histories reminds us of the permanent potential for liberal democracies to take a reactionary turn.

GOLD-PLATED POPULISM

The victory of the Leave campaign in the June 2016 referendum on whether Britain should exit the European Union (Brexit) and the election of Donald Trump as President of the United States five months later have been greeted with consternation by seasoned political observers. Their surprise at the results was shared by the central figures in both campaigns, perfectly captured in a now iconic photograph taken in the gold-plated elevator to Trump's penthouse apartment in Trump Tower in New York. It was shot just after leading personalities in the Leave EU campaign had come out of an hour-long meeting with the president-elect, the first British political actors to be granted an audience. At first sight it appears to be the latest addition to a long line of photographs projecting the assumed "special relationship" between Britain and the United States through warm personal encounters between successive prime ministers and presidents, from Winston Churchill and Franklin Roosevelt, to Margaret Thatcher and Ronald Reagan and Tony Blair and George Bush. Except that it is an image of displacement and redirection. The British prime minister at the time, Theresa May, had been well down the list of world politicians that Trump telephoned once his election had been confirmed, and the easy informality of the Trump Tower photograph contrasts sharply with the visibly awkward intimacy revealed in photographs of May posing, holding hands with Trump during his visit to London, an occasion met with mass protest demonstrations in the streets of the capital and a giant inflatable blimp depicting Trump as an obese baby in nappies flying over Parliament Square (see Ewen, 2020).

The official "remain"' campaign was headed by the then British prime minister, David Cameron, who had called the referendum in the expectation that winning would finally silence the long-standing demands to leave the EU from his Eurosceptic backbench MPs. The officially designated leave campaign was organized by Vote Leave, fronted by Boris Johnson, the flamboyant former Conservative mayor of London and political journalist. Nigel Farage, the driving force behind the United Kingdom Independence Party (UKIP), led the parallel campaign, Leave UK, as a political outrider. In common with Trump he advanced a strident authoritarian populist platform, castigating the political and cultural establishment for dismissing and denigrating popular concerns with immigration, cultural liberalism, declining national power and prestige, and the sense of opportunities and choices being unduly circumscribed by overbearing international agreements. Both Farage and Trump enjoyed lives of privilege, far removed from the straightened circumstances of their core supporters. Trump took over his father's property empire. Farage had been a successful commodities trader on the London metals market and was heading a campaign largely financed by an insurance entrepreneur with interests in South African mining. They were all beneficiaries of the financialized capitalism that had dismantled the postwar welfare settlement, redirecting wealth and income to the top social tier and eroding the living standards and life chances of those at the bottom. Their platforms were informed by a commitment to radical deregulation, removing the remaining restrictions on corporate freedom to operate unhindered. They diverted attention from the inevitable widening of social inequalities this would produce by "performing ordinariness," employing live performances and direct media to construct a personalized relationship with their core supporters and present themselves as men of the people (Murdock, forthcoming)

Their ideological affinity was anchored by a network of social relations and connections. Farage wrote a regular column for the right-wing US newsletter, *Breitbart News*, whose editor, Raheem Kassam, was later appointed his chief of staff. *Breitbart*'s executive chairman, Steve Bannon, managed Trump's election campaign. At a Trump campaign rally in Jackson, Mississippi, Farage was hailed as "the Brexit guy" and invited to address the crowd from the podium.

The Trump Tower photo shows a laughing Farage holding out an open hand to Trump, relaxed in an open shirt, smiling broadly, and giving the thumbs up. They appear as two men who have bet against long odds and beaten the bookies, and are reveling in their unexpected win. As Farage told a journalist at the time, "They thought they were probably going to lose, if we are being honest about it. We were both roaring with laughter. We were two people who had been through quite an ordeal. But suddenly, you know, we'd won" (quoted in Knight, 2016).

Both results were close. Having failed to insist that the winning margin must reach a supermajority of two-thirds, David Cameron was obliged to accept the 51.9% endorsement for leaving the EU as binding and discount the 48.1% who voted in favor of remaining. He immediately resigned, and Theresa May became the new leader of the Conservative Party and prime minister. In the US presidential election Hillary Clinton commanded 48.2% of the popular vote while Trump received 46.1%, a shortfall of almost 2.9 million, more than any other losing presidential candidate in American history, but Trump went on to secure a decisive majority in the Electoral College giving him the presidency.

Attempts to explain these outcomes have generated an ever-growing volume of commentary and analysis in search of novel forces that have altered contemporary political communication in ways that have opened renewed space for the resurgence of right-wing populist platforms. Efforts to identify a "Trump effect" on the conduct of politics and political communication have focused on his rejection and denigration of mainstream media and reliance on the direct connections with citizens, provided by staged rallies and social media. They point to the combative performative styles he has borrowed from his involvements in reality television and professional wrestling (see Klein, 2017, pp. 51–55) to his unprecedented manipulation of voters' personal information harvested, without their knowledge, from social media sites to microtarget electoral appeals (Wylie, 2019), and his incessant use of Twitter to bypass media outlets and post his personal comments on unfolding events (Ott, 2017). Carefully staged public performances and direct media appeals also played central roles in the Brexit campaigns.

Boris Johnson came to the Vote Leave campaign from a long and highly visible career as a journalist with finely honed skills of news management. Dismissed from his first post at the *Times* for fabricating a quotation, he moved to the right-of-center broadsheet the *Daily Telegraph* as its Brussels correspondent. Over the five years he spent covering EU affairs he developed a distinctive performative style that combined humor with provocation, posting a series of openly misleading assertions on policy proposals "mocking, lampooning, and ridiculing the EU" with claims that "Brussels recruits sniffers to ensure that Euro-manure smells the same," and that one of Britain's favorite snacks, prawn-flavored crisps, was about to be banned (Fletcher, 2016). As he later recounted in a BBC interview "[I] was sort of chucking these rocks over the garden wall and I listened to this amazing crash from the greenhouse next door over in England . . . and it really gave me this, I suppose, rather weird sense of power" (quoted in Fletcher, 2016). The continuous stream of "euro myths" depicting unaccountable Brussels bureaucrats devising unnecessary regulations that wasted pubic money and eroded personal liberties provided the Eurosceptic wing of the Conservative Party with added ammunition and pushed other newspapers to follow suit, embedding negativity as the default position for British coverage of European affairs. Johnson continued to write a regular column for the *Daily Telegraph* after moving into politics, first as mayor of London and later as a Conservative member of parliament, giving him a guaranteed and direct public platform for his views. Recalling Johnson's tenure at the *Telegraph*, his editor Max Hastings acknowledged that he was "a brilliant entertainer" but added that he "would not recognize truth, whether about his private or political life, if confronted by it in and identity parade" (Hastings, 2019). Johnson's tendency to be economical with the truth was on very public display during the referendum campaign when he toured Britain in a red bus bearing the message "We send the EU £350 million a week. Let's fund our NHS instead" emblazoned in large print on the side. Evoking Britain's most cherished public institution guaranteed saturation news attention, but the quoted figure took no account of the EU money paid into Britain each week and the publicity forgot to mention that the bus was German built.

Johnson's fabricated image of the EU as a force attacking national freedoms also featured prominently in Vote Leave's targeted Facebook ads. One widely distributed example featured a fist inside a glove draped in the EU flag threatening to smash a brimming cup of tea decorated with a small union jack with a miniature iconic red London bus and public telephone box balanced on the saucer. Borrowing from Johnson's earlier promotion of the prawn cracker as an essential ingredient in the British diet it was captioned "The European Union Want to Kill Our Cuppa."

Evoking notions of nation inevitably imposes definitions of who can legitimately claim membership. Labeling migrants as an alien incursion polluting an idealized national culture and bringing disease and disorder is a central motif in all right-wing populist platforms. It was activated in another of Vote Leave's Facebook ads captioned, "Turkey has a population of 76 million. Turkey is Joining the EU. Good Idea?" showing a solid wedge of people assembled in Turkey with a red arrow sweeping across Europe directed at the southern coast of England. The large number quoted invokes powerful images of invasion and plays on the embedded assumption that since Turkish culture has been indelibly shaped by Islam its citizens do not "belong" in a country defined by state sanctioned Christianity. This assumption surfaced in a more intense form during the Leave EU campaign when Nigel Farage was photographed standing in front of a billboard poster captioned "Breaking Point: The EU has failed us All" filled with a deliberately provocative image of a long column of Syrian refugees nearing the border with Croatia. As critics were quick to point out, the composition was almost identical to footage of Jewish refugees in a Nazi propaganda film of the 1940s shown earlier in a British television documentary on the holocaust captioned "parasites undermining their host communities, threatening thousand-year-old cultures and bringing with them, crime, corruption and chaos" (quoted in Bartlett, 2016). No longer being bound by a commitment to the free movement of labor within the EU and taking back control of national borders was promoted as one of the main advantages of leaving.

Trump shared both Leave campaigns' distrust of Muslim migrants singling out Syrian refugees as a particularly potent threat during his presidential campaign, telling his supporters in 2015 that "They could be ISIS. I don't know. They could make the Trojan Horse look like peanuts" (quoted in Johnson & Hausloher, 2017). Soon after assuming office he issued Executive Order 13769 (later overturned by the Court of Appeal) canceling entry to all migrants from Syria and six other countries with Muslim majorities. He located the other major unwanted incursion on the southern border claiming in his June 2015 speech in Trump Tower announcing his decision to enter the contest for the presidency, that "When Mexico sends its people, . . . they're bringing drugs, they're bringing crime, they're rapists. And it's got to stop" (quoted in CBS News, 2015). His proposed solution, which became a favored chant at his campaign rallies, was to build a solid wall along the entire length of the border.

The central roles played by public performances and direct media appeals in the Trump and the Brexit campaigns are all too easily seen as marking an unprecedented break with the past. This is a mistake. To fully grasp the present crisis of liberal democracies on both shores of the Atlantic we need to return to its origins at the turn of the twentieth century to the political fault line that appeared in mass democratic systems and its complex entanglements with the rise of popular journalism and the realignment of global power. It was precisely at this crucial moment of formation that the processes and contradictions that echo so powerfully in the present were set in motion.

One instructive point of departure is provided by the writings of William Stead the most famous British journalist of the Victorian and Edwardian eras.

PLATFORMS AND POPULAR MEDIA: LINEAGES OF THE PRESENT

As editor of the *Pall Mall Gazette*, Stead forged a new style of sensational and crusading journalism. In pursuit of his most famous campaign, against child prostitution in London, he purchased the thirteen-year-old daughter of a chimney sweep and was sent to prison for three months for failing to secure the father's consent. His general news coverage drew heavily on the innovative use of interviews, dramatic headlines, and gossip already current in popular American reporting. Where his contemporaries among Britain's intellectual elite viewed this Americanization of the press as a force for trivializing the serious discussion of issues, Stead saw it as an essential resource for articulating the popular concerns and preoccupations of the emerging mass electorate.

"It is," he argued, "the fashion among English people . . . to sneer at American newspapers but . . . from the first [they] represented far more faithfully than [their] English contemporaries the aspirations, the ideas, and the prejudices of the mass of the people" (quoted in Goodwyn, 2018, p. 415).

In a piece provocatively entitled "Government by Journalism" he pointed to a growing disconnect between proceedings in Britain's elective parliamentary chamber, the House of Commons, and "the nation which it represents," which if left unchecked would, he argued, inevitably result in "despotism." He saw the solution lying with the "direct and living contact with the people" provided by "the power of the Press and the Platform" bound together in a symbiotic relation. "If a statesman now wants to impress the nation" he argued "the last place in the world he will make his speech is in Parliament." The future lay with carefully orchestrated rallies and personal appearances and the blanket coverage they received in the popular media (Stead, 1886). The advent of radio took this relation a stage further, sidelining the gatekeeping and editorial roles previously monopolized by press journalists and allowing political actors to address audiences directly. Commercial radio in 1940s America supported a plethora of programs, giving a platform to right-wing populist evangelicals and political agitators. They included Gerald K. Smith. In a startlingly similar platform to Trump he claimed that the government was "controlled by undesirable and immoral bureaucrats" intent on sacrificing the country's national sovereignty by conceding too much control to the United Nations and other international institutions and that the solution lay with his America First Party (Janowitz, 1944).

The tension between representative and direct democracy is a permanent structural fault line running through mass democracies, opening space for authoritarian populist movements that claim to speak for "the people," voicing concerns ignored or derided by the supposedly self-serving career politicians and bureaucrats at the heart of government. Donald Trump's repeated election promises to "drain the Washington swamp" and put "America First" and his continual resort to the unmediated personal connection with voters provided by Twitter, stand in an unbroken line of descent from Smith's radio broadcasts and Stead's original formative conception of the new politics.

Its manifest departure from the ideal of informed, reasoned, and even-handed debate exercised many of Stead's contemporaries. Their concerns were voiced with particular force by Victorian England's leading cultural critic, Matthew Arnold who saw politicians in mass democracies being pulled inexorably toward crafting performance that played well to the gallery. "Practical politics" he lamented, was increasingly characterized by "a mass of insincerity, of phrase, fiction and claptrap, useful for purposes of party or faction" but ill-suited to serving the common good (Arnold, 1887, p. 629). This novel performative style was, he argued, nourished and amplified by Stead's "new journalism," which, while "full of ability, variety and sensation . . . throws out assertions at a venture because it wishes them to be true; does not correct them or itself if they are false; and to get to the state of things as they truly are seems to feel no concern whatever" (p. 638).

Arnold's alternative was to cast intellectuals and journalists as educators. The son of a reforming headmaster and a long-serving inspector of schools himself, he placed public education at the heart of democratic practice. In his influential broadside *Culture and Anarchy*, published in 1869 in the wake of the Hyde Park riots in support of extending the right to vote, he called on "men of culture" to ensure that mass democracy was rooted in reasoned debate rather than emotional reaction informed by "a passion for diffusing, for making prevail, for carrying from one end of society to another, the best knowledge, the best ideas of their time" and making them "efficient outside the clique of the cultivated and learned" (Arnold, [1869] 1966, p. 70). This drive to democratize expert and specialist knowledge found its fullest institutional expression in the practices of public service broadcasting, but it was also central to social responsibility conceptions of the press which charged newspapers with serving democracy by providing the comprehensive information, informed analysis, and plural argumentation that underpinned citizens' full and effective participation in social and political life. As Barbie Zelizer reminds us, since its inception this "model of inspiring conduct" has played a central role in mainstream "journalism's Anglo-American imaginary" bolstering its claims to authority (Zelizer, 2018, p. 140). But as she points out, it was the "massive failure" of this imaginary "that helped usher in Brexit and Trump" (p. 152).

Thomas Patterson's audits of the mainstream US press and television news coverage demonstrate how comprehensively Trump commanded the news agenda. "From the time he announced his candidacy until he received his party's presidential nomination, he received 63 percent of the coverage compared to 37 percent for his most heavily covered rival," and once the election campaign was under way, "week after week," he received 15 percent more press coverage than his democratic rival, Hillary Clinton (Patterson, 2016, p. 7). At the same time, the majority of the coverage he generated, 56 percent, was negative (p. 3), with only two out of the hundred top-circulation newspapers prepared to endorse him (Sillito, 2016). British press coverage was characterized by an even stronger antipathy to the content and style of Trump's campaign with 66 percent of the articles sampled by Lars Nord and his colleagues adopting a negative stance and only 8 percent presenting a positive view (Nord, Mancini, & Gerli, 2017, p. 8). Mainstream media commentary failed to understand that Trump's rejection of the accepted conventions of public discourse was central to his success.

Listening to right-wing radio agitators during his war-time exile in the United States in the 1940s, the critical cultural theorist Theodore Adorno argued that their appeal lay in their willingness to "violate the taboos which middle-class society has put in expressive behaviour on the part of the normal matter-of-fact citizen" and their ability to dramatize their arguments in immersive performances "reminiscent of sport and so called religious revivals" (Adorno, [1946] 1994, p. 166). Trump's mastery of exactly these strategies, with his constant denigration of opponents, the ritual chants at his rallies, and his uncensored stream-of-consciousness commentary on Twitter, bound platform and popular media together in a new configuration. For mainstream news outlets under increasing financial pressure from the migration of advertising revenues to the major internet companies, it proved irresistible. As Les Moonves, chair of the CBS network admitted, Trump's bid for the presidency "may not be good for America, but it's damn good for CBS. . . . The money's rolling in and this is fun. I've never seen anything like this, and it's going to be a very good year for us" (quoted in Collins, 2016). The constant stream of negative publicity provided Trump with visibility and free promotion.

He capitalized on the hostility of the mainstream American media by incorporating it into his worldview of a self-interested left-leaning establishment intent on ignoring or misrepresenting the "true" interests and voice of the people, repeatedly denouncing negative coverage of him as "Fake News." In an angry tweet he singled out the *New York Times,* CNN, and the three established broadcasting networks for particular condemnation declaring that "the FAKE NEWS media is not my enemy, it is the enemy of the American People" (quoted in Greenwood, 2017). It was an argument that had enjoyed currency on the radical right for some time. In 2009, the veteran right-wing radio commentator Rush Limbaugh used his program to present universities, science, government, and the mainstream media as "Four Corners of Deceit," constructing a cultural universe "run, dominated and controlled by the left" where everything "is an entire lie." Pitched against this complex he celebrated "the other universe where we are, and that's where reality reigns supreme" (quoted in Roberts, 2017). In 2020 Trump interrupted his State of the Union address to award Limbaugh the Medal of Freedom, the country's highest civilian honor. For sympathetic coverage and commentary, he could rely on Rupert Murdoch's Fox News channel, which since the abolition of the Fairness Doctrine in 1987 was under no obligation to provide space for contending views and free to be resolutely partisan and partial.

Broadcast news in Britain is still bound by the requirement to be impartial, but the national press is not and is strongly skewed toward the right of the political spectrum. Only three titles supported the Remain position in the Brexit referendum, the broadsheet *Guardian* and tabloid *Mirror*, both with long traditions of supporting parties of the center and left, and the *Financial Times*, voicing the concerns of the business community. With the exception of the *Times* the remainder, accounting for 80% of total daily circulation (Media Reform Coalition, 2015), all endorsed the Leave position. After allowing for "the proportion of the newspaper's audience likely to be exposed to each article," the comprehensive analysis of press reporting conducted by David Levy and his colleagues found that overtly pro-Brexit items accounted for 48 percent of the total referendum coverage as against just 22% for Remain, with the rest not adopting a position (Levy, Aslan, & Bironzo, 2016, pp. 17–18). Although the then prime minister, David Cameron, was the most quoted source, he was run a close second by Boris Johnson, with Nigel Farage quoted considerably more times than Jeremy Corbyn, the leader of the main opposition Labour Party campaigning for Remain (pp. 28–29). These figures point to attention being diverted from parliamentary figures to the platform performances of Johnson's bus tour of Britain and Farage's "Breaking Point" poster.

Their ability to capture the agenda during the referendum debate is confirmed by the more comprehensive inventory of media coverage conducted by Martin Moore and Gordon Ramsay, which included broadcast news and internet sites alongside the press. As they argue, although the Remain campaign's emphasis on the negative consequences for the British economy of leaving the EU was the lead issue overall, the Leave side successfully reframed projections of severe losses as "Project Fear" and politically motivated scaremongering. The

Treasury estimate that every household would be £4,300 a year poorer if Britain left the EU was discussed, mostly in hostile terms, in 365 of the articles sampled, whereas the fallacious Leave claim of a £350 million pound national weekly bonus emblazoned on Boris Johnson's tour bus was examined in only 147 (Moore and Ramsay, 2017, p. 8). This skewed attention, coupled with the emergence of the Leave campaigns' focus on immigration control as the dominant issue in the later stages of the debate, severely limited the Remain side's initial agenda-setting advantage (2017, p. 61).

The immediate arguments over the future of the economy and the imagined community of the nation dominating both the Brexit and Trump campaigns spoke to a deeper anxiety over how to respond to the shifting composition of global power. Remain supporters saw Britain's future lying primarily with continued membership of a European-wide confederation. Leave supporters campaigned under the slogan "Take Back Control," arguing that Britain needed to retrieve national sovereignty over key decisions affecting its future and seek independent trade deals around the world, with the United States as the first port of call, capitalizing on the supposed "special relationship.'" At the same time. Trump was promising to put "America First," and to disengage from international agreements and associations where he claimed the United States had conceded and given more than it had gained and to renegotiate alliances on more favorable terms.

The post–World War II global order, outside the Communist Bloc, was anchored by a settlement devised primarily by the United States and Britain. General cooperation was organized through the various agencies of the United Nations inaugurated in 1945, while the launch of the International Monetary Fund and the precursor of the World Bank the following year was designed to regulate the global economic system and avoid the beggar-my-neighbor competition that had characterized the interwar period. The growing tensions in relations between Britain, Europe, and the United States, dramatized in the Trump and Brexit campaigns, represent a radical break from this settlement. To understand their popular purchase, however, we need to recognize that they activate deeply embedded assumptions, fears, and desires with roots dating back to the turn of the twentieth century when American power was consolidating. Once again, William Stead is an illuminating guide.

THE FATEFUL TRIANGLE

Reflecting on his travels around Europe in 1898, Stead concluded that "the menacing ascendency of the American producer" compels "the Old World to adopt the New World conditions, or give up the struggle" and that only a United States of Europe would enable the continent "to hold its own in the struggle for existence in the markets of the world" (Stead, 1899, pp. 10–11). He imagined this association as both a free-trade zone and a political formation based around a "federal centre . . . which can not only deliberate, but on occasion act" (p. 24). Helping to construct a European confederation that would reproduce a variant of the federal system of the United States was one ambition he had for British foreign policy. The other was to "unite all branches of the English-speaking race in an Anglo-Saxon Bund" (p. 33). He developed this theme three years later in *The Americanisation of the World* arguing that now that America was overtaking Britain as the world's premiere economic power "common sense teaches us that, seeing we can never again be the first, standing alone, we should lose no time in uniting our fortunes with those who have passed us in the race" (Stead, 1902, pp. 5–6). This new alliance would be based, he argued, on the unity of "the two sections of the English-speaking world" (p. 4). It was a deeply racialized conception that defined the boundaries of shared culture by adding "to the population of the United Kingdom every white-skinned person in the British Empire" and "deducting from the population of the United States all men of colour" (p. 4).

Stead was drowned when the *Titanic* sunk on its maiden voyage in 1912 on the North Atlantic route between England to New York. But his project of forging a privileged connection between Britain and the United States was already being roundly rejected in the United States. In 1894, the Republican Party had campaigned on the slogan "America first, the rest of the world afterward." In 1915, President Woodrow Wilson revived the phrase, defending the US refusal to enter Word War I in support of Britain and its European allies by claiming that "Our whole duty for the present, at any rate, is summed up in the motto 'America First'" (quoted in Churchwell, 2016). Following German attacks on US shipping, however, he oversaw America's entry into the conflict in April 1917 and in 1919 was awarded the Nobel Peace Prize for his role in establishing the League of Nations, precursor of the United Nations. The United States, however, never became a member of the League, with Republicans denouncing it for undermining the commitment to "America First." In 1940, the main organization lobbying against US entry into World War II, another conflict presented as an exclusively European concern, chose to call itself the America First Committee.

At the same time, the phrase insistently raised the question of who counted as "American." In 1919, the leader of the Ku Klux Klan used his Fourth of July speech to give an unequivocal answer, insisting, "I am for America first, last and all the time. And I don't want any foreign elements telling us what to do" (quoted in Churchwell, 2016). America's Black population was excluded from full citizenship under the Jim Crow laws instituted after the Civil War. Denied the right to vote, they became de facto "foreign elements." Banners bearing the slogans "America First" and "White Supremacy" became standard accompaniments at Klan rallies. Almost a century later, in August 2017, a coalition of extreme right-wing groups converged on Charlottesville in Virginia to protest the removal of a statue of the Confederate general Robert E. Lee from the city center. Displaying Klan and Nazi slogans and regalia they provoked violent confrontations with anti-Nazi protestors during which a young woman was killed by a car deliberately driven into the crowd. While regretting the death, Trump refused to condemn the instigators of the march.

This incident, which attracted widespread condemnation in the British media, demonstrates very clearly the continuity between Stead's overtly racialized vision of "an Anglo-Saxon Bund" (Stead, 1902, p. 33) and militant contemporary assertions of white supremacy.

Stead's version of relations between Britain and the United States is also marked by another motif that has proved remarkably enduring. "We may," he argues, "lose our primacy in the forging of iron and steel, but no 'invasion' can deprive us of the indestructible renown possessed by the land which gave birth to Shakespeare and Milton" (Stead, 1902, p. 3). This worldview sets up an opposition that remains active in contemporary discourse, between the immediate brute force of American money and industrial production and the enduring symbolic value of English "high" culture and its central role in defining the nation. The word *invasion* also suggests that economic power may spill over into the cultural domain as a force for colonization and annexation, precisely the sense in which the term *Americanization* came to be most widely used in later debates.

In September 1943, Britain's wartime leader, Winston Churchill, traveled to Harvard University to accept an honorary degree. The United States had entered the war following the Japanese destruction of the Pacific Fleet at Pearl Harbor in December 1941, and Churchill took the opportunity of addressing military allies under a unified command to promote a "doctrine of the fraternal association of our two peoples." "You will," he told his audience, find the "English-speaking people" of Britain and the Empire "good comrades to whom you are united by ties . . . of blood and history" and "the priceless inheritance" of the "gift of a common tongue" (Churchill, 1943). This reconstruction of Stead's "English-speaking world" is softer edged but establishes boundaries that are no less resilient. Churchill reiterated the argument in March 1946 in a speech accepting an honorary degree from Westminster College at Fulton, Missouri, insisting that there was a "fraternal association of the English-speaking peoples" rooted in "a special relationship between the British Commonwealth and Empire and the United States" (Churchill, 1946).

At the same time, Churchill, like Stead, had also been reflecting on Britain's future relations to Continental Europe. In 1930, in an article for the *Saturday Evening Post*, he had revived Stead's notion of a United States of Europe, arguing that "national hatreds and distrust from the First World War could best be dispelled by mutual cooperation and dependence" (quoted in Mauter, 1998, p. 67). In March 1946, having lost the British general election to the Labour Party's radical reforming platform, he was leading the parliamentary opposition but still campaigning vigorously for a united Europe. In the Fulton speech's most famous passage, he characterized the Soviet annexation of Eastern Europe as "an iron curtain [that] has descended across the Continent." In this changed context, he argued, "the safety of the world requires a new unity in Europe, from which no nation should be permanently outcast" (Churchill, 1946). He went on to argue forcefully that "a united Europe was the best means to heal residual hatreds from the Second World War, prevent future wars, and ensue economic prosperity" (Mauter, 1998, p. 67). He imagined the postwar global order outside the Soviet sphere of influence resting on three pillars, the United States, the British Empire, and a United States of Europe. Britain, however, would not join this new union, since, as he noted, "We are with Europe but not of it. We are linked but not compromised. . . . We have our own dreams" (quoted in Mauter, 1998, p. 68). Economic considerations forced a reconsideration of this position.

Britain's original application to join the European Community was rebuffed by General de Gaul, the president of France, but entry was finally ratified in 1972 under a Conservative prime minister, Edward Heath. It was a pragmatic decision, driven by economic calculation. Successive decolonization struggles had consigned the British Empire to history, propelling an urgent search for new markets for British goods. Europe's Common Market offered a solution, and Britain played a major role in eroding its original basis in the old welfare consensus and promoting neoliberalism's core demands for liberalization and privatization as the new economic orthodoxy (see Streeck, 2019). Britain was now in Europe but still not of it, however, with the political establishment displaying little interest in the wider political and cultural projects of reconciliation and imaginative exchange. This insistence on maintaining separation and distance opened the door to Brexit's populist platforms that cast a resurgent Germany as the new pivot of European power, intent on further eroding Britain's national sovereignty and creating a super state, a concern encapsulated in the Brexit slogan "Take Back Control."

A month before the referendum vote, Boris Johnson reminded *Daily Telegraph* readers that "Napoleon, Hitler, various people tried [unifying Europe] and it ended tragically" (quoted in O'Toole, 2019, p. 40). The choice of historic references is instructive. As Linda Colley has argued, it was mobilization against an expected Napoleonic invasion that finally cemented British national identity (Colley, 2005), while Churchill's 1940 wartime speech, exhorting citizens to fight Hitler's expected landing on the south coast on the beaches, fields, and landing grounds and to never surrender, is one of the most frequently quoted evocations of national will. In 2014 Johnson, a self-proclaimed admirer, published a biography of Churchill (Johnson, 2014).

Britain's continuing anxieties over the terms of its membership of the EU and the prospects of greater political integration have coincided with successive postwar prime ministers' efforts to strengthen the "special relationship" with the United States. Margaret Thatcher and Ronald Reagan found common ground in their joint promotion of minimal state intervention in economic affairs and maximum freedom of operation for corporations. Tony Blair, alone among the major European powers and in the face of concerted opposition from Germany and France endorsed George Bush's invasion of Iraq. This breach between the United States and the EU has widened under Trump, who casts Europe as more of an enemy than an ally, presenting it as another major economic power, together with China, trading on unfair terms. When asked in interview in 2018 to name his biggest foe globally right now, he replied, "Well we have a lot of them. . . . I think the European Union is a foe. . . . Now you wouldn't think of the European Union, but they're a foe . . . in a trade sense they've really taken advantage of us" (quoted in Roth, Smith, Helmore, & Pengelly, 2018). For Trump, as for earlier American populists, it is America first, last, and always. In an economic competition viewed as a zero-sum game, delivering on the promise to Make America Great Again necessarily involves rewriting the rules to secure maximum advantage.

The Brexiteers' assumption that leaving the EU opens the way for a new privileged trade deal and alliance with the United States ignores the obvious fact that the "special relationship" was always highly asymmetric and informed by "a persistent inclination to pursue empire vicariously by clambering like a mouse on the American eagle's head" (Colley, 2002, p. 376). In his original formulation, William Stead was honest enough to recognize that Britain would always be in a subordinate position, but asked, "What sacrifices are there which can be regarded as too great to achieve the realization of the ideal of unity of the English-speaking race?" (Stead, 1902, p. 6). Nor is the other plank in Stead's original vision, which resurfaced in the Brexit debate, any more sustainable, fueled as it is "by fantasies of a reconstructed global mercantilist trading empire in which the old white colonies will be reconnected to the mother country," a project dismissed as "Empire 2.0" by critics (O'Toole, 2019, p. 3).

THE TRUMP EFFECT

The election campaign and presidency of Donald Trump and the British vote to exit the European Union mark the resurgence of authoritarian populism in the world's two oldest established modern democracies and its migration from the margins to the center of political debate. Both campaigns illustrate the pivotal role now played by digital media and spectacle in political communication (Kellner, 2017). Trump's raucous rallies and Johnson and Farage's carefully staged photo opportunities, combined with both campaigns' use of digital platforms to micro-target appeals, tapped into popular anxieties and resentments in ways that were emotionally engaging. The visibility and popular currency of their interventions set the agenda for debate, pulling the mainstream media into territory they had mapped out.

As a group of distinguished political scientists observed, faced with these multiple disruptions to political business as usual, "One is tempted to proclaim something dramatic: the end of an era, the beginning of one" (Wells, Shah et al., 2016, p. 1). To adopt this stance is to abandon any hope of a full understanding of our present condition. I have argued here that this requires us to see Trump and Brexit, not as unprecedented and exceptional, but as the latest articulations of deep-seated reactionary ideological constructions of national identities and destinies and fears of national decline and forceful reminders of the permanent structural tension between representative and direct conceptions of democracy that propels these constructions into the political mainstream. The primary "Trump Effect" is to illuminate the dark institutional and imaginative underbelly of liberal democracies and to compel us to confront authoritarian populism's permanent potential to construct an "illiberal democracy" that preserves the formal apparatus of electoral politics while hollowing out the checks on the arbitrary exercise of power provided by an independent judiciary and civil service and a media system dedicated to providing the full range of cultural and communicative resources that support informed deliberation and political engagement.

REFERENCES

Adorno, T. W. (1994). Anti-Semitism and Fascist propaganda. In T. W. Adorno, *The stars down to earth and other essays on the irrational in culture*. Edited with an introduction by Stephen Crook (pp. 162–171). Routledge.

Arnold, M. (1869/1966). *Culture and anarchy*. Cambridge University Press.

Arnold, M. (1887, May 21). Up to Easter. *The Nineteenth Century, 123*, 629–643.

Bartlett, E. (2016, June 16). People are calling out UKIP's new anti-EU poster for resembling "outright Nazi propaganda." *Independent*. https://www.indy100.com/article/people-are-calling-out-ukips-new-antieu-poster-for-resembling-outright-nazi-propaganda—WkTYUB18EW

CBS News. (2015, June 16). Transcript: Donald Trump announces his presidential candidacy. https://www.cbsnews.com/news/transcript-donald-trump-announces-his-presidential-candidacy/

Churchill, W. S. (1943, September 6). The gift of a common tongue speech at Harvard University. https://winstonchurchill.org/resources/speeches/1941-1945-war-leader/the-price-of-greatness-is-responsibility/

Churchill, W. S. (1946, March 5). The sinews of peace speech at Westminster College, Fulton, Missouri. https://winstonchurchill.org/resources/speeches/1946-1963-elder-statesman/the-sinews-of-peace/

Churchwell, S. (2016, April 21). End of the American dream? The dark history of "America First." *The Guardian*. https://www.theguardian.com/books/2018/apr/21/end-of-the-american-dream-the-dark-history-of-america-first

Colley, L. (2005). *Britons: Forging the nation 1707–1837*. Yale University Press.

Colley, L. (2002). *Captives: Britain, Empire and the world, 1600–1850*. Jonathan Cape.

Collins, E. (2016, February 29). Les Moonves: Trump's run is "damn good for CBS." *Politico*. https://www.politico.com/blogs/on-media/2016/02/les-moonves-trump-cbs-220001

Ewen, N. (2020). Holding hands as the ship sinks: Trump and May's special relationship. I. B. Brickman, D. Jermyn, & T. Trost (Eds.), *Love across the Atlantic: US-UK romance in popular culture*. Edinburgh University Press.

Fletcher, M. (2016, July 1). Boris Johnson peddled absurd EU myths—and our disgraceful press followed his lead. *New Statesman*. https://www.newstatesman.com/politics/uk/2016/07/boris-johnson-peddled-absurd-eu-myths-and-our-disgraceful-press-followed-his-lead

Goodwyn, H. (2018). A "new" journalist: The Americanisation of W. T. Stead. *Journal of Victorian Culture, 23*(3), 405–420.

Greenwood, M. (2017, February 17). Trump tweets: "The media is the 'enemy of the American people.'" *The Hill*. https://thehill.com/homenews/administration/320168-trump-the-media-is-the-enemy-of-the-american-people

Hastings, M. (2019, June 24). I was Boris Johnson's boss—he is utterly unfit to be prime minister. *The Guardian.* theguardian.com/commentisfree/2019/jun/24/boris-johnson-prime-minister-tory-party -britain

Janowitz, M. (1944). The technique of propaganda for reaction: Gerald L. K. Smith's radio speeches. *Public Opinion Quarterly, 8*(1), 84–93.

Johnson, B. (2014). *The Churchill factor: How one man made history.* Hodder and Stoughton.

Johnson, J., and Hausloher, A. (2017, May 20). I think Islam hates us: A timeline of Trump's comments about Islam and Muslims. *Washington Post.* https://www.washingtonpost.com/news/post -politics/wp/2017/05/20/i-think-islam-hates-us-a-timeline-of-trumps-comments-about-islam-and -muslims/?noredirect=on&utm_term=.9761df81df42

Kellner, D. (2017). Donald Trump, media spectacle, and authoritarian populism. *Fast Capitalism, 14*(1), 75–87.

Klein, N. (2017). *No is not enough: Defeating the new shock politics.* Allen Lane.

Knight, S. (2016, November 20). Nigel Farage on the story behind his friendship with Trump. *New Yorker.* https://www.newyorker.com/culture/persons-of-interest/nigel-farage-on-the-story-behind-his -friendship-with-trump

Levy, D. A., Aslan, B., & Bironzo, D. (2016). *UK press coverage of the EU referendum.* Oxford University, Reuters Institute for the Study of Journalism.

Mauter, W. R. (1998). Churchill and the unification of Europe. *The Historian, 61*(1), 67–84.

Media Reform Coalition. (2015). *Who owns the UK media?* Media Reform Coalition. www.mediare form.org.uk

Moore, M., & Ramsay, G. (2017). *UK media coverage of the 2016 EU referendum campaign.* Kings College London University, Centre for the Study of Media, Communication and Power.

Murdock, G. (forthcoming). Profits of deceit: Performing populism in polarized times. *European Journal of Cultural Studies.*

Nord, L., Mancini, P., & Gerli, M. (2017). *The exceptional election: Press coverage of Clinton and Trump in Italy, Sweden and the UK.* Mid Sweden University.

O'Toole, F. (2019). *Heroic failure: Brexit and the politics of pain.* Head of Zeus.

Ott, B. L. (2017). The age of Twitter: Donald J Trump and the politics of debasement. *Critical Studies in Media Communication, 34*(1), 59–68.

Patterson, T. E. (2016). *News coverage of the 2016 general election: How the press failed voters.* Harvard University, Shorenstein Center on Media, Politics and Public Policy.

Roberts, D. (2017, May 19). Donald Trump and the rise of tribal epistemology. Vox. https://www.vox .com/policy-and-politics/2017/3/22/14762030/donald-trump-tribal-epistemology

Roth, A., Smith, D., Helmore, E., & Pengelly, M. (2018, July 15). Trump calls European Union a "foe"—ahead of Russia and China. *The Guardian.* https://www.theguardian.com/us-news/2018/ jul/15/donald-trump-vladimir-putin-helsinki-russia-indictments

Sillito, D. (2016, November 14). Donald Trump: How the media created the president. BBC News. https://www.bbc.co.uk/news/entertainment-arts-37952249

Stead, W. T. (1886, May). Government by journalism. *The Contemporary Review, 49*, 653–674.

Stead, W. T. (1899). *The United States of Europe: On the eve of the parliament of peace.* Doubleday & McClure.

Stead, W. T. (1902). *The Americanisation of the world: The trend of the twentieth century.* Horace Markley.

Streeck, W. (2019, July–August). Progressive regression: Metamorphoses of European social policy. *New Left Review*, 118, 117–139.

Wells, C., Shah, D. V., et al. (2016). How Trump drove coverage to the nomination: Hybrid media campaigning. *Political Communication, 33*, 669–676.

Wylie, C. (2019). *Mindf*ck: Inside Cambridge Analytica's plot to break the world.* Profile Books.

Zelizer, B. (2018). Resetting journalism in the aftermath of Brexit and Trump. *European Journal of Communication, 33*(2), 140–156.

ENGLAND

9

Donald Trump: Balloon Baby or Toilet Head?

Satire and Protest in the Press and on the Streets of London

Jane Stokes, University of East London

INTRODUCTION

Readers will probably have seen the images of the Donald Trump "baby blimp" or "balloon baby," which made its debut in London in 2018 and has since appeared at a number of protests around the world. The balloon baby has a snarl on his face and is naked save for a diaper and the cell phone he carries in his hand. This helium-filled manifestation clearly alludes to the figuration of Trump as infantile: irrational, selfish, and lacking control. It also bears a strong resemblance to the images that political cartoonist Steve Bell has created of Trump especially in regard to the shape and color of the eyes, lips, and face. Some, especially British readers, may be familiar with Steve Bell's work in the British newspaper, *The Guardian*. Bell's more recent caricatures of Trump typically show him wearing a long red tie to symbolize his links to Russia; his small hands peeking from within an ill-fitting business suit; his eyes like a cartoon bandit's mask and his twisted mouth set in a face the bizarre color of orange television makeup. The balloon baby wears a diaper that, while signaling infancy, also carries a connotation of the fecal; Bell's manifestation of POTUS shows him with a head shaped like a toilet, his unmanageable hair depicted as a sometimes ajar, sometimes closed, toilet seat. Besides the physical resemblance, there is, then, a shared implication of something scatological about the man. These two representations of Trump, from street activism and editorial cartoons respectively, emanate from the same British traditions of burning effigies and theatrical pantomime attacks on authority. What do they say about the representation of the United States of America and its 45th president from the perspective of the United Kingdom?

Donald Trump is recognized by Douglas Kellner, and others, as "the *master of media spectacle*" (Kellner, 2016, p. 1). His inherited wealth and family real estate and casino businesses, often bearing his name, as in Trump Tower and the Trump Taj Mahal in Atlantic City, helped to launch "Trump" as an avaricious brand enhanced by the self-aggrandizement in his 1987 book:

Trump: The Art of the Deal. These qualities of pompous self-aggrandizement were used (maybe even exploited) by the British born television producer, Mark Burnett, who built a successful television franchise around Trump's persona, the NBC reality television show *The Apprentice* (NBC: 2004–2015) (Littleton, 2017). In the television show, contestants vie for an opportunity to work in the Trump organization by completing business-oriented tasks for the cameras. *The Apprentice* has been franchised around the world, and the UK version (launched in 2005) features the British entrepreneur, Alan Sugar, as the man doing the hiring and firing. Audience numbers for the UK show have grown steadily, so that now *The Apprentice* is not only one of the BBC's top-rated shows but it has become a staple of the television calendar. In Britain (as in the United States), Trump was known as the person who fronted this popular, if ruthlessly neoliberal, television show long before he stood for election. The brand "Trump" was further consolidated in Britain by his highly contested purchase of land in Scotland where he built a golf course, Trump International Golf Links, near Aberdeen, Scotland (opened in 2012). Local people mounted fierce opposition to the development, and while it was originally scheduled to host the Scottish Open in 2017, the tournament was moved elsewhere in response to Trump's offensive comments about Muslims. In 2014 he bought a second course, Turnberry, Scotland, home of many British Opens, which he renamed "Trump Turnberry." In the United Kingdom, as in the rest of the world, Trump is known for being a racist, misogynistic, right-wing bully. But he is also known in Britain for his association with British real estate—specifically the golf courses in Scotland—and for his connection with one of the most successful shows on British television. Scottish people took to the streets to protest against his visit in 2018 and thousands of people protest against his presence when he comes to London, or to Scotland. The cry of "no Trump, no racist USA" accompanies the protests (Brooks L., 2018).

   During his campaign, and subsequently, Trump has always endeavored to capitalize on any publicity and has been a powerful manipulator of the media circus that surrounds him. "Trump's rise to global celebrity and now political power is bound up with his use of media spectacle" (Kellner, 2016, p. 1). If we are in an age of the spectacle, we are also living in an age where a strong relationship to the truth seems no longer required. Matthew d'Ancona is one of many who claims that we are in a "post-truth" world. "As candidate and President, Donald Trump has demeaned the assumption that the leader of the free world should have at least a passing acquaintance with the truth" (D'Ancona, 2017, p. 8). Many commentators have noted Trump's at best tangential relationship to the truth. This was perhaps first apparent at the hugely satirized claim that his inauguration speech was attended by massive audiences—bigger than any previously (Hunt, 2017). Satirists and newspaper editors delighted in comparing the crowds at Obama's inauguration with those of a significantly more sparsely populated Washington Mall for Trump's. His dangerously ambivalent, if not antipathetic relationship to the truth often parodied.

   The US satirical television shows, *Saturday Night Live* and *The Daily Show*, have provided cutting critiques of Trump. In the case of *Saturday Night Live*, Alec Baldwin's impersonations of him have hit home, prompting Trump to rise to the bait and tweet responses. In the UK, Nish Kumar fronted up *The Mash Report* (BBC 2017–2019), loosely based on *Saturday Night Live*; other UK television programs such as *The Last Leg* and *Have I Got News for You* also pitch satirical barbs at Trump, targeting his extreme right-wing politics, racism, misogyny, grandiosity, and general ignorance of the affairs of state. These do seem to aggravate Trump, but really, are they harmful? Matthew D'Ancona thinks so: "Trump is right to be bothered: the forces that created him could yet destroy him. A politician so dependent upon emotional resonance cannot afford to become a figure of general ridicule. Clearly, the satirists are doing their job" (D'Ancona, 2017, p. 139).

In their discourse analysis of news reports about Trump, Will Penman and Doug Cloud investigated the ways news reports discussed Trump and are especially interested in the way discussions around Trump address (or not) issues of race and racism and ideas of white supremacism, for example implicit in the slogan: "Make America Great Again." When they coded the media content, they found some 500 different actions or attributions associated with "Trump," from which they identified four rhetorical archetypes: Trump the Authoritarian, Trump the Acclaim-Seeker, Trump the Idiot, and Trump the Sick Man (Penman & Cloud, 2018, p. 112). The latter category, "Trump the Sick Man," includes the diagnosis of Trump as having "arrested development" of some kind: "Critics call him a 'baby,' an 'infantalist' or a 'little boy' with 'juvenile' behaviour and a propensity for 'blow ups' and 'tantrums'" (Penman & Cloud, 2018, p. 118).

An example of news articles about Trump being infantile would be David Brooks's piece in the *New York Times*, headed: "When the World Is Led by a Child" (Brooks, 2017). He is renowned for his propensity to be impulsive and for his brutal nastiness and it is this quality that has attracted the attention of satirists and the Trump balloon creators.

SATIRICAL RESPONSES

Lamenting the decision of the *New York Times* to no longer run political cartoons in its international edition, the British cartoonist Martin Rowson wrote:

> Cartoons have been the rude, taunting part of political commentary in countries around the world for centuries, and enhance newspapers globally and across the political spectrum, in countries from the most tolerant liberal democracies to the most vicious totalitarian tyrannies. As we all know, they consequently have the power to shock and offend. That, largely, is what they are there for, as a kind of dark, sympathetic magic masquerading as a joke. (Rowson, 2019)

Martin Rowson and Steve Bell are two of the most influential cartoonists in Britain today. Steve Bell is renowned for his long-standing series *If. . .* in the *Guardian*, which has chronicled the activities of successive prime ministers and their cabinets, while his editorial cartoons respond to news events from around the world including, of course, America. Bell first gained acclaim as a cartoonist for his depictions of Margaret Thatcher in his series, *Maggie's Farm*, published in the London left-wing magazine *City Limits* in the 1970s and 1980s. Ever since, he has been tirelessly satirizing the British political establishment. His acerbic attacks on Margaret Thatcher and her entourage of "animals" in the cabinet take the caricature skills of James Gillray and combine them with the social conscience of William Hogarth to ruthlessly critique the British establishment. Subsequently, Prime Minister John Major, a mild-mannered and quiet man, was depicted with his underpants over his trousers as if he somehow forgot to get dressed properly and conjuring a sartorial reference to a kind of negative Superman. David Cameron, he of the Brexit debacle, was always depicted with a condom for a head, while Boris Johnson, Britain's current prime minister, is almost always depicted with a rear end where his face should be. Johnson's persona is of someone slightly unkempt and bumbling yet engorged on his own self-importance, a quality he shares, along with his unusually blond hair, with Trump and makes him a sitting target for cartoonists.

Trump is an absolute gift for cartoonists, and Bell especially delights in drawing him. In a cartoon from 2015, "Assholes Awake," Bell drew him with his head simply the shape of a bottom with a firecracker between the cheeks and the slogan "assholes awake!" His eyes are slits and his mouth small and strangely square (see www.belltoons.co.uk 3916-9-12-15). Later images by Steve Bell have consistently depicted him with a garish orange skin color with pink lips and eyes like slits within graying eye sockets. Bell styles Trump's head in the likeness of a toilet, which we sometimes see open to reveal the contents of his brain to be largely excrement. A recurring motif is the henchmen swathed in the *Stars and Stripes* in the shape of a Klansman's gown standing behind Trump, symbolizing the support of the racist right in America. In August 2019 two mass shootings in America—in El Paso and in Dayton—left more than 29 people dead, but Trump showed very little empathy. On *Last Week Tonight* John Oliver launched a scathing attack on Trump's apparent disinterest in the loss of lives, especially among the largely Hispanic community, and demanded an investigation into racism in the White House. Steve Bell responded with a cartoon in which the two Klansmen in their *Stars and Stripes* gowns stand either side of Trump who is also figured wearing a wizard's hat decorated with stars from the American flag atop his toilet seat hair (www.belltoons.co.uk, 4400-7-8-19). This image, with Trump's tiny hand in a gesture of "O.K." includes a slogan behind them which reads: "Hate has no place in America." From the British perspective, then, the depiction of links with the Klan are symbolic of the right-wing, racist actions of the president.

The Steve Bell cartoon commenting on Donald Trump's impeachment hearings in January 2020 again shows him with two characters at his side, shrouded in the Stars and Stripes KKK gown identifiable by the triangular shape and the eye slits cut into the flags. He has the red tie, spilling over the White House desk in tribute to Trump's "ties" to the Russian state and to Putin hidden in plain sight. He is reading a children's book with the words: "Me in Peech" and a picture of him as a cross between a peach and a backside "with apologies@TrumpDraws" (www.belltoons.co.uk, 4453-170120). His issues with literacy are further commented on in the cartoon on January 9, 2020, in which he addresses a White House briefing with the words: "The Muslamic Revolution will not be Tolerised."

When it comes to the "special relationship" between Britain and the United States, there are no holds barred. On December 7, 2019, Boris Johnson is shown lying face down on an inflatable bed, his fat bottom dressed in Union Jack shorts, floating in a swimming pool of feces contained in the toilet of Donald Trump's head—the smelly maelstrom replacing any brain tissue that might be there. Trump's eyes are just visible at the bottom of the frame strained in an expression of mild anxiety (belltoons.co.uk, 4390.12.7.19). On January 23, 2020, in the build up to Britain's exit from the European Union, Bell chooses to depict Donald Trump appearing behind Johnson—who has an arse for a head (www.belltoons.co.uk, 4455-230120). The following day, he shows Johnson making a running jump off the white cliffs of Dover, Union Jack behind him making a bee line for the toilet head of Donald Trump—just visible from the eyes up. (www.belltoons.co.uk, 4456-240120). The commentary on the function of the "special relationship" in relation to the exit of the UK from the European Union is being directly critiqued here. The deluded leader of the Conservative party imagining that he can get some special favor from Trump as the country bumbles into post-Brexit chaos.

Steve Bell does not hold any punches in depicting the US president as mean spirited, spiteful, childish, and with excrement for brains. His editorial cartoons also make acerbic attacks on specific persons and their policies. On February 25, following the conviction of Harvey Weinstein, the *Guardian* carried a cartoon by Steve Bell that had two frames—to the left an image of Weinstein being escorted from the court in handcuffs after his convictions for sexual assault, and the opposite panel showing Trump, with his characteristic small hands grossly exaggerated in front of the American flag, his red tie dangling and next to him the logo: "#menext."

TRUMP IN THE UK AND THE BABY BALLOON

Before the visit of the president to the United Kingdom in 2018 there were debates in parliament about whether he should even be allowed to come and some public anxiety opposing the visit, so strong is the anti-Trump feeling in the UK (Elgot and Weaver, 2019). There were many groups opposed to Trump, several of which united under the umbrella organization Together Against Trump, which helped to co-ordinate the actions of several protest groups (Topping, 2018; O'Grady, 2018). The idea for the original blimp baby came from Matt Bonner, a graphic designer from London, who issued a crowdsourcing post to fund its creation:

"Make Trump Baby Fly.
   "Donald Trump is a big, angry baby with a fragile ego and tiny hands.
   "So when Trump visits the UK on Friday the 13th of July this year, we want to make sure he knows that all of Britain is looking down on him and laughing at him. That's why a group of us have chipped in and raised enough money to have a 6-meter-high blimp made by a professional inflatables company, to be flown in the skies over Parliament Square during Trump's visit"
   "He's also a racist demagogue who is a danger to women, immigrants and minorities and a mortal threat to world peace and the very future of life on earth. Moral outrage is water off a duck's back to Trump. But he really seems to hate it when people make fun of him." (Crowdfunder.co.uk)

Bonner told Joe Shute and Mark Molloy: "Our motivation is quite clearly mockery. . . . It is the only language Donald Trump understand" (Shute & Molloy, 2018). The Mayor's Office did not at first recognize the balloon as legitimate protest and were wary of the potential public health issues and possibly concerned about counterdemonstrations. A petition was signed by 100,000 people to allow the balloon to fly and the Greater London Authority gave permission pending approvals from the Metropolitan Police and National Air Traffic Service (Penman M., 2018). Leo Murray told *The Telegraph*:

We didn't get off to the best start with the Mayor's office over this, who originally told us they didn't recognise Trump Baby as legitimate protest. But, following a huge groundswell of public support for our plan, it looks like City Hall has rediscovered its sense of humour. Trump Baby will fly. (*The Telegraph*, 2018)

The balloon was allowed to fly over Parliament Square Gardens at a low height, for two hours, from 9 a.m., before many protestors had arrived. It was nonetheless part of one of the largest protests seen in Britain, as 250,000 protesters came out on the streets in a noisy "Carnival of Resistance" to show their disdain and disgust for Trump. The balloon's sojourn was reported widely in the national and international press and on television newscasts and gained a lot of attention for the anti-Trump protests. Politicians and public figures joined the protest against Trump. Owen Jones was one of many who addressed the crowd:

A historic day beckons, one that will get under the skin of not just Trump, but the entire bigoted movement he represents, and which will help galvanise the fightback against it. As a bonus, as

Trump—a man who ridicules and demonises anyone who dares to challenge him—is feted by the British establishment, he will know that somewhere up above him, in the sky, is a giant blimp of the president as a howling baby. (Jones, 2018)

Trump Baby has since appeared in various places in the United States, thanks to crowdfunding, and the balloon represents a new way of protesting against the president. He appeared at the July 4 celebrations in Washington despite protests that it should not be permitted (Gambino & Weaver, 2019). The Associated Press reported a story that there had been some protests about Trump's appearance at a Louisiana-Alabama football game in November 2019, where Robert Kennedy had brought the "baby balloon" and was serving as its "babysitter." The crowd was evidently divided about the presence of Trump at their football game. It is unclear what exactly happened, but there were some angry scenes and the baby balloon received the brunt of it all, as protestors stabbed and deflated the balloon. (Associated Press, 2019). Baby Trump balloons can now be bought in more manageable sizes and as an adult costume suit. The figuration has entered the public imagination. But are we in danger of reducing a serious menace to so many communities and to world stability as a bit of a joke? Or is the depiction of Trump in this populist, humorous way supporting and encouraging democratic debate?

CONCLUSION

The danger in characterizing Trump as a child, as a person with mental retardation or, as Penman and Cloud say, "sick" (Penman & Cloud, 2018) is that such images may be preventing us from wrestling with the serious fact that he is racist, misogynistic, and of apparently limited intelligence but nonetheless holds the reins of power in one of the most important and powerful countries in the world. The problem with Trump the demagogue, and to a lesser extent Johnson in Britain, is a systemic one—the structure of contemporary politics contains a massive lacuna into which populist leaders are able to inveigle themselves. With no adequately functioning alternative, and with the left intelligentsia increasingly removed from their traditional bases in the working classes, we are not going to be able to put up serious, credible challenges. Slavoj Žižek claims: "What happened in the US is that the Trump victory triggered a process of radicalisation in the Democratic Party—and this process is our only hope" (Žižek, 2019). Trump, then, may be helping to contribute to changing the perception of the problem and engaging with the public, except that it is not ordinary working-class voters who read *the Guardian* or who attend mass public rallies. The problem is how to orchestrate political debate in an engaging, exciting, and practical way that reclaims the political arena for the forces of positive change and improvement. Is the correct response to engage with him at the level of the spectacle? The two responses we look at are certainly very much engaged with the issue of definition and depiction—how we show something, how we challenge the self-representation is an important counter to the position to power. Has Trump become something of a pantomime villain by virtue of these representations? A weird, misshapen bully who we can bait and tease but who is, in the end, just a lot of hot air. Or is he an extremely dangerous person we have to challenge in a more direct way. Satire itself does not make changes (Rifkind, 2017). The role of the satirist in holding power to account is vitally important in the spectacular economy in which Trump seems to dominate as a monopoly player. We can use the British sense of humor to laugh at Trump, but nowhere in the world can we afford to laugh him off.

REFERENCES

Associated Press. (2019, November 10). Trump swaps baseball boos for cheers at Louisiana-Alabama football game. *The Guardian*.

Brooks, D. (2017, May 15). When the world is led by a child. *New York Times*, p. sec. Opinion.

Brooks, L. (2018, July 14). Thousands protest across Scotland as Trump plays golf. *The Guardian*.

D'Ancona, M. (2017). *Post truth: The new war on truth and how to fight back*. Ebury Press.

Elgot, J., & Weaver, M. (2019, June 4). Labour says Trump does not deserve special honours. *The Guardian*.

Gambino, L., & Weaver, M. (2019, July 3). Trump baby blimp may not fly over president's Fourth of July extravaganza. *The Guardian*.

Hunt, E. (2017, January 22). Trump's inauguration crowd: Sean Spicer's claims versus the evidence. *The Guardian*.

Jones, O. (2018, July 6). The Trump baby blimp is the perfect riposte to the snowflake right. *The Guardian*.

Kellner, D. (2016). *American nightmare: Donald Trump, media spectacle and authoritarian populism*. Sense Publishers.

Littleton, C. (2017, January 19). Mark Burnett's ties to Trump put him in a tricky situation. *Variety*.

O'Grady, S. (2018, July 5). A giant blimp depicting Trump in a diaper is likely to greet the U.S. President when he visits London. *Washington Post*.

Penman, M. (2018, July 5). London mayor says "Trump Baby" blimp can fly in protest of President Trump's visit. National Public Radio.

Penman, W., & Cloud, D. (2018). How people make sense of Trump and why it matters for racial justice. *Journal of Contemporary Rhetoric*, 8(1–2), 107–136.

Rifkind, H. (2017, February 7). Laugh all you like but satire changes nothing. *The Sunday Times*.

Rowson, M. (2019, June 12). The *New York Times* political cartoon ban is a sinister and dangerous over-reaction. *The Guardian*.

Shute, J., & Molloy, M. (2018, July 14). "Trump Baby" blimp flies outside Parliament as thousands of protesters march through London. *The Telegraph*.

The Telegraph. (2018, July 12). Angry "Trump Baby" blimp to fly in London during president's UK visit. *The Telegraph*.

Topping, A. (2018, July 9). Donald Trump to face "carnival of resistance." *The Guardian*.

Žižek, S. (2019, June 26). Was I right to back Donald Trump over Hillary Clinton? Absolutely. *The Independent*.

GERMANY

10

Mediated Populism

The US Image in German Media

Regina Cazzamatta and Kai Hafez, University of Erfurt

THE SYMBIOSIS BETWEEN MEDIA AND RIGHT-WING POPULISM

Independent of the analyzed media system, one of the most exploited news factors by current right-wing populists is "controversy" through their provocative political style, polemical declarations, and confrontations. In Schulz's (1976) news value's catalog, one classifies this variable under the category crisis, or a nonviolent form of conflict. Certainly, personification, elite status, and drama also play an essential role. Considering the case of Donald Trump, one can identify another layer of news value—unexpectedness—since the president does not act as a leader and "step outside normal political discourse" (O'Loughlin, 2019). Trump's unpredictability and arbitrariness certainly catch the press attention. He and other right-wing populists "break the routine" (Mazzoleni, 2008) in the political scene using communication strategies that guarantee media coverage in a kind of "supply-demand" interdependence.

Nowadays, these right-wing figures have indeed taken advantage of the news values of modern media and mastered their populist strategies to an inconceivable level (Hafez, 2019). A fundamental characteristic of populist political groups is their potential to convey the exasperation and emotions that will reverberate among dissatisfied audiences (Freedman, 2018). By populism, we understand a political ideology that highlights the primary role of regular citizens in the political process (Mazzoleni, 2015), focused on "bad manners and performance of crisis" (Destradi & Plagemann, 2019). The current debate on populism is based on ideational approaches and deems populism as a "thin-centered ideology" (anti-elitism and anti-pluralism). However, this "thin-ideology" coexists with "thicker" ideological variables—that is, nationalism, socialism, religious fundamentalisms (Destradi & Plagemann, 2019), and even neoliberal capitalism. Mediated populism, in its turn, refers to the results of the pronounced interdependence between media logic and the upsurge of populist attitudes (Mazzoleni, 2015).

The role of the media in promoting—intentionally or unintentionally—the right-wing populism has been discussed by scholars from several backgrounds (Boomgaarden & Vliegenthart, 2007; Burack & Snyder-Hall, 2012; Freedman, 2018; Hafez, 2017, 2019; Major, 2012; Mazzoleni, 2008, 2015). For instance, Boomgaarden & Vliegenthart (2007) show that the prominence of immigration's issues has an impact on people's political attitudes. By emphasizing specific topics and setting the agenda for the central questions of populist parties such as anti-immigration policies, the media create an information framework that contributes to the electoral support of these populist anti-immigration parties (Boomgaarden & Vliegenthart, 2007). Although a few authors analyze the role of the conservative media in promoting populists (Burack & Snyder-Hall, 2012), our main concern here is with the liberal press that paradoxically takes part in hyping such right-wing movements due to its persistent criticism and state of shock. According to Hafez (2017, 2019), even the most earnest and prestigious media have the propensity to merge the Trump-sensationalism with real and substantial politics. The prestigious and elite media, characterized by Mazzoleni (2008) as "the mouthpiece of the ruling class," have a more critical stance toward populists; however, they are comparably fundamental to the legitimizing of populist views.

Freedman (2018) criticizes the literature of mediated populism for setting the media logic as the chief variable to explain the construction of right-wing movements and for insufficient understanding of the media environment as a policy result. Thus, the author associates the spread of right-wing populism also with four primary media policy failures: the fiasco in addressing concentration ownership, supervising tech-companies, protecting an efficacious fourth state, and cultivating an independent public media service (Freedman, 2018). In any case, based on the democratic deliberation theory and its understanding of the public sphere, Hafez (2017) considers this marital interaction between right-wing populism and media an outrageous feature of our times. According to him, the media have turned into the "mouthpiece of populist manipulators," and thus, they are co-responsible for the current renaissance of illiberal democracy. It is urgent for journalism not to be susceptible to the right-wing staged pseudo-events and to resist the compulsion of propagating as a loyal vassal every single controversial word and tweet of populist actors (Hafez, 2019).

FOREIGN NEWS MAKING AND THE ROLE OF RIGHT-WING MEDIA EVENTS AS PARADOX INTERVENTIONS

The issue of German media coverage of the United States in the Trump era projects the media's right-wing fixation into the sphere of foreign news making. This examination of the US-image under the Trump administration in Germany is pivotal for the relationship of both nations, considering that decision-makers—as Boulding (1959, p. 120) has already acknowledged—do not react to the "factual" reality but to its constructed image. Several studies have demonstrated that the force of media messages tends to be intensified when there is no direct experience or a previous audience's knowledge (Happer & Philo, 2013). Since not many people have direct experience and deep familiarity with several foreign nations, the agenda-setting effect is even stronger in the case of global news, and the media remain for most individuals the primary source of information about international events (Hafez & Grüne, 2015; Wilke, 1989). Regarding the media's effect on public perception of foreign countries, the salience—that is, the amount of coverage—is crucial for the awareness of a specific state's importance (Wanta et al., 2004). The reader perceives the relative relevance of an issue or a nation from its quantity of coverage. Considering the position of the United States in the global news flow as a consistent news maker, its importance is undoubtedly recognized. However, new developments in the agenda-setting studies, often combined with frame analyses, reveal that protuberant attributes in the mass media also have the propensity of being pronounced in the audiences' minds (McCombs, 2014; Wanta et al., 2004). This means that the more negative the media frame a country, the more likely the audience will perceive them negatively (Wanta, Golan, & Lee, 2004).

By reducing the complexity of the "factual" world, the media can offer a limited number of reconstructions, more or less adequate according to a bunch of variables from micro-, meso-, and macro-level of analysis (Hafez, 2002; Shoemaker & Reese, 2014). That leads us to the question of how global news is selected. The *Foreign News Study*, which emerged from the NWICO debate, was the first global analysis dealing with the matter (Sreberny-Mohammadi & Grant, 1985). The research identified five main features of international news coverage: regionalism, conflict perspective (negativity), the dominance of politics, focus on elite, and decontextualization (Hafez, 2005; Sreberny-Mohammadi & Grant, 1985). In general, further benchmark publications on international news flow evaluate either context- (countries' attributes and their relationship) or event-oriented (internal characteristic inherent to the occurrence) variables. Within the news value theory, concerned with the question of what turns an event into the news—the work of Galtung and Ruge (1965) and their 12 proposed factors was a relevant starting point. Their core results outlined four specific conditions—namely, whether the event involves elite states, elite people, personal action, or negative consequences. Another groundbreaking work in the field was the analysis from Schulz (1976), which expanded the catalog of Galtung and Ruge and operationalized the news factors empirically, measuring their impact in the German media. The author distinguished between geographical, political, and cultural proximity.

As a result of that relatively old research tradition, one can reasonably explain why the US image in German media has been comparatively balanced and stable for decades. As the most powerful country in the world, it takes center stage in German media with an enormous amount of usually highly diversified coverage on all types of political, economic, and cultural events (Benkert, 2018; Breunlein, 2008; Kopper, 2006). Unlike other countries from Asia, Africa, and Latin America, negativity has hardly been a dominant news factor in German US coverage after World War II. However, with the advent of a massive political tendency such as right-wing populism, the linkage discourse between domestic politics and foreign policy proposed by Rosenau (1967, 1969) seems on the rise. In that sense, one can understand the issue of right-wing populism as an interacting discursive field between the American and German domestic politics since the escalation of right-wing populism is a global phenomenon also manifested in Europe and Germany. From the journalistic perspective, as Cohen (1993) pointed out, domestic and foreign news coverage is deemed as a commodity with similar criteria of selection and depiction. Thus, the merging of both perspectives is entirely possible under specific circumstances (Hafez, 2002, p. 1:144). The question is now whether the fundamental negativity of right-wing reporting might be able to overshadow the structural diversity of the US image in the German press. It is theoretically plausible that a giant media event such as the election of Trump causes shifts in otherwise relatively stable cultural discourse and serves as a paradox intervention (Couldry et al., 2010; Weichert, 2008) since it was in nature massive and unexpected.

For this reason, we intend to clarify how a leading European magazine debates Trump's agenda and discusses the framing of potential consequences regarding not only domestic politics but also the foreign policy. We will not be able to analyze the complete coverage of the United States within this chapter, and therefore we will focus solely on reports concerning the Trump presidency, which certainly poses some limitations to the evidence presented here. However, even though we will only be capable of discussing the portrayal of a US president and not the whole nation, the findings presented here still provide valuable insights and a broad understanding of a possible negative shift in the image of the United States in German media.

METHODOLOGY

Unit of Analysis

To investigate the US image under the Trump administration and its mediated populism in Germany, we selected every article published by the weekly magazine *Der Spiegel* from January 2016 until October 2019 in which the name of the US president appeared in the title or the introduction of the text, totaling 360 news items. We appointed *Der Spiegel* mainly due to its influential role as an intra-media agenda-setter. As part of the "leading media," it influences the coverage of other editors and journalists, according to the hypothesis of co-orientation (Brosius et al., 2016). Therefore, it is plausible to say that one finds approximately the tone of reporting of the prestige press, such as *Der Spiegel* in the smaller newspapers and media landscapes (ibid.). On top of that, the magazine attaches great importance to foreign reporting, especially in the area of politics (Bieber, 2011).

The Main Categories of the Quantitative Content Analysis

The news items were firstly classified according to their focus on the United States. We excluded 10 articles in which President Trump was quoted solely as an example in another political context with no relation to the USA whatsoever (for instance, the expression "Trump of the Tropics" to describe the Brazilian president). Afterward, we systematized the texts between small and significant focus. In the next step, we analyzed the other 360 articles according to their major subject areas and key theme to acquire a first judgment of the media agenda (we provide the resulted list in the findings section). Furthermore, we categorized every piece concerning the tone of reporting—positive, negative, or neutral. One defines these three described categories as following:

1. Positive: success, economic aid, positive developments, cooperation, inventions, discoveries, attempts at reconciliation, peace negotiations, settling disputes, unification, justice, bilateral agreements, peace efforts, state improvement, dialogue between opponents, survival, release of hostages, rating agencies' grading improvements, agreements, cultural exchanges or travel recommendations.
2. Negative: violence, failures, crime, disaster, war, electoral fraud, political unrest, interruption of peace negotiations, repression, aggression, destruction, damage, protests, demonstrations, conflicts, economic crises, trade conflicts, controversies.
3. Neutral: general social processes such as state visits, conferences, stock market events, memories of historical facts, Jubilees (without protests or arguments), and fair elections.

Apart from that, we coded the first five described actors—state representatives, organized social groups, ordinary people, celebrities/authors/artists, and supranational organizations. This category should not be confused with the sources quoted by journalists (US-media, international media, Twitter, and other social media, polling institutes, think tanks, among others). It is not related to interviewees, but external sources cited in the articles. Concerning specific news factors, we analyzed whether the articles brought any controversy (yes or no as category) and who were the targets of such debates (immigrants, women, LGBT+, Trump himself, among others). Regarding the factor of personification, we measured its level, according to the following definition:

0. Not at all. No person mentioned.
1. Small. People are quoted illustratively, without relevance for the reporting
2. People are mentioned in the foreground, but the main event concerns abstract processes, or it can be expressed through their actions. People's behavior or statements illustrate the situation.
3. People are the cause and the main focus of the article. The event revolves around them or their family members.

Qualitative Content Analysis: Frames Identification

During the quantitative content analysis, we selected at least three text passages per article with a problem definition, a causal interpretation, or a moral evaluation related to the United States or President Donald Trump, according to the frame elements proposed by Entman (1993). Afterward, we transferred all these selected articles' excerpts to the NVivo program of qualitative data analysis. Using the three steps' method—paraphrase, generalization, and reduction, proposed by Mayring (2010)—we looked deductively for discursive patterns within the frame elements mentioned above. "*To frame is to select some aspects of a perceived reality and make them more salient in a communication context, in such a way as to promote a particular problem definition, causal interpretation, moral evaluation, and/or treatment recommendation for the item described*" (Entman, 1993, p. 52). The identified frames—for example, American isolationism, the crusade against Germany, among others—will be discussed thoroughly in the finding section. Our goal here is not to quantify but identify discursive, cognitive patterns of interpretations. Since frames are socially shared, they are suggestive for both those producing the news coverage (the German journalists) and those acquiring it—that is, the German audience (Carter, 2013).

FINDINGS

As stated by Hafez (2019), the prestigious German media are, in general, most critical to right-wing populism. Indeed, if we look to the *Der Spiegel* frames to describe Donald Trump, there is no doubt that the magazine adopts tones of outrage and ridicule to portray the president. One identifies seven frames of moral evaluation related to his figure: (1) an unreliable partner; (2) anti-democratic and despot; (3) populist, racist, and sexist; (4) personality disorder; (5) unprepared and inept; (6) corrupt and dishonest; and (7) disdain for science. The word cloud below (Figure 10.1) exemplifies the most used terms (mostly adjectives and substantives)

Figure 10.1   Word cloud of most frequent words used to Describe Trump

to depict the US head of state, based solely on the sentences classified under the category "Trump's moral evaluation."

So, it seems that the factual dilemma of mediated populism is not necessarily the media framings, but its news agenda (Hafez, 2019). Thus, we analyzed the main topics and themes associated with US coverage, as displayed in Table 10.1. In total, we evaluated 360 news items—285 with a significant focus and 75 with a small emphasis on the United States and its president. During the campaign in 2016, the United States was responsible for eight title stories in the German magazine. However, the actual president at the time, Barack Obama, appeared on two covers, while the still-candidate Trump appeared on six. Even if the journalistic discourse proved to be extremely critical as demonstrated above, one could assure that the weekly overexposed the figure of Trump, dedicating entire cover stories—for instance "The Trumps," "The End of the World," or "Madness"—to an extremely polemical candidate. For populists, "bad news is good news" (Hafez, 2019), and precisely this over-attention is their goal. As the factual president in 2017, Trump was responsible for seven covers of the magazine,

Number of published articles per annum

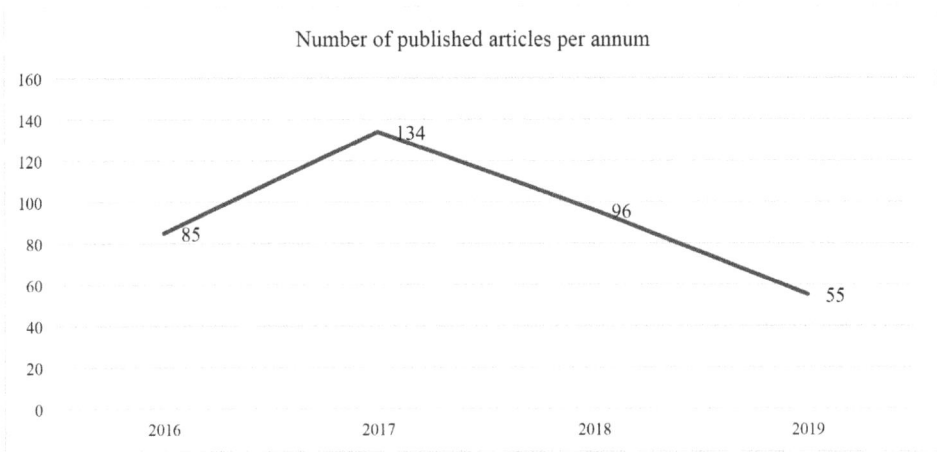

Figure 10.2 Development of coverage in *Der Spiegel* on the United States 2016–2019

and we can notice an attention peak regarding the number of total news stories, that has been decreasing in the next two following years, as shown in Figure 10.2.

Considering now the major subject areas, one can see a strong focus on politics (36.9% of domestic policies and 34.7% of international affairs), followed by the coverage of culture and society (34.7 %), in which half of the issues amid the category were dealing with the American zeitgeist, trying to explain and understand the Trump phenomenon and the upsurge of right-wing populism (Table 10.1). The areas of environment and environmental policies and catastrophes and accidents received less attention, with 1% each, as Figure 10.3 demonstrates.

MAJOR SUBJECT AREAS

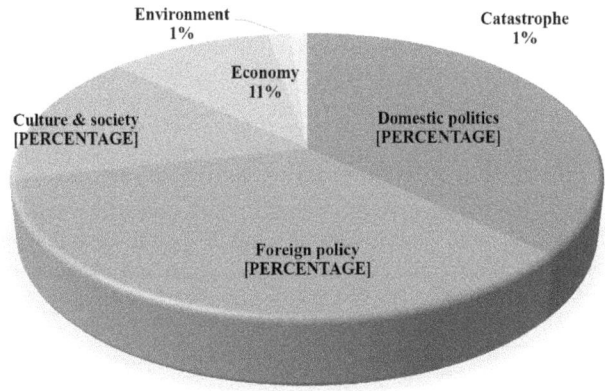

Figure 10.3 Key covered areas of foreign reporting on the United States

Table 10.1.   Main Themes Related to US Foreign Reporting in the German Press 2016–2019.

Themes	N	%	Amid the Respective Areas of Coverage
European/German-American relationship	45	12.5	36% within foreign policy
Presidential election campaign and transfer of power	39	10.8	29.3% within domestic politics
Mideast conflicts	28	7.8	22.4% within foreign policy
(American) global zeitgeist	27	7.5	50% within culture & society
The US in the global economy	25	6.9	65.8% within economy & finance
Profile, comments, and interviews from/related to people in the administration	24	6.7	18% within domestic politics
Political scandals	21	5.8	15.8% within domestic politics
Questions related to NATO, G20, and international agreements	21	5.8	16.8% within foreign policy
Media, media freedom, social media, and the public sphere	15	4.2	11.3% within domestic politics
Literature	15	4.2	26.8 % within culture & society
Conflict with North Korea	14	3.9	11.2 % within foreign policy
Conflict within the administration	11	3.1	8.3% within domestic politics
China affairs	10	2.8	8.0 % within foreign policy
German-American economic relationship	7	1.9	18.4 % within economy & finance
Political analyses in general	6	1.7	4.5% within domestic politics
Legislature elections	5	1.4	3.8 % within domestic politics
Demonstrations, marches, and protests	5	1.4	3.8 % within domestic politics
US economic developments	5	1.4	13.2 % within economy & finance
Human rights and treatment of opposition	4	1.1	3.0 % within domestic politics
US-Russian/Ukrainian relationship	4	1.1	3.2 % within foreign policy
TV, cinema, and series	4	1.1	7.1% within culture & society
Sports and tourism	4	1.1	7.1% within culture & society
Environmental policies and agreements	4	1.1	80 % within environment
Immigration and immigration policies	2	0.6	1.5 % within domestic politics
US relation to Latin America / Mexico	2	0.6	1.6 % within foreign policy
Opera and theater	2	0.6	3.6 % within culture & society
Music and concerts	2	0.6	3.6 % within culture & society
Mass shootings	2	0.6	50% within catastrophes & accidents
Natural disasters	2	0.6	50% within catastrophes & accidents
Bills in the House of Representatives and Senate	1	0.3	0.8% within domestic politics
US foreign policy analyses in general	1	0.3	0.8 % within foreign policy
Exhibition and architecture	1	0.3	1.8 % within culture & society
Trump's private business	1	0.3	2.6 % within economy & finance
Climate change / global warming	1	0.3	20 % within environment
Total	360	100	

FRAMES AMID INTERNATIONAL AFFAIRS

Table 10.1 displays the most discussed US themes in the German press both in the complete coverage and within the thematic areas of reporting. On the top of the list is the European and German-American relationship with 12.5% of the total US foreign reporting (or 36% within international politics). Trump's foreign policy comportment shocks the journalists and perpetuates a "new normal" constant state of anxiety (O'Loughlin, 2019). Accordingly, we identified six frames, mostly related to the foreign policy and international affairs: (1) demolishing the global order; (2) the crusade against Germany and the expectation to divide Europe; (3) the US-renouncing of global responsibility and role as guarantor of global stability; (4) the influence of Trumpism in Europe; (5) disregard of Obama's policies (also within domestic politics); and (6) the American protectionism and isolationism. This last one appears in the economic coverage as well, within topics such as the United States in the global economy. The central news values associated with the reporting of foreign affairs are generally personification, elite status, drama, and conflict. Trump adds the variable unexpectedness since he breaks all the diplomatic protocols and escalates international conflicts, contributing to an uncertain global order. It is vital to notice that these frames appear not only within the European-American relationship but also within other foreign policy themes such as the Mideast conflicts, the conflict with North Korea, or the China affairs. In all these examples, one has the type of discursive interaction classified as a reactive process (Rosenau, 1969) in which actors of national systems (the German press) react to the maneuvers of actors of other political systems (the ruling class of the United States) and generate a condemnatory response.

The idea that Trump was going to "destroy the international system" was expressed through several events. For instance, his critics related this idea to the INF-treaty and the nuclear nonproliferation agreements, the recognition of Jerusalem as Israel's capital, the dispute related to the role of NATO and security issues, the dismissal of the Iran nuclear deal, the provocations of North Korea's leader Kim Jong-un, the disregard of traditional Western partners and the transatlantic alliance, and the pullout of the Paris Agreement on climate to give a few examples. Thus, Trump is an "unreliable partner" and "unprepared," "ignorant," or "inept." The fact that Trump turns himself against the global order can be read in several articles: "*The existing order, as we were used to since the end of the Cold War, will be radically transformed. . . . This President will make every effort to weaken confederations such as the UN, the EU, or the G20 to make room for bilateral deals just like his Kremlin counterpart*" (*Spiegel*, January 1, 2017). The drama of having a president with no foreign policy experience and the vocabulary of a "fourth-grader" in charge of a nuclear power state is also often described: "*On the other side of the globe, in Washington, sits Donald Trump, a democratically elected President who knows little about the world, but in addition to the nuclear weapons' codes also has an account on Twitter, which he uses rather thoughtlessly*" (*Spiegel*, April 22, 2017).

Furthermore, the magazine conveyed the "crusade against Germany" reporting Trump's battle against the German foreign trade surplus (also amid the area of economy and finance), security questions, and the fragile relationship between Washington and Berlin: "*Trump has made the NATO summit a showdown . . . Trump against Merkel, Trump against Germany . . . Germany of all countries, one of the closest allies of the United States for decades, the front state of the Cold War, has become Trump's number one enemy. . . . Perhaps it is the mixture of economic strength, military restraint, and moral hubris that makes Germany the object of hatred for the US President,*" wrote the weekly (*Spiegel*, July 15, 2018). The publication defends the German interests, but to do so, it has to echo Trump's populist performance and cover the show. The entire description—even if it holds absolute truth—sounds apocalyptic: "*He has also shown that he cares little about the rules of Western politics. His plans could tear the European Union apart and cause serious economic damage to Germany. Trump has announced he will fight Germany's export surplus*" (*Spiegel*, March 11, 2017). In this case, besides the conflict, one has direct European-German involvement in the events that ascribe more news values to the report: "*He wants to put an end to the low-cost security that he believes Germany has enjoyed so far. He wants to break Germany's export power and dictate to the Germans where they have to get their gas*" (*Spiegel*, June 9, 2018).

These above-described frames are also connected to "American protectionisms and isolation-ism," depicted in a catastrophic style as a severe risk to the global monetary order. Events such as the trade war with China, the increase of custom tariffs on steel and aluminum from the EU without the endorsement of the WTO, or the withdrawal from the Transpacific Partnership (TPP) exemplifies where these discursive patterns occur. It is common to pinpoint how the international and monetary order with Trump is upside-down: "*The entrepreneur and capitalist Trump wants to raise tariffs and build walls, the communist Xi presents himself as an advocate of a liberal economic order*" (*Spiegel*, February 21, 2017). The peculiar protectionist behavior of the president is also oft highlighted: "*Trump is an avowed protectionist; he accuses supporters of free trade of abandoning America to plunderers*" (*Spiegel*, June 16, 2018). On the other hand, the weekly does not criticize radical neoliberalism and market fundamentalism in the United States. For instance, the Transatlantic Trade and Investment Partnership (TTIP) has been condemned to a certain extent by several trade unions, NGOs, and environmental associations for lacking labor principles and consumer and environment defense (Stelzel, 2019).

Apart from that, another discursive structure that appeared oft is the "US-renounce of its global responsibility" either politically or economically. The magazine notes that for Trump, "*America is no longer the leading power of liberal democracies*" (*Spiegel*, January 12, 2019) or that "*the role of the USA as a guarantor of global organizations such as the International Monetary Fund (IMF) can no longer be taken for granted*" (*Spiegel*, September 9, 2017). From the German perspective and its historical relation with the United States, this kind of discourse might be comprehensible (e.g., the West Berlin air corridor). However, from a Latin American point of view, for example, it might seem to depict the United States as the guarantor of global demo-cratic values. The strong US support for brutal military dictatorships in several countries in the region guaranteed the "global order" in Latin America during the Cold War (Simon & Brian, 2018). Lastly, other frames identified within the foreign policy's subject area were the way Trump dismantled the legacy of his predecessor and the danger of right-wing populism in Europe.

Dominant News Factors of Trump's Foreign Reporting

Considering the above-discussed symbiosis between media and right-wing populism—that is, how populists reinforce the media's appetite for news factors—in this subsection we will look at these components of the US foreign reporting. Amid domestic politics, the most covered themes were presidential election campaign (29.3% within the category), profiles from people inside the administration (18%), and political scandals (15.8%). While the most covered topic in 2016 was the presidential election, in 2017, the central theme was general portrayals of people in Trump's administration. The magazine gave greater importance to the characterization of Steve Bannon, Ivanka Trump and her spouse Jared Kushner, First Lady Melania Trump, and the president himself, showing how media prefer stories based on real people rather than monotonous political speeches or conceptual matters described in an official style (Mazzoleni, 2008). They are all strong and flamboyant personalities that satiate the hunger for spectacular and outrage feelings.

Thus, the substantial level of the factor of personification is not surprising. If one considers the 360 published articles altogether, the US-Trump foreign reporting shows a personification average of 2.14 (intensity from 0 to 3), since 63.9% of the texts boast middle and 25.8% significant personification levels. In addition to this strong personification of *Der Spiegel's* coverage, the orientation on elites is also a valid premise, taking into consideration that only 7.1% of the reported actors describe ordinary people. In general, the US-coverage is focused on state representatives (59.1%); organized social groups (15.1%); and celebrities, authors, and artists (14.2%). Besides, as expected, based on German public opinion (Pew Research Center, 2019), the factor of "negativity" is hugely pronounced, considering that 65.6% of the published items were about adverse events (the other 26.1% were neutral and 8.30% positive).

Furthermore, the US image is strongly marked by controversial discussions, seeing that 80% of the articles depicted polemical issues. The focus of these controversies or polemic statements was related to the global political system or leader of other countries, followed by the American president himself and the members of his family and matters concerning environmental problems and trade wars (Table 10.2). Within this category, Trump is the target of the controversy, but indirectly. Considering that a substantial amount of the US coverage in Germany comprises foreign policy and international affairs, it is plausible that the main subjects of polemics are the global order or leaders of other nations. Besides, in almost 39% of the articles, the journalist reproduced Trump's rhetoric or that of people linked to him to criticize or contextualize the discussed controversy. In any case, Trump's questionable statements, mostly from social media (35.2%) and the US media (51.7%) found an echo in the German press, even if they were not necessarily the main reason for the article. Here it is reasonable to think about Hafez's (2019) argument that the media are possibly promoting the populist posture, certainly with a "critical twist," but it is still promoting it.

The result of this strong orientation on news factors such as personification, elite status, political scandals, and dramatic controversies or polemics is that the press does not report about processes of American domestic politics in depth, regarding the entire political spectrum.

Table 10.2. The Principal Targets of Controversies in the US-News Coverage in Germany

Target of Controversies	Frequency	Percentage
(International) political systems/leaders of other states	120	32.0
Trump himself or his family	83	22.1
Others issues (environment, currency war)	47	12.5
More than one quoted together	30	8.0
Media and journalists	19	5.1
The opposition, other candidates	18	4.8
Muslim communities	14	3.7
Women	10	2.7
US government	9	2.4
Immigrants from Central America/Mexico	8	2.1
Palestinians	5	1.3
Right-wing extremists	5	1.3
African Americans	4	1.1
LGBT+	2	0.5
Scientist and academics	1	0.3
Total	375	100.0

Frames Within Domestic Politics

Besides the described news factors, one also identifies a few frames (causal attribution), amid domestic politics, used to explain Trump's victory. The first one—"the American dream is over"—indicates how social ascendancy has become arduous: "*The American dream promises that anyone can be successful, regardless of origin or skin color. . . . The American dream is the cement that has so far held a diversified and fragmented nation together. However, when two jobs are not enough to feed a family, the promise is no longer valid*" (*Spiegel*, March 5, 2016). Another pronounced frame is how Trump took advantage of the "losers of globalization" to win the campaign and exploited their fear of social decline and feelings of marginalization. The argument is that several of Trump's voters are not necessarily radical Tea Party followers, but just citizens dominated by the fear of the future: "*Trump is targeting white middle-class men, workers who feel marginalized by globalization and fear further job exodus*" (*Spiegel*, May 21, 2016). The main explanation is that even though people have chosen Trump, "*that does not mean that they want to get rid of democracy, freedom, and human rights*" (*Spiegel*, November 19, 2016).

These two frames are indeed tightly related to the social division and its cultural struggle between conservatives and liberals: "*It is a vote of no confidence against globalized capitalism, an expression of America's division into liberal cities and backward regions*" (*Spiegel*, November 12, 2016). One can also find discourses such as "*the white uprising against colorful America*" (*Spiegel*, November 19, 2016). The "crisis of democracy" discourse denotes the fragility of American democracy, the illusion of political reality, and the infotainment society: "*The election reporting was mainly about quotas, hardly about politics. However, if elections are only infotainment, then a reality TV star is the better candidate than an ordinary politician*" (*Spiegel*, July 8, 2017). The last identified discursive structure—"zeitgeist"—deals with the post-truth era of populism and appears not only within domestic politics but also within culture and society. The main argument here is that populists such as Trump "*conquer an America that can no longer agree on historical truths*" (*Spiegel*, April 2, 2016).

Even the role of the Republican Party becomes unclear in light of the populist rhetoric. The press framed the party as divided regarding Trump's controversial attitudes and its image damaged. The party of Abraham Lincoln, previously established against slavery, turned into a movement of "*white and crazy Jesus-following conservatives*" (*Spiegel*, April 2, 2016). The coverage concentrates on how Washington looks like a chaotic circus amid the absurdities of Trump's antidemocratic extravagancies but, on the other hand, undervalues or ignores the reluctance of the Republican Party to respect electoral results. For instance, when they lost the governorship elections in North Carolina in 2016 and Wisconsin in 2018, the legislative bodies of the states still controlled by Republicans approved several regulations to limit draconianly the power of the arriving Democratic governors (Stelzel, 2019). Lastly, besides the frame "Washington is a circus," we identified—though less frequently—arguments related to the solidity of the American democracy and its system of checks and balances.

CONCLUSION

As demonstrated in our empirical analysis, the current US-image in Germany, as reflected in the coverage of Trump's presidency, is indeed captured and overshadowed by the demagoguery of the president's sensationalist staged politics. Since the more negative coverage a state obtains, the higher the odds that the audience will think negative about that country (Wanta et al., 2004), it is not surprising that 73% of German interviewees judge the US-German relationship as bad (Pew Research Center, 2019). The negative effect of Trump is manifested in 65.6% of the coverage, across different areas. Besides, as shown in Table 10.3, the reporting of US domestic politics concentrates mostly on elections (29.3%), personalized profiles of flamboyant figures (18%), and political scandals (15.8%). Thus, we do not get much information about the deepest structures of US-American politics and society.

In the era of Trump, news factors such as personification, controversy, crisis, and polemics play a vital role in the US coverage. As our frames analysis indicates, the magazine was extremely critical of the upsurge of US right-wing populism. However, by reproducing and echoing (39% of the articles) Trump's controversial statements—even with a critical twist—the publication might be helping to set his agenda and spread his populist messages and provocative political posture in Germany. Years before Trump, Sponholz (2018) also identified this opposite effect of counter speeches in her case study concerning the publication of Thilo Sarrazin's book in 2010 (*Deutschland schafft sich ab*). Despite predominantly negative reporting and massive criticism of the politician's position about migrants from Islamic countries and German immigration policies, the controversy was responsible for the establishment of Islamophobic and Xenophobic beliefs in the media. Both examples—Trump in the United States and Sarrazin in Germany—demonstrated that it is possible to set the media agenda through hate speech controversies since they prompt enormous press attention (Sponholz, 2018). In this chapter, we demonstrated that the same agenda-setting mechanism—forced through negative, conflicted-oriented, and controversial discourse—also characterizes the foreign-reporting of right-wing populism.

Lastly, one should not forget that 78.90% of the articles identified as "foreign news abroad" (events that happened in the United States without German participation) also might retain through discursive connections elements of home news in Germany—that is, the dangers represented by far-right extremists, racism, and populism. This issues' interconnectedness certainly ascribes even more news values to the Trump phenomenon. For all these reasons, we confirm an extremely negative Trump effect on the US image in Germany and hope that the democratic institutions will be able to cope with the dilemma. In the meanwhile, as recommended by several authors, the press worldwide should resist the waterfall of news values staged by right-wing populists and concentrate on debates based on pure political substance.

APPENDIX

Table 10.3. Identification of Frames' Dimensions and Coding Examples

Frame Element	Variables	Description	Examples
Problem definition	Reputation of Republicans	Abraham Lincoln's honored party is transformed into a movement of white racist and conservatives	Trump becomes the gravedigger of this once-proud party.
	Global order demolition	Foreign policies controversies, i.e., INF-treaty, the role of NATO, Iran deal, Paris climate pullout, etc.	This president will make every effort to weaken confederations like the UN, the EU, or the G20 to make room for bilateral deals just like his Kremlin counterpart.

(continued)

Table 10.3. *Continued*

Frame Element	Variables	Description	Examples
	Isolationism protectionism	Monetary order controversies, i.e., trade wars with China, EU-US trade disputes, etc.	The wrong world: The entrepreneur and capitalist Trump wants to raise tariffs and build walls, the communist Xi presents himself as an advocate of a liberal economic order.
	Loss of democratic values	Attack on media, minorities, justice and political scandals	Nixon's contempt for the Washington establishment and the institutions can be found today in Donald Trump, and his followers. He puts the Western model, indeed the entire liberal democracy, at risk.
	Crusade against Germany	Trump's fragile relationship with Berlin	Trump wants to put an end to the cheap security that he believes Germany has enjoyed so far. He wants to break Germany's export power and dictate to the Germans where they have to get their gas from.
	Renouncing of global responsibility	The US gives up its role as the leading power of liberal democracies	It is not about the defense of Western values; it is about the protection of American interest. The role of the US as a guarantor of global organizations (. . .) can no longer be taken for granted.
	Influence of Trumpism in Europe	The danger of right-wing populism in Europe	In the right-wing scene, AfD and Pegida sympathizers are thinking about which instruments from the counterfeit trumpet workshop can best be transferred to Germany.
	Discard Obama's policies	Dismantle the legacy of the predecessor	We do not believe that Trump has a problem with Iran, but with everything, his predecessor left him.
Causal attribution	The American dream is over	Social rise and security has become difficult	A great myth of the United States is threatened: the American dream; the worse the American economy goes, the more radical the president's actions would be.
	Losers of globalization	Trump's voters feel marginalized by globalization and fear a social decline	Trump is targeting the white middle-class men, the workers who feel marginalized by globalization and fear further job emigration.
	Society's division and cultural struggle	Expression of America's division into liberal cities and backward regions	It is a vote of no confidence against globalized capitalism, an expression of the division of America into liberal cities and backward areas.
	Crisis of American democracy	Fragile democracy, infotainment, the illusion of political reality	The election reporting, for example, was mainly about quotas, hardly about politics. However, if elections are only infotainment, then a reality TV star is the better candidate than an ordinary politician.

Frame Element	Variables	Description	Examples
	Zeitgeist	America can no longer agree on historical truths. Post truth and populism	Trump-brand populists conquer an America that can no longer agree on historical truths. Trump has already blurred the line between truth and lie.
Moral evaluation	Trump		
	Negative	Unreliable partner	In any case, we can no longer rely on being involved in decisions, on being consulted. America is no longer reliable.
	Negative	Sympathy for dictators	Donald Trump's 12-day tour of Asia was a pilgrimage to anti-democrats.
	Negative	Populist, hate-preacher, racist, sexist, fascist	The face of racism and exclusion, the president with whom you sit at the table discriminates against women, Muslims, and minorities.
	Negative	Autocratic behavior, despot, antidemocratic	Donald Trump's flirt with violence is a threat to democracy/ he decrees, he determines, he rules like an autocrat.
	Negative	Personality disorder, e.g., psychopath, egomaniac, arsonist, narcissist, vulgar, violent, unpredictable, etc.	Dominance behavior of male chimpanzees/sociopaths suffered from a defect in the fundamental nature of their humanity.
	Negative	Unprepared, ignorant, brainless, clown, stupid, inept	The rumbling, foreign-policy less experienced president/ the vocabulary of a fourth-grader/ Trump is unsuitable for any public office.
	Negative	Corrupt, dishonest, player, unscrupulous, elitist, liar, relation to criminals	Trump puts the interests of billionaires above those of hard-working Americans/ Trump is a cheater who only feels comfortable among liars who admire him.
	Negative	Disdain for science and environmental issues	There is hardly a place where Trumpism flourishes as much as in Pruitt's EPA, this mixture of incompetence, paranoia, hostility to science, and politics of interest.
	USA		
	Positive	Trust in the American institutions	Under Donald Trump, the USA did not turn into an autocracy because the judiciary and Congress are still resisting the president's impulses.
	Negative	Washington is a huge circus / democratic crisis	Or will the United States of America become a banana republic, a country in which a clan dominates business and politics?/ The president makes politics as if he were a guest on a reality show

(continued)

Table 10.3. *Continued*

Frame Element	Variables	Description	Examples
	Negative	Society's moral decline / intolerant America	Trump has unleashed the terrible part of America/ Make America great again means in the social Darwinist USA: Natives rule migrants again, heterosexuals over homosexuals; white rules black again, men over women.
	Positive	Multifaceted America	Young America is diverse, believes in tolerance, accepts same-sex marriages, believes in integration. But young people are not as likely to vote as older people.

REFERENCES

Benkert, V. (Ed.). (2018). *Feinde, Freunde, Fremde? Deutsche Perspektiven auf die USA* (1. Auflage). Nomos.

Bieber, L. (2011). *China in der deutschen Berichterstattung 2008: Eine multiperspektivische Inhaltsanalyse* (1. Auflage). VS Verlag für Sozialwissenschaften.

Boomgaarden, H. G., & Vliegenthart, R. (2007). Explaining the rise of anti-immigrant parties: The role of news media content. *Electoral Studies, 26*(2), 404–417. https://doi.org/10.1016/j.electstud.2006.10.018

Boulding, K. E. (1959). National images and international systems. *Journal of Conflict Resolution, 3*(2), 120–131. https://doi.org/10.1177/002200275900300204

Breunlein, M. (2008). *Das Nationenbild der USA in deutschen Tageszeitungen: Eine vergleichende Inhaltsanalyse vor und nach dem 11. September 2001.* VDM-Verl., Müller.

Brosius, H.-B., Haas, A., & Koschel, F. (2016). *Methoden der empirischen Kommunikationsforschung: Eine Einführung* (7., überarbeitete und aktualisierte Auflage). Springer VS.

Burack, C., & Snyder-Hall, R. C. (2012). Introduction: Right-wing populism and the media. *New Political Science, 34*(4), 439–454. https://doi.org/10.1080/07393141.2012.729736

Carter, M. J. (2013). The hermeneutics of frames and framing: An examination of the media's construction of reality. *SAGE Open, 3*(2), 215824401348791. https://doi.org/10.1177/2158244013487915

Cohen, B. C. (1993). *The press and foreign policy.* University of California Press.

Couldry, N., Hepp, A., & Krotz, F. (Eds.). (2010). *Media events in a global age.* Routledge.

Destradi, S., & Plagemann, J. (2019). Populism and international relations: (Un)predictability, personalisation, and the reinforcement of existing trends in world politics. *Review of International Studies, 45*(5), 711–730. https://doi.org/10.1017/S0260210519000184

Entman, R. M. (1993). Framing: Toward clarification of a fractured paradigm. *Journal of Communication, 43*(4), 51–58. https://doi.org/10.1111/j.1460-2466.1993.tb01304.x

Freedman, D. (2018). Populism and media policy failure. *European Journal of Communication, 33*(6), 604–618. https://doi.org/10.1177/0267323118790156

Galtung, J., & Ruge, M. H. (1965). The structure of foreign news. The presentation of the Congo, Cuba, and Cyprus crises in four Norwegian newspapers. *Journal of Peace Research, 2*(1), 64–90. https://doi.org/10.1177/002234336500200104

Hafez, K. (2002). *Die politische Dimension der Auslandsberichterstattung. Bd.1.* (1. Aufl, Vol. 1). Nomos.

Hafez, K. (2005). *Mythos Globalisierung: Warum die Medien nicht grenzenlos sind* (1. Aufl). VS Verlag für Sozialwissenschaften.

Hafez, K. (2017). A complicated relationship: Right-wing populism, media representation and journalism theory. *Global Media Journal-German Edition*, *7*(2). https://www.db-thueringen.de/servlets/MCRFileNodeServlet/dbt_derivate_00039851/GMJ14_Hafez_final.pdf

Hafez, K. (2019). The staging trap: Right-wing politics as a challenge for journalism. *Journalism*, *20*(1), 24–26. https://doi.org/10.1177/1464884918807352

Hafez, K., & Grüne, A. (2015). Chaotische Fernwelt—getrennte Lebenswelten: Auslandsberichterstattung zwischen negativem und positivem Journalismus. In *Positiver Journalismus* (pp. 99–112). Herbert von Halem. https://content-select.com/de/portal/media/view/598c6f89-e750-4a45-a376-745bb0dd2d03

Happer, C., & Philo, G. (2013). The role of the media in the construction of public belief and social change. *Journal of Social and Political Psychology*, *1*(1), 321–336. https://doi.org/10.5964/jspp.v1i1.96

Kopper, G. G. (2006). Korrespondententätigkeit, US.-Amerika-Bild und U.S-Amerika-Berichterstattung—Analyse und Handlungshinweise. In G. G. Kopper & J. Lönnendonker (Eds.), *How are you, Mr. President? Nachrichtenarbeit, Berufswirklichkeit und Produktionsmanagement an Korrespondentenplätzen deutscher Medien in den USA; Arbeitsbuch für Medienpraxis und Forschung* (pp. 19–38). Vistas-Verlag.

Major, M. (2012). Objective but not impartial: *Human Events*, Barry Goldwater, and the development of the "liberal media" in the conservative counter-sphere. *New Political Science*, *34*(4), 455–468. https://doi.org/10.1080/073931410.2012.729737

Mayring, P. (2010). *Qualitative Inhaltsanalyse: Grundlagen und Techniken* (12., überarbeitete Auflage). Beltz Verlag.

Mazzoleni, G. (2008). Populism and the media. In D. Albertazzi & D. McDonnell (Eds.), *Twenty-first century populism: The spectre of Western European democracy*. Palgrave Macmillan.

Mazzoleni, G. (2015). Mediated populism. In W. Donsbach (Ed.), *The concise encyclopedia of communication* (p. 376). Wiley Blackwell.

McCombs, M. E. (2014). *Setting the agenda: The mass media and public opinion* (2nd ed.). Polity Press.

O'Loughlin, B. (2019). The big standoff: Trump's handshakes and the limits of news values. In C. Happer, A. Hoskins, & W. Merrin (Eds.), *Trump's media war* (pp. 143–157). Springer International Publishing. https://doi.org/10.1007/978-3-319-94069-4_10

Pew Research Center. (2019). Americans and Germans disagree on the state of bilateral relations, but largely align on key international issues. https://www.pewresearch.org/global/2019/03/04/americans-and-germans-disagree-on-the-state-of-bilateral-relations-but-largely-align-on-key-international-issues/

Rosenau, J. N. (1967). Foreign policy as an issue-area. In J. N. Rosenau (Ed.), *Domestic Sources of Foreign Policy*. Free Press.

Rosenau, J. N. (1969). *Domestic sources of foreign policy*. Free Press.

Schulz, W. (1976). *Die Konstruktion von Realität in den Nachrichtenmedien: Analyse der aktuellen Berichterstattung* (1. Aufl). Alber.

Shoemaker, P. J., & Reese, S. D. (2014). *Mediating the message in the 21st century: A media sociology perspective* (3rd ed.). Routledge/Taylor & Francis Group.

Simon, R., & Brian, W. (2018). Trumpism comes to Brazil. *Foreign Affairs*. https://www.foreignaffairs.com/articles/brazil/2018-10-28/trumpism-comes-brazil

Sponholz, L. (2018). *Hate Speech in den Massenmedien*. Springer Fachmedien Wiesbaden. https://doi.org/10.1007/978-3-658-15077-8

Sreberny-Mohammadi, A., & Grant, N. (Eds.). (1985). *Foreign news in the media: International reporting in 29 countries: Final report of the "Foreign Images" study*. United Nations Educational, Scientific, and Cultural Organization.

Stelzel, P. (2019). Transatlantic relations, the liberal democratic order, and the populist challenge. In *Cooperation or Division? The German-American relationship in a changing world* (pp. 7–14). American Institute for Contemporary German Studies.

Wanta, W., Golan, G., & Lee, C. (2004). Agenda setting and international news: Media influence on public perceptions of foreign nations. *Journalism & Mass Communication Quarterly, 81*(2), 364–377. https://doi.org/10.1177/107769900408100209

Weichert, S. A. (2008). Krisen als Medienereignisse: Zur Ritualisierung mediatisierter Kommunikation im Fernsehen. In C. Winter, A. Hepp, F. Krotz, & Deutsche Gesellschaft für Publizistik- und Kommunikationswissenschaft (Eds.), *Theorien der Kommunikations- und Medienwissenschaft: Grundlegende Diskussionen, Forschungsfelder und Theorieentwicklungen* (1. Aufl, pp. 311–320). VS, Verlag für Sozialwissenschaften.

Wilke, J. (1989). Imagebildung durch Massenmedien. In D. Schmidt-Sinns & Bundeszentrale für Politische Bildung (Germany) (Eds.), *Völker und Nationen im Spiegel der Medien* (pp. 11–21). Bundeszentrale für Politische Bildung.

GREECE

11

Does Trump Represent America?

The Image of the United States in Greek Online News During the Trump Presidency

Thimios Zaharopoulos, The American College of Greece

INTRODUCTION

The image of the United States in the international press has been the subject of hundreds of studies. The image of a country is important because it is its national reputation (Lee, Toth, & Shin, 2008, p. 273). Normally, the image held by people abroad of the United States is directly tied to the perception of its president. The long-term communication goal of any nation is to have a good reputation internationally, regardless of who the president happens to be at the time. A country's positive image abroad can lead to trade and foreign policy successes. For example, the evaluation of a nation's products is often based on a nation's reputation. Similarly, a nation's reputation is an integral part of a nation's foreign policy interests. Regardless of the approach one chooses, either the communication or the marketing approach, this image includes at least the following dimensions: The affective dimension, which captures feelings and emotions, and the cognitive dimension, which includes knowledge and observations.

As Lippmann (1922) indicated, in the case of a distant country, the image perceived is primarily through the media. Even though people can better form an image of a country based on their own knowledge and experiences, the media is the main determinant of how the country will be perceived, especially for people without related personal experiences. In many cases, the mediated image might be the only source of information that the public has about a country. Kunczik (1997) has said that the image of a nation in people's minds is a result of the news media agenda, as it disseminates most information about the world affairs. By creating a positive image in the foreign media, a country can ensure the foreign public's positive perception.

The author wishes to acknowledge the help of ACG graduate students Vasiliki Tzifopoulou, Lampros Koitsanos, and Kyriaki Patsialidi in assisting with this project.

145

Kunczik (2009) defines the national image as the cognitive depiction that an individual has of a country, and more specifically, as what a person assumes to be accurate regarding a nation and its people. According to Kunczik, a national image is formed by a complicated communication process involving numerous sources, including the mass media, which can define the image of a country or a culture by simply reporting an event.

This study examines the current portrayal of President Donald J. Trump in the Greek press, to see how it relates to the overall image of the United States over the years.

ELEMENTS OF A NATION'S IMAGE

In a study of US and Japanese perspectives toward foreign products, Nagashima (1970) stated that "country image is the reputation, picture and stereotypes which consumers and professionals of the industry attach to a specific country's products" (pp. 67–68). Variables such as national characteristics, representative products, political and economic background, traditions, and history might contribute to this image. In later years, experts widened that definition to include such elements as culture, relationships and historical events, political and economic maturity, and the degrees of technological progress and industrialization (Allred, Chakraborty, & Miller, 1999).

A nation's portrayal in the foreign news media is often an outcome of its international communication strategy and the prevailing journalistic practices of a nation's media. As Samaras and Balomenos (2010) have stated, the mediated image of a nation is an interaction of the unplanned events happening within the country and its strategic communication process.

Journalistic practices, and not necessarily intentionality, tend to result in news framing of people, places, and events. An essential and inevitable part of the news-making process is the concept of framing, which can affect the perceived image of a country. According to Entman (1993), framing is the process that results in making more salient some features of a specific reality, and this might promote defined interpretations, definitions, or moral evaluation. Influenced by the effects of framing, people can acquire a specific opinion of an issue or reinforce their already existing beliefs (Chong & Druckman, 2007).

During the process of framing, journalists "select some aspects of a perceived reality and make them more salient in a communicating text, in such a way as to promote a specific problem definition, causal interpretation, moral evaluation, and/or treatment recommendation for the item described" (Entman, 1993, p. 52). Journalists try to make foreign news relevant and appealing to their readers by using the appropriate frames. As a consequence of journalistic practices, the readers shape a favorable or unfavorable image about a country and a specific interpretation of events happening there.

Manhein and Albritton (1984, p. 645) have defined two dimensions of a nation's image depicted in the news media: "visibility" and "valence." Visibility is the amount of media coverage a country receives, while valence is either the favorable or unfavorable tone reflected by the media content. Zaharopoulos (1986) has stated that the image of a country can be influenced not only by the positive or negative coverage in the foreign press, but also by the amount and type of coverage. However, both the quantity and the quality of the content are relatively subjective, therefore a framework is needed to evaluate the coverage. Pasadeos (1986) has listed some of the basic news selection criteria, which provide a basis from which the news media's treatment of a country can be assessed, explained, or interpreted. These are timeliness, conflict, cultural and economic proximity, prominence of the person or place, impact, and human interest. These factors can help us determine the type and amount of coverage a nation receives in the host country's press. Therefore, through this selection process, the media helps to set the public's agenda. By selecting to promote certain issues about a foreign nation as more newsworthy than others, they influence the public's perception.

IMAGE OF THE UNITED STATES IN INTERNATIONAL NEWS MEDIA

A study conducted in 2010 regarding the image of the United States in the Chinese media shows that generally the Chinese press covered topics related to the United States in a balanced and neutral fashion. The most frequently covered issues had to do with the US economy (46.6%) or politics (30.7%), with more than half of them adopting a neutral tone. The political image of United States contained plenty of conflicting attributes, such as democratic but hypocritical, aggressive but strong (He, Xianhong, & Xing, 2012).

In most cases US news in international media becomes domesticated. For example, for foreign events to be perceived as more relevant by local audiences, news is given a more national angle. Media in countries like Iran, Russia, China, and Egypt offered a lot of coverage to issues like the Ferguson events or other human rights–related topics since this type of attention might be a way to point out that it is better for America to not point any fingers at the human rights record of other nations (Clausen, 2004).

During the Trump presidency, Trump's character has also received a lot of press coverage. What most news pieces found around the world seem to agree on is that although they criticize Trump, they simultaneously seem to criticize Americans and their political choices. For example, in 2015, the German global broadcaster *Deutsche Welle* wrote about how Europeans are baffled by Trump's personality and criticized how US media cover the news. On the other hand, the *Irish Times* took a stronger view and tended to portray Trump as egocentric, with a strange haircut, and only appealing to Americans for his personality and his populist ideas (Simpson, 2015).

According to Wike et al. (2018), there is a correlation between how the United States is presented in international media and its image around the world. In an international survey conducted in 2017 among 40,448 participants by the Pew Research Center, it seems that the image of United States has suffered a decline since Trump was elected president.

THE US PRESIDENT AND THE IMAGE
OF THE UNITED STATES ABROAD

Many studies relate the negative image of the United States to its foreign policy over the years. The Bush presidency especially had a detrimental effect on the overall image of the United States. However, the Obama candidacy may have changed this overall negative image. This is called the "leadership effect," which is the process of transferring the leader's characteristics to the whole country (Samaras & Balomenos, 2010). In this case, the good reputation of Obama could affect the reputation of the nation. As Samaras and Balomenos stated, the Obama campaign was framed by the Greek media as a departure from the Bush presidency, and Obama was portrayed as an agent of hope and change.

Samaras and Balomenos (2010) studied the assumption that the Obama presidency could help the US image to be disassociated from the negative connotations and attributes that the Greek media was giving it over the years. They questioned whether the power of the "Brand

USA" would be enough to rehabilitate the US image, and if the Obama candidacy could restore it. Overall, they found that the evaluation of the United States was less negative under Obama than under Bush. This confirmed the leadership effect, as the Obama presidency helped improve the overall image of the United States as portrayed in the Greek media.

In addition, the blame for negative image effects was much more limited for Obama in comparison to Bush (blame to Obama was found in 6.3% of the articles, whereas blame to Bush in 34.2%). Moreover, Obama was represented with the hope frame twice as frequently as with the fear frame. Interestingly, the articles with a positive tone toward Obama came from various sources, whereas with Bush, the positive-toned articles were those that carried his own statements (Samaras & Balomenos, 2010).

At that time, the change in presidential leadership decreased the negativity toward the United States and balanced the nation's image. The overall negative US evaluation and its impact on the image decreased during the Obama presidency. Therefore, Obama contributed to the restoration of the image of America. After many years of negativity toward the United States, the representation of the US image in the Greek press changed for the better and the overall use of anti-Americanism master frames decreased.

The election of Donald Trump as president of the United States may have reversed these gains once again. In a survey conducted by the European Council on Foreign Relations, 60,000 people across 14 European Union countries were asked if Trump and the United States is a reliable ally. The result was that most Europeans do not have the same confidence in the alliance that they once had. The research shows that only 4% of Europeans trust Donald Trump (Keating, 2019).

Similarly, a Pew Research Center "global attitudes survey" on the confidence people around the world have in the "US president doing the right thing regarding world affairs" shows that there is a significant decrease in people's confidence regarding President Trump, compared to the confidence they had about President Obama. In fact, even the confidence in President Bush was a bit higher than that for Trump. Specifically, people in the United Kingdom, Germany, France, and Spain almost immediately lost their confidence in the US president to make the correct decision or do the right thing regarding world affairs as soon as he was elected (Bialik, 2019). Among citizens of EU countries, the Greek people have some of the lowest opinions of the US president, with only 36% of the population having a favorable view of President Trump (Bialik, 2019).

IMAGE OF THE UNITED STATES IN GREEK PRESS

Being a considerable economic and political power, the United States receives an extended amount of coverage in the foreign press. The Greek press also dedicates a significant part of its space and time to the affairs of the United States, not only because the United States influences global politics, but also due to its historical relationship with Greece.

Undoubtedly, the US involvement in the Greek civil war, its relationship with the Greek military junta of 1967–1974, the Cyprus dispute, the Yugoslavian crisis, and various events involving Turkey have affected the US image in the Greek media and among the Greek public. For years, the United States has had an overall negative image, because the Greek media coverage of the United States has been constructed using frames linking the US portrayal with what Greeks perceive to be negative events (Samaras & Balomenos, 2010).

A study by Zaharopoulos (1989) examined the image of the United States presented by seven Greek newspapers during 1986–1987. Given that the Greek press is politically oriented, he expected that left-wing papers would have less favorable coverage than right-wing papers. Overall, the amount of coverage about the United States showed that the Greek press considers the news about the United States as very important to their readers. Comparing news categories, an association was found between the right-wing-oriented papers and US domestic news, and the left-wing oriented newspapers with foreign news. However, he also found that there was a difference in the amount of coverage, as left-wing papers carried more such news items than right-wing papers. However, this may have been related to circulation size.

As such, the politically oriented environment of the Greek press affected the type of news coverage. Overall, over 75% of the Greek papers during that period portrayed the image of the United States as a global force that affects the rest of the world. An important element missing from the US news items was geographic diversity, as most news items were coming from Washington.

The candidacy of the Greek American Michael Dukakis during the 1988 US presidential election was an opportunity for Zaharopoulos (1990) to test the effect of cultural proximity in the news-making process. A content analysis examined whether Greek newspapers would offer more coverage about Dukakis than George H. W. Bush, and whether the coverage would be affected by the political orientation of the newspaper. Overall, more news items and photographs were dedicated to Dukakis; therefore, cultural proximity affected the news selection process. Moreover, the elements controlled by the gatekeepers such as photographs and headlines emphasized the importance of the Dukakis candidacy in the Greek press. Photographs of Dukakis and headlines containing his name were significantly greater in number than those of Bush. Lastly, the tone of the coverage was neutral for both candidates. Regarding the political orientation of the publication, the overall coverage showed little difference between the left-wing and the right-wing papers.

Samaras (2005) identified some dominant "master frames" that the Greek media have used extensively to construct the US image. More specifically, as Rachlin (1988, as cited in Samaras, 2005) has stated, the meaning of global events is influenced by the host country's national interests, and cultural and political perspectives. American presidents in their statements frame the various events based on US interests. Even though these statements find their way to a world audience, the host country's media can reframe them. The "counter-frame" refers to the phenomenon of reframing US statements by the foreign media, because of the media's ethnocentric perspective (Samaras, 2005, p. 4).

The Greek mass media, especially after the NATO bombardment of Serbia, enhanced the "anti-Americanism" master frame (Samaras, 2005, p. 1), which had been used for a long period. Even after the 9/11 terrorist attacks, when the United States developed and started to use the "War on Terrorism" master frame, the Greek media continued to report the US news through the "anti-Americanism" master frame (Samaras, 2005, p. 1). The use of this "counter-frame" created a negative image of the United States, especially during the Bush presidency (Samaras, 2005).

Samaras (2005) also examined how Greek newspapers framed the terrorist attack and the reactions of the Bush government one month after September 11, and the week after the US attack on Afghanistan. He explored the anti-Americanism master frame in four different politically oriented newspapers. He concentrated on the editorial columns because their tone is set mostly by the writer, whereas the tone of other news stories is usually the outcome of the objectivity norm and similar journalistic practices. The results were evaluated in three levels: the evaluative comments on the different parts, the attribution of responsibility for the attack, and the framing of the US reactions to both the 9/11 and the Afghanistan attack. Overall, the anti-Americanism master frame is confirmed in the portrayal of the United States in the Greek media. The level of anti-Americanism varied depending on the political orientation of the newspaper. A comparison between the left-wing newspapers with the others indicates that the anti-Americanism content was considerably higher in the left-wing newspapers.

Regarding the first level of evaluation, the comments on the United States are mostly negative. The level of negative criticism was higher than the positive in every newspaper. However, the left-wing newspaper had the highest percentage of negative comments. Moreover, the left-wing paper was the only one to emphasize the violation of human rights by the US government's reaction to the 9/11 attack, while the terror attack was presented as a consequence of US policy. The left-wing and center-left newspapers pointed to the responsibility to the United States, whereas the center-right's judgment was more balanced. Regarding the framing of the US reaction, only the center-right newspaper portrayed the reactions as a defense policy. The others presented the American reaction as an act aimed to extend American dominance.

Another opportunity for research on the anti-Americanism frame was the 2004 US presidential elections. Samaras and Koutrouli (2007) examined how powerful the anti-Americanism master frame was, how the US image was presented in the Greek press during the 2004 elections, and how intrusive journalists were toward the issue. They collected data from five mainstream newspapers (177 articles in total) during a one-month period. Overall, the coverage was negative toward the United States; therefore, the Anti-Americanism counterframe is confirmed again.

The neutral evaluation of the US elections was 43.5% in comparison with the negative which was 40.7%. So, the anti-Americanism frame remained in the representation of the United States. Furthermore, the U.S. president was heavily associated with negative feelings, and the idea of a change in leadership did not seem to change this negativity. Regarding the dominant issues, US partisan politics was first, and the external affairs of the United States was second.

METHOD

This study is an updated examination of the image of the United States in the Greek press, through the study of the coverage of President Trump in Greek online newspapers. For the quantitative part of this study, a content analysis of two online newspapers was used. *Proto-Thema* and *Kathimerini* are hard-copy newspapers, but they have two of the most popular online versions as well. Politically, their hard-copy versions have a center-right orientation, but generally tend to be more objective than most. These electronic papers generally carry more news items and longer articles than their print counterparts. Two constructed weeks (14 days) were used to cover the first 10 months of 2019. Using the search engine of each of the two sites, any article with a headline or major content having the word "Trump" became part of the sample. A coding procedure created for this purpose coded each article for the paper, topic, month of issue, whether a Trump tweet was included, whether photographs were included and how many, the length of the article in paragraphs, the tone toward Trump, and the tone toward the United States. Two coders coded each article. When there were disagreements between the two coders, a third coder was used to choose one of the two codes of the initial coders.

FINDINGS

Over the 14 days sampled, there were a total of 138 articles identified and coded. These represent about 10 news items about the United States per day in the two publications, which is considerably heavy coverage. The length of these articles was also long: 19% were more than 10 paragraphs in length, while 49% were 6 to 10 paragraphs long, and 30% were up to 5 paragraphs in length.

The months with the heaviest coverage of president Trump were the months of January, June, and October. Most topics dealt primarily with the United States or the Trump foreign policy. US relations with Turkey, which are important to Greece, also received extended coverage. On the other hand, about 10% of the topics covered by these two ePapers dealt directly with Trump scandals involving Russia and Ukraine (see Table 11.1).

About 17% of the news articles in these online newspapers included Trump's Twitter message. Similarly, around 90% of the news items included at least one photograph. Most photographs (53%) were of President Trump, followed by photos of other foreign leaders (10%).

This study finds a high degree of association between the tone of coverage toward Trump and the tone toward the United States (X^2 = 22.5; df = 4; p < .001). As Table 11.2 indicates, most of the tone of the coverage of Trump was neutral. However, 18% of it was negative, while only 1.4% was positive. There was no difference between the two news sites regarding the

Table 11.1. Topics in Trump Coverage by Major Greek News Sites

Topics	Kathimerini #	Kathimerini %	Proto Thema #	Proto Thema %	TOTAL #	TOTAL %
Trump's/US Foreign Policy	13	20	24	33	37	27
Trump's Immigration Policy	8	12	7	10	15	11
Relations with Iran	8	12	4	5.5	12	9
Relations with Turkey	8	12	4	5.5	12	9
Trump Family	5	8	4	5.5	9	6.5
Ukraine Impeachment Issues	2	3	7	10	9	6.5
Relations with the EU	4	6	3	4	7	5
Russian Collusion Issues	3	5	2	3	5	4
Relations with Russia	3	5	2	3	5	4
Trump's US Economic Policy	1	1.5	4	5.5	5	4
Relations with Congress	1	1.5	2	3	3	2
Other	9	14	9	12.5	18	13
TOTAL	65	100	72	100.5	137	101

X^2 = 11.2; df =11; p = .43

Table 11.2. The Tone of Trump Coverage by Major Greek News Sites

Tone toward Trump	Kathimerini #	Kathimerini %	Proto Thema #	Proto Thema %	TOTAL #	TOTAL %
Positive	1	1.5	1	1.4	2	1.4
Negative	11	16.7	14	19.4	25	18.2
Neutral	54	81.8	57	79.2	111	80.4
TOTAL	66	100	72	100	138	100

X^2 = .181; df = 2; p = .91

tone toward Trump. Similarly, the study did not find a relationship between the topic of the coverage and the tone toward Trump (X^2 = 25.9; df = 22; p = .25). Nevertheless, the articles with the most negative tone appeared during the month of October, when the impeachment issues about Ukraine were being discussed in Congress (X^2 = 37; df = 18; p = .005).

From a qualitative standpoint, the early morning news programs of two major television stations were monitored throughout 2019. One of these stations has a daily morning report from a correspondent in Washington, D.C. In addition, a major evening newscast of a major television station, the morning news and information program of a major radio station, and an electronic newspaper (*iephimerida*) were monitored daily for news about the United States. Generally, the image of President Trump presented via the Greek news media is not necessarily much different than his image portrayed in media around the world. It is just that in Greece, for obvious geopolitical reasons, there is an emphasis on his relationship with Turkey's president Recep Tayyip Erdogan. President Trump's positive relations with many of the world's authoritarian figures gets the attention of the Greek news media, as it does in the US news media. The particular relationship between Trump and Erdogan is especially important to the Greeks for obvious reasons. Erdogan's increasing attempts to make Turkey a regional power and Turkey's relationship with Greece, as well as with Russia, are especially covered by the Greek news media.

While Congress is portrayed by the Greek news media as taking the side of Greece in the various disputes the two countries have with each other, they portray President Trump as taking the side of Turkey. They often wonder about the Trump family's business dealings in Turkey and whether this is related to Trump's very friendly relationship with Erdogan. This leaves the Greek news media to accept the view that in a dispute between Greek and Turkey over Cyprus or the Aegean, Greece will not get any support from the United States, even though Greece is perceived as the more faithful ally in the United States. Of course, another important topic in the Greek news coverage of the Trump and the United States in general is the impeachment process. The news media and the public in general show a great deal of fascination over the process and wonder how it will end, even though experts inform them that there is no way Trump will be found guilty in the US Senate.

General themes running in the Greek news coverage of Trump include Trump's unpredictability and his narcissistic personality. They often portray him as not listening to his aids, and as one correspondent reported, "Trump seems to be making last-minute decisions during a phone call." The Greek media coverage also embodies a voyeuristic theme, in terms of Trump's relationship with women or his current wife's appearance. They focus on his relationship with the rest of the government, which according to the Greek news media reflects a conflict between Trump and the American "Deep State." And while Trump and his supporters refer to the deep state in derogatory terms, the Greek news media tend to feel grateful for its presence. The media in Greece also show an admiration that the balance of power between the branches of government in the United States tend to work more or less as designed, implying that they do not do so in Greece. At the same time, they are negative about the degree that business and major corporations play in the public life and policies of the United States, and particularly how important the personal business interests of Trump interfere with official US affairs. Overall, the Greek media portray President Trump as a different type of US president, and this is presented in a negative manner.

CONCLUSION

This study of the coverage of President Trump in two electronic newspapers in Greece by the amount of coverage shows that the Greek media continue to treat the United States as the major news and global affairs superpower. This study is reinforcing other previous studies about the negative tone of coverage regarding the United States, and in this case, Donald Trump. In fact, there is evidence that the negative portrayal of President Trump is negatively affecting the portrayal of the United States. At the same time, however, there is evidence that President Trump is portrayed somewhat separately from the rest of the US government, primarily because of his unique personality and of his impeachment troubles. At the same time, unlike the coverage of past presidents, there is a voyeuristic examination of Trump, because of his background as a personality before he became president, because of his wife, and his because of his unsteady personality. President Trump's coverage in Greek media is not that different from his coverage in other nations' media except for the particular attention Greek media pay to his relationship with Turkey's president, which is worrisome to the Greeks.

Thus, in response to the question of whether Trump represents America, the answer is complex. On one hand the Greek media seem to say that someone like Trump could only be elected in the United States, which leaves them scratching their head, as they worry about the country and its people. On the other hand, they portray the United States as a stable and important democracy, which will survive the attitude and behavior of President Trump.

REFERENCES

Allred, A., Chakraborty, G., & Miller, S. J. (2000). Measuring images of developing countries: A scale development study. *Journal of Euromarketing, 8*(3), 29–49. doi: 10.1300/j037v08n03_02

Bialik, K. (2019). How the world views the United States and its president in 9 charts. Pew Research Center. Retrieved from https://www.pewresearch.org/fact-tank/2018/10/09/how-the-world-views-the-u-s-and-its-president-in-9-charts/

Chong, D., & Druckman, J. N. (2007). Framing theory. *Annual Review of Political Science, 10*(1), 103–126. doi: 10.1146/annurev.polisci.10.072805.103054

Clausen, L. (2004). Intercultural encounters in the global transmission of news: Perception and production of cultural images. Paper presented at the 54th Annual International Communication Association Conference. ICA 2004, New Orleans, LA.

Entman, R. M. (1993). Framing: Toward clarification of a fractured paradigm. *Journal of Communication, 43*(4), 51–58. doi: 10.1111/j.1460-2466.1993.tb01304.x

He, Z., Xianhong, C., & Xing, W. (2012). The image of the United States in the Chinese media: An examination of the evaluative component of framing. *Public Relations Review, 38*(5), 676–683. doi: 10.1016/j.pubrev.2012.09.001

Keating, D. (2019). Only 4% of Europeans trust Donald Trump. *Forbes.* https://www.forbes.com/sites/davekeating/2019/09/12/only-4-of-europeans-trust-donald-trump/#7a2aa11a6a5f

Kunczik, M. (1997). *Images of Nations and International Public Relations.* Lawrence Erlbaum.

Kunczik, M. (2009). Transnational public relations by foreign governments. In K. Sriramesh & D. Vercic (Eds.), The global public relations handbook. Theory, research and practice (expanded and revised ed., pp. 842–871). Routledge.

Lee, S., Toth, E. L., & Shin, H. (2008). Cognitive categorization and routes of national reputation formation: US opinion leaders' views on South Korea. *Place Branding and Public Diplomacy, 4*, 272–286.

Lippmann, W. (1922). *Public Opinion.* Harcourt, Brace and Company.

Manheim, J. B., and Albritton, R. B. (1984). Changing national images: International public relations and media agenda-setting. *American Political Science Review, 78,* 64–657.

Nagashima, A. (1970). A Comparison of Japanese and U.S. Attitudes toward Foreign Products. *Journal of Marketing, 34*(1), 68–74. doi: 10.2307/1250298

Pasadeos, Y. (1986). A context for assessing the image of Greece in the U.S. press. In M. Paraschos (Ed.), *Greece and the American Press observations, implications, strategies* (pp. 3–8). Krikos.

Rachlin, A. (1988). *News as hegemonic reality: American political culture and the frame of news accounts.* Praeger.

Samaras, A. N. (2005). Représentations du 11-Septembre dans quatre journaux grecs. Une question de cadrage. *Questions de Communication, 8,* 367–388 (English translation).

Samaras, A. N., & Balomenos, K. P. (2010, October). The mediated nation-image of the USA and the dynamic of events in the Obama era: A quantitative content analysis of the Greek press. Poster presented at the 3rd Conference of ECREA, Hamburg/Germany.

Samaras, A. N., & Koutrouli, M. (2007, July). Anti-Americanism and the 2004 USA presidential campaign in the Greek press: A case study in nation image making. Poster presented at the IAMCR Conference, Paris/France.

Simpson, L. (2015, September 11). How Donald Trump is covered by media around the world. https://abcnews.go.com/Politics/donald-trump-covered-media-world/story?id=33539306

Wike, R., Stokes, B., Poushter, J., Silver, L., Fetterolf, J., & Devlin, K. (2018, December 6). America's international image continues to suffer. Pew Research Center, Global Attitudes and Trends. https://www.pewresearch.org/global/2018/10/01/americas-international-image-continues-to-suffer/

Zaharopoulos, T. (1986). The image of Greece in the U.S. press: A study of six major American newspapers. In Paraschos, M. (ed.), *Greece and the American press observations, implications, strategies* (pp. 9–22). Krikos.

Zaharopoulos, T. (1989). The image of the U.S. in the Greek press. *Journalism Quarterly, 66,* 188–192.

Zaharopoulos, T. (1990). Cultural proximity in international news coverage: 1988 U.S. presidential campaign in the Greek press. *Journalism Quarterly, 67,* 190–194.

IRAN

12

Iranian Media Coverage and Views of the United States and Trump

Saeedeh Moradifar, University of Isfahan
Ali Omidi, University of Isfahan
Kourosh Ziabari, Fair Observer Correspondent and UK Chevening
Scholarship Alumnus

INTRODUCTION

The roots of the current skirmishes between Iran and the United States should be traced to several decades ago, starting with the US-backed 1953 coup d'état against the democratically elected prime minister Mohammad Mosaddegh and culminating in the 1979 Islamic Revolution. However, the 9/11 attacks represented a watershed moment in the bilateral relations, as it changed the dynamics of mutual relations into a state of reciprocal threat. With the deployment of the American forces in the Middle East region, envisioning the strategic goal of establishing military bases on Iran's doorsteps in Afghanistan, Iraq, and the Persian Gulf countries, Washington turned into an existential threat for Iran's national security. Even though Iran's regional rivals on the eastern (Taliban) and western borders (Saddam Regime) were trounced, the United States replaced them and functioned as a serious security challenge. In addition, regional crisis in countries such as Afghanistan, Iraq, and some other Arab countries signified that both sides had varying and at times contradicting strategic and geopolitical interests (Barzegar, 2010).

With the outburst of determining regional developments in the Middle East in the form of the Arab Spring, differences between Iran and the United States became more evident. Each side adhered to a distinct narrative of developments in countries such as Egypt, Tunisia, Libya, and Syria. The coming to power of Donald Trump, the firebrand Republican president in 2016 accelerated the growth of confrontation between Iran and the United States. These differences manifested themselves while Iran's media, as the representatives of different strata of the society, exponentially focused on depictions and storytelling about the new US president. In fact, newspapers, as one of the most popular media outlets, have immensely influenced public opinion and political alignments in Iran at the same time as representing the political streams and the public perception of other nations.

Three recent polls of Iranian people conducted by the Center for International and Security Studies at Maryland underscore this fact. Since 2014, this center has been regularly surveying Iranians' public opinions, and its early polls were done in 2006. The 2019 poll was conducted while Iranians were being subjected to the "maximum pressure" campaign by the United States. According to this poll, Iranian people's perception of the United States hit a 13-year low as there is no indication for tendency for negations with the United States. At the moment, 86% of the Iranian people do not have positive feelings about negotiations with the United States, showing a 10% increase in the number of people who were pessimistic about talks with the United States in 2016. While the official US policy has been to exempt medicine from the list of sanctioned goods being exported to Iran, 57% of the respondents say the procurement of these goods has become more difficult as compared to the preceding year, and 70% of them are of the opinion that this is a deliberate policy adopted by the United States to block Iranian people's access to medicine (Ramsay, 2019).

On this basis, the authors have attempted to choose newspapers that were long-running, somewhat well-known, and boasted a high circulation at the same time as representing the different sociopolitical leanings of the Reformists and Principalists (conservatives),[1] reflecting a range of beliefs held by the Iranian people. In the present study, four newspapers, namely *Kayhan* and *Resalat* (Principalist) and *Etemad* and *Sharq* (Reformist), were scrutinized.

In the present study, the authors employed the theoretical framework proposed by Robert Jervis to respond to the research question. Jervis believes the understanding or perception of the world and the actions of other players can be distinct from the reality based on comprehensible and discoverable reasons (Jervis, 2017). To decipher the perceptions and misperceptions, it is important to note that different players look at a single subject or incident from different perspectives while their perceptions and imaginations of that phenomenon are different and diverse. Newspapers, as media players, approach different events and subjects with different mindsets, based on their intellectual filters, system of beliefs and thoughts, and ideological values.

THEORETICAL FRAMEWORK

Actions and reactions are not embedded in reality; rather, they are rooted in the perceptions of rivals of each other's image. Before Jervis, there were other scholars who had come up with ideas on this theme. The "Image Theory" proposed by Lee Roy Beach and Michael A. Hogg is one of the theories by which personal knowledge is expressed through mental images (Patalano, 2003). Robert Jervis is one of the scholars who, at the same time as laying emphasis on bureaucratic variables, domestic policies, and international system, draws attention to personal-level perceptions such as world leaders' understanding of threats and opportunities.

Jervis mostly highlights the idea of cognitive psychology. Cognitive psychology is focused on how the individuals and groups get involved in the decision-making processes. Ole Rudolf Holsti argues that individual behavior is shaped, to a great extent, based on the way the individual understands, identifies, and assesses the physical and social environment. Similarly, it has been made clear that in order to experience and face the complex and confusing realities of the environment, individuals should formulate simple and structured beliefs about the

---

1. Principalists in Iran are not necessarily mainstream conservative, because they take sometimes hardline and revolutionary attitudes.

nature of their surroundings. The understanding of the individuals, in turn, is filtered through a conglomerate of thoughts and cognitive maps pertaining to the different segments of physical and social environment (Holsti, 1976). In his 2017 book *Perception and Misperception in International Politics*, Jervis postulates that if we consider players in the international arena a monolith who all act in accordance with a certain model, it is again important to figure out the cognitive differences of the players and their imagination of the real world.

Jervis believes that perceptions and misperceptions are spectacularly important in systems where the role of individuals in decision-making and policy-making is more prominent than that of entities and structured authorities. In these systems, the perception of individuals of themselves and their roles, the significance and power of the nation, national interest, other players, and the structure of international system are immensely effective. Whenever the misperceptions are coupled with miscalculations, irretrievable damage will be inflicted on the country and the political system (Shokouhi, 2017). Perception and misperception are important from the standpoint that the understanding of a leader or a nation of the image or beliefs of another player influences their perspective of an event or a behavior that is expected of that player under different circumstances (Jervis, 2017).

In other words, the significance of understanding and perception lies in the fact that they powerfully impact the modality of the reception and interpretation of information about others and the external world. How the leaders interpret the threats emerging from the behavior of others is to a great extent dependent on their understanding of the adversary (Sharifi & Karami, 2018). Even so, Jervis warns that a distinction should be drawn between the two psychological and operational realms. The psychological realm is a universe that the politician and the actor behold, and the operational realm is a universe in which policies are implemented. The decisions and policies of politicians are swayed by their goals, calculations, and perceptions. A leader or a nation may describe the events, circumstances, and interaction between governments without exploring their nature and the consequences their future behavior might entail (Jervis, 2017).

By building on cognitive psychology as a foundation, Jervis believes the main factors involved in perception include belief, image, and intention. Understanding is a process by which a player takes action to devise or produce an understanding (belief) about other players (image) and how they conduct themselves under certain circumstances (intention). Intention comprises the set of actions a government takes in a certain situation or is inclined to take. Intentions are sometimes different from what the governmental decision makers think they want to do. This is important in that they should predict how other actors will behave. One might imagine the actor can always precisely predict its behavior; however, this is not accurate, because actors may not know how to behave under different circumstances. A lot of events may happen that the actor cannot envision (Jervis, 2017). For example, even if two actors evaluate each other in a precise manner, perceptions and misperceptions still play a leading role in the emergence of disputes or even outbreak of war between them. Of particular importance are reliable and unreliable judgments about the intentions of the other party (Jervis, 1988).

To lessen the problems resulting from misunderstandings and render the other actors' behavior predictable, leaders and governments attempt to send signals to carve the players' imagination of themselves, lead their actions and reactions toward themselves in certain directions, and make them predictable. Jervis argues that actors need two things: first to predict how others will behave or what actions they will take; second, to ensure others make the predictions that are favorable to them. The actor not only attempts to understand and perceive the environment, but it dispatches signals to portray images that might be accurate or inaccurate. Moreover, when they interpret the behavior of the others, they realize that others are also endeavoring to portray their favored images (Jervis, 2002). Cognitive adaptability contributes to the facilitation of this process. Through this psychological mechanism, leaders and governments aim at simplifying concepts. In this process, mental logic is more effective than pure logic.

Jervis is of the opinion that researchers have found people's belief structures to be inclined toward adaptability and moderation. This means data that contradict the comprehension-related belief structures of the decision makers (governments) do not enter the decision-making stream. This process is referred to as cognitive adaptability. Cognitive adaptability means the decision makers put aside certain information that is at odds with previous perceptions and understandings and, on the other hand, pay excessive attention to information that is adaptable to their previously held beliefs and understandings (Mintz & DeRouen, 2010). In Jervis's view, we tend to hold the opinion that the countries we love do actions that are favorable to us, advocate for our goals, and oppose the countries we are against. We tend to believe the countries that are our nemeses propose ideas that harm us, are against the interests of our allies, and help our contenders (Jervis, 2017).

As a conclusion, it can be noted that the news reports and analyses of newspapers do not merely describe the current events and their possible repercussions, but also portray the actions and expression of viewpoints and political, economic, and military beliefs of the policy makers and the public and add to the negative and positive dimensions of these portrayals (Van Dijk, 1989). These beliefs result in selective attention to and selective choice of parts of these messages, and other parts that belie the dominant stream and the stabilized portrayals are removed. Therefore, newspapers can perform the role of a strainer to present special (here negative) perceptions toward special countries and statesmen.

Sample Size

Topics and contents related to President Trump's policies and the United States have been selected from four newspapers, *Etemad*, *Kayhan*, *Sharq*, and *Resalat*, spanning the 2016–2019 period. Considering the high volume of the newspaper texts, these samples have been selected completely randomly and also purposefully, which means the authors have chosen 24 editions of each of these newspapers to be studied within the four-year period.

Methodology

The present study has been carried out using a qualitative and quantitative content analysis method in order to expose latent text connotations about the United States and President Trump. At the outset, the authors selected and gathered the relevant texts and in the next stage dissected and analyzed the selected texts. The variables studied include (1) news resources and (2) text analysis of news, interviews, reports, articles, editorial, and op-eds.

Analysis of Findings

Frequency of Stories

As Figure 12.1 shows, a total of 487 stories from the four newspapers discussing the United States and Donald Trump have been selected. Out of the total stories selected, 27.3% (133 stories) were published by *Kayhan*, 24% (117 stories) were run by *Sharq*, 28.7% (140 stories)

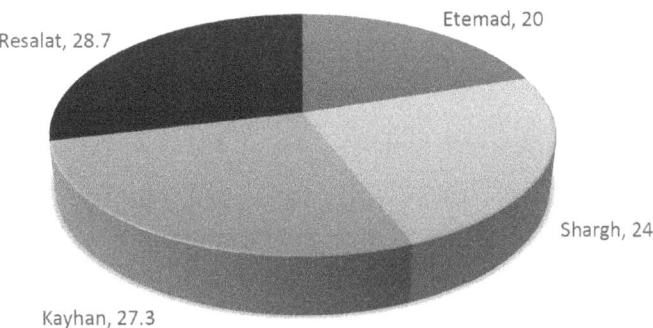

Figure 12.1   Frequency of stories

were featured by *Resalat*, and 20% (90 stories) were printed by *Etemad*. *Resalat* had the most stories on the United States and Trump, and the smallest portion belonged to the *Etemad* daily. Overall, 44% of the stories were printed by the Reformist newspapers and 56% were released by Principalist dailies. This is indicative of the disproportionate emphasis of the Principalists, as opposed to the Reformists, on the United States and President Trump.

News and Reports Resources

In this section, "news and reports resources" implies the origin of the content that is presented at the beginning of each news story. The authors have defined five categories in line with the data in Table 12.1. By coding the references of the lede, or the opening paragraphs, the authors concluded that for the *Etemad* daily, the newspaper's own reporters and experts were the predominant resources cited. This is while 54.9% of the stories of *Kayhan* newspaper and 39.3% of the stories of *Sharq* lacked any reference to the resources at the beginning of the texts. Moreover, the overriding resources used by the *Resalat* newspaper (37.1%) were Iran's domestic news agencies such as Mehr, Tasnim, Fars, and ISNA news agencies. The important point in reviewing the codes of Principalists and Reformists was that the first one minimally gave any reference to their own reporters and experts.

The other important point surrounding the coverage of the United States and President Trump is these newspapers' use of American news agencies and news outlets as resources to describe Trump. The aim was to validate their specific image-making for the audience. Out of the total 487 news stories, 40 stories (8.2%) were extracted from American news agencies. Taking into account Figure 12.2, *Kayhan* cited American media outlets at a 45% rate, principally giving reference to reporting by the *Washington Post* and the *New York Times*. It was followed by *Sharq*, which used American media outlets as a reference, mostly citing the *Los Angeles Times* and CNN at a rate of 27.5%. *Resalat*, with 25% and *Etemad* with 2.5% represented the smallest use of American sources. As a matter of fact, the goal

Table 12.1. News Resources

News Agencies and News Outlets		Ledes/Opening Paragraphs of the Newspaper Stories					Reformists Total	Principalists Total
		Etemad	Kayhan	Sharq	Resalat	Total		
Newspaper's reporters and experts	Frequency	56	15	39	21	131	95	36
	Columnar Percentage	57.7	11.3	33.3	15	26.9	44.4	13.2
	Linear Percentage	42.8	11.4	29.8	16	100	72.5	27.5
Iran's domestic news agencies and news outlets	Frequency	3	19	13	52	87	16	71
	Columnar Percentage	3.1	14.3	11.1	37.2	17.9	7.5	26
	Linear Percentage	3.5	21.8	14.9	59.8	100	18.4	81.6
American news agencies and news outlets	Frequency	1	18	11	10	40	12	28
	Columnar Percentage	1	13.5	9.4	7.1	8.2	5.6	10.2
	Linear Percentage	2.5	45	27.5	25	100	30	70
Other foreign news agencies	Frequency	3	8	8	21	40	11	29
	Columnar Percentage	3.1	6	6.9	15	8.2	5.1	10.6
	Linear Percentage	7.5	20	20	52.5	100	27.5	72.5
Unspecified	Frequency	34	73	46	36	189	80	109
	Columnar Percentage	35.1	54.9	39.3	25.7	38.8	37.4	40
	Linear Percentage	18	38.6	24.3	19.1	100	42.3	57.7
Total	Frequency	97	133	117	140	487	214	273
	Columnar Percentage	100	100	100	100	100	100	100
	Linear Percentage	20	27.3	24	28.7	100	44	56

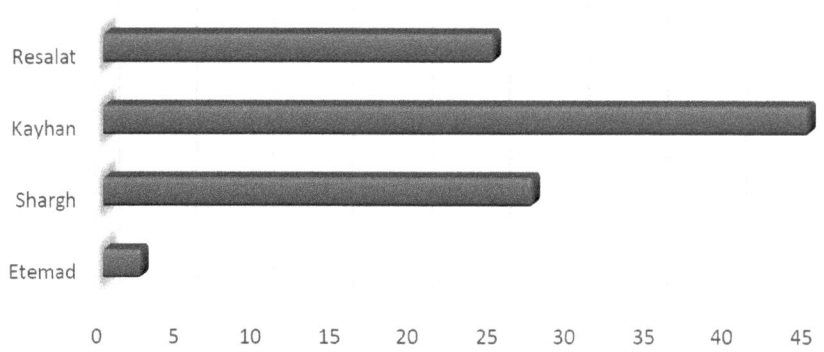

Figure 12.2   American news agencies and news outlets used as references across two spectrums of newspapers

of the Principalists in making these references (70%) was to underline the criticisms levied against President Trump's activities and policies by the American media and news agencies. This would mean the shortcomings of Trump's policies have made him a subject of severe criticism even inside the United States.

TEXT ANALYSIS

After analyzing the texts of four newspapers, this research arrived at 46 code categories, which in sum amounts to 4,931 codes.[2] Of this total, the pro-reform *Sharq* daily boasted the largest coding with 1,420 codes, while the Principalists retained the smallest number of codes at 939. It is noteworthy that the order of coding in the following table is random.

In sum, the Principalist newspapers represented 2,348 codes while the Reformist newspapers represented 2,583 codes, the reason for which has to be found in the positive approach of the Reformists to the Hasan Rouhani administration. Of the entire codes included in the following table, there are four frequently used codes that the Reformist and Principalist newspapers gave reference to. The most frequent code was the reinstatement and enforcement of sanctions (old and new), which the Principalists alluded to 511 times and the Reformists mentioned 385 times. Second is the code denoting the violation of commitments and abrogation of Joint Comprehensive Plan of Action (JCPOA), which the Principalist newspapers cited 295 times and the Reformists gave reference to 186 times. The code of JCPOA (Iran nuclear deal) as Iran's biggest achievement is the fourth-most-frequent code, which the Reformists mentioned 199 times and the Principalists cited 37 times.

Table 12.2 is a general overview of the codes extracted from the texts selected from the four newspapers. For the purpose of differentiation, the cells containing codes belonging to the Principalist newspapers are highlighted with dark background. It should be taken into consideration that both the Principalists and Reformists almost unanimously agree about these codes; however, each of them puts a greater emphasis on a specific code or a certain aspect of Trump's presidency.

Table 12.2.   Codes Extracted from the Newspapers

Orientation in Text	Code	Etemad	Kayhan	Sharq	Resalat	Reformists Total	Principalists Total
Direct negative orientation toward Trump and the United States	Travel ban against the citizens of seven Muslim-majority countries	14	14	8	2	22	16
	Regime-change policy vis-à-vis Iran	7	19	20	13	27	32
	Maximum pressure campaign	30	19	29	11	59	30

(continued)

---

2. A code is a word or short phrase that symbolically assigns a summative, essence-capturing attribute for a portion of language-based or visual data. The data can consist of interview transcripts, participant observation field notes, journals, documents, literature, artifacts, photographs, video, websites, e-mail correspondence, and so on (Saldaña, 2009).

Table 12.2. *Continued*

Orientation in Text	Code	Etemad	Kayhan	Sharq	Resalat	Reformists Total	Principalists Total
	Blocking the entry of investors and cutting off trade channels with Iran	15	30	3	8	18	38
	Reinstatement and enforcement of sanctions (old and new)	156	377	229	134	385	511
	Iran's quest for nuclear arms	8	28	32	15	40	43
	Global consensus and coalition against Iran	17	1	8	6	25	7
	Iran destabilizing the Middle East and the world	49	24	31	27	80	51
	Iran's violations of human rights and democracy	8	15	4	3	12	18
	Iran's destabilizing missiles program	20	61	29	27	49	88
	Iran, a sponsor of terrorist groups	15	26	24	22	39	48
	Violation of commitments and abrogating the Iran Nuclear Deal	72	193	118	102	190	295
	Trump's inattention to ethical considerations	4	15	4	3	8	18
	Trump's limited political knowledge	14	2	17	7	31	9
	Trump, a liar	3	18	20	7	23	25
	Trump as a thoughtless and illogical person	10	2	14	5	24	7
	Trump's unpredictability	—	5	4	11	4	16
	Trump' narcissist attitude	—	4	2	4	2	8
	Trump's unreliability	—	55	8	15	8	70
	Impeachment of Trump	—	72	9	14	9	86
	Trade, economic and psychological war (against Iran)	14	21	15	20	29	41
	Indirect warmongering policies (internationally)	69	25	78	47	147	72

Orientation in Text	Code	Etemad	Kayhan	Sharq	Resalat	Reformists Total	Principalists Total
	Trump's sponsorship of terrorism on the global scale, particularly in the Middle East	2	5	4	5	6	10
	Safeguarding the security of Israel in the Middle East region	14	16	16	25	30	41
	Iran, the most important priority in policy-making	6	3	4	5	10	8
	Intervention in the internal affairs of other countries (such as the presence of American troops in Syria)	24	42	27	48	51	90
Indirect negative orientation toward Trump and the United States	Collusion of Trump's 2016 presidential campaign with the Russian government	18	15	43	9	61	24
	Negotiations with and extracting concessions from Iran	109	92	95	94	204	186
	Withdrawing from multiple international and regional treaties & agreements	19	3	35	8	54	11
	Illegitimacy and unacceptability of Trump's policies in the realm of international relations	5	9	6	8	11	17
	Diminishing the supranational expenditures of the United States and bequeathing them to other nations	20	7	2	8	22	15
	Rupture between the United States and its European partners and their independence	87	13	108	36	195	49

(continued)

Table 12.2. Continued

Orientation in Text	Code	Etemad	Kayhan	Sharq	Resalat	Reformists Total	Principalists Total
	US quest for new Middle East allies (Arab nations)	43	9	31	19	74	28
	Trump claiming to lead the fight against ISIS in the Middle East	16	4	5	7	21	11
	Trump swayed and influenced by his entourage and family	28	10	18	7	46	17
	Trump's removing and appointing of officials	9	2	20	8	29	10
	Importance of personal relationships and interests in politics	5	17	24	4	29	21
	Growth of racism in the US society	29	33	34	19	63	52
	Growth of populism in the US society	11	—	16	2	27	2
	Trump's lack of credibility and acceptability in the US society	6	36	9	30	15	66
	Intensification of intra-party and intra-government disputes in the United States	5	35	21	10	26	45
	Undermining the achievements of President Barack Obama	9	2	19	12	28	14
No orientation	Trump's close relationship with Russia	—	—	9	21	9	21
	Economy, the most important priority in the US policy	27	1	27	22	54	23
	Improvement of the economic conditions of Iran	50	10	38	11	88	21
	JCPOA as Iran's biggest breakthrough	96	19	103	18	199	37
	Total codes	1163	1409	1420	939	2583	2348

Within the total of 46 code categories, this research has identified three general orientations regarding the main research theme. These orientations include: (1) Direct negative orientation toward Trump and the United States, (2) Indirect negative orientation toward Trump and the United States, and (3) Directionless or neutral orientation.

There are 26 code categories (18 Principalist code categories and 8 Reformist code categories) for direct negative orientation toward Donald Trump and the United States. Considering Figure 12.3, the Principalist newspapers demonstrated greater direct negative orientation in their emphasized codes as compared to the Reformists. The Principalist newspapers revealed greater intensity in 18 out of the 26 code categories.

There are 16 code categories (13 Reformist code categories and 3 Principalist code categories) for indirect negative orientation toward Trump and the United States. The Principalist newspapers revealed greater intensity in 13 out of the 16 code categories.

There are two neutral code categories (2 for Principalists and 2 for Reformists). In fact, it is possible to note a more favorable emphasis by the Reformist newspapers on the performance of the moderate Rouhani administration. The orientations of the Reformist and Principalist

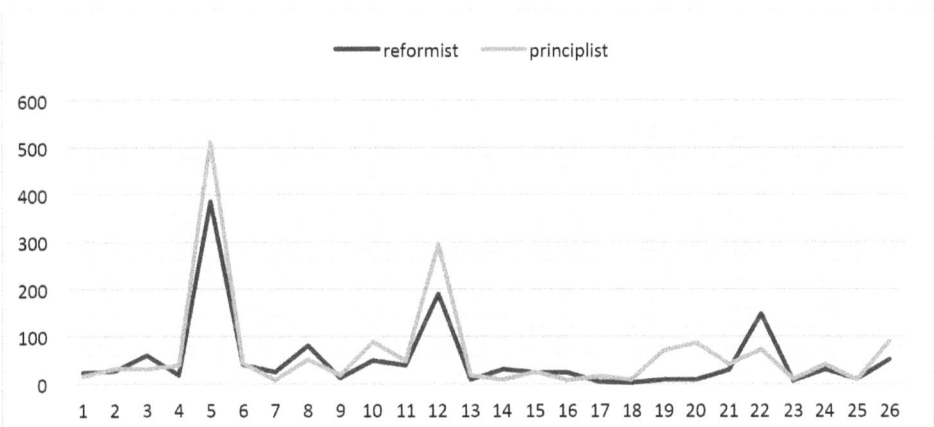

Figure 12.3   Direct negative orientation toward Donald Trump and the United States

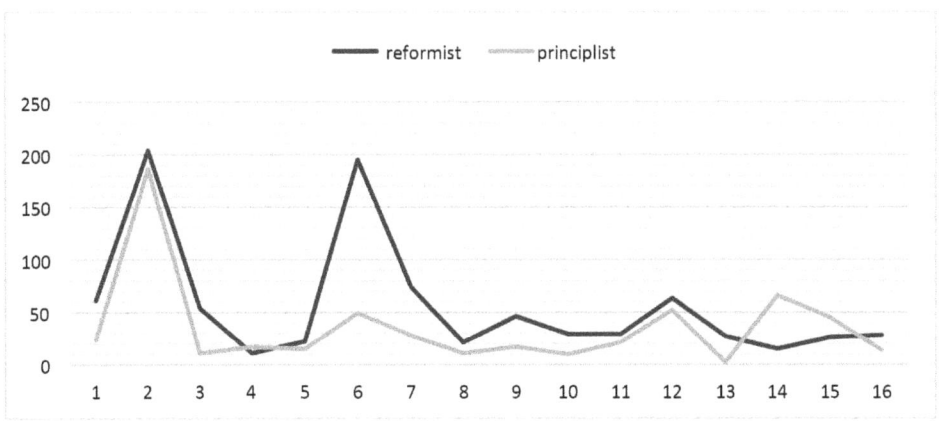

Figure 12.4   Indirect negative orientation toward Donald Trump and the United States

newspapers are predicated on their worldview and ideological beliefs. Therefore, they might be inattentive to the parts of messages that have been inconsistent with their orientation. On this basis, it is possible to observe two different narratives about Trump and the United States in the two different spectrums of newspapers studied: the soft and indirect orientation of the Reformist newspapers and the harsh and direct orientation of the Principalist newspapers. However, these narratives subscribe to the anti-American paradigm dominating Iranian politics. In what follows, these orientations are investigated with reference to the words and terms that are presented in Table 12.2.

Orientation of the Reformist Newspapers

Essentially, the Iranian Reformists subscribe to a more positive understanding and interpretation of the West and this is due to their intellectual foundations, which have commonalities with the Western intellectual tradition. The Reformist discourse came under spotlight after the Islamic Revolution of 1979, particularly with the election of Mohammad Khatami as president on May 23, 1997. In terms of concepts such as civil society, democracy, freedom of expression, human rights, social justice and rule of law, this discourse shares many features with the Western thought tradition.

The outcome of the existence of such commonalities was that after rising to power as president, Mohammad Khatami built on détente as a basis for his government's relationship with the outside world, particularly the West, because in the preceding years, as a result of events such as the Islamic Revolution and the Iran-Iraq War (1980–1988), there was no positive perception of the West in Iran. By proposing a culture-oriented rhetoric and "Dialogue of Civilizations" within the framework of Islamic Revolution, Khatami founded his foreign policy based on mutual respect among nations and the absolute rejection of the clash of civilizations (Shariati, 2004). One of the dimensions of Khatami's détente was manifested in his efforts to lower tensions and confrontation between Iran and the United States in such a way that he tried to engage in direct dialogue with the American people and indirect dialogue with the US government. Therefore, on January 7, 1998, in an address to the American people, which was aired on CNN, he admired the American nation at the same time as expressing his respect for them, and extolled the religious foundations and freedoms of the United States, noting that the principles of liberty and religious freedom that have reinforced the essence of the American republic have also articulated the establishment of the Islamic Republic of Iran (Darvishi, 2015).

With the coming to power of the moderate administration of Hassan Rouhani, which had actually inherited many of its intellectual origins from the reform era of Khatami, a new climate emerged for the initiation of positive understanding and comprehension between Iran and the West, because akin to Khatami, the Rouhani administration had envisaged moderation and peaceful coexistence as its foreign policy motto. The main promises made by Rouhani during his presidential terms were: Iran should seriously engage in negotiations with the Western countries; it must reduce the regional tensions through constructive interaction with its neighbors, and that it should concentrate on the improvement of the economic situation and general welfare of the Iranian public. He believed for the Iranian people to enjoy welfare, Iran must be integrated in the global economy and attract foreign investment. Moreover, Rouhani was trying to convince his domestic political rivals that they should not see Iran's relations with its opponents as a zero-sum game. From Rouhani's perspective, this demanded immediate action to strike a nuclear deal with the P5+1. Therefore, it was based on this positive comprehension that a new round of negotiations with the US government under President

Barack Obama began. In addition, the Rouhani administration's positive approach to the West underpinned indirect cooperation between Iran and the United States on some of their shared concerns in the Middle East. Rouhani was trying to paint a picture of Iran as an independent and moderate country. This was unachievable without changing the general orientations of Iran's foreign policy. Rouhani maintained the general orientation; however, he applied subtle changes to improve Iran's global public image, particularly in the West (Haji-Yousefi, 2018).

With the election of Trump, and the aggressive policies he adopted against Iran subsequently, many Reformists and the Rouhani administration moderated their approach to relations with the West and the United States, and this was reflected in the Reformist newspapers' reporting. The election of Trump was not merely a big blow to the Democrats, but it also undermined the Rouhani administration's nuclear deal and resulted in a transformation of the moderate Iranians' approach to the United States and Trump. For example, Trump believed that the JCPOA as Obama's achievement gave Iran ample opportunity for aggression and violence in the region, so the United States had to abrogate it and institute new sanctions against Iran. Actually, the election of Trump gripped the Reformists in a state of paradox. Therefore, several Reformist media, including pro-reform newspapers, embarked on assigning many of the US actions to Trump as a person, as they believed he was not notably popular in the United States. For example, they saw that Trump had pledged to his base to further the "America First" strategy, and refuse to be the president of the world, and to advance his agenda, he unilaterally withdrew from a number of international treaties and organizations, including the Paris Agreement on climate change, the Intermediate-Range Nuclear Forces Treaty, Trans-Pacific Partnership Agreement, the UN Human Rights Council, UNESCO, and the Joint Comprehensive Plan of Action. This is while most of these conventions were founded by the United States. On this basis, many Reformists believe the withdrawals represented an integral part of Trump's foreign policy.

The Reformist media were trying to show that the reason behind Trump's withdrawal from the nuclear deal was his typical approach to the majority of multilateral agreements and his vanity, and that the agreement resulting from the work of the pro-reform administration in Iran by itself did not have flaws. For example, in its June 12, 2018, edition, *Sharq* daily quoted the Wall Street Journal and wrote, "One of the methods used by Trump in his foreign policy decision-making is the "I'll fix it myself" method. Twenty-two months after being elected president, on May 8, 2018, Trump appeared before the cameras sitting at a wooden desk, and by signing a few documents, pulled the United States out from the nuclear deal with Iran (*Sharq*, 2018b). Moreover, in their view, Trump's withdrawal from and violation of international agreements has caused fissures between the United States and its European and non-European partners and created mistrust between them (*Sharq*, 2018a).

Disregarding his allies and building on his businessman's attitude, Trump has been intent on extracting concessions from others, including Iran, and has defined new negotiations with Iran as his foreign policy priority so that he can claim this achievement as his own breakthrough in US history. Therefore, after pulling out from the JCPOA, enforcing the maximum pressure campaign, and issuing the executive order banning the nationals of seven Muslim-majority countries from entering the United States, including Iranian citizens, Trump is trying to establish a channel to put pressure on Iran and engage in new negotiations with Iran or restoring the JCPOA with the 12 preconditions for talks with Iran earlier put forward by Secretary of State Mike Pompeo.

In the eyes of the Reformists, all of these characteristics corroborate the point that Trump is a self-important and bullying individual with little political knowledge and is unaware of the consequences of the majority of decisions he makes. He is someone who does not spend time on reading books and studying and is always swayed and influenced by people around him, his advisors (Mike Pompeo and John Bolton) and his family. As a result, his mental structure is chaotic, and he deals with political issues including agreements and other people in an illogical, unpremeditated manner and by merely considering his own interests. Trump has made several appointments and dismissals based on his personal views. In political affairs, he gives priority to personal relationships and personal interests over the US national interests and handles ties with countries and different agreements the way only he deems appropriate. Trump's mental turbulence extends to focusing on nationalism and populism; he targets the communities of Mexican immigrants and America's Hispanics and engages in erecting a wall at the southern borders of the United States. By promoting racism, Trump has affected the livelihoods of the ethnic minorities of the United States, tightening the noose around the necks of the people of color in America. In this regard, Ramezan Ali Sobhanifar, the spokesperson of the Iranian Moderation and Development Party said, "indubitably, as a businessman and merchant, in his time as the US President, Trump has demonstrated that he is an amateur who has entered the world of politics" (*Etemad*, 2017:6).

Trump's resorting to a businessman's attitude and his U-turn in picking new partners in the Middle East, as well as his indirect warmongering policies, have been censured by many critics. This warmongering spirit also applies to Iran; however, he follows that path in an indirect way.

Unlike the Iraq war in 2003 when the Americans took direct military action and paid heavy costs for war, this time Trump is intent on stoking Iranophobia and exaggerating the threat of Iran so as to sell more weapons to the Arab states. On the other hand, under the pretext of fighting ISIS, Trump is demanding his own share of oil resources in the Middle East region. This policy, while implicating US partners in paying the costs of militarism in the region and the world, is predicated on militarism and warmongering across the globe. Trump is trying to form an international and regional consensus and coalition against Iran with the help of the old and new US allies.

By calling Iran a destabilizing player in the region, Trump is trying to eliminate Iran's presence in Syria, Yemen, and Iraq and undermine the Islamic Republic's influence in these countries. However, what has so far precluded the emergence of this global consensus is the Rouhani administration's calmness and its adherence to a policy of prudence, diplomacy, engagement, and moderation. On this theme, after the downing of the US RQ-4A Global Hawk BAMS-D surveillance drone by Iran on 20 June 2019, Gholamreza Nazarboland wrote in an op-ed in *Sharq* daily:

> Evidence suggests that the country's diplomatic apparatus has shown a satisfactory performance in this regard and has fulfilled its prime responsibility. The downing of the US drone and its consequences should be considered as a turning point in the highly fraught relations between Iran and the United States and it is possible that from its ashes, a phoenix rises, creating a golden opportunity, serving to diffuse the tensions between the two sides. (Nazarboland, 2019, p. 1)

Orientation of Principalist Newspapers

Unlike the Reformists, the Principalist media maintain a more negative conception and understanding of the West in general, and the United States in particular, and express their anti-American convictions explicitly. They look at the United States as a monolithic entity with no difference between Trump and Obama. It is for the same reason that many Principalists consider every compromise with the United States a deviation from the Islamic values and the revolution maxims. To the Principalists, there is no difference between the American leaders because they have a problem with the existential nature of an "evil" which is the United States, blaming it as the main culprit for the injustices of the world and the difficulties of Iran. Therefore, when Trump came to power and imposed new sanctions against Iran subsequent to his withdrawal from the JCPOA, the Principalists branded the US government untrustworthy and criticized the Rouhani administration in different ways, insisting on the correctness of their intellectual principle in considering the United States an absolute evil.

Principalists are of the opinion that Trump is the representation of the true image of the United States: A narcissistic, unpredictable, and unreliable individual who has an unusual penchant for demonstrating and acquiring power. It is for the same reason that during the presidential campaign in the United States, Principalist media in Iran insisted that the American voters had to know how their future president was deceiving them.

From the standpoint of these newspapers, Trump lies 16 times a day and this is how he has forfeited his social capital in the government and the society. He has called into question his acceptability and credibility in the American society as a result of making abrupt decisions. Therefore, it can be said that Trump is not only loathed by his own people but has been defeated domestically. Intra-party disputes and standoff between Republicans and Democrats over the "Ukraine-gate" and the revelation of moral scandals has put Trump on the brink of impeachment. Trump's loss of credibility is not confined to the borders of the United States, for Trump, due to his peculiar foreign policy and disagreement with the world, particularly his allies, has challenged the acceptability and legitimacy of US policies as the so-called benevolent hegemon. Indubitably, this growing incredibility of the United States in the world has been predicated on Trump's performance and the implementation of his campaign promises.

After rescinding the Iran deal, Trump's second campaign promise was to increase support for Israel in the Middle East. Recognizing Jerusalem as the capital of Israel, moving the US embassy from Tel Aviv to Jerusalem, and recognizing Israel's sovereignty over the Golan Heights belonging to Syria are in line with the same policy of backing Israel. The latest support offered by Trump to Israel was to reverse the 40-year US policy vis-à-vis the Israeli settlements. To announce that Israeli settlement constructions in the occupied parts of the West Bank do not violate the international law was the other gift the US president gave to Israelis. The new announcement by the United States drew negative reactions from the international community and even US partners. In the eyes of the Principalists, this is all that should be expected of the United States.

Principalists, particularly the *Kayhan* newspaper and its managing director Hossein Shariat-madari, also believe that Trump sponsors terrorism in the Middle East. It is the US strategy to sponsor terrorism in the Middle East. It was on this basis that the United States sent 90,000 mercenaries to Syria and dispatched 4,900 trucks carrying arms to northern Syria to support terrorist groups. As claimed by the Principalists, during the 2016 presidential campaign, Trump called Obama the founder of ISIS, the terror group that was weakened significantly in 2017, but there is a possibility that it might be revitalized in the Middle East with the US assassination of General Qassim Suleimani in Iraq.

Trump's interventionism has unfolded while he continues to have no precise strategy for withdrawal from Syria. Sometimes, Trump claims that the American troops will be returned from Syria, and sometimes he claims that if their expenses are paid, they will remain there. This is while Trump has been seeking very close and cooperative relations with Russia in order to solve the Syrian crisis, praising President Vladimir Putin during the presidential campaign several times. This can be indicative of America's dissociation from its erstwhile partners.

Hossein Shariatmadari, the managing director of *Kayhan* newspaper, who is the most outspoken detractor of the JCPOA and Iran's negotiations with the United States, criticized the diplomacy of the Rouhani administration in an interview with Euronews, saying that JCPOA was a "slouchy hat" which the United States and Europe put on the Rouhani administration's head (ironically meaning that they deceived the Rouhani administration) and that the proposals put forward by Europe so far have been the same as Trump's proposals (*Kayhan*, 2019). In Shariatmadari's view, these proposals and Trump's withdrawal from the JCPOA provided excuses for restraining Iran's ballistic missiles program, highlighting Iran's democracy and human rights issues and portraying Iran's regional activities in supporting the resistance axis as terrorism. By exaggerating Iran's missile activities, Trump has been intent on pressuring Iran to back away from its position to lay the groundwork for the introduction of JCPOA 2.0 or adding amendments to the existing Iran deal. Trump claims that some of Iran's missile launches are "inconsistent" with the UN Security Council resolution 2231. On this basis, the United States has always resorted to the excuse of democracy and human rights in Iran instrumentally, while the state of democracy and human rights in Iran significantly outpaces the record of the Arab allies of the United States. Trump has claimed that Iran has expended the money it gained after the JCPOA on sponsoring terrorism. He has designated the Islamic Revolutionary Guard Corps as a foreign terrorist organization and called Iran a "terrorist nation."

Mohsen Pirhadi, the managing director of the *Resalat* newspaper, contemplates on the designation of IRGC as a terrorist organization in an op-ed:

> The terrorist-nurturing regime of the United States, or as said by Imam Khomeini, this state felon, has officially put IRGC on its blacklist of terrorist organizations. What has happened is not new. The behavior of the US government vis-à-vis the Iranian people, whether at the time of the Shah regime or in the Islamic Republic period, has always been pivoted on hostility. The 1953 coup, the Capitulation and the humiliation of Iranians in the age of the Pahlavi Dynasty and countless US crimes and interventions in the period following it are not unknown to anyone. Operation Eagle Claw (Tabas), martyring several hundred Iranians by attacking the passenger plane, directly supporting Saddam Hussein in the war against Iran, playing an active role in the 1999 and 2009 seditions, imposing economic sanctions and tens of other wicked actions have painted an ugly picture of the United States in the minds of Iranians. (Pirhadi, 2019a, p. 1)

Also, in another piece, he notes that the United States government retains complex decision-making layers, which in the Trump administration are exactly as calculating as in the Obama administration and ponder upon the consequences of war with Iran. If the current US administration demonstrates a tough and aggressive appearance, this is not a decision made by a few individuals or one person, but it is the output of a system that has decided to adopt the approach of coercion, pressure, use of force and bullying under the current world circumstances. He wrote: "It is possible for the American officials to have different methods in different areas of policy-making, but they don't have any difference with each other on major issues, and as they say, containing Iran—read regime change or changing its nature—is one of the large-scale and definite goals of all US administrations" (Pirhadi, 2019b, p. 1).

Above all of what has been said, Trump has claimed that JCPOA was a very bad deal and made Iran's access to nuclear arms easier. The expansion of Iran's nuclear might poses a serious threat to Israel in the Middle East region. Therefore, by abrogating the JCPOA, Trump laid the groundwork for imposing sanctions and putting pressure against Iran. In this time period, with Trump's withdrawal from the Iran deal, the institution of sanctions has entered a new phase. Trump not only resurrected all the suspended sanctions, but is demanding the minimization of Iran's oil sales so that tensions are generated inside Iran. Aside from the secondary oil and banking sanctions, Trump has put many Iranian entities and politicians including Iran's leader and foreign minister in the sanctions blacklist. In a general overview, these sanctions violate human rights and place great economic pressure on the Iranian people. Pressuring banks into not cooperating with Iran has prevented the entry of investors and blocked the global trade relations channels with Iran. Even several European firms such as Total S.A. and Peugeot have suspended their activities in Iran. According to the Principalists, by imposing maximum pressure on the Iranian government, Trump is not merely looking to force Iran into accepting a modified deal with more concessions but to change the political regime of Iran and topple Iran's Islamic system. Even though Trump denies this, he has not spared any effort to support Iran's domestic and foreign opponents on this path. In addition to these activities, Trump has waged an economic warfare against Iran and through imposing more pressure and sanctions is endeavoring to initiate a psychological and economic war against Iran so as to turn Iran into a weak country to be attacked by the United States and its regional and international allies.

Hamidreza Taraghi, a Principalist figure and one of the members of the central council and the head of the International Bureau of Islamic Coalition Party stated:

> the definite option of the Iranian nation is resistance against the United States, and in this confrontation, in this resistance, it will be forced to retreat, and the idea of resistance is not the idea of military confrontation. We are not looking for war, and they know it's not cost-effective for them to look for war, and they know it. We, too, are not intent on military action—we never were and are not now. This clash is the clash of determinations. This face-off is the face-off of determinations, and our determination is stronger than theirs. In addition to strong determination, we have faith in God, as well. (Taraghi, 2019, p. 1)

CONCLUSION

Based on their orientations and ideologies, the newspapers of the two Reformist and Principalist wings present special discourses to help their audiences perceive the happenings and events. Belief systems of these two groups of newspapers constantly interact with the new information resulting from events. However, chances are that the new information are manipulated by changes and restrictions. Therefore, this understanding can be of importance considering the beliefs and ideological systems of newspapers influencing how these outlets represent the events.

The findings of the present study indicate that the Reformist and Principalist newspapers portray a negative image of the United States and Donald Trump based on the anti-American discourse existing in Iran; however, their tones differ slightly. The Principalist newspapers, since they have standpoints close to the state, have adopted a more stringent, severe, and direct orientation toward the United States and Trump. The Principalists were opposed to negotiations with the United States and the Iran deal since the very beginning, and even after the JCPOA was agreed demanded Iran to withdraw from the accord. In sum, they maintain an essentialist opinion toward the US political entity in which it makes no difference who is in the White House. The Reformist newspapers, on the other hand, have had a relatively mild and indirect orientation to Trump and the United States. It should not be ignored that JCPOA was the outcome of the Rouhani administration and the pro-administration newspapers have also perpetually supported it. The Reformists generally have a pluralistic opinion of the US political entity, in which different parties and presidents make some difference in its foreign policy.

The four newspapers all represent their understanding of the United States as an unreliable government, and following the adoption of highly rigorous anti-Iranian policies by Trump and the emergence of severe economic difficulties in Iran, the four newspapers converged in their views more notably. However, it is quite clear that these media depict their understandings as the realities of Iran-US relations, citing Trump as either an excellent archetype of the United States, or not really the ideal epitome of American politics. Here, the Jervis theory positing that media sell their own ideological understandings and perceptions to the audiences, rather than objective and impartial data, appears to be more relevant.

REFERENCES

Barzegar, K. (2010). Roles at odds: The roots of increased Iran-US tension in the post-9/11 Middle East. *Iranian Review of Foreign Affairs, 1*(3), 85–114.

Darvishi, J. (2015). *The influence of the character of Seyed Mohammad Khatami on the behavioral pattern of foreign policy in the reform era.* [Master's thesis, Faculty of Social Sciences, Razi University, Iran].

Etemad Daily (2017, September 21). The failed address of the American merchant. http://www.Etemad newspaper.ir/fa/Main/Detail/86959

Haji-Yousefi, A. (2018). Political culture and Iran's foreign policy: A comparative study of Iran's foreign policy during Ahmadinejad and Rouhani. *World Sociopolitical Studies, 2*(2), 225–245.

Holsti, O. R. (1976). Cognitive process approaches to decision-making: Foreign policy actors viewed psychologically. *American Behavioral Scientist, 20*(1), 11–32.

Jervis, R. (1988). War and misperception. *The Journal of Interdisciplinary History, 18*(4), 675–700.

Jervis, R. (2002). Signaling and perception: Drawing inferences and projecting images. In K. R. Monroe (Ed.), *Political psychology* Lawrence Erlbaum, 293–312.

Jervis, R. (2017). *Perception and misperception in international politics.* Princeton University Press.

Kayhan Newspaper (2019, September 11). From JCPOA to INSTEX: Referendum and negotiations with the United States in an interview with *Kayhan*'s managing director by Euronews. http://Kayhan .ir/fa/news/169642

Mintz, A., & DeRouen K. Jr. (2010). *Understanding foreign policy decision making.* Cambridge University Press.

Nazarboland, Gh. (2019, June 23). The trigger of threat, the trigger of opportunity. *Sharq Daily.* http:// *Sharq*daily.com/fa/Main/Detail/223372

Patalano, R. (2003). *Beyond rationality: Images as guide-lines to choice* (Working Paper 5). University of Torino, Department of Economics.

Pirhadi, M. (2019a, April 9). The US anger is natural. *Resalat Daily.* https://*Resalat*-news.com/?p=1852

Pirhadi, M. (2019b, May 20). Tarred with the same brush. *Resalat Daily.* https://*Resalat*-news .com/?p=3250.

Ramsay, C. (2019, Oct. 29). New surveys show Trump's Iran policy has opposite of intended effect. *Baltimore Sun.* Retrieved from https://www.baltimoresun.com/opinion/op-ed/bs-ed-op-1030-iran -policy-20191029-67bxz7x5sbfavp5vfytnbwn4xq-story.html

Saldaña, J. (2009). *The coding manual for qualitative researchers.* SAGE.

Shariati, Sh. (2003). *Idealism in Iran's foreign policy during the term of Khatami.* [Master's thesis, Faculty of Humanities, Tarbiat Modares University].

Sharifi, M. M., & Karami, A. S. (2018). The leaders' core beliefs, perceptions of threat, and the US-North Korea hostility. *International Relations Research Quarterly, 8*(3), 125–158.

Sharq Daily (2018a, May 9). JCPOA without the United States. http://*Sharq*daily.com/fa/main/de tail/187105/

Sharq Daily. (2018b, June 12). Trump's decision-making for withdrawal from the JCPOA. http://Sharq daily.com/fa/Main/Detail/189202

Shokouhi, S. (2016). The role of the interpretations of elites in the Iran-Saudi Arabia tensions. *World Politics, 5*(4), 40–63.

Taraghi, H. (2019, May 25). Our war with the United States is the war of willpowers. *Resalat Daily.* https://*Resalat*-news.com/?p=3394

Van Dijk, Teun A. (1989). Structures of discourse and structures of power. *Annals of the International Communication Yearbook 12*(1), 18–59.

KOREA

13

News Coverage about the United States in Korea During the Bush, Obama, and Trump Administrations

Trump as an Outlier?

Hyelim Lee, Seoul National University
Seulgi Jang, Seoul National University
Kadir Jun Ayhan, Hankuk University of Foreign Studies

INTRODUCTION

South Korea (hereafter, Korea) is one of the countries with the highest favorability scores toward the United States. US favorability was less than 60% under President George W. Bush, and reached over 80% with President Barack H. Obama, and remained around there under Donald Trump's presidency. However, confidence in the US president in Korea dropped to even lower than the Bush era (around 30%) under Trump (17% in 2017), following the high level of confidence enjoyed by Obama. This discrepancy suggests that Korean people treat the United States and its president separately under Trump, which was not necessarily the case for the Bush and Obama administrations.

To gain more in-depth understanding of how the United States and its presidents are portrayed in Korea, we turn to media coverage in Korea about the United States and the US presidents. Following this volume's main concern, we specifically explore if there is a "Trump effect."

To demonstrate changes over time in Korean news coverages' patterns, text analysis techniques are employed. We collect news article titles that were published in 10 daily Korean newspapers, from 2001 until 2019. Using this data, we analyze the word frequencies and create a semantic network related to the news articles about individual presidents (Bush, Obama, Trump). Furthermore, we explore the divergences and convergences between news coverage in conservative (*Chosun Ilbo, JoongAng Ilbo*, and *Dong-A Ilbo*) and progressive (*Hankyoreh* and *Kyunghyang Shinmun*) Korean newspapers.

STRONG PRO-AMERICANISM IN
SOUTH KOREA, BUT NOT FOR TRUMP?

For the United States, Korea is an unusual ally. In the last decade, there were a lot of voices concerned about globally widespread anti-Americanism (Rubin & Rubin, 2004), yet Koreans' favorable feelings for the United States has remained high. As shown in Figure 13.1, Korea's favorability toward the United States fell slightly below 50% only once in 2003 and continued to rise, with the figure hitting 84 percent in 2015. Although some scholars are worried by occasional crises of the US-Korea alliance and sudden eruption of anti-US feelings (e.g., Cummings, 2005; Kim, 2002; Woo & Lee, 2013), globally, Korean publics' fondness of the United States is remarkable (Chiozza & Choi, 2012).

In Korea, favorability toward the United States often directly reflects favorable or unfavorable attitudes toward its presidents. Yet Trump's election caused an interesting trend: unpairing of favorability toward the United States and confidence in the US president. According to the 2017 report of the Pew Research Center (Poushter & Bialik, 2017), Korean people sharply lost their confidence in President Trump even if they maintain positive views on the United States. Only 17% of Korean respondents are confident in the US president Trump, although 75% of them keep their favorable views about the United States. As compared with Bush (36%) and Obama (81%), the approval rate for the first year is very low. This result is parallel with the polling outcome conducted by Gallup Korea in 2017 (Gallup Korea, 2017).

This discrepancy of favorability could be attributed to the peculiarity of how Trump is viewed in Korea. Generally, Korean citizens used to think the United States and its leaders as a package, and they have constructed their congruent stances about the United States. As his market-oriented policy stance derails the previous politically engaged relationship of two states, however, Koreans cannot support him as much as the predecessors. One good example is that a large portion of Korean people disagree with Trump's policy related to South Korea

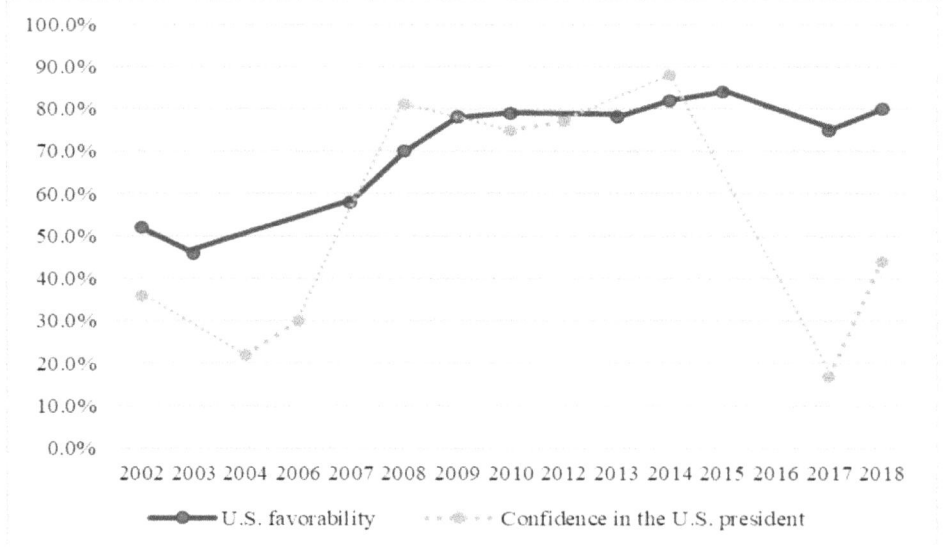

Figure 13.1   U.S. favorability and confidence in the US president (2002–2018, the Pew Research Center)

on defense cost, while they still strongly support the US-Korea alliance. According to the latest poll of the Chicago Council of Global Affairs, 92% of the Korean public show their strong support for Korea's alliance with the United States, but 74% of respondents say that Korea "should not contribute to the costs of US forces stationed in the Pacific, but outside of South Korea" and 68% say that Korea "should negotiate a lower (defense) cost than the $4.7 billion request made by the United States" (Friedhoff, 2019).

Before turning to the news coverages of three presidents with the aim of figuring out if Trump is an outlier in Korean politics and the media sphere, we will give a historical background of US-Korea relations. This will help readers understand the United States and its leaders' images in Korean media, as the distinctive features of ideological conflicts in Korean political elites and the Korean press polarize the perceptions or sentiments toward the United States.

A Brief Trajectory of Korean Ambivalent Sentiments Toward the United States

South Korea–US relations have been quite stable since Korea's independence from Japan in 1945, with the alliance being one of the strongest alliances in the world. Except for small and temporary deviations, the alliance has been the unshattered fundamental aspect of relations between the two countries (Snyder, 2018). The countries had foreign policy disagreements from time to time, particularly when it comes to how to deal with North Korea.

The division of Korea into South and North was not the will of Koreans themselves, but rather initiated by tension between the United States and the Soviet Union at the beginning of the Cold War. The division, which brought about a US-friendly regime in the South and a socialist anti-US regime in the North, played a deterministic role in the ideological landscape of South Korea's local politics, constituting the dividing line between progressives and conservatives (Ayhan & Kim, 2019; Ryu, 2012). This ideological dividing line also became an imperative gauge of the contemporary relationship between South Korea and the United States.

After its liberation from Japanese colonial rule, the pro-American and anti–North Korea stance were dominant in the first government of President Rhee Syngman. The early dominance of pro-America provided the root of contemporary conservative parties. The origin of progressive parties is intertwined with the process of democratization. The conservatives mainly had a pro-America and anti–North Korea discourse. On the other end of the Korean political spectrum, the left parties have positioned themselves with mild anti-Americanism and support for social democracy, including some sympathy toward North Korea.

Moon (2005) suggests that, unlike many people's universal beliefs, Korea's feelings toward the United States have changed continuously over time and are divided into *chinmi* or pro-US and *banmi* or anti-US by one's ideological propensity. People who stand for pro-Americanism have the idea that the US military presence is safeguarding them from the extant menace from North Korea. Moreover, as many elites educated in the United States have taken over as the ruling elites, the admiration of the United States is widespread.

Anti-Americanism is rather a novel mindset that the progressive or leftists have built after democratization movements. Moon (2005, p. 143) argues that the Gwangju uprising in the 1980s was a trigger of anti-US sentiment due to American failure to deter Chun Doo-hwan's military from killing of civilians. More importantly, the group called "The National Liberation (NL)" leading the 1980s student movements against dictatorship, which is one branch of the leftist coalitions, precipitated anti-Americanism. Ideologically, they believe that the United States exploited South Korea as its capitalistic ground and interrupted the unification of the country. Some more recent events threw the US-Korea relationship into turmoil. One of the turning points of anti-US sentiments was in June 2002, when demonstrators condemned the tragedy of the death of two middle school girls hit by a US armored vehicle (Bong, 2004; Jung, 2010). Another peak in anti-US sentiments was during the final stages of the Korea-US free trade agreement in 2008. The candlelight protestors voiced their concerns against the import of US beef.

These two ideological lines polarize Korean views on the United States. The polarized political ideologies steered the Korean public's ambivalent perceptions toward the United States. The images have been formed and reinforced by political rhetoric and campaigns. Media also plays an important role in shaping public opinions. Many domestic scholars observe the robust partisanship in Korean newspapers owing to the same background and history behind polarization of Korean political realm (Choi, 1994; Park & Jang, 2000; Yang, 1995; Yoon, 2001). This is largely because of close ties between mass media outlets and the politicians (Yoon, 2001). The conservative newspapers such as *Chosun Ilbo* and *Joongang Ilbo* furnish the supportive reports of the conservative parties' political stance on the United States, whereas the progressive newspapers such as *Hankyeoreh* and *Kyunghyang Shinmun* advocate the progressive parties' or governments' policies unfavorable to the United States. Such ideological pairing of media and politics has been tenacious for many years.

In summary, Korean views of the United States appear ambivalent or polarized. This two-sided US image in Korea is actually not distant from polarized Korean local politics. Understanding why Korea has such ambivalence toward the United States requires an appropriate grasp of how Korean political ideologies have developed and how they are linked with the Koreans' image of the United States.

Method

An exploratory approach using text analysis is applied to analyze news articles that have been published during the respective administrations of Bush, Obama, and Trump. We are interested in which words Korean newspapers used in their coverage of three American presidents. Furthermore, we look at the differences in coverage based on ideological stances (conservative versus progressive versus nonpartisan) of newspapers.

We collected the articles of two newspapers, *Hankyoreh* and *Donga-Ilbo*, from the most extensive news portal in Korea, the Naver. These papers are selected due to their symbolic meaning as representative media outlets; *Hankyoreh* for the progressive and *Donga-Ilbo* for the conservatives. They are also available back in the first Bush administration. We only took the first two years of the respective presidents because Trump was only through half of his first term. The starting and final date of the data are January 20, which is the official inauguration day. Specifically, the Bush data starts on January 20, 2001, and ends on January 20, 2003. The Obama data starts on January 20, 2013, and ends on January 20, 2014, we chose to look at his second term for its visibility then in relation to both South and North Korea compared to his first term. Only Trump data has a different end date, December 31, 2019, because the data collection was implemented then, and the data after this date were not accessible.

The data collection was operated by the python crawler based on the Naver keyword search engine. It provides a keyword search algorithm that automatically suggests related articles when users look for news articles and makes it possible to designate which media the users intend to search for. We only used the keywords related to three American presidents instead of using "US" or "South Korea–US relation" for two reasons. First, searches of "US" have too many published articles in the given period, with lots of noise demanding manual work-

Table 13.1.   The Number of News Stories Collected

	Trump (2017–2019)	Obama (2011–2013)	Bush (2001–2003)
Conservative	2,356	1,460	2,401
Progressive	1,962	1,150	1,429
Total	4,318	2,610	3,830

arounds and thereby hindering the selection of the proper news articles. A multiple keyword search still has more tasks in choosing which keywords would be valid together for finding the politically related news coverage. Second, this study has the purpose of verifying the distinctive pattern of Trump coverage as compared to the former presidents' coverage. Analytically, the news articles related to the United States easily contain articles about American presidents. The news coverages about American presidents are much more proper sources for testing Trump's effects because the intention of published news stories is already well defined.

The collected data includes 4,318 Trump stories, 2,610 Obama stories, and 3,830 Bush stories, and the total number of the articles used is 10,758. The conservative newspaper coverage frequency about the United States tends to be higher than the liberal newspaper. A slight gap in the number of articles by president is due to the difference in the richness of the Korea-US relation. The eventful circumstances such as North Korea–US Summit of the Trump era and the "axis of evil" comment of the Bush era are given plentiful coverage from the Korean media compared to the era of President Obama.

We also collected the articles of 10 daily newspapers[1] from Big Kinds,[2] the news archive system run by the Korea Press Foundation, for comparing the tone between the conservative and the liberal newspapers in the Trump administration. We did not use this system for the entire analysis due to its inconsistency of the data; they do not have the conservative newspapers before 2018. Since they do cover from the second year of President Trump, this additional data enables us to have richer analysis with much more data for the Trump era. Finally, 97,061 Trump stories were collected from the system for the same period we set for the data crawling from the Naver.

On tracking trends of the newspapers' coverages on three US presidents, we tapped into the text analysis methods. We used the python package called "Konlpy,"[3] enabling the natural language processing (parsing, tokenization, and lemmatization). This package grants a Korean-language parser/tagger and one of the most commonly used packages for NLP in Korean. We chose Kkma model as a parser/tagger to process the raw data. We focus on an exploratory approach and then check the frequencies of nouns and then their semantic networks.

The frequencies of nouns are automatically calculated after identification of tokens and lemmas by tags. We manually selected the most frequent 50 words out of the initial outputs based on its frequency and relevancy. For example, words indicating the journalist names or the section names were dropped as stop words. This criterion applied to all outputs of the three presidents' data. Mapping the semantic networks is also based on this frequency output.

---

1. Most of the previous works studying the Korean newspapers' coverage categorize *Chosun Ilbo, Joongang, Ilbo* and *Dong-A Ilbo* as the conservative newspapers and *Hankyoreh* and *Kyunghyang Shinmun* as the progressive newspapers (e.g., Han, 2001; Kim & Noh, 2011; Koh, 2007; Lee & Koh, 2009; Park, 2011). Moreover, others are regarded as not strongly partisan. The other newspapers included in this study are *Seoul Shinmun, Segye Ilbo, Hankook Ilbo, Moonhwa Ilbo*, and *Kukmin Illbo*.

2. https://www.bigkinds.or.kr/

3. http://konlpy.org/en/latest/

We calculated the co-occurrence of the top 50 words and operationalized the co-occurrence as "how frequent words follow one another even if we would skip two words in between in the same document or title."

Findings

In the first part, we discuss how the news stories on American presidents have changed over time. In the next part, we discuss the results of the Trump news coverages in more detail explicating the ideological difference by newspapers' partisanships.

Changes in Korean News Coverage About American Presidents Over Time

The frequency of news articles fluctuates by the events related to South Korea's relationship with North Korea and the United States. The pattern of periodic fluctuations is not distinctive according to the news outlets. In the Trump period, the two highest peaks were generated in November 2017 and June 2018. The former is when the 65th Korea-US summit meeting was held, and the latter had two momentous events—the Second Inter-Korean summit and the US-North Korea summit. All the peaks are engendered by the presence of notable events such as the summit meeting of the three countries. February and May in 2019 are also the months where the historic US–North Korea summit meetings were held. Trump brought a dramatic transition and somewhat of a breakthrough with North Korea, so the summit meeting coverage amounts to the majority of news stories.

Obama and Bush had more formulaic responses from the Korean newspapers up to the relatively regular events such as North Korea's nuclear missile launching or the G20 summit meetings or annual South Korea–US summit talks. Three peaks in August 2009, November 2009, and November 2010 were attributed to the South Korea–US summit talks.

In the case of the Bush administration, February 2002 has the highest peak when Bush declared several nations to be an "axis of evil," including North Korea. This critical moment aggravated the US relationship with North Korea, and Korean newspapers kept reporting the potential provocations from the North.

The most frequently occurring words of each administration shows the relations between South Korea, the United States, and North Korea and summarize the perspectives of the Korean media toward the United States. In Table 13.2, the top 20 frequent words give us an opportunity to look into how the Korean media covers the United States and its presidents, presented with the frequency and percentage against the number of articles.

The topics related the United States in the Korean news media have been mainly on international affairs, as expected. The most reoccurring words are the names of nations or terminology that shows the US main foreign policy focus from a Korean perspective in those years: "North Korea" (291 times, 7.6%), "Iraq" (153 times, 3.99%), and terrorism (66 times, 1.72%), for the Bush presidency, "North Korea" (127 times, 4.87%), "Syria" (63 times, 2.41%) and China (57 times, 2.18%) for the Obama presidency, and "North Korea" (375 times, 8.68%), "denuclearization" (167 times, 3.87%), "Kim Jong-un" (153 times, 3.54%) for the Trump presidency. These topics drew the most attention during each era and all keywords are related to foreign policies. The US news is dominantly related to the foreign policies of all three presidents.

Table 13.2. Top 20 Nouns Frequency and Ranking by the Administration

	Trump				Obama				Bush		
Rank	Key	Freq.	%	Rank	Key	Freq.	%	Rank	Key	Freq.	%
1	Trump	1221	28.28	1	Obama	411	15.75	1	Bush	656	17.13
2	North Korea	375	8.68	2	US	173	6.63	2	North Korea	291	7.60
3	US	206	4.77	3	North Korea	127	4.87	3	Iraq	153	3.99
4	denuclearization	167	3.87	4	president	72	2.76	4	US	126	3.29
5	Kim Jong-un	153	3.54	5	Syria	63	2.41	5	president	86	2.25
6	President	143	3.31	6	China	57	2.18	6	terrorism	66	1.72
7	North Korea Nuclear	112	2.59	7	summit	43	1.65	7	Kim Daejoong	60	1.57
8	Korean Peninsula	107	2.48	8	NK Nuclear	40	1.53	8	attack	59	1.54
9	summit	101	2.34	9	Iraq	39	1.49	9	summit	56	1.46
10	Xi Jinping	97	2.25	10	Xi Jinping	36	1.38	10	The White House	52	1.36
11	China	94	2.18	11	diplomacy	35	1.34	11	Colin Powell	50	1.31
12	negotiation	92	2.13	12	Vladimir Putin	35	1.34	12	Kim Jong-il	44	1.15
13	The White house	86	1.99	13	Korea Peninsula	34	1.30	13	war	43	1.12
14	against North Korea	80	1.85	14	The White House	34	1.30	14	diplomacy	41	1.07
15	sanction	75	1.74	15	Republican	32	1.23	15	against NK policy	39	1.02
16	pressure	64	1.48	16	negotiation	31	1.19	16	the Senate	35	0.91
17	Mike Pompeo	64	1.48	17	pressure	31	1.19	17	economy	33	0.86
18	talk	61	1.41	18	Abe Shinzo	30	1.15	18	Afghanistan	32	0.84
19	THAAD	56	1.30	19	failure	30	1.15	19	Korean Peninsula	30	0.78
20	trade war	55	1.27	20	six-party talks	29	1.11	20	media	29	0.76

What is most notable is how frequently presidents' names appear in each era. Each of the presidents' names are the most repeated words in all three presidencies, of course, occurring 1,221 (Trump, 28.28%), 411 (Obama, 15.75%), and 656 (Bush, 17.13%) times. President Trump appears in almost one-third of the articles in his first two years, which shows the enormous interest and attention of the Korean media to him in comparison with two other presidents. Trump appears almost two times as much compared to his predecessors. These results may have something to do with Trump's peculiar character attracting media interest, such as his controversial tweets and speeches. However, taken together with the word co-occurrences in Table 13.3, which we explain below, the greater interest seems to be due to the fact that he has been the most outspoken and most active American president vis-à-vis North Korea.

Now, we turn to word co-occurrences with the name of each president, looking into whether there is a critical disparity of how the three presidencies are portrayed in the Korean media. In Table 13.3, the most repeated 20 words with each presidents' name are presented with frequency and ratio to the rate of occurrence of the names.

As international affairs get the most attention in Korean news market surrounding the United States, most of the words that co-occur with the name of the president are also foreign policy–related. The most co-occurring words are "president" (5.64%) and "North Korea" (5.64%) for Bush; "Xi Jinping" (3.65%), "North Korea" (3.16%), and "Republican" (3.16%) for Obama; and "Kim Jong-Un" (5.73%) and "North Korea" (4.67%) for Trump. Trump, who became the first sitting American president to meet a North Korean leader and having done this three times, gets the most mentions regarding North Korea. This comes after the presidency of Obama who apparently had less interest in North Korea.

What is peculiar to the Trump era are the co-occurrences of the words "negotiation" (2.13%), referring most probably to his trade deals with China and other countries, and "tweet" (2.13%), referring to Trump's highly scrutinized and unprecedented use of social media for presidential communication.

Korean News Coverage During the Trump Presidency

In this section, we compare conservative and liberal newspapers' coverage for the Trump period. Considering the Korean newspapers' bias in the US stories discussed above, the news coverage on Trump would have discrepant coverage based on the news outlets' ideologies. These differences can grant us a better pathway to apprehend the Korean media's relationship with the US-related topics.

In the frequency results, firstly, the news stories about Trump demonstrate ideological reporting style of partisan media. When looking at the top 50 frequent words in each newspaper group, the word with the highest frequency is "US" in both conservative newspapers (17.2%), and non-partisan newspapers (17.6%). Meanwhile, "US" is used in the progressive newspapers' titles with very low frequency, which is ranked as 13 out of 50 (2.1%) and has a lower frequency than "North Korea–US" (3.5%). Instead, they used "president" (8.3%) most often, and Korean president, "Moon Jae-In" (6.5%) appears at the forefront. "China" is interestingly an indicator of difference: the progressive papers' frequency rate of the word is much higher (4.8%) than the conservative (3.1%) and nonpartisan newspapers (2.2%). The conservative papers often use trade or economy-related words—"trade," "trade war," "trade negotiation," "tariff," and "economy." Mainly "economy" is found with more than 1% frequency in conservative newspapers, implying that they covered the United States or presidents more often than others from the economic angle.

Table 13.3. Top 20 Co-occurrence Words with the Presidents' Names

	Trump				Obama				Bush		
Rank	Key	Freq.	%	Rank	Key	Freq.	%	Rank	Key	Freq.	%
1	Kim Jong-un	70	5.73	1	Xi Jinping	15	3.65	1	president	37	5.64
2	North Korea	57	4.67	2	Republican	13	3.16	1	North Korea	37	5.64
3	president	49	4.01	2	North Korea	13	3.16	3	Iraq	32	4.88
4	Xi Jinping	41	3.36	4	summit	11	2.68	4	war	16	2.44
5	US	31	2.54	4	Syria	11	2.68	5	administration	13	1.98
6	negotiation	26	2.13	6	Abe Shinzo	10	2.43	5	summit	13	1.98
6	tweet	26	2.13	6	president	9	2.19	5	attack	13	1.98
8	The White House	25	2.05	6	Vladimir Putin	9	2.19	8	diplomacy	12	1.83
10	NK Nuclear	25	2.05	9	yield	8	1.95	9	The White House	11	1.68
10	China	24	1.97	9	diplomacy	8	1.95	9	Kim Daejoong	11	1.68
10	Vladimir Putin	24	1.97	9	attack	8	1.95	11	Vladimir Putin	10	1.52
10	denuclearization	24	1.97	11	national debt	7	1.70	12	The Senate	9	1.37
14	Russia	22	1.80	11	war of nerves	7	1.70	12	media	9	1.37
14	summit	22	1.80	11	limitation	7	1.70	12	Kim Jeong-il	9	1.37
15	pressure	21	1.72	11	The White House	7	1.70	12	warning	9	1.37
15	against NK	21	1.72	11	strategic	7	1.70	12	criticism	9	1.37
17	James Comey	19	1.56	11	air raid	7	1.70	17	Bill Clinton	8	1.22
17	trade war	19	1.56	11	Hillary Clinton	7	1.70	17	Europe	8	1.22
19	talks	18	1.47	19	gun control	5	1.22	17	Tony Blair	8	1.22
20	discard	17	1.39	19	negotiation	5	1.22	20	gossip	7	1.07

Table 13.4. Centrality of Top 15 Nouns (Trump, 2018–2019)

Conservative Newspapers				Progressive Newspapers				Other Five Newspapers			
Noun	Degree	Btw.	Eig.	Noun	Degree	Btw.	Eig.	Noun	Degree	Btw.	Eig.
US	22	217.3	1	China	10	85	0.20	US	22	93	1
North Korea	9	24.3	0.70	South Korea	9	4	1.00	North Korea	11	20	0.91
denuclearization	7	28.7	0.51	NK-US	8	19	0.95	summit meeting	8	0	0.42
tariff	5	63	0.36	North Korea	7	42	0.05	denuclearization	7	26	0.52
defense cost	5	28.7	0.26	denuclearization	6	15	0.14	defense cost	4	7	0.17
negotiation	4	48	0.41	US-China	5	7	0.26	negotiation	4	8	0.21
sanction	4	11	0.30	defense cost	3	0	0.54	the second	3	0	0.22
trade war	3	0	0.18	the second	3	31	0.20	sanction	3	8	0.13
Trump	2	0	0.28	against NK	3	8	0.08	president	3	0	0.13
trade negotiation	2	0	0.18	tariff	3	0	0.06	trade war	3	0	0.13
summit meeting	2	0	0.17	president	3	2	0.00	trade negotiation	3	0	0.13
China	2	0	0.06	conversation	3	2	0.00	South Korea	2	0	0.24
against NK	2	0	0.06	addition	2	0	0.21	US-China	2	0	0.03
pressure	2	0	0.05	Moon Jae-In	2	0	0.20	China	2	0	0.03
US	22	217.3	1	China	10	85	0.20	US	22	93	1
North Korea	9	24.3	0.70	South Korea	9	4	1.00	North Korea	11	20	0.91
denuclearization	7	28.7	0.51	NK-US	8	19	0.95	summit meeting	8	0	0.42
tariff	5	63	0.36	North Korea	7	42	0.05	denuclearization	7	26	0.52
defense cost	5	28.7	0.26	denuclearization	6	15	0.14	defense cost	4	7	0.17
negotiation	4	48	0.41	US-China	5	7	0.26	negotiation	4	8	0.21

To be sure, there is some similar pattern discovered among the groups. "North Korea" is placed in the high ranks (11.0% in the conservative, 6.1% in the progressive, and 10.9% in the nonpartisan). These results disclose that the US news is linked with North Korea no matter what partisan bias works in the news production. The other common term is "denuclearization," which is in the same context of "North Korea," and this word is located in the upper group of ranking in all three groups.

We also discovered a difference between the three groups in a variance in the distributions. The conservative (582.48) and other five newspapers' (793.05) standardized deviation of frequency is much higher than the progressive newspapers (138.75). That is, only a small group of words is used in the title in the case of the conservative and other newspapers, yet the progressive newspapers do not have predominant words in the news stories. "The US," ranked as number one in the conservative, and the other group amounts to more than 17 percent. This means that except the liberally biased newspapers, the news coverage related to Trump is reported in the North Korea–related frame in the vein of the previous findings.

The co-occurrence of the frequent nouns gives us a clear picture of comprehending the news outlets' approaches. The conservative and nonpartisan newspapers' networks are plotted with the one big cluster surrounding the word "US" and "North Korea." In both data, the degree centrality, betweenness centrality, and eigenvector centrality of "US" have the largest number. Notably, "North Korea" is located in the center with the second-highest degree centrality in both groups but in the case of the conservative newspapers, "tariff" has a higher number of betweenness centrality than "North Korea" and the other five newspapers put "denuclearization" at a higher rank than "North Korea" in betweenness.

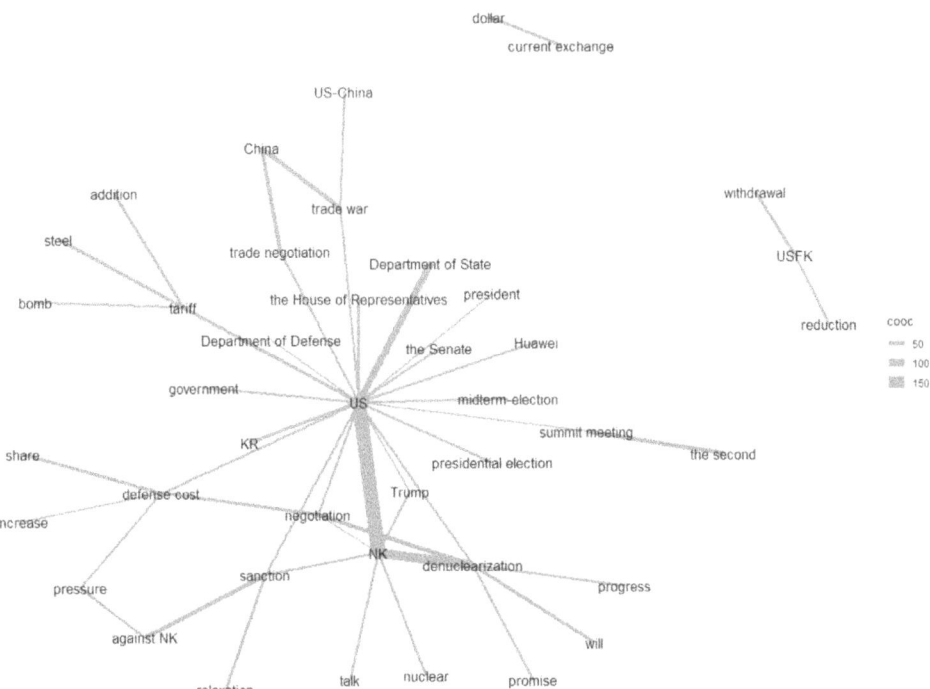

Figure 13.2   Co-occurrence network of top 50 nouns (Trump, conservative newspapers, 2018–2019)

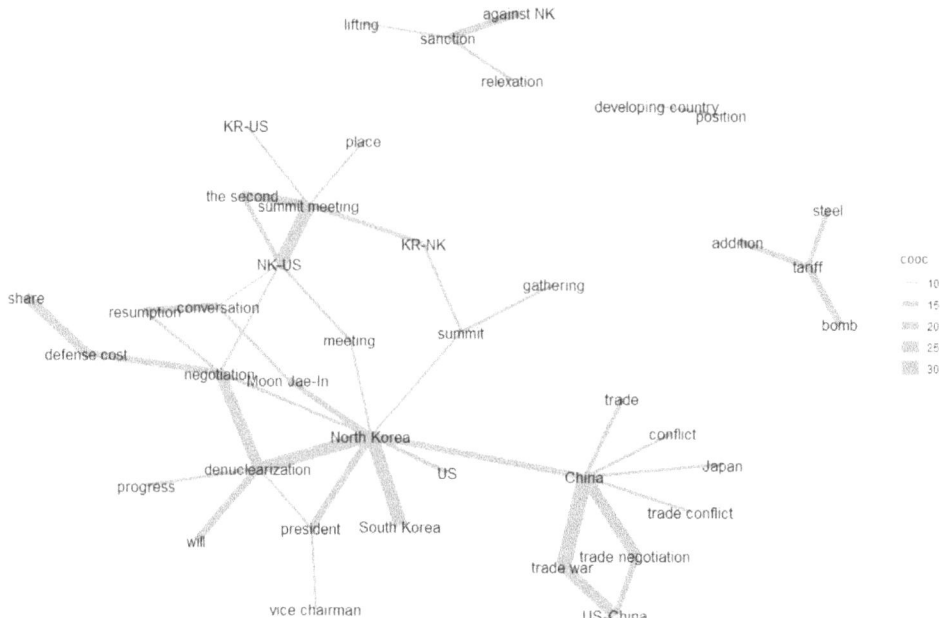

Figure 13.3   Co-occurrence network of top 50 nouns (Trump, progressive newspapers, 2018–2019)

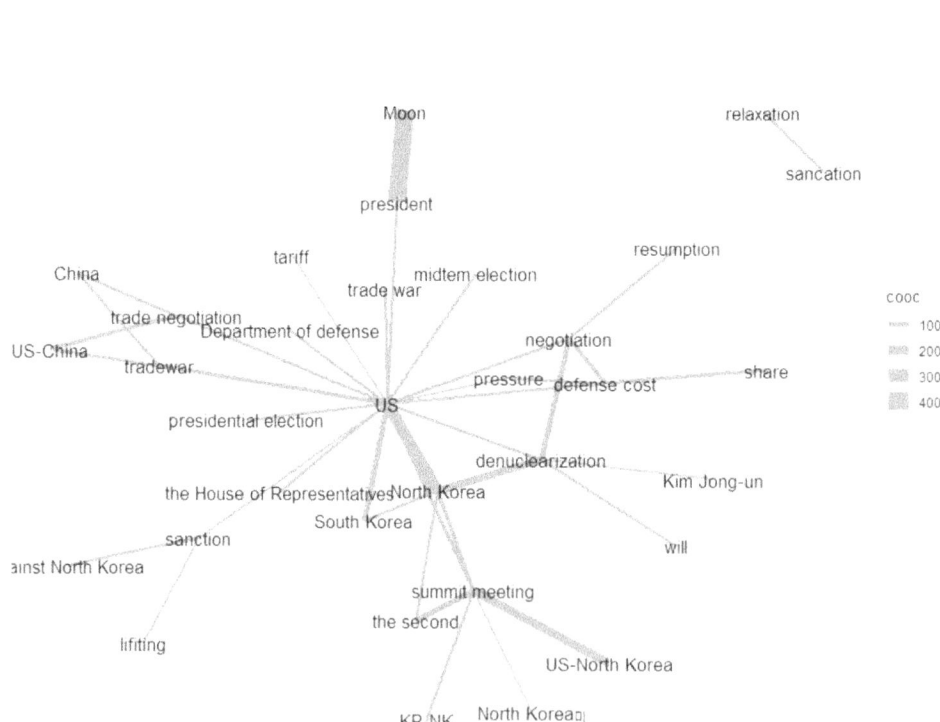

Figure 13.4   Co-occurrence network of top 50 nouns (Trump, nonpartisan newspapers, 2018–2019)

On the other hand, the progressive newspapers generate more than three clusters, not converged into one or two. "China" is surprisingly the word with the highest centrality of degree and betweenness. "China" in the progressive newspapers has noticeable importance in terms of trade conflicts with the United States. Nevertheless, this issue cannot be expanded to its connections with the other cluster associated with the other topics regarding the United States. "North Korea" is the word with the second-highest betweenness. This clarifies the perspective of the progressive newspapers about the US governments, with regard to international relations dynamics. Although the news stories are talking about the United States or its government, the news reports put more emphasis on geopolitical dynamics rather than the US-Korea bipartite relationship.

CONCLUSION

In this chapter, we tried to figure out whether Trump is treated as a deviant leader by Korean news media. To do this, we employed the computational text analysis of 10 Korean daily news articles for three presidents, Trump, Obama, and Bush. In the first part of comparing the change over time, it provides mixed results. The results of frequency analysis about partisan and non-partisan newspapers, in particular, illustrate that Trump appears a less critical figure than his two immediate predecessors. However, the co-occurrence analysis shows that the three US presidents' news coverage still shares the key terms "US or" "North Korea." As this study is designed to take a simple snapshot of change over time concerning the United States and its leaders' images in Korean news outlets by computational methods with an exploratory goal, further work using qualitative contents analysis is necessary.

REFERENCES

Ayhan, K. J., & Kim, Y. (2019). *Ideas matter in inter-Korean relations: An analysis of ideological changes in South Korea's North Korea policies.* ISA Asia-Pacific Conference 2019, Singapore.

Bong, Y. (2004). Yongmi: Pragmatic anti-Americanism in South Korea. *Brown Journal of World Affairs, 10*(2), 153–165.

Chiozza, G., & Choi, A. (2012). Going the American way: The surprising case of Korean pro-Americanism. *The Pacific Review, 25*(2), 269–292.

Choi, J. J. (1994). Hanguk Minjujueuiwa Eonron. *EonrongwaSahwei, 6,* 40–64.

Cummings, B. (2005). The structural basis of "anti-Americanism" in the Republic of Korea. In D. I. Steinberg (Ed.), *Korean attitudes toward the United States: Changing dynamics* (pp. 91–115). Routledge.

Friedhoff, K. (2019 December, 6). *While positive toward US Alliance, South Koreans want to counter Trump's demands on host-nation support.* The Chicago Council on Global Affairs. https://www.thechicagocouncil.org/publication/while-positive-toward-us-alliance-south-koreans-want-counter-trumps-demands-host-nation

Gallup Korea. (2017 May, 25). *Daily opinion issue 260.* Gallup Korea. http://www.gallup.co.kr/gallupdb/reportContent.asp?seqNo=834

Han, D. S. (2001). Bukhangwanryeon bodoae natanan ideology jihyunggwa silchunbangsik. *EonronGwahakYeongu, 1*(2): 250–294.

Jung, H. J. (2010). The rise and fall of anti-American sentiment in South Korea: Deconstructing hegemonic ideas and threat perception. *Asian Survey, 50*(5), 946–964.

Kim, K. H., & Noh, G. Y. (2011). Hanguk shinmunsaeui eenyeomgwa bukhan bodobangsikae daehan yeongu. *HangukEonronHakbo, 55*(1), 361–387.

Kim, S. H. (2002). Anti-Americanism in Korea. *Washington Quarterly, 26*(1), 109–122.

Koh, Y. S. (2007). Junggwoneui seonggyuk byeonhwawa eonronbodo: Daetongryung chininchuk biri-bodoeui news frameeul jungshimeuro. *Communication Yron, 3*(1), 156–196.

Lee, G. H., & Koh, H. S. (2009). Chuijaewon hwalyongeul tonghae salpyeobon hankook shinmuneui bodosigak gochal: Miguk sogogi suip gwanryun gisaae natanan chuijaewon shinroidowa yuinga bun-sukeul jungsimeuro. *Haguk Eonron Hakbo, 53*(3), 347–368.

Moon, C. I. (2005). Between banmi (anti-Americanism) and sungmi (worship of the United States). In D. I. Steinberg (Ed.), *Korean attitudes toward the United States: Changing dynamics* (pp. 139–152). Routledge.

Park, G. S. (2011). 4daegang saeop newsae daehan bodo frame yeongu: Kyunghyang Shinmun, Dong-A Ilbo, Hanguk Ilbo deung 3gae jonghapilganjireul jungsimeuro. *Hanguk Eonron Hakbo, 55*(4), 5–26.

Park S. G., & Jang G. S. (2000). Hankookeu jeongchibyeondonggwa eonrongwonryuk: Gukgga-eunron gwangye mohyung byeonhwa. *Hanguk Bangsong Hakbo, 14*(3), 81–111.

Poushter J., & Bialik K. (2017 June, 26). *Around the world, favorability of the U.S. and confidence in its president decline.* Pew Research Center. https://www.pewresearch.org/fact-tank/2017/06/26/around-the-world-favorability-of-u-s-and-confidence-in-its-president-decline/

Rubin, B., & Rubin, J. C. (2004). Anti-Americanism re-examined. *The Brown Journal of World Affairs, 11*(1), 17–24.

Ryu, J. S. (2012). Jeongchiinyeome jeongchaekseonho Kyeoljeonge Isseo Jeonchijisike Yeokhal. *Hanguk Jeongchi Yeongu, 21*(2), 53–86.

Snyder, S. (2018). *South Korea at the crossroads: Autonomy and alliance in an era of rival powers.* Columbia University Press.

Woo J. Y., & Lee, S. W. (2013). Hankook kookmineui hanmi dongmaengae daehan jiji byeonhwaae daehan yeongu. *Gukje-Jiyeok Yeongu, 24*(3), 41–65.

Yang, S. M. (1995). Hangukeui minjuhwawa eonroneui seonggyuk byeonhwa. In J. C. Yoo (Ed.), *Hanguksaheoi byeondonggwa eonron* (pp. 93–141). Sohwa.

Yoon, C. Y. (2001). *Hanguk mijujueuiwa eonron.* The Yumin Cultural Foundation.

MALAYSIA

14

The Image of Donald Trump in Major Malaysian Newspapers

A Deeper "Mistrust" Than Obama's Time

Abbas Ghanbari Baghestan, University of Tehran
Mohd Nizam Osman, Universiti Putra Malaysia

INTRODUCTION

The "images" of countries held by the people of other countries have long been of interest to many scholars in different disciplines to understand how they perceive each other and how they think about each other. In the process of constructing an image, the mass media play a crucial role and there is no doubt that the way society thinks about other countries is the product of the mass media. According to McNelly and Izcaray, the mass media can contribute toward the people's understanding or misunderstanding of each other's countries (McNelly & Izcaray, 1986, p. 546). Therefore, as Navasky noted, "it is based largely on journalism that we make up our national mind" (Navasky as cited in Zelizer & Allan, 2002, p. 1). The purpose of this study is first to capture the image of Donald Trump and from there, the image of the United States in Malaysian major ethnic newspapers and secondly, to investigate the major discourses used in the selected newspapers of the country in order to portray Donald Trump and the United States.

MALAYSIAN MEDIA REGULATION POLICIES AND ACTS

The freedom of the media and the press in Malaysia is regulated strongly by policies and acts that primarily seek to ensure the media do not unnecessarily publish news or stories that might be offensive to other ethnic groups or the monarchy and secondly, to maintain peace and harmony

Acknowledgment: The authors would like to thank Aishah Elena Binti Shaari, Nurulhayati Binti Ariffin, Thachainee A/P Lingam, and Tang Hui Li for their assistance in collecting and translating news from Malay, English, Tamil, and Chinese languages in this study. We also thank Elaheh Farahmand and Topic Peremobowei Akoje for their research assistance.

among the multiethnic and multiracial citizens of Malaysia. The Malaysian constitution guides and legislatures restrict media freedom through several acts, policies, and regulations, which include acts like the Internal Security Act (ISA), the Sedition Act (SA), and the Printing Presses and Publications Act (PPPA). Apart from these acts, which provide strong media regulation in Malaysia in terms of its freedom of speech and expressions, Malaysia also has implemented several other media acts, such as the Broadcasting Act, the Malaysian Communications and Multimedia Commission Act, the Communications and Multimedia Act, the Control of Imported Publication Act, the BERNAMA Act, and the FINAS Act. These acts and policies are implemented largely to control and to regulate the function, role, and freedom of the media industry in Malaysia when reporting and disseminating news and stories to the general public.

After Malaysia achieved its independence from the British in 1957, the government under the then ruling party of the National Front (Barisan Nasional) introduced various policies and acts to regulate the freedom of the press in reporting news and stories to the general public. One of the acts that was introduced by the government under the ruling party of the National Front after Malaysia achieved its independence was the Internal Security Act (ISA). The introduction of the ISA resulted in the press losing much of its freedom in reporting news and stories in Malaysia (Sani, 2008). Apart from the ISA, the government at the time also introduced a number of other acts and policies, such as the Sedition Act (SA) and the Printing Presses and Publications Ordinance as a means of further regulating the media content in the country. Under these acts, stern actions were taken against a few major leading newspapers in the country that were found to have published news articles that were seen to bring major implications to the country's security. One example is the banning of the Socialist Front newspaper under the Printing Presses and Publications Ordinance for showing clear indications in having a strong pro-communist stand. Apart from having the newspaper banned from publication, some leaders of the Socialist Front party leaders were also arrested in connection to the party's strong support for the communist party.

The policies and acts regulating the media in Malaysia were revised and strengthened by Mahathir Mohamad who became the fourth Malaysian prime minister in 1981. Prime Minister Mahathir Mohamad believed rather strongly in the need to implement laws, such as the ISA and the Printing Presses and Publications ACT and the Sedition Acts in a multiracial country like Malaysia to avoid racial conflict and political instability.

Theoretical Perspective

This study has adopted two interrelated theories, agenda setting and framing theory, as a main conceptual framework in order to figure out the image of Donald Trump and the United States in Malaysian major ethnic newspapers. Agenda setting and framing theory have been applied to the media coverage of a wide array of different issues across the world; among them, "the Middle East and Islam: from the Iraq war of 2003 to the battle against the 'ISIS'" (Isakhan, 2014; Mulherin & Isakhan, 2019), "The coverage of the Arab Spring" (Al-Rawi, 2015; Guzman, 2016; Oz, 2016), "The publication of the Prophet Mohammad cartoons in European newspapers" (Bowe & Makki, 2015; Strömbäck, Shehata, & Dimitrova, 2008), and "Onto the conflation of terrorism and the Islamic religion in the mainstream global media" (Powell, 2011; Rane & Ewart, 2012).

According to the agenda-setting theory, the intensity of discussion in the mass media can affect human perceptions about the importance of any given events. This theory was first formulated based on data from the US presidential election campaign in 1968 when researchers discovered a link between human perceptions about the most significant problems in the programs of candidates and the frequency of mentions of these problems in the media (Mc-Combs & Shaw, 2006). In the future, the core idea of agenda setting was confirmed by many diverse empirical studies worldwide.

Agenda-setting hypotheses have been extended to some changes in substance. For instance, as a supplement to the idea of media discussion that influences social perceptions about the importance of the problem, it was suggested that attention be paid to the fact that focusing on certain characteristics of a situation or a public figure shapes public opinion (Wanta, Golan, & Lee, 2004). Such substance change in the theory later on is called, "second-level agenda setting" or "framing theory." In this context, framing is a process by which political actors, policy makers, campaign managers, and journalists are able to distil otherwise complex positions on a particular issue to deliver an easily understood and remembered message (Pan & Kosicki, 1993). For instance, during an electoral campaign, framing is a vehicle where the media can offer a set of interpretative schema or an unfolding narrative that enables the audience to interpret the complexities of a candidate's policy agenda (Gitlin, 1980; Tuchman, 1978; Nwokora & Brown, 2017). Therefore, frames also serve to obfuscate at least as much as they illuminate with much being left out of the picture in the interest of penetrating through to, and resonating with, the intended audience (Entman, 1993). In fact, the way certain issues or events are framed has a significant impact on public awareness, given that citizens may have few other sources of information (Entman, 1991).

Methodological Insights

There are two distinct approaches for the agenda setting and framing analysis that both are equally important for an in-depth analysis of the topic. The first is a quantitative content analysis, which typically uses computer programs to search for a set of keywords and isolate sets of frames before determining their prominence and frequency (Miller, 1997). This "frame mapping" has the advantage of being capable of analyzing a large amount of data to provide various statistical analyses. However, a purely quantitative method is not adequate, as it may tell the researcher that a particular newspaper has mentioned "Trump" and the "Muslim ban" hundreds of times over a given period, but without a careful qualitative analysis of the articles in question, the overall tone or context cannot be understood. The second approach is qualitative discourse analysis of the source material. In media and communication contexts, prominent discourse analysis scholar van-Dijk states, "Discourse analysis emerged as a new transdisciplinary field of study between the mid-1960s and mid-1970s" (Van-Dijk, 1991, p. 108). Discourse analysis has theoretical and methodological roots in a number of academic traditions, including linguistics and literary studies, which try to analyze different aspects of language usage and its impacts on the users in the process of communication (Van-Dijk, 2001). In discourse analysis, the researchers should apply their "expertise to induce the meaning of texts," including their familiarity with the topic, their ability to identify the evolving structure and narrative of the frames employed, and the "essential question about what could have been in the content but was not" (Hertog & McLeod, 2001, p. 154). This study applied a mixed method (including both quantitative content analysis and qualitative discourse analysis) to examine the ways in which Donald Trump and the United States was covered and framed in Malaysian major ethnic newspapers.

Because Malaysia is a multicultural society, this research was conducted based on the following ethnic publications: (1) *The Star* (English newspaper), (2) *Berita Harian* (Malay Language), (3) *Sin Chew* (Chinese Language), and (4) *The Malaysian Naban* (Tamil/Indian Language). The time span of the study at the early stage was six months from March to September

Table 14.1. Characteristics of the Four Selected Newspapers in Malaysia

Name of Newspaper	First Issue	Month Analyzed	No. of News Materials
Star Online	1971	March 2019	158
Berita Harian	1957	August 2019	117
Sin Chew	1929	Jun 2019	105
The Malaysian Naban	1986	May 2019	22

2019. At the second stage, and due to having plenty of news material related to the topic, for each publication, one month of full coverage was selected randomly for further content analysis (Table 14.1). The unit of the analysis was "news material," which could be "news," "report," "opinion," "interviews," "editorial," and so on. The coding protocol of the study consisted of five variables validated by three experts in the field of media and communication. In terms of the reliability, the test and re-test mechanism of 10% of all the collected "news materials" was used in the three-week time frames for the two most important variables, namely, "Direction of the news material toward U.S." and "Direction of the news materials toward Donald Trump". Finally, to measure the intercoder reliability (test and re-test), the results of the Kappa test, 0.79 and 0.84, respectively, showed the results of the study to be valid and reliable.

Results and Discussion

This study focused mainly on quantitative content analysis to identify Malaysian media coverage of the United States and Donald Trump and secondly, to critically analyze the content of Malaysian newspapers to reveal the major "themes" portraying the United States and Donald Trump in the major Malaysian ethnic newspapers.

The first research question of this study was: How did Malaysian newspapers portray the United States and Donald Trump in their daily coverage? In order to answer this question, four mainstream Malaysian newspapers were selected and analyzed accordingly.

As can be seen in Table 14.1, altogether 402 news materials were collected, out of which 158 news materials were collected from the *Star Online*, 117 news materials from *Berita Harian*, 105 news materials from *Sin Chew*, and 22 news materials from *The Malaysian Naban*.

Regarding the topic of the news materials, 88% of the news materials were in the format of the "News." This was followed by "Report" at 6.2%, and "Opinion" at 4% in sequence. In terms of the topic of the news materials, as shown in Table 14.2, the majority of the news materials, 290 items (66.6%), were related to the "US global policy," mainly related to "US–China Trade War," "North Korea Issue," "Palestine Issue," "Iran's Nuclear Deal," "War in Syria," "Anti-Terrorism War in Iraq and Afghanistan."

While 22.4% (90 news materials) were related to internal issues in the United States, 5.5% (22 news materials) were also about the impact of the United States on the Malaysian economy, mainly the "Malaysian Bursa & Currency."

Regarding the direction of the news material, there is a distinction between the two positions highlighted in the news materials: one toward Donald Trump as a person (in this case,

Table 14.2. News Materials of the Four Selected Topics in Malaysia

No.	Topic	Frequency	Percentage
1	US impact on the Malaysian Economy	22	5.5
2	US Global Policies	290	66.6
3	US Internal Affairs	90	22.4
4	Total	402	100

Table 14.3. Direction of the News Materials toward the US and Donald Trump

Direction	Toward Donald Trump		Toward the US	
	Frequency	%	Frequency	%
Positive	24	6	59	14.7
Negative	202	50.2	87	21.6
Neutral	174	43.3	250	62.2
Ambiguous	2	0.5	6	1.5
Total	402	100	402	100

the president and head of the current government of the United States) and second toward the United States, as the most powerful country in the world. However, it is notable to mention that in many cases, the role of Donald Trump, especially his personality and his policies, were highlighted in a very specific manner whereby it seems without "him being president" there would not be such controversial cases.

As can be seen in Table 14.3, half of the news materials (50.2% or 202 items) have taken a "negative" position toward Donald Trump, followed by 43.3% (174 news materials) being "Neutral" and 6% (24 items) as "Positive." In contrast, when it comes to the United States, 62.2% (250 items) had a "neutral" position toward the country, followed by 21.6% (87 items) as "negative," and 14.7% (59 items) being "positive."

Narrowing down to only the image of Donald Trump portrayed in Malaysian newspapers, Table 14.4 shows the exact issues as being covered very negatively pertaining to the respective topics. In this regard, *The Star*, which is an English-language leading newspaper in Malaysia seems to focus on the protests and critics against Donald Trump's policies inside the United States. The news stories covered by *The Star* clearly are seen to be more negative in nature, which suggests that not only other countries around the world seem to protest Donald Trump's policies, but a significantly large percentage of the American citizenship as well as politicians are also against him.

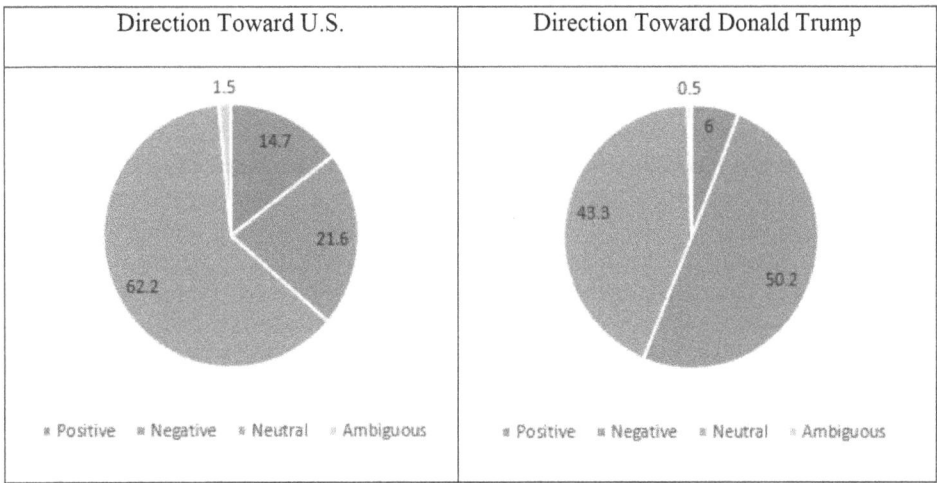

Figure 14.1 The direction of news materials toward the United States and Donald Trump. Four selected Malaysian media had a more "negative" direction toward Donald Trump in comparison to the United States overall, where the majority of the items were "neutral."

Table 14.4. Main Issues Highlighted Negatively Due to Donald Trump

No.	Topic	Issues
1	US impact on Malaysian/ Asian economy	Plummeting Malaysia share/stock Lower performance of the currency (RM) Restrictions on the export of Malaysian products into the USA
2	US global policies	Palestine-related issues and Trump's Pro-Israel moves War in Syria and anti-terrorism war in Iraq and Afghanistan US-China Relations Iran's nuclear deal North Korea issues Anti-immigration policy (visa ban)
3	US internal affairs	Raising "hate" related crimes Criticism and protests against Donald Trump's policies inside the United States

Berita Harian, the Malaysian national language newspaper was chosen to portray Donald Trump's policies toward Muslim nations with a very aggressive expression on issues like visa bans for seven Muslim nations, the war in Syria, and Palestine-related matters. *Sin Chew*, which is the leading Chinese-language newspaper in Malaysia, was chosen to focus mainly on issues pertaining to relations between the United States and China. The news stories covered by *Sin Chew* are clearly negative toward the United States in the framework of the "Trade War" initiated by Donald Trump.

The second research question of the study was: "What are the main discourses that emerged from analyzing the news material regarding the issues related to the United States and Donald Trump?" To address this question, using qualitative discourse analysis, a careful thematic analysis of all the news materials was carried out. Based on this in-depth analysis, the Malaysian media landscape of the image of the United States and Donald Trump is marked by three main themes.

1. The Islamophobia Rhetoric of Donald Trump

It was observed that most of the Malaysian mainstream newspapers tend to use very negative captions/titles/content to highlight news stories pertaining to Donald Trump's policies toward Muslim nations. Two of the four selected newspapers (*The Star* and *Berita Harian*, with over 150 news pieces), especially, seem to focus on the key issues highlighted by Donald Trump that are not favorable to Islamic countries. Central to this theme are the "visa ban for seven Muslim countries"; "labeling Muslims as terrorists"; "supporting all Israeli activities against Palestinians"; and "war in Syria, Iraq, and Afghanistan"; which can be traced in the framework of Trump's "Islamophobia rhetoric."

The reason the Malaysian media are very sensitive about Donald Trump's "Islamophobia rhetoric" is because the majority of the country's population is Muslim. In addition, the country has a strong self-image as a moderate force within the Islamic world. Under the framework of "moderate Islam," Malaysian leaders always criticize the Western military intervention in Muslim nations as well as all the United States' support of Israel, arguing this intervention in a broader sense generates support for Islamic militancy. From the Malaysian point of view, these policies create the perception that Western countries and the United States in particular are "anti-Islam." Although one ought to acknowledge that this perception of America as being "anti-Islam" is not new, it is obvious that Donald Trump's anti-Islamic policies have changed the Malaysian perception dramatically, especially when compared to Barack Obama's time as president. In this regard, Harding and Sutton (2017) have reported that during Barak Obama's time, Malaysian perceptions of the United States underwent sharp swings due to his "personal popularity" as well as his administration's strategic "rebalancing" of foreign policy toward Muslim nations. According to their report, "Malaysian perception toward America is driven mainly by two events: the Iraq War and Barack Obama's first presidential election. In 2007 (the Iraq War), only a quarter of Malaysians, and only 10 percent of Malaysian Muslims had a favorable view of the United States. By 2013, the percentage of Malaysians who viewed the United States in a positive light had increased to more than 55 percent. As in Indonesia, the personal popularity of Obama, the first US president to visit Malaysia since Lyndon Johnson, likely accounts for much of this turnaround. Mutual interest in regional stability, bilateral trade, and countering violent extremism, along with a shared wariness about the prospect of Chinese hegemony in East Asia have provided a durable basis for economic, military, and diplomatic cooperation across a range of domains" (Harding & Sutton, 2017).

Therefore, it can be concluded that Trump's embrace of Islamophobia as a rhetoric and, certainly most troubling, his "executive order 13769,"[1] which was widely covered by Malaysian media, not only make him very unpopular, but also have create a negative climate toward the United States in the political and ideological sphere of the country.

2. US-China Competition in East Asia

In 2019, the world witnessed a trade war between two major global powers: the United States and China. Perhaps more interesting for our purposes are the concerns expressed over US policy toward China by Malaysian newspapers in the frame of issues like "imposing tariffs," "Huawei Ban," "product boycotts," and so on. A careful in-depth analysis of the "themes" highlighted in covering the news material pertaining to the US-China trade war, also reveals that the Malaysian media traces it in the broader sense of a framework of "U.S.-China" competition in East Asia. In this regard, the leading Chinese-language newspaper in Malaysia has shown keen interest in the issue, as can be seen in the following excerpts captured from the *Sin Chew* newspaper:

> U.S. acting defence secretary John Shanahan, without naming China by name, blamed a series of destabilizing activities in Asia, citing issues ranging from the South China Sea to Taiwan as threats to regional stability. He also warned China against threatening the sovereignty of its neighbours and said Washington was investing in new military technology over the next five years to keep Asia stable." (*Sin Chew*, 1 June 2019)

The same newspaper published another opinion, citing the acting US defense secretary:

> "Under the leadership of the Chinese communist party, the People's Republic of China has sought to re-establish a regional order to take advantage," . . . using military modernisation, sway operations and "predatory economics" to oppress others. (*Sin Chew*, 7 June 2019).

A more notable outcome of this study is that the selected newspapers clearly stood on the opposite site of the United States and in favor of China, whereby more than 50% of the news

---

1. Executive Order 13769, titled "Protecting the Nation from Foreign Terrorist Entry into the United States," was politically labeled as a Muslim ban.

articles related to US-China relations were negative toward the United States. One possible reason for such positioning in coverage of the conflict might be the significant proportions of ethnic Chinese in Malaysia. However, there is no doubt that, as quoted and stated by many newspapers in Malaysia, this also might be a major political shift in the country mainly due to Donald Trump's unpredictable and unstable policies. Of this political shift, Mahathir Moham-mad, the current prime minister of Malaysia who took power again after winning the 2018 general election, is a central figure. For example, *The Star* had an article, "Malaysia Prefers China over 'Unpredictable' U.S." and quoted Mahathir stating: "Well, it depends on how they behave. . . . Currently, I think the U.S. is very unpredictable as to the things that they do. At this moment, we have to accept that China is close to us. And it is a huge market. We want to benefit from China's growing wealth. So at this moment, economically, we would prefer China" (March 28, 2019).

To understand the importance of this political shift, it is important to highlight that Ma-laysia has always had a policy of alignment behavior vis-à-vis the United States and China. In their article titled "Malaysia between the United States and China," the researcher reviewed the nature and the extent of the relationship between Malaysia and the United States as well as between Malaysia and China and argued,

> Relations with the United States and China are among the most vital facets of Malaysia's external policy. . . . Given Malaysia's past problems with the giant to its north as well as the unresolved, overlapping territorial claims over the Spratly Islands in the South China Sea, one would expect Malaysia to balance against China. Yet it has opted to hedge, a position that has endured three different leaderships—Mahathir Mohamad (1981–2003), Abdullah Ahmad Badawi (2003–2009), and Najib Tun Razak (2009–2018). . . . Under Abdullah Ahmad Badawi, Mahathir's immediate successor, Putrajaya's ties with Washington made progress on multiple fronts. More notable prog-ress has been made under the current Prime Minister, Najib Razak, where Malaysia's U.S. policy has been more cooperative in gesture and more pragmatic in tone. Substance-wise, he has made a more concerted effort than all his predecessors to cultivate a stronger partnership with the global superpower, with marked progress in all key domains. U.S. President Barack Obama's visit to Malaysia in April 2014 was a testimony to this transformed relationship. (Cheng-Chwee, 2016)

Put succinctly: Even though many of the barriers to warmer bilateral ties between Malaysia and the United States eased during the past 10 years, particularly during the time when Barack Obama and Najib Razak held office, the emergence of Donald Trump and his personal popularity as an unpredictable and unstable president create a critical climate between the two countries. Alternatively stated, as highlighted by many media and newspapers, the emergence of Donald Trump in the United States has caused significant damage to perceptions of the United States and its government among the people of Malaysia.

3. Asian Values vs. Western Values

Going beyond the context of Donald Trump's recent discourse in the United States, Malay-sia historically is a leading country behind the call for an "Asian Value System," which one can-not ignore in any attempt to analyze the political sphere of Malaysia through the discourses of its media. The idea of "Asian values" and having a type of "Asian-only" institution emerged in Southeast Asia around the late 1980s, where a central figure and one of its strongest advocates was Mahathir Mohamad, who was at the time the Malaysian prime minister. Mahathir, who remained the Malaysian prime minister until 2003, has structured and shaped a more Asian-based society and system in Malaysia whereby multiethnic races can coexist in the country in peace and harmony. In the framework of promoting an "Asian Value," he also aggressively criticized such things as "Western democracy" and gay sexuality, among other Wester values.

In the context of the "Asian Values" movement in the country and region, Malaysia witnessed a historic election in 2018 when the political opposition party, with its charismatic hero, Mahathir Mohammad, won the Malaysian general election and once again took over the leadership of the country as prime minister. As observed in much of the media coverage of Donald Trump and the United States, the four selected newspapers in Malaysia reported that Mahathir's return to power in 2018 created a very critical climate regarding Donald Trump and the United States. For instance, *The Star* online wrote:

> "It is important to promote and accept the diversity of culture and value for the sake of world peace," says Tun Dr Mahathir Mohamad. He said there should not be just one single value system for the world because many countries were not prepared for it. "We need to tolerate different cultures and values," he said at a leader's roundtable session at the Second Belt and Road Forum for International Cooperation here on Saturday. The Prime Minister said although the world had made tremendous progress in technology, there was no commensurate progress in forging better understanding between peoples. Dr Mahathir said, "Asians should be allowed to preserve their own values. We should not impose one single value (on others). When certain values are (forcefully) imposed, it will be disruptive, resulting in violence," he pointed out. (*Star Online*, April 27, 2019)

Mahathir's vision and views on Western values have been very clearly stated at major international platforms, such as at world summits, international conferences, dialogues, and talks. He has always advocated Eastern values to spearhead the development of the nation, largely due to the spirit of Asian values in terms of the high level of respect Asians have toward the family, friends, and for one another. This is largely the reason why Mahathir has established the 'Look East' policy, whereby he very strongly advocated for Malaysians, especially Malaysian government officers, to learn from the values of the Japanese, who have a high level of respect for one another and who have a high commitment toward work and responsibilities. Mahathir has always believed strong Asian values are largely rooted by a strong belief in religious teachings that require everyone to do good things for other people.

CONCLUSION

This study overall focused on a quantitative content analysis and qualitative discourse analysis toward the identification of Malaysian media coverage of the United States and its current president, Donald Trump, and the ways in which they portrayed them. An in-depth analysis of the four selected Malaysian newspapers yielded significant and rich insights into perceptions of the United States and Donald Trump in Malaysia. Based on the results and discussions highlighted here, it can be concluded that the Malaysian media coverage of the United States, especially when it comes to Donald Trump's administration is complex. While the economic and technological aspects of the relationship in terms of imports and exports between the two countries are well acknowledged, in a political sphere, there is a deep "mistrust," as can be revealed from the way Malaysian newspapers portray the current government of the United States. Even though this image of mistrust does not seem to be new, it has become deeper than during Barack Obama's administration. Therefore, the major conclusion is that the rehabilitation of the United States' image in Malaysia during Obama's time is in danger because of Trump's Islamophobia rhetoric and related actions and policies.

Further discourse analysis of the collected news materials disclosed three major themes behind such mistrust articulated in these media: (1) Trump's Islamophobia rhetoric: the majority Muslim nation of 32 million people is sensitive on the issues related to Muslim nations, chief among them Palestine, which put Malaysians strongly on the opposite side of all Donald Trump's actions against the Muslim nations. (2) Competition in East Asia between the United States and China: The country has a considerable Chinese ethnic population that favors China, when it comes to the US-China trade war. Their view has become stronger after the 2018 general election, with the new government led by Mahathir Mohammad. (3) Asian values versus Western values: Malaysia, historically, is the leading country behind the voices for a type of "Asian-only" regional institution. This "Asian-only" initiative put Malaysia at the center of the "anti-Western values" movement in the region. As a result, one finds a complex perception about the United States in Malaysian mainstream media.

We need to acknowledge, however, that the systematic interpretive analysis of the four Malaysian newspapers has limitations as well. These four newspapers do not represent all of Malaysia's voices, as this multiethnic country has a vast variety of media and news channels representing different points of view. In addition, the limited amount of collected news materials means that its conclusions cannot be generalized to the ways in which Donald Trump and the United States were covered in the broader Malaysian press and media. To assist in developing more robust insights into media framing of perceptions toward the United States and Donald Trump, future research should involve a broader array of newspapers and media coverage, including more local language related media as well as broadcast media.

REFERENCES

Al-Rawi, A. K. (2015). Sectarianism and the Arab Spring: Framing the popular protests in Bahrain. *Global Media and Communication, 11*(1), 25–42.

Bowe, B. J., & Makki, T. W. (2015). Muslim neighbours or an Islamic threat? A constructionist framing analysis of newspaper coverage of mosque controversies. *Media, Culture & Society, 38*(4), 540–558.

Cheng-Chwee, K. (2016). Malaysia between the United States and China: What do weaker states hedge against? *Asian Politics & Policy, 8*(1), 155–177.

Entman, R. M. (1991). Framing US coverage of international news: Contrasts in narratives of the KAL and Iran air incidents. *Journal of Communication, 41*(4), 6–27.

Entman, R. M. (1993). Framing: Toward clarification of a fractured paradigm. *Journal of Communication, 43*(4), 51–58.

Gitlin, T. (1980). *The whole world is watching: Mass media in the making and unmaking of the new left.* University of California Press.

Guzman, A. L. (2016). Evolution of news frames during the 2011 Egyptian Revolution. *Journalism & Mass Communication Quarterly, 93*(1), 80–98.

Harding, B., & Sutton, T. (2017, June 5). U.S-Indonesia and U.S-Malaysia relations in the Trump era. Center for American Progress. https://www.americanprogress.org/issues/security/reports/2017/06/05/433540/u-s-indonesia-u-s-malaysia-relations-trump-era/

Hertog, J. K., & McLeod, D. M. (2001). A multiperspectival approach to framing analysis: A field guide. In S. Reese, O. H. Gandy, A. E. Grant (Eds.), *Framing Public Life: Perspectives on Media and Our Understanding of the Social World* (pp. 139–161). Lawrence Erlbaum.

Isakhan, B. (2014). The politics of Australia's withdrawal from Iraq. *Australian Journal of Political Science, 29*(4), 647–661.

McCombs, M. E., & Shaw, D. L. (2006). The agenda-setting function of mass media. *Public Opinion Quarterly, 36*(2), 176–187.

McNelly, J. T., & Izcaray, F. (1986). International news exposure and images of nations. *Journalism Quarterly, 63*(3), 546–553.

Miller, M. (1997). Frame mapping and analysis of news coverage of contentious issues. *Social Science Computer Review, 15*(4), 367–378.

Mulherin, P., & Isakhan, B. (2019). The Abbott government and the Islamic state: An elitist foreign policy discourse. *Australian Journal of Political Science, 54*(1), 82–98.

Nwokora, Z., & Brown, L. M. (2017). Narratives of a race: How the media judged a presidential debate. *American Politics Research, 45*(1), 33–62.

Oz, M. (2016). Mainstream media's coverage of the Gezi protests and protesters' perception of mainstream media. *Global Media and Communication, 12*(2), 177–192.

Pan, Z., & Kosicki, G. M. (1993). Framing analysis: An approach to news discourse. *Political Communication, 10*(1), 55–75.

Powell, K. A. (2011). Framing Islam: An analysis of U.S. media coverage of terrorism since 9/11. *Communication Studies, 62*(1), 90–112.

Rane, H., & Ewart, J. (2012). The framing of Islam and Muslims in the tenth anniversary coverage of 9/11: Implications for reconciliation and moving on. *Journal of Muslim Minority Affairs, 32*(3), 310–322.

Sani, M. A. M. (2008). Freedom of speech and democracy in Malaysia. *Asian Journal of Political Science, 16*(1), 85–104.

Strömbäck, J., Shehata, A., & Dimitrova, D.V. (2008). Framing the Mohammad cartoon issue: A cross-cultural comparison of Swedish and US press. *Global Media and Communication, 4*(2), 117–138.

Tuchman, G. (1978). *Making news: A study in construction of reality.* Free Press.

Van-Dijk, T. A. (1991). Media contents: The interdisciplinary study of news as discourse. In K. Bruhn-Jensen & N. Jankowksi (Eds.), *A handbook of qualitative methodologies for mass communication research* (pp. 108–120). Routledge.

Van-Dijk, T. A. (2001). Critical discourse analysis. In D. Tannen, D. Schiffrin, & H. Hamilton Hamderab (Eds.), *Handbook of discourse analysis* (pp. 352–371). Oxford: Blackwell.

Wanta, W., Golan, G., & Lee, C. (2004). Agenda setting and international news: Media influence on public perceptions of foreign nations. *Journalism & Mass Communication Quarterly, 81*(2), 364–377.

Zelizer, B., & Allan, S. (2002). *Journalism after September11.* Routledge.

MEXICO

15

Coverage of Donald Trump in Three Mexican National Newspapers

El Universal, Reforma, and *La Jornada,* 2017–2019

José Carlos Lozano, Tecnológico de Monterrey
Francisco Javier Martínez-Garza, Universidad Autónoma de Nuevo León

INTRODUCTION

> The Free Trade Agreement, the most ambitious project of understanding [of Mexico] with the northern neighbor, has been much more than a commercial agreement; now it depends on the whim of a demagogue . . . [and on] the xenophobia of the next tenant of the White House. . . . Enrique Peña is trying to respond to the threat of hurricane Trump, overwhelmed by distrust in the future and preparing us to protect our national interests from the US aggressor. Is Mexico's admiration for the laws, wealth and prosperity of the United States over? Is greed from the north the worst danger? Is Trump a big bad wolf? (Cárdenas, 2016)

The above quote, by one of the most respected journalists and radio anchors in Mexico, José Cárdenas, illustrates the general tone of Mexican news stories and op-ed pieces on Donald J. Trump during the first three years of his administration. First in the primaries, then during the general election, and later as president of the United States, Trump decided to fiercely attack Mexico as a way to attract votes and to get support for his nationalist, protectionist, and anti-immigrant policies. In fact, the very first speech of Trump announcing his candidacy, on June 16, 2015, was a strong attack on Mexico. After arguing that Mexico was laughing at the United States for its lack of control of the border between the two countries, Trump said:

> They are not our friend, believe me. But they're killing us economically. The U.S. has become a dumping ground for everybody else's problems. . . . When Mexico sends its people, they're not sending their best. . . . They're sending people that have lots of problems, and they're bringing those problems with us. They're bringing drugs. They're bringing crime. They're rapists. And some, I assume, are good people. (Reilly, 2016, August 31)

That attack on Mexico would be repeated dozens of times in the primaries and the general election and would become officialized by a persistent policy of building a big wall on the border with Mexico as the most efficient way to contain the increasing threat posed, according to him, by the undocumented immigrants coming from the neighbor on the south. "Build the Wall!" became a rallying cry of Trump supporters.

The coverage of Trump's visit to Mexico on August 30, 2016, to meet with then Mexican president Enrique Peña Nieto, was characterized by vitriol and contempt. An *El Universal* columnist, Mario Melgar, wrote: "Trump is an enemy to Mexicans. He's worse than a persona non grata. He never should have been welcomed."

On July 1, 2018, Andres Manuel Lopez Obrador, a left-of-center and populist opposition candidate running for the third time in a row, won the Mexican presidency in a landslide election with 53% of the popular vote. On December 1 of that year, Lopez Obrador took office as president. During his first year in office, while maintaining a firm but discrete position against Donald Trump's proposed wall and his tough immigration policies and actions against Mexicans, Lopez Obrador decided not to antagonize the president of the United States.

On December 20, 2018, less than three weeks after Lopez Obrador' inauguration, the Trump administration declared its intention to implement a plan in which asylum seekers had to wait in Mexico before they could be admitted into the United States for an asylum hearing, a plan that was enacted with the name of the Migration Protection Protocols (MPP) (Arriola Vega, 2019). In January 2019, the first Central American migrants seeking asylum in the United States were returned to Mexico, a unilateral act by which the US government considered Mexico as a de facto safe third country. Instead of rejecting and opposing the US move, the Lopez Obrador administration announced he would support, temporarily and for humanitarian reasons, the asylum seekers returned to Mexico. By late June 2019, the National Institute of Migration Issues (INM) claimed that more than 16,000 Central Americans had been returned to Mexico as part of the MPP (p. 11). By February 2020 that number had risen to 57,000 (Rivlin-Nadler, 2020).

In June 2019, President Trump threatened to impose tariffs on Mexican goods if Mexico kept allowing Central American migrants to enter Mexico and reach the US-Mexico border. To avoid these tariffs, the Lopez Obrador administration deployed around 6,000 national guard troops to the Guatemala border to stop migrant caravans from entering Mexico and from moving to the north of the country (Miroff, Lynch, & Sieff, 2019). From that moment, up to 2020, the initial policy of welcoming Central American immigrant caravans to Mexico and helping them reach the border with the United States turned dramatically into a tough, stringent stance against the caravans. By January 2020, the *New York Times* was reporting that the Mexican national guard was consistently stopping migrant caravans from Central America, "using a combination of carrots and sticks—the lure of possible employment for those who chose to enter legally, and pepper spray, detention, and deportation for those who did not" (Semple & McDonald, 2020).

THE MEXICAN PRESS

Classified by Hallin and Papathanassopoulus (2002) as historically clientelist,[1] the Mexican press has experienced significant changes in the last two decades, becoming more critical of the government and more independent from the political class. According to Hughes (2003), most

---

1. Clientelism, according to Hallin and Papathanassopoulus (2002), refers to "a pattern of social organization in which access to social resources is controlled by patrons and delivered to clients in exchange for deference and various kinds of support."

of the main national and regional Mexican newspapers moved from an authoritarian tradition in which journalists "took a passive, noncritical approach to reporting and forged subordinate relationships" with politicians (p. 94) to a form of civic journalism with the potential to enable democratic citizenship. Hughes argues that Mexican newspapers moved from clientelism to the civic approach through three different routes: (a) owners pushed change from above; (b) new cohorts of journalists pushed from below; or (c) change "moved horizontally as staffs deserted publications when faced with dilemmas brought on by a clash of values or government intervention" (p. 99). The first wave was in the 1970s and 1980s when the traditional authoritarian regime was still in force. Some publishers decided to push change from above, like in the case of Monterrey newspaper *El Norte*, which defied the ruling party and managed to become commercially successful despite the lack of governmental subsidies, tax audits, cuts in the state-controlled newsprint supplies, and the like (Hughes & Gil, 2004). In other cases, like *La Jornada*, left-of-center journalists, academics, and artists inspired by international newspapers like *El País* (Spain) decided to join forces and create a newspaper able to question the authoritarian government. Following the dramatic political changes in Mexico's political system in the 1990s (increased democratization and frequent electoral triumphs by opposition parties at the local, state, and federal levels), more newspapers followed the new civic-oriented model and abandoned their clientelist relationship with the ruling party (Lawson, 2002). Among these dailies was *El Universal*, the oldest Mexico City newspaper. By the mid-1990s, the paper had adopted the new approach, becoming more critical and independent.

In 2000, after 71 years of uninterrupted PRI presidents, Mexico had a major political upheaval. For the first time, an opposition candidate (Vicente Fox), from the right-of-center Acción Nacional party (PAN) won the presidency of Mexico, and other oppositional political parties increased their representation in the Mexican congress. In 2006, in a close election, Felipe Calderón, another PAN candidate, won the presidency. During these 12 years of PAN rule, Mexican newspapers enjoyed a never-before-experienced freedom and autonomy from the political elite, although in many instances they keep benefiting from official advertising and subsidies. Daily newspapers like *El Universal*, *La Jornada*, and *Reforma* (founded in Mexico City in 1993 by the owner of Monterrey's *El Norte*) became even more critical and professional and commercial advertising and income coming from subscriptions and sales soared. These changes were so significant and lasting that when the former ruling party (the PRI) returned to power in 2012, with Enrique Peña Nieto as president, these Mexican newspapers, and many others, kept their independence and critical stance toward the political class despite the renewed efforts by the Peña Nieto administration to return to a clientelist model.[2]

The Mexican Press and the Coverage of the United States

While there are many more studies on the images of Mexico in the United States' news media than the image of the United States in their Mexican counterparts, the few content analyses available show the significant amount of coverage received by the United States in the Mexican news media and an ambivalent but mostly critical view of the neighbor to the north, especially in the op-ed pages. John C. Merrill (1962) in a content analysis of 10 regional Mexican dailies in 1960, concluded that the United States was by far the country receiving the highest attention in the foreign news sections, with 37% of the total space, a higher percentage

---

2. The Mexican scholar Mireya Marquez-Ramirez (2014), however, describes how, despite unquestionable changes and professionalization of Mexican journalism in the last decades, some traditional clientelist practices survived and still coexist with the new civic-oriented model.

than the combined coverage of all Latin American countries (p. 204), and that opinion genres were negative and critical toward the United States (p. 209).

More recently, Muñiz (2011) has shown how Mexican newspapers covering the topic of undocumented migration center most of their attention on what happens to migrants in the United States, strongly denouncing the American government's disregard for human rights and its harsh policies on undocumented persons, while local coverage associate frames of "criminality" and "threats to Mexican jobs" when discussing Central Americans residing or passing through Mexico. A more recent content analysis of the coverage of migrants in transit (Ramos, 2014), confirms Munoz's conclusions about news stories relating these migrants to increased criminality and abuses. While there are no content analyses yet about the coverage of Central American migrant caravans after Lopez Obrador took office in December 2018, an informal review of Mexican newspapers during the last 14 months shows this same trend in their coverage. The same seems also to be true for any other topic. While main national and regional newspapers may be highly critical of the Mexican president or his administration on economic, political or social internal issues, when the US government or American political actors attack Mexico or try to pass legislation against Mexican interests, the same news media may furiously criticize the neighbor on the north, siding with the national position. This was evident in the reactions of Mexican news media about the shooting in a Wal-Mart store in El Paso that left 14 Mexicans dead. The BBC reported that

> in editorials and commentaries, several leading Mexican media outlets and pundits squarely blamed US President Donald Trump's incendiary rhetoric against undocumented migrants and in particular Mexicans. They said his language played a part in encouraging the anti-immigrant feelings that reportedly motivated the suspect in the El Paso attack. Major Mexican dailies widely reflected the Mexican government position, expressed in a tweet that said: "We condemn this act of terrorism against the Mexican-US community and nationals from Mexico in the USA." (US mass shootings 2019)

The objective of this chapter is to discuss and analyze the way main national newspapers in Mexico have covered the Trump administration, and how they have reacted to its harsh and controversial policies toward the country.

METHOD

The findings discussed in this chapter come from a content analysis of news stories and op-ed pieces about Trump published during 2017–2019 in three of the leading daily newspapers in Mexico City: *Reforma* (conservative), *El Universal* (centrist), and *La Jornada* (leftist). While these newspapers are not "national" in the sense of newspapers in many European nations that are widely read everywhere in the country, they are extremely influential at the political level and represent the spectrum of left-to-right news media in Mexico. Furthermore, as argued in the literature review, these three dailies were pioneers in what Hughes (2003) calls the transformation of the Mexican press into a civic-oriented model potentially able to enable democratic citizenship.

A sample of five composite weeks was determined to represent the period of January 2017 through June 2019 (two composite weeks for 2017; two composite weeks for 2018, and one composite week for the first semester of 2019). The coding book included variables like topics in the news story, sources, origin of the story, and main frames in relation to

Trump and to Mexico. The unit of analysis was the news story and op-ed piece mentioning Donald J. Trump in 150 words or more. The search for the units of analysis was conducted in the database Proquest Latin American Newsstand. Graduate students from Tecnológico de Monterrey and Universidad Autónoma de Nuevo León participated as coders: Ana Laura Maltos Tamez (Tecnológico de Monterrey), Jessica Loana Ferreira Lara (UANL), and Hiram Garrido Ledezma (UANL).

A reliability check among the coders was conducted on a sample of the news stories, achieving a .87 reliability coefficient (Holsti).

RESULTS

Number of Stories and Length

How much attention did the sampled newspapers pay to Donald Trump and his campaign and administration during 2017–2019? Table 15.1 shows that during the sampled five composite weeks, each medium published around 85 stories, for a combined total of 253. Most of these stories were news reports, although the papers on the right and left sides of the political spectrum tended to publish more op-ed pieces than the one in the center. In contrast with the 1960s when according to Merrill (1962) the Mexican press depended heavily on international news agencies for its coverage of the United States, the three papers mostly relied during 2017–2019 on their own staff to report on the United States, with *Reforma* depending the least on foreign news services and *La Jornada* depending the most, but with only 28% of its total number of stories mentioning Trump coming from agencies like the Associated Press (AP). The mean number of words per story was 515, with a combined total of 130,869 words in the sample of dates (Table 15.2).

Table 15.1. Origin of News Stories about Trump in Three Mexican National Dailies

Origin	El Universal	Reforma	La Jornada	Total
Reporter or correspondent	75	55	33	163
	89.3%	*65.5%*	*38.8%*	*64.4%*
Op-ed writer	4	29	28	61
	4.8%	*34.5%*	*32.9%*	*24.1%*
Foreign news services	5	0	24	29
	6.0%	*0.0%*	*28.2%*	*11.5%*
Total	84	84	85	253
	100%	*100%*	*100%*	*100%*

Chi square test 69.005, df= 4, p .000

Table 15.2. Number of Words in Stories about Trump in Three Mexican National Dailies

Newspaper	Mean	N	Words	%
El Universal	453.2	84	38,070	33.1
Reforma	458.1	84	38,477	33.1
La Jornada	631.7	86	54,322	33.9
Total	515.2	254	130,869	100

Geographical Origin

What was the geographical origin of the stories about Donald Trump and his policies toward Mexico or any other country? According to Table 15.3, most stories originated in Mexico, signaling that they were to a great extent the reactions of Mexican politicians and other actors to Trump's comments, threats, or actions. Only a third of the stories came directly from the United States as opposed to 55% originated in Mexico. Mexican readers of the three newspapers, thus, were more familiar with the reactions and perceptions of Trump's policies and comments in their own country than with the original messages coming directly from the president of the United States or his administration.

Table 15.3.   Geographical Origin of News Stories about Trump in Three Mexican National Dailies

Geographical Origin	El Universal	Reforma	La Jornada	Total
US	27	27	37	91
	32.1%	32.1%	43.0%	35.8%
Mexico	46	55	39	140
	54.8%	65.5%	45.3%	55.1%
Latin America	6	0	4	10
	7.1%	0.0%	4.7%	3.9%
Other countries	5	2	6	13
	6.0%	2.4%	7.0%	5.1%
Total	84	84	86	254
	100%	100%	100%	100%

Sources

US sources, however, were cited slightly more often in the stories than Mexican ones. As we can see in Table 15.4, 55% of all sources were American sources, starting with Donald Trump himself, followed by White House officials and US congresspersons. Most cited Mexican sources, on the other hand, were president Andres Manuel Lopez Obrador (AMLO), officials in his administration, and pundits. Curiously enough, the leftist newspaper *La Jornada* was more likely to cite US sources than either the centrist *El Universal* or the right-of-center *Reforma*. The latter was the paper with the best balance of US and Mexican sources of the three. In line with what the media sociology approach has found for the US press (Shoemaker & Reese, 1991), Mexican papers were also dependent on public officials (whether American or Mexican) in their coverage of Trump and his actions (or words) and devoted minimal space to nongovernmental sources like civic, social, or activist organizations; victims; and the general public. Mexican readers of these three dailies, thus, were much more likely to know about and perceive the main issues revolving around Donald Trump (whether bilateral or internal to the United States) from politicians' and public officials' frames and biases from both countries, than from alternative and independent views. Even when publishing in-depth analyses by experts on bilateral issues, the dailies tended to favor current or former public officials, like an essay reviewing and analyzing the three years of negotiations devoted to the new trade agreement between Mexico, Canada, and the United States (USMCA) in *Reforma*, written by the former Mexican ambassador to the United States and former vice minister for North American and Latin American trade Gerónimo Gutiérrez (2019).

The paper providing the highest access to Donald Trump as a source was the left-of-center *La Jornada*, with 20% of its total stories citing Trump directly, as opposed to *El Universal*

Table 15.4. Sources in News Stories about Donald Trump in Three Mexican National Dailies

Source	El Universal	Reforma	La Jornada	Total
Donald Trump	18	7	21	46
	14.2%	7.9%	20.2%	14.4%
White House official	8	4	5	17
	6.3%	4.5%	4.8%	5.3%
Andrés M. López Obrador	8	7	2	17
	6.3%	7.9%	1.9%	5.3%
Mexican government official	7	7	3	17
	5.5%	7.9%	2.9%	5.3%
US senator or representative (Republican)	2	4	9	15
	1.6%	4.5%	8.7%	4.7%
US senator or representative (Democrat)	3	5	5	13
	2.4%	5.6%	4.8%	4.1%
Other US public officials	7	4	8	19
	5.5%	4.5%	7.7%	6.0%
Mexican experts or pundits	4	6	4	14
	3.1%	6.7%	3.8%	4.4%
Mexican residents in the US	3	4	6	13
	2.4%	4.5%	5.8%	4.1%
Mexican business organizations	7	4	2	13
	5.5%	4.5%	1.9%	4.1%
Mexican senators or deputies (Representatives)	4	4	4	12
	3.1%	4.5%	3.8%	3.8%
US civic, social, or religious organizations	5	5	1	11
	3.9%	5.6%	1.0%	3.4%
Mexican civic, social, or religious organizations	3	6	2	11
	2.4%	6.7%	1.9%	3.4%
Foreign heads of state	6	0	4	10
	4.7%	0.0%	3.8%	3.1%
Other foreign sources	9	2	1	8
	7.1%	3.3%	2.0%	4.4%
Other US sources	19	12	18	49
	14.9%	13.4%	17.4%	15.4%
Other Mexican government sources	7	3	4	14
	5.5%	3.4%	3.8%	4.4%
Other Mexican sources	7	1	1	9
	5.5%	1.1%	1.0%	2.8%
Journalists, editorial staff of the newspaper	0	3	3	6
	0.0%	3.4%	2.9%	1.9%
Total	127	89	104	320
%	100%	100%	100%	100%
Total US sources	62	41	67	170
	55.4%	47.7%	68.4%	57.4%
Total Mexican sources	50	45	31	126
	44.6%	52.3%	31.6%	42.6%
Total	112	86	98	296
	100%	100%	100%	100%

Table 15.5.   Focus of Stories about Trump in Three Mexican National Dailies

Focus of Story	El Universal	Reforma	La Jornada	Total	Chi-Square	df	p.
Main focus	17	22	28	67	15.522a	4	0.004
	20.2%	26.2%	32.6%	26.4%			
Trump not main focus	57	37	46	140			
	67.9%	44.0%	53.5%	55.1%			
Trump and other heads	10	25	12	47			
	11.9%	29.8%	14.0%	18.5%			
Total	84	84	86	254			
	100%	100%	100%	100%			

(14%) and *Reforma*, which quoted Trump directly in a meager 8% of the stories about him or his administration. *La Jornada* was also the paper focusing its stories more directly on Trump, followed by *Reforma* and *El Universal* (Table 15.5). The controversial president, however, was not the main focus per se of most stories in the Mexican press, but issues, persons, or facts indirectly related to him or his administration. In one story reacting to Trump's threat on setting a 5%–20% tariff on Mexican imports unless the country stopped migrant caravans from reaching the US-Mexico border, for example, the story in *El Universal* quoted spokespersons from the Canada and the Mexican-American Chambers of Commerce, as well as the Mexican Business Coordinating Board, who talked extensively about the likelihood of the implementation of the tariffs as well as their repercussions in the Mexican economy (Saldaña, 2019).

One-fifth of the stories discussed Trump in the context of his dealings and problematic and controversial relationships with other heads of state in Europe, North Korea, or the Middle East. The meetings, agreements, and disagreements between Trump and Kim Jong-un were widely covered by the Mexican newspapers, as well as Trump's visits to Europe for the D-day memorial or the G-20 summits, and his visits to Israel, and South Korea, among others. Most of the stories focused on the controversies, the awkwardness, the conflict, or the mocking of Trump for his lack of professionalism and diplomacy. A story in *El Universal* about Trump's meeting with Queen Elizabeth on July 2018, after criticizing the American president for not following protocol, made reference to the "hidden messages" sent by the queen by wearing a brooch given to her by President Obama in 2011 one day, and another brooch given by the government of Canada in 2017, at the time involved in controversies with the US administration (El mensaje oculto, 2018).

Tendency

About half the news stories about Trump or his administration in the three Mexican dailies referred to ways in which his policies or actions were affecting Mexican interests (Table 15.6). Trump's attacks and insults against Mexico or undocumented migrants were also an important focus of the stories, although less so in comparison with the broader category of Mexican interests which included trade, border relations, tourism, politics, drugs, and so on.

It is important to see how more than half the stories mentioning Trump made reference to his inability or fitness to be president (Table 15.6). Reflecting the critical perception of a president considered an enemy of Mexico, the three papers continuously pointed out Trump's defects and shortcomings in terms of the qualities a president of the United States should have. Table 15.7 shows these tendencies in the coverage of Trump in the three Mexican papers did not change significantly from one Mexican administration (Enrique Peña Nieto) to the next (Andrés Manuel López Obrador). Table 15.8 shows that the three papers tended to describe President Trump as irresponsible, disrespectful, dishonest, uneducated, and tactless

Table 15.6. Tendency of Stories about Trump in Three Mexican National Dailies

Mention	El Universal	Reforma	La Jornada	Total	Chi-Square	df	p.
Trump is affecting Mexican interests							
Mentioned	49	42	34	125	6.039a	2	0.049
	58.3%	*50.0%*	*39.5%*	*49.2%*			
Not mentioned	35	42	52	129			
	41.7%	*50.0%*	*60.5%*	*50.8%*			
Total	84	84	86	254			
	100%	*100%*	*100%*	*100%*			
Trump attacks, insults, denigrates Mexicans							
Mentioned	36	24	19	79	8.925a	2	0.012
	42.9%	*28.6%*	*22.1%*	*31.1%*			
Not mentioned	48	60	67	175			
	57.1%	*71.4%*	*77.9%*	*68.9%*			
Total	84	84	86	254			
	100%	*100%*	*100%*	*100%*			
Trump not fit to be president of the US							
Mentioned	46	43	52	141	1.503a	2	0.472
	56.8%	*51.2%*	*60.5%*	*56.2%*			
Not mentioned	35	41	34	110			
	43.2%	*48.8%*	*39.5%*	*43.8%*			
Total	81	84	86	251			
	100%	*100%*	*100%*	*100%*			

Table 15.7. Tendency of Stories about Trump during the Administrations of Enrique Peña Nieto and Andrés Manuel López Obrador

Mention	EPN	AMLO	Total	Chi-Square	df	p.
Trump is affecting Mexican interests						
Mentioned	106	18	124	2.651a	1	0.103
	51.5%	*38.3%*	*49.0%*			
Not mentioned	100	29	129			
	48.5%	*61.7%*	*51.0%*			
Total	206	47	253			
	100%	*100%*	*100%*			
Trump attacks, insults, denigrates Mexicans						
Mentioned	67	11	78	1.493a	1	0.222
	32.5%	*23.4%*	*30.8%*			
Not mentioned	139	36	175			
	67.5%	*76.6%*	*69.2%*			
Total	206	47	253			
	100%	*100%*	*100%*			
Trump not fit to be president of the US						
Mentioned	119	21	140	3.010a	1	0.083
	58.6%	*44.7%*	*56.0%*			
Not mentioned	84	26	110			
	41.4%	*55.3%*	*44.0%*			
Total	203	47	250			
	100%	*100%*	*100%*			

Table 15.8. Depiction of Trump in Three Mexican National Dailies

Tendency in the News Story	Newspaper	N	M	SD	F	Sig.
Trump presented as responsible	El Universal	60	4.22	0.993	1.234	0.294
	Reforma	46	4.2	1.108		
	La Jornada	45	4.49	0.92		
	Total	151	4.29	1.011		
Trump presented as respectful	El Universal	57	4.32	0.985	2.537	0.083
	Reforma	48	4.19	1.214		
	La Jornada	42	4.67	0.874		
	Total	147	4.37	1.048		
Trump presented as honest	El Universal	47	4.04	0.932	6.542	.020
	Reforma	37	4.08	1.14		
	La Jornada	30	4.77	0.504		
	Total	114	4.25	0.965		
Trump presented as intelligent	El Universal	47	4.02	1.032	4.469	0.014
	Reforma	31	4.03	1.08		
	La Jornada	30	4.67	0.844		
	Total	108	4.2	1.03		
Trump presented as diplomatic	El Universal	60	4.18	6.49	0.909	0.405
	Reforma	47	4.11	1.255		
	La Jornada	47	4.83	0.67		
	Total	154	4.75	4.13		

Note. Mean is in the scale: 1 *Total agreement*; 2 *Agreement*; 3 *Neutral*; 4 *Disagreement*; 5 *Total disagreement*.

in their stories and news analyses reflecting a clear antipathy and critical stance toward him. *La Jornada*, for example, covered a controversial exchange between Trump and Macron in November 2018, when the former tweeted several insults against the French president, mocking him for proposing the creation of a European army independent of NATO. Contrasting the "irrational, irascible, and rude" attitude of Trump with the calm, diplomatic, and friendly response from Macron, the story in *La Jornada* made clear who the bad guy in this incident was (Macron pide respeto, 2018).

Topics

The preferred topic of the Mexican newspapers in relation to Trump during the three years in the sample was not undocumented immigration but international trade and tariffs (Table 15.9). The Mexican economy being so dependent on trade with the United States (and on twin plants and American manufacturing plants in Mexico), and given Trump's threats to impose tariffs or not sign a new trade agreement with Mexico, *El Universal*, *Reforma*, and *La Jornada* devoted almost half of its stories to cover this topic.

Immigration was the second topic most mentioned in the stories, with 67,089 words devoted to it (28% of total words). The coverage of this topic in the dailies was in tune with the findings of Muñiz (2011) and Ramos (2014) of Mexican news being very critical of US policies against migrants but critical of migrants-in-transit during their stay in Mexico. An editorial published by *La Jornada* after Trump's administration granted troops guarding the border authority to use lethal force, reflected the typical revulsion of Mexican journalists to such actions:

> At a minimum, we can use the term "exorbitant" to the idea of opposing the most powerful army in the world to a group of unarmed and particularly vulnerable people, but the order is also alarming because it establishes . . . murder as [an appropriate] response to the search for asylum and of a better life. (Trump: Licencia para Matar, 2018)

Table 15.9.   Topics in News Coverage of Trump in Three Mexican National Dailies

Topic	M	N	Words	%
International trade, tariffs	545.44	123	67,089	48.60
Immigration	481.63	70	33,714	27.70
US politics	549.25	24	13,182	9.50
Trump's personality	544.64	14	7,625	5.50
Reactions to Trump	350.31	13	4,554	5.10
World economy	536.14	7	3,753	2.80
Drug trafficking	257.5	2	515	0.80
Total	515.54	253	130,432	100.00

While these editorials and stories on Trump's actions tended to strongly defend migrants, citing their human rights and their vulnerability and justification to flee from violence and threats in their countries, the coverage on Central American caravans in-transit was much more negative. National polls showing Mexican citizens' association of migrants with criminality and displacement of jobs made front-page news frequently (Se desploma el apoyo, 2018). While Trump's insults to Mexicans as rapists and criminals, his insistence on building a big wall on the US border with Mexico, and his unilateral actions and policies against migrants were extremely newsworthy, the long renegotiation of NAFTA (three years) and the potential impact of tariffs on trade and the Mexican economy displaced the topic of immigration to second place in the coverage.

Internal US politics occupied a distant third position in the coverage, followed by references and analyses of Trump's personality and national or international reactions to his tweets, actions, or policies (Table 15.10). The Trump administration's reactions to the Mexican War on

Table 15.10.   Topics in News Coverage of Trump by Newspaper

Topic	M	N	Words	%
El Universal				
International trade, tariffs	508.62	34	17,293	41.0
Immigration	468.47	32	14,991	38.6
Reactions against Trump	259.67	6	1,558	7.2
US politics	370.83	6	2,225	7.2
Trump's personality	350.33	3	1,051	3.6
Drug Trafficking	257.5	2	515	2.4
Total	453.41	83	37,633	100
Reforma				
International trade, tariffs	447.76	46	20,597	54.8
Immigration	421.76	17	7,170	20.2
US politics	539.63	8	4,317	9.5
World economy	540.67	6	3,244	7.1
Reactions against Trump	376	5	1,880	6.0
Trump's personality	634.5	2	1,269	2.4
Total	458.06	84	38,477	100
La Jornada				
International trade, tariffs	679.05	43	29,199	50.0
Immigration	550.14	21	11,553	24.4
US politics	664	10	6,640	11.6
Trump's personality	589.44	9	5,305	10.5
Reactions against Trump	558	2	1,116	2.3
World economy	509	1	509	1.2
Total	631.65	86	54,322	100

Drugs or the violence coming from it, surprisingly, was not a significant topic in the coverage in any of the three papers. The agenda put forward by the Mexican dailies for their readers gravitated more around the economic implications of Trump's trade policies and the closely related issue of undocumented migration to the United States than around equally sensitive topics on security or environmental and health bilateral issues.

CONCLUSION

The coverage of the three first years of Donald Trump's presidency in three leading Mexican national newspapers was uniformly negative and critical, reflecting the fixation of Mexican journalists on his polarizing discourse and policies. Regardless of their ideological tendencies (left-of-center, center, or right-of-center), stories and news analyses mentioning the president of the United States concurred both on the degree of attention paid to him and in their depiction of his personality and the harsh criticism of his policies, actions, or tweets.

It is not clear how influential this coverage may have been on regular Mexican citizens, in a country in which only 22% of the population reads newspapers every day (Porcentaje de personas, 2016). But the nationalist position adopted by the dailies seems to be part of a dialogue between Mexico's political elite and the most prominent economic actors, and helps amplify internal attitudes and policies that may contribute to legitimize the measures, tactics, and reactions of Mexico to the powerful neighbor on the north. While these three media tend to be critical of the new left-of-center administration in the country and defend and promote the particular interests of their respective ideological constituencies, there is hardly any difference between them in their criticism of Trump and their rejection of his policies and positions against Mexico.

While historically the Mexican press has tended to be critical of the United States due to the asymmetrical relationship between the two countries and the vulnerability of the Mexican economy (Merrill, 1962; Lawson, 2002), it is clear that with Donald Trump, this tendency has intensified and Mexican journalism has turned even more explicitly nationalist and adversarial to the perceived external threats. While in general the news coverage maintained the resemblance of objectivity, our content analysis shows how in their depiction of Trump's personality, and the prioritization of certain topics over others, the three newspapers were extremely critical of Trump's administration. If this was true for news stories, op-ed pieces were even more disapproving and demeaning, with Mexican analysts reacting frequently in visceral terms to the constant attacks and threats to Mexico coming from the US president or his team.

An interesting and novel fact, however, is the frequent critical stance of these three papers toward the new president of Mexico. Instead of openly and unconditionally defending the Mexican administration's actions and policies, like they used to in the clientelist period of the Mexican press just a few years ago, the papers have also condemned first President Peña Nieto and later President Lopez Obrador for not standing against Trump and for yielding to his requests, as in the recent Mexican actions to stop Central American caravans from entering Mexico.

The coverage of Trump in the Mexican press may not end up being too different from his coverage in other countries or even in the American news media. Animadversion to Donald Trump, and critiques of his personality and actions seem to be widespread all over the world. What makes the Mexican coverage particular is the unique situation of Mexico as a neighbor and its asymmetrical relationship with the United States, with an economy extremely vulnerable to the unilateral policies and positions adopted by its powerful neighbor.

REFERENCES

Arriola Vega, L. A. (2019). *Lopez Obrador's initial policies toward Central American migrants: Implications for the U.S.* Baker Institute Center for the United States and Mexico. Rice University.

Cárdenas, J. (2016, November 22). Peña, el Peje . . . y el Lobo Feroz [President Peña, President-elect Lopez Obrador, and the Big Bad Wolf]. *El Universal.* https://www.eluniversal.com.mx/entrada-de -opinion/columna/jose-cardenas/nacion/2016/11/22/pena-el-peje-y-el-lobo-feroz

El mensaje oculto de la reina Isabel II para Trump. (2018, July 18). *El Universal.* https://www.eluniversal .com.mx/mundo/el-mensaje-oculto-de-la-reina-isabel-ii-para-trump

Gutiérrez, G. (2019, December 16). TMEC [USMCA]. *Reforma.* https://www.reforma.com/aplicacio neslibre/preacceso/articulo/default.aspx?__rval=1&urlredirect=https://www.reforma.com/tmec-2019 -12-16/op170395?referer=—7d616165662f3a3a6262623b727a7a7279703b767a783a—

Hallin, D., & Papathanassopoulus, S. (2002). Political clientelism and the media: Southern Europe and Latin America in a comparative perspective. *Media, Culture and Society, 24,* 175–195.

Hughes, S. (2003). From the inside out. How institutional entrepreneurs transformed Mexican journalism. *Press & Politics, 8*(3), 87–117.

Hughes, S., & Gil, J. (2004). The civic transformation of Mexican newspapers. *NACLA Report on the Americas, 37*(4), 26–28.

Lawson, C. (2002). *Building the fourth estate: Democratization and the rise of a free press in Mexico.* University of California Press.

Macron pide respeto a Donald Trump. (2018, November 14). *La Jornada.* https://www.jornada.com .mx/ultimas/mundo/2018/11/14/macron-pide-respeto-tras-criticas-de-donald-trump-661.html

Marquez-Ramirez, M. (2014). Professionalism and journalism ethics in post-authoritarian Mexico: Perceptions of news for cash, gifts, and perks. In W. Wyatt (Ed.), *Individual, institutional and cultural bases of journalism ethics.* I.B. Tauris, Reuters Institute for the Study of Journalism, University of Oxford.

Merrill, John C. (1962). The image of the United States in 10 Mexican dailies. *Journalism and Mass Communication Quarterly, 39*(2), 203–209.

Miroff, N., Lynch, D. J., & Sieff, K. (2019 June 6). Mexico aims to avoid tariffs with potential deal limiting migrants going north, allowing U.S. to deport Central American asylum seekers. *Washington Post.* https://www.washingtonpost.com/business/economy/trump-reports-headway-in-us-mexico-talks-on -migrants-but-renews-tariff-threat/2019/06/06/bb0801e4-8860-11e9-98c1-e945ae5db8fb_story.html

Muñiz, C. (2011). Encuadres noticiosos sobre migración en la prensa digital mexicana: Un análisis de contenido exploratorio desde la teoría del *framing* [Immigration frames in the Mexican digital press: An exploratory content analysis based on framing]. *Convergencia, 18*(55). http://www.scielo.org.mx/ scielo.php?pid=S1405-14352011000100009&script=sci_arttext&tlng=en

Porcentaje de personas que leía periódicos según la frecuencia de lectura en México en 2015. (2016, November 22). *Statista.* https://es.statista.com/estadisticas/619738/frecuencia-de-lectura-de-periodicos -de-la-poblacion-mexico/

Ramos, D. N. (2014). Encuadres noticiosos en la cobertura mediática de la transmigración en México (2009–2011). *Razón y Palabra,* (90), 388–404.

Reilly, K. (2016, August 31). Here are all the times Donald Trump insulted Mexico. *Time,* https://time .com/4473972/donald-trump-&/

Rivlin-Nadler, M. (2020, Feb 14). A year of Trump's "Remain in Mexico" policy leaves migrants desperate, vulnerable. KPBS. https://www.kpbs.org/news/2020/feb/14/border-has-descended-darkness -year-remain-mexico/

Saldaña, I. (2019, June 5). Ven inminente arancel de 5% [Experts consider 5% tariff is imminent]. *El Universal.* https://www.eluniversal.com.mx/cartera/ven-inminente-arancel-de-5-contra-mexico

Semple, K., & McDonald, B. (2020, January 24). Mexico breaks up a migrant caravan, pleasing White House. *New York Times.* https://www.nytimes.com/2020/01/24/world/americas/migrant-caravan -mexico.html

Shoemaker, P., & Reese, S. D. (1991). *Mediating the message: Theories of influences on mass media content.* Longman.

US mass shootings: Trump condemns racism and white supremacy. (2019, August 5). *BBC News.* https://www.bbc.com/news/world-us-canada-49240310

16

Media Coverage of the United States and Trump in Nigeria

A Mixture of "Greatness" and "Arrogance"

Abbas Ghanbari Baghestan, University of Tehran
Topic Peremobowei Akoje, University of Benin

INTRODUCTION

The images of countries held by the people of other countries have long been of interest to many scholars in different disciplines to understand how they perceive and think about each other. In the process of constructing a popular image, the mass media plays a crucial role and there is no doubt that the way its respective society thinks about other countries is a product of its mass media. According to McNelly and Izcaray, the mass media can contribute toward the people's understanding or misunderstanding of each other's countries (McNelly & Izcaray, 1986). Therefore, as Navasky noted, "it is based largely on journalism that we make up our national mind" (Navasky as cited in Zelizer & Allan, 2002, p. 1).

The purpose of this study is first to capture the public image of Donald Trump as well as the image of the United States as depicted in six Nigerian major newspapers and, secondly, to investigate the major discourses used in the selected newspapers of the country in order to portray Donald Trump and the United States.

THEORETICAL PERSPECTIVE

This study has adopted two interrelated theories, agenda-setting theory and framing theory, as the main conceptual framework to figure out the image of Donald Trump and the United States in six mainstream Nigerian newspapers. Agenda setting and framing theory have been applied to the media coverage of a wide array of different issues across the world. Among these

Acknowledgment: The authors would like to thank Sanitei Ebierin Akoje and Ebenezer Adaralegbe for their assistance in collecting news materials in this study.

are: the Middle East and Islam from the Iraq war of 2003 to the battle against ISIS (Isakhan, 2014; Mulherin & Isakhan, 2019), the coverage of the Arab Spring (Al-Rawi, 2015; Guzman, 2016; Oz, 2016), "The publication of the Prophet Mohammad cartoons in European newspapers" (Bowe & Makki, 2015; Strömbäck, Shehata, & Dimitrova, 2008), and the conflation of terrorism and the Islamic religion in the mainstream global media (Powell, 2011; Rane & Ewart, 2012).

According to the agenda-setting theory, the intensity of discussion in the mass media can affect human perceptions about the importance of any given event. This theory was first formulated based on data from the US presidential election campaign in 1968 when researchers discovered a link between human perceptions about the most significant problems in the programs of candidates and the frequency of mentions of these problems in the media (Mc-Combs & Shaw, 2006). In the future, the core idea of agenda setting was confirmed by many diverse empirical studies worldwide.

Agenda-setting hypotheses have been extended to some changes in substance. For instance, as a supplement to the idea of media discussion about its influence on social perceptions about the importance of the problem, it was suggested that attention be paid to the fact that a focus on certain characteristics of a situation or a public figure shapes public opinion (Wanta, Golan, & Lee, 2004). Such substance change in the theory is later called "second-level agenda setting" or "framing theory." In this context, framing is a process by which political actors, policy makers, campaign managers, and journalists can distil down otherwise complex positions on a particular issue to deliver an easily understood and remembered message (Pan & Kosicki, 1993). For instance, during an electoral campaign, framing is how the media can offer a set of interpretative schema or an unfolding narrative that enables the audience to interpret the complexities of a candidate's policy agenda (Gitlin, 1980; Tuchman, 1978; Nwokora & Brown, 2017). Therefore, frames also serve to obfuscate at least as much as they illuminate with much being left out of the picture in the interest of penetrating through and resonating with the intended audience (Entman, 1993). In fact, the way certain issues or events are framed has a significant impact on public awareness, given that citizens may have few other sources of information (Entman, 1991).

METHODOLOGICAL INSIGHT

There are two distinct approaches for the agenda-setting and framing analysis because both are equally important for in-depth analysis of the topic. The first is a quantitative content analysis, which typically uses computer programs to search for a set of keywords and isolate sets of frames before determining their prominence and frequency (Miller, 1997). Frame mapping has the advantage of being capable of analyzing a large amount of data to provide various statistical analyses. However, a purely quantitative method is not adequate. It may tell the researcher that a particular newspaper has mentioned "Trump" and the "Muslim ban" hundreds of times over a given period, but without a careful qualitative analysis of the articles in question, the overall tone or context cannot be understood. The second approach is a qualitative discourse analysis of the source material (van-Dijk, 2001). In media and communication contexts, prominent discourse analysis scholar van-Dijk states, "Discourse analysis emerged as a new transdisciplinary field of study between the mid-1960s and mid-1970s" (van-Dijk, 1991, p. 108). Discourse analysis has theoretical and methodological roots in several academic traditions, including linguistics and literary studies, which try to analyze different aspects of language usage and its impact on the users in the process of communication. In discourse analysis, researchers should apply their "expertise to induce the meaning of texts," including their familiarity with the topic, their ability to identify the evolving structure and narrative of the frames employed, and the "essential question about what could have been in the content but was not" (Hertog & McLeod, 2001, p. 154). This study applied a mixed method (including both quantitative content analysis and critical discourse analysis) to examine the ways in which Donald Trump and the United States were covered and framed in major Nigerian newspapers.

Regarding the quantitative content analysis, six major Nigerian newspapers were selected. Also due to the highly politically oriented nature of the media in the country, three newspapers (*The Nation, Leadership*, and *Daily Trust*) represent the pro-government media and three newspapers (*The Vanguard, Daily Independent*, and *This Day*) represent the anti-government media. The time span of the study was six months (March 20, 2019, until September 20, 2019). The unit of the analysis was "news materials," which could be either news, reports, opinions, interviews, or editorial. Due to the limited time frame, the researchers did not carry out a sample selection. In fact, all the "news materials" of the aforementioned newspapers, as much was possible, were collected within the time frame for further analysis (Table 16.1). The coding protocol of the study consisted of seven variables validated by four experts in the field of media and communication. In terms of the reliability, the test and re-test mechanism of 10% of all the collected "news materials" was used in the three-week time frames for the two most important variables, namely, "direction of the news material toward the United States" and "direction of the news materials toward Donald Trump." Finally, to measure the intercoder reliability (test and re-test), the results of a Kappa test, 0.89 and 0.86 respectively, showed the results of the study to be valid and reliable.

Regarding the critical discourse analysis, Fairclough's and van-Dijk's discussions of critical discourse analysis (CDA) was used. Norman Fairclough offers a three-dimensional model of applying CDA to communicative events. According to Fairclough, every language has three dimensions or layers: (1) text, which is the actual content of communication message (e.g., the text of the article); (2) discursive practice, or established discourses drawn on in production and consumption of the text (e.g., the neoconservative discourse permeating the article); and (3) social practice, or larger (nondiscursive) social structures within which the communicative event happens (Fairclough, 1993). Although the three layers/dimensions are inevitably intertwined, Fairclough emphasizes that CDA research should address all of these (Jorgensen & Phillips, 2002, p. 69). Van-Dijk (1991) offers helpful insights for the conduct of CDA as well. He introduces the concept of global coherence, which refers to the text's overarching topic/theme. In fact, van-Dijk's method focuses on the search for those general themes/topics that structure the discourse/message behind the text: "global coherence is described by what we all intuitively know as themes or topics. Topics conceptually summarize the text and specify its most important information" (p. 113).

RESULTS AND DISCUSSION

This study unfolds in two stages: (1) Quantitative content analysis toward identification of Nigerian media coverage about the United States and Donald Trump; and (2) critical discourse analysis of their publications to reveal the major discourses portraying the United States and Donald Trump in Nigerian newspapers.

Stage 1: Quantitative Content Analysis

The first research question of this study was: "How does the Nigerian mainstream media portray issues related to the United States and Donald Trump?" To answer this question, six mainstream Nigerian newspapers were selected and their content was analyzed accordingly (Table 16.1).

Table 16.1. Characteristics of the Six Mainstream Newspapers in Nigeria

No.	Media	First Issue Date	Political Orientation	Collected News Materials
1	*The Nation*	2006	pro-government	101
2	*The Leadership*	2004	pro-government	79
3	*The Daily Trust*	2001	pro-government	121
4	*The Vanguard*	1983	anti-government	70
5	*Daily Independent*	2001	anti-government	115
6	*This Day*	1995	anti-government	64

Overall, 550 "news materials" were collected from the six mainstream media outlets in Nigeria. Out of these, most, 357 (64.9%), were in the format of "news," followed by "report" at 128 (23.3%), and "editorial" at 54 (8.6%). In terms of the topic of the "news materials," the majority of them at 410 (74.5%) items were related to "US global policy," where issues like "US influence all around the world," "US economy and trade policy," "US battleground competition with China in Africa," "US visa ban for Muslims," and "Iran's nuclear deal" highly came to the picture overall. This was followed by 126 items (22.9%) related to "bilateral relations" between the United States and Nigeria and 14 items (2.5%) were related to "Nigeria's foreign policy." In terms of the "bilateral relation between the United States and Nigeria," the majority of the news items were about the "US position toward the new president of Nigeria," "US position toward bad governance in Nigeria," "US position toward terrorism in Nigeria," and so on.

As can be seen in Table 16.2, the majority of the direction of the news material toward the United States in Nigerian mainstream media were either "negative" or "neutral." Whereas, when it comes to Donald Trump, the majority of the news materials stand as either "negative" or "ambiguous." In regard to the United States, 227 items (42.3%) stand "negative" followed by 215 items (39.1%), which were "neutral." In contrast, for Donald Trump, 215 items (39.1%) stand for "negative," followed by 149 items (27.1) as "ambiguous." In both cases, the "positive" direction was very low, at 15.1% and 7.8%, respectively.

The second main question was, "Is there a difference between the two groups of newspapers (pro-government versus anti-government newspapers in Nigeria) in portraying issues related

Table 16.2. Direction of the News Materials toward the United States and Donald Trump

Direction	Toward the US		Toward Donald Trump	
	Frequency	%	Frequency	%
Positive	83	15.1	43	7.8
Negative	227	41.3	215	39.1
Neutral	215	39.1	143	26
Ambiguous	25	4.5	149	27.1
Total	550	100	550	100

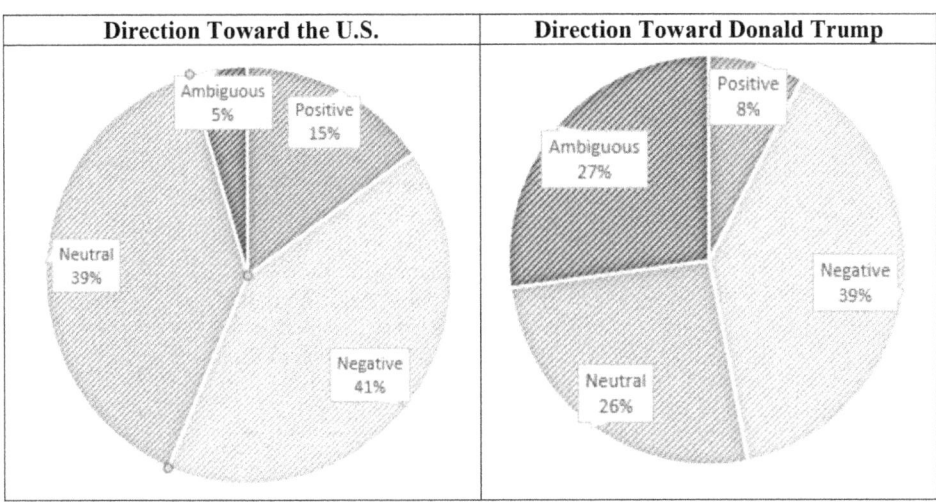

Figure 16.1   The direction of news materials toward the United States and Donald Trump. Nigerian mainstream media had more "negative" and "ambiguous" directions toward Donald Trump compared to the United States itself, where the majority of the items were "negative" or "neutral."

to the United States?" To answer this question, the chi-square statistic test was applied for both directions of the news material toward the United States and Donald Trump.

As can be seen in Table 16.3, even though there were differences between pro-government and anti-government media in Nigeria and the ways they portray issues related to Donald Trump (X^2 : 10.748 and Sig., .013), however, based on the Phi/Cramer's V value (.112), this difference was too low. This means that, overall, the Nigerian mainstream media on both sides (pro-government and anti-government) are in the same direction when it comes to the issues and topics related to the United States and Donald Trump.

Table 16.3.   Difference between Two Groups of the Media in Portraying Issues Related to United States and Donald Trump

	Chi-Square P. Value	df	Sig.	Phi / Cramer's V
Toward the US	6.947	3	.074	—
Toward Donald Trump	10.748	3	.013	.112

Stage 2: Qualitative Discourse Analysis

The third research question of the study was: "What are the major discourses that emerged from analyzing the news material regarding the issues related to the United States and Donald Trump?" To address this question, a careful textual discourse analysis of five purposefully selected "editorials" in a longer time frame (2018–2019) was carried out (Table 16.4). The reason these "editorials" were chosen was because these type of news materials are considered to be the leading articles and normally are written by senior editorial staff of the newspaper. Also these five selected editorials had some criteria: (1) They are from both "pro-government," "anti-government," and "independent" mainstream newspapers in Nigeria; (2) They published ahead of top official visitations of each other's countries; and (3) they offer an in-depth analysis (either in general or specific case studies) regarding the issues related to the United States and Nigeria relations.

Table 16.4.   Title and Details of the Editorials

Name of Newspapers	Type of Newspapers	Title of Editorials	Date
The Guardian	independent	China, Africa and Washington's Weird Worry	30 January 2019
The Nation	pro-gov	Donald Trump and the Post-American World Order!	29 March 2019
The Vanguard	anti-gov	U.S., China and Africa: Issues in Tillerson's Visit	19 March 2018
This Day	anti-gov	Muhammadu Buhari and Donald Trump in Nigeria-U.S. Relations: A Prolegomena to Their April 30 Meeting	22 April 2018
Daily Independent	anti-gov	Buhari's Visit to USA	10 May 2019

The first stage of the three-dimensional model by Fairclough (1993) is "text," which is the actual content of message communicated. This stage also refers to the first step of the three interrelated processes of Fairclough's discourse analysis, which is description. By a detailed analysis of the linguistic characteristics of a text using certain tools, it is possible to highlight how discourses are activated textually, arrive at, and provide backing for a particular inter- pretation. Fairclough proposes a few tools for textual analysis. Those with a background in linguistics will probably recognize the following selection: interactional control, ethos, meta- phors, wording, and grammar.

Table 16.5 shows the main concepts, metaphors, words, and phrases portraying the im- age of the United States in three different layers, namely, (1) people of America; (2) Donald Trump; and (3) government of the United States. All of these give insight into the ways in which texts treat events and social relations and thereby construct specific versions of reality, social identities, and social relations.

Table 16.5.   Main Concepts, Metaphors, Words, and Phrases Portraying the Image of the United States

Layers	Portrayed of	Main Concepts	Sub-Concepts for Description	Impact
1	American people	Great*	Role model	Civilized
2	Donald Trump	Ultra-nationalistic	America first, racist, zero tolerance, intellectually lazy, narcissistic, infinite nuisance value, one-man riot squad, authoritarian-minded, arrogant	Death of democracy in United States & worldwide
3	Gov. of United States	Empire of control	Concentric of the world, sensationalism, paranoia, ideological hankerings, ideological contestations	Shift to: post-American world order / new multinational blocks worldwide

*Note: Despite the fact that much of the commentary by Donald Trump and his administration in Nigerian newspapers are largely covered negatively and they warn of the danger of his policies toward the globe, some news and articles were found to emphasize various positives of the American peoples' culture, divinations, and its proud "history of peaceful democratic transition."

Further analysis of the above-mentioned editorials of the respective newspapers reveals that three broad discourses can be deployed to interpret and explain, as the second and third steps of the Fairclough discourse analysis, the image of the United States in Nigerian Newspapers: (1) a core inner circle versus many outer circles, which is, a manifestation of US global policy; (2) sensationalism and paranoia, which is the manifestation of US policy toward Africa overall; and (3) hegemony and dependency syndrome, which is a manifestation of US policy specifically toward Nigeria.

Discourse 1: A Core Inner Circle versus Many Outer Circles

Based on the above discourse, to understand Donald Trump's global policy, his main mantra of "America First" within the framework of global concentricity should be analyzed. The immediate implication of this is in President Trump's mind, the whole globe is a concentric circle, where the United States is the epicenter. Alternatively stated, America is following a global-centricity policy where the United States is located at the core. There is no place for multilateral diplomacy or diplomatic courtesies to other countries:

> In the possible thinking of President Trump, there is no need differentiating between or among many foreign policy concentric circles. At best, we can talk about two, inner and outer circles. In this regard, the inner circle is America or the United States, while the outer circle is the rest of the world. President Trump only has one priority, and that is anything American, that is, anything with American character, and anything considered American. (*This Day*, April 22, 2018)

In these regards, and most troubling according to Nigerian newspapers, is that such ways of treating the world are a product of Donald Trump's leadership that can easily lead to demolition of democracy. Therefore, from the perspective of the Nigerian media, this way of approaching the world by Donald Trump could result in the "death of democracy" and consequently, "an end of American hegemony in the whole world." On several occasions, the authors of the editorials describe Trump's personality as "a one-man riot squad with infinite nuisance value," "a single authoritarian-minded elected leader," "intellectually lazy," "narcissistic," "Racist," and with "zero tolerance" as illustrated from the following passage:

> America is deliberately encouraging the death of democracy around the globe! . . . The focus of this editorial, however, is on how its foreign policy is shaping contemporary world affairs, its impact on global configuration of power, in particular the fast-receding American influence on the world stage. . . . Now it is truer than ever, the era of American domination of global affairs which had begun at the end of the Cold War is fast coming to an end. And it is not only because of the rise of other rival powers . . . but much more importantly due to Donald Trump's deliberate policies and actions. (*The Guardian*, January 30, 2019)

However, what is most interesting for our purposes, is the extent to which the Nigerian media finds Trump's mantra of "America First" in stark contrast to "American ideals." In this regard, the most provocative conclusion is the emergence of "Post-American World Order," which is predicted accordingly:

> In less than two years under Trump, America has withdrawn from several multilateral engagements. . . . These developments are causing other great powers to have a rethink of their relationship with America and their future in a post-American world order. In Europe, China, Russia, Japan and India, New multinational blocs are also in the process of challenging the U.S. . . . By

the time all these fully unfold, the world order would have changed in spectacular ways, and there would have been a thorough diffusion of political, economic, technological and military power. [The U.S.] hegemonic hold will weaken considerably in the multi-polar global order, and the American empire as we know it will go the way of all previous empires! . . . [The American] global hegemonic stranglehold is fast coming to an end, and a truly post-American world order is in the offing, although its exact outlines remain fluid. And it is America's deliberate retrenchment from multilateralism and global commitments in the Trump era that is hastening it. A truly polycentric world order is inexorably dawning on us. (*The Nation*, March 29, 2019)

Discourse 2: Sensationalism and Paranoia

From the government of the United States' point of view, to understand where the whole world is going, it is necessary to understand that Africa is a significant part of the future.

Africa by the year 2030 will represent about one-quarter of the world's workforce. And by the year 2050, the population of the continent is expected to double to more than 2.5 billion people—with 70% of them under the age of 30. . . . Africa is experiencing significant growth. The World Bank estimates that six of the 10 fastest growing economies in the world this year will be African. (*The Vanguard*, March 19, 2018)

In 2019, African countries witness two major initiatives by the United States: (1) President Trump's administration of a new Africa strategy themed, "Prosper Africa"; and (2) then US secretary of state Rex Tillerson's five-nation African tour. What is perhaps more interesting for our purposes is that the expressed US policy toward Africa throughout the selected editorials also includes an ongoing critique of American attitudes toward the "Africa-China Partnership." For example, the *Guardian*'s editorial referred to "Africa featuring only as a mere battle ground for America to contain China":

The West [mainly represented by the U.S.] can help by gaining a more realistic picture of China's engagement, avoiding sensationalism and paranoia, admitting our shortcomings, and perhaps exploring the notion that China's model of consistent non-intervention may be preferable to one that regularly intervenes in other countries' domestic affairs or uses of military force to foster political change. (*Guardian*, January 30, 2019)

In these regards, it is highly significant that John Bolton mentioned "China" 17 times in six pages of documents discussing the United States' new strategy toward Africa. In this perspective, by describing China's engagement with Africa as "predatory action," China invariably is considered to be an ideological adversary for America.

With such robust view and understanding of the strategic potential of Africa, the United States of America . . . should readily mean business by engaging Africa more productively than into a battle-ground for ideological contestations by the unsolicited and false alarm of China's so-called "predatory practices." As former Head of State, Murtala Muhammed affirmed in 1976, "Africa has come of age, and it's no longer under the orbit of any extra continent power. . . . The time has come when we [Africa] should make it clear that we can decide for ourselves, that we know our own interests and how to protect those interests; that we are capable of resolving African problems without presumptuous lessons in ideological dangers, which, more often than not have no relevance for us, nor for the problem at hand. (*Vanguard*, March 19, 2018)

Discourse 3: Hegemony and Dependency Syndrome

When it comes to Nigeria itself, the country is going to have a larger population than the United States in the year 2050. Moreover, by the geopolitical position of the country in the continent, Nigeria is considered to be the biggest democracy in Africa, of which its leadership can advance mutual benefit to the United States and Nigeria itself. However, considering the US policy toward the world as well as Africa, Nigeria is not exceptional at all. The in-depth analysis of the mentioned editorials at the respective newspapers did yield significant and rich insights into the US perceptions of Nigeria that can be summarized in the concept of "dependency." Indeed, as mentioned in the quantitative content analysis, throughout their coverage, the newspapers published many criticisms of the United States and especially Donald Trump's policies toward the rest of the world.

> The mania of foreign policy management under Donald Trump is another problem entirely: it is without extension of diplomatic courtesies to other sovereign leaders, but with use of arrogant foul language. In the eyes of Donald Trump, other elected presidents can be talked to, and not necessarily talked with. Donald Trump addresses the Nigerian leader as a sub-president, and this has precisely been a major dynamic of the relationship between Donald Trump and Muhammadu Buhari in their individual capacities as leaders of their two countries. (*This Day*, April 22, 2018)

The second issue that portrays the way the United States perceives Nigeria is the business mindset of Donald Trump's "America First" mantra. In this regard, while Donald Trump only has one priority, Nigeria cannot be more than another "outer circle," among many others, in the globe.

> President Trump only has one priority, and that is anything American, that is, anything with American character, and anything considered to be American. . . . Explained in other words, President Trump should not be expected to negotiate away any U.S. interest, implying that Nigeria has been boxed to the corner before negotiations even begin. . . . It is our belief that, contrary to popular diplomatic belief, Nigeria's relationship with the United States under President Donald Trump and President Buhari is neither warm nor deep. Before the advent of the two leaders, the relationship was fairly warm in attitudinal disposition and deep in scope of areas of cooperation. Beyond that, the relationship has been that of crises and conflicts. (*This Day*, April 22, 2018)

Put succinctly, the relations between the United States and Nigeria should not come at the expense of a powerful and independent country like Nigeria. Further elaborating on this, one editorial argues that Nigeria should never be able to challenge the United States in bilateral relations:

> The foregoing is strongly advised given the ultra-nationalistic posture of Donald Trump with his "America First" mantra. . . . The goodness in, and development of, the bilateral ties must not be to the extent of enabling Nigeria to be strong enough to be able to effectively challenge the directives or positions of the United States in inter-state relations. (*Daily Independent*, May 10, 2019)

Table 16.6.   The Perception of US-Nigeria Relations

America	Type of Interaction	Nigeria
Core inner circle, great power	Hegemonic (talk to vs. talk with) and dependency	Outer circles, sub-president, diaspora, suspicion, corrupt

CONCLUSION

Before briefly assessing the results, we must acknowledge that the systematic interpretive analysis of the six Nigerian newspapers has limitations. These include that these six newspapers may not represent all of the Nigerian voices and that the limitation of collected news materials means that any conclusions cannot be generalized to the ways in which the United States and Donald Trump were covered in the broader Nigerian press and media. To assist in developing more robust insights into media-framed perceptions of the United States and Donald Trump, future research should involve a broader array of newspapers and media coverage, including local-language media as well as broadcast media. These limitations aside, the in-depth analysis of the six mainstream Nigerian newspapers did yield significant and rich insights into perceptions of the United States and Donald Trump in Nigeria. Overall, this study unfolds in two stages: (1) quantitative content analysis for identification of Nigerian media coverage of the United States and Donald Trump and (2) critical discourse analysis of their publications to reveal the major discourses portraying the United States and Donald Trump. Based on the above results and discussions, it can be concluded that the perception of Nigerians on the United States and Donald Trump can be summarized as a mixture of "greatness" and "arrogance." It is great, because the American people are considered to be exemplary, and because the technological feats and industrial development are seen to be a major source of such inspirations. Aside from these positive comments about the Americans, the Nigerian media were also host to many substantive criticisms and discussions of three broader discourses: (1) a core inner circle vs. many outer circles; (2) sensationalism and paranoia; and (3) hegemony and dependency syndrome confronting the earlier perception. Therefore, when it comes to the US government, especially under the Donald Trump administration, they see it to be very arrogant and that it can carry this arrogance to the international arena as well.

REFERENCES

Al-Rawi, A. K. (2015). Sectarianism and the Arab Spring: Framing the popular protests in Bahrain. *Global Media and Communication, 11*(1), 25–42.

Bowe, B. J., & Makki, T. W. (2015). Muslim neighbours or an Islamic threat? A constructionist framing analysis of newspaper coverage of mosque controversies. *Media, Culture & Society, 38*(4), 540–558.

Entman, R. M. (1991). Framing US coverage of international news: Contrasts in narratives of the KAL and Iran air incidents. *Journal of Communication, 41*(4), 6–27.

Entman, R. M. (1993). Framing: Toward clarification of a fractured paradigm. *Journal of Communication, 43*(4), 51–58.

Fairclough, N. (1993). Critical discourse analysis and the marketization of public discourse: The universities. *Discourse and Society, 4*, 133–168.

Gitlin, T. (1980). *The whole world is watching: Mass media in the making and unmaking of the new left.* University of California Press.

Guzman, A. L. (2016). Evolution of news frames during the 2011 Egyptian revolution. *Journalism & Mass Communication Quarterly, 93*(1), 80–98.

Hertog, J. K., & McLeod, D. M. (2001). A multiperspectival approach to framing analysis: A field guide. In S. Reese, O. H. Gandy, & A. E. Grant (Eds.), pp. 139–161. *Framing public life: Perspectives on media and our understanding of the social world.* Lawrence Erlbaum.

Isakhan, B. (2014). The politics of Australia's withdrawal from Iraq. *Australian Journal of Political Science 29*(4), 647–661.

Jorgensen, M. W., & Phillips, L. (2002). *Discourse analysis as theory and method.* SAGE.

McCombs, M. E., & Shaw, D. L. (2006). The agenda-setting function of mass media. *Public Opinion Quarterly, 36*(2), 176–187.

McNelly, J. T., & Izcaray, F. (1986). International news exposure and images of nations. *Journalism Quarterly, 63*(3), 546–553.

Miller, M. (1997). Frame mapping and analysis of news coverage of contentious issues. *Social Science Computer Review, 15*(4), 367–378.

Mulherin, P., & Isakhan, B. (2019). The Abbott government and the Islamic state: An elitist foreign policy discourse. *Australian Journal of Political Science, 54*(1), 82–98.

Nwokora, Z., & Brown, L. M. (2017). Narratives of a race: How the media judged a presidential debate. *American Politics Research, 45*(1), 33–62.

Oz, M. (2016). Mainstream media's coverage of the Gezi protests and protesters' perception of mainstream media. *Global Media and Communication, 12*(2), 177–192.

Pan, Z., & Kosicki, G. M. (1993). Framing analysis: An approach to news discourse. *Political Communication, 10*(1), 55–75.

Powell, K. A. (2011). Framing Islam: An analysis of U.S. media coverage of terrorism since 9/11. *Communication Studies, 62*(1), 90–112.

Rane, H., & Ewart, J. (2012). The framing of Islam and Muslims in the tenth anniversary coverage of 9/11: Implications for reconciliation and moving on. *Journal of Muslim Minority Affairs, 32*(3), 310–322, doi: 10.1080/13602004.2012.727292.

Strömbäck, J., Shehata, A., & Dimitrova, D. V. (2008). Framing the Mohammad cartoon issue: A cross-cultural comparison of Swedish and US press. *Global Media and Communication, 4*(2), 117–138.

Tuchman, G. (1978). *Making news: A study in construction of reality.* Free Press.

van-Dijk, T. A. (1991). Media contents: The interdisciplinary study of news as discourse. In K. Bruhn-Jensen & N. Jankowksi (Eds.), *A handbook of qualitative methodologies for mass communication research* (pp. 108–120). Routledge.

van-Dijk, T. A. (2001). Critical discourse analysis. In D. Tannen, D. Schiffrin, & H. Hamilton (Eds.), *Handbook of discourse analysis* (pp. 352–371). Blackwell.

Wanta, W., Golan, G., & Lee, C. (2004). Agenda setting and international news: Media influence on public perceptions of foreign nations. *Journalism & Mass Communication Quarterly, 81*(2), 364–377.

Zelizer, B., & Allan, S. (2002). *Journalism after September 11.* Routledge.

PAKISTAN

17

Pakistani Perceptions of Trump's America

A Troubled Relationship with Pakistan and Islam

Ejaz Akram, Southwestern University of Politics & Law, Chongqing
Ayesha Khan, Shanghai University, Shanghai

INTRODUCTION

Pakistan and the United States have had a bumpy mutual relationship. Since its independence, Pakistan has seen good times and bad times in its relationship with the United States. Good times were only there when the United States needed Pakistan's cooperation during Soviet times and the post 9/11 so-called Global War on Terror (GWOT), and bad times were all of the remaining times. Today, Pakistan sees the United States of America as an unreliable ally. A vast majority of Pakistanis also see the group of Western nations led by the United States as their civilizational foes from the days of crusades to colonialism to neocolonialism. This view of the United States by Pakistan is more or less constant and not affected by change of governments. President Trump's leadership and his peculiar political discourse have only exacerbated this view but have not created it ex nihilo. The Pakistani liberal elite is Westernized and in habitual subservience to anything Western, and it does not represent the views and aspirations of the society. This elite can sometimes give a false view of Pakistan's cordial relationship with the United States and the Trump administration because it is very small but very visible in media, academia, and policy circles. This chapter will look at the Pakistani society as a whole and its perceptions of Trump's America and propose that negative perceptions of America are not due to Trump, but rather are a continuation of manipulative and violent foreign policy in and around Pakistan.

In order to examine the perceptions of Pakistani society about America and President Trump, it is imperative to investigate why the United States of America does not like Pakistan. The reasons are many. Pakistan is a country with nuclear weapons and a professional military that is opposed to American destruction of Muslim countries, most notably Afghanistan. Pakistan's mortal enemy, India, is a deep strategic partner of the United States and Israel from where it gets weapons and guidance for offenses against Pakistan.[1] Pakistan has the closest partnership with China, which is America's declared (and undeclared) enemy on the global geopolitical chessboard. Overcoming the disagreements of the past, Pakistan has forged cordial relations with Iran; one-third of Pakistan being adherent to Shia Islam has spiritual attachment to Iran. Pakistan has formed a close relationship with Russia, while its relationship with Turkey, Qatar, and the Afghan resistance against foreign occupation have been rooted deeply in history, ethnicity, and religion.[2] Recently, Pakistan has been blackmailed by the Saudis for starting another Muslim block of which Iran's Rouhani, Turkey's Erdoğan, and Malaysia's Mahathir are a part. The Saudis used to enjoy considerable respect in Pakistani circles, but because of recent events, this has changed. A vast majority of Pakistanis now see that the Saudi royal family are puppets of the Americans, the American administration are puppets of the Israelis, who in turn are the custodians of the aims of political Zionism. These are the building blocks of American antagonism toward Pakistan. These foundational factors cannot be changed so easily; therefore, the US antipathy toward Pakistan is not likely to change. These can only change from the American side if the goals of global Zionism change.

Pakistan, on the other hand, disapproves of the United States for its fascist mindset, its bullying of small countries, its destruction of Muslim states and societies, its demands to "do more" all the time, its demands to bow down to the Indian pressure, the rampant Islamophobia oozing out of Western channels of information, and its opposition to the China Pakistan Economic Corridor (CPEC), which will take away Chinese dependence on the United States as far as the latter's monopoly of shipping sea lanes (GLOCs) and roaming of the high seas is concerned. Most recently, President Trump has taken certain actions vis-à-vis the Muslim world that do not sit well with Pakistan. Since the Trump era, most Pakistanis have hated Trump's facilitation of the illegal Israeli occupation of Palestine and usurpation of Jerusalem and the Golan Heights. Add to this Trump's double-cross diplomacy on the Kashmir issue. All these, again, are not likely to change because these aspects are foundational to Pakistan's identity and policies safeguarding its existence.

Pakistan is a country that came into existence in the name of Islam. Four big nationalities (Punjab, Pushtun Frontier of the British Empire, Baluchistan, and Sindh) and a few smaller ones (in northern parts of Pakistan) came together in the name of Islam to form a union. Pakistani politics and transnational behavior cannot be understood without the knowledge of the ideals and realities of Muslims. This may be true for other Muslim countries as well, but it is particularly true for Pakistan because it is etched into the national ideology and psyche of Pakistani people. It would be accurate to state that Pakistan's perceptions of Trump's America are a function of global Muslims' perceptions of the same. Trump's immigration policies, Islamophobic discourse, and subservience to Israel put an unbridgeable

---

1. India regularly egresses from across the Line of Control (LOC) in Kashmir routinely killing the civilian population of Pakistan. From the Afghan side of the border, its external intelligence organization Research and Analysis Wing (RAW) is notorious for funding terrorist activity across the border in Pakistan's Baluchistan and KP provinces. Indian spy Kalbhoshan Yadev, a serving Indian military officer, has been in the Pakistani custody for a few years now, convicted on the charges of espionage and sabotage. The ICJ in Hague has passed a judgment against him.

2. We do not use the word *Taliban* to describe the Afghan armed resistance against foreign occupation because the United States has over the decades created fake Taliban groups (such as Tehrik-i-Taliban Pakistan or TTP) to unleash terror in Pakistan in order to portray a nasty image of the Afghan Taliban who finally defeated the United States in Afghanistan just as their earlier Mujahideen defeated the Soviet Union. Indian officials have openly acknowledged supporting TTP as their proxy terror group as well as other terror groups operating inside Baluchistan, part of Pakistan under the Baluchistan Liberation Front (BLF). See Ajit Duval's speech about Indian support to TTP and BLA. See Sirajuddin Haqqani's article. (February 20, 2020): *What we, the Taliban, Want. New York Times*, https://www.nytimes.com/2020/02/20/opinion/taliban-afghanistan-war-haqqani.html.

gap between the reality perceptions of Muslims and those who are systematically vilifying them. This idea is further explored below.

ISLAMIC WORLD'S RELATIONS WITH THE UNITED STATES

Traditional Muslims have resisted the perceived onslaught of modernism. It is true that Muslim regions have either sought modernization voluntarily or faced modernization in the form of colonialism. The defense of Muslim nations requires industrial development, which requires modernization. Muslims' drive toward modernization is not because of a love of modernity but to safeguard their identity, which issues forth from their religious tradition. It is equally true that Muslims have resisted modernism whether in its communist/atheistic form or its Western secular form. The alliances of the Muslim world with the United States do not exhibit a consensus on basic values and outlook on life but are only a function of their strategic imperatives. The strategically expedient American policy of supporting US-friendly dictators in the Muslim world has led to suppression of democracy on one hand and anti-American sentiment on the other. The president of Malaysia, Dr. Mahathir Mohamad (Irshad, 2003) stated the following at the 10th summit of the Organization of the Islamic Conference (OIC):

> Today, we, the whole Muslim *ummah* are treated with contempt and dishonor. Our religion is denigrated. Our holy places are desecrated. Our countries are occupied. Our people starved and killed. Today, if they want to raid our country, kill our people, destroy our villages and towns, there is nothing substantial that we can do. (p. 85)

In the quote above "they" alludes generally to the West, but particularly the United States. Pakistan reflects that same sentiment. Pakistan sees itself as part of the four-nation coalition that constitutes legitimate leadership in the Muslim world. These nations are Iran, Turkey, Pakistan, and Malaysia. One could add to this cluster Qatar from among the Arab states and Afghan resistance from among the southern part of Central Asia.

ISLAM AND THE WEST: BETWEEN COLLISION AND DIALOGUE

Many voices within the West have asked for a dialogue, just like President Mohammad Khatami of Iran convinced the United Nations to declare the first year of the second Christian millennium as the year of dialogue of civilizations. The reason chances of dialogue seem tenuous is the enormous disparity of political and military power between the Muslim world and the United States.

The modern world system led by the United States continues to dwindle, but Islam is spreading rapidly around the world. Not only is Islam continuing to spread among the dispossessed, it continues to spread even among the privileged. Therefore, to think that economic marginalization of the masses alone is the cause of the global spread of Islam is rather superficial. Islamic fundamentalism spreads because of the atrocities and stupidities of US foreign policy. Osama bin Laden was not an economically marginalized person, but rather part of the Saudi elite who thought that the world of Islam had been singled out, castigated, and attacked. On the surface, Islam seems to accommodate modernity, but if Islam indeed remains Islam (i.e., the Quran, its law, prophet as the exemplar), the clash is imminent because of its diametrical opposition to the philosophical foundations of modernity. The modern world is less likely to clash with the world of Islam if the conditions of modernity transform into a justice-based system (Nasr, 1987). From the Muslim point of view, the West must come to terms with its own religious tradition before it can recover the capacity to understand other traditions, whereas from the Western point of view, the Muslim world must accept modernism and realize that they have little choice because of the enormous power differences between the United States and the Muslim world.

From the Western point of view, the Muslims have remained backward as compared to other groups who joined the race of modernization and became successful economically and militarily. Historically, the earliest Christian missionaries tried to convince the Muslims that the West has been able to progress because Christianity is a superior religion. At a later colonial period when Europe had become fully secular and the Muslim world won de jure independence, it became apparent that Western material progress was not due to the superiority of the Christian religion; rather, it was due to the jettisoning of religion, including Christianity. However, many Western analysts errantly ascribe this economic backwardness to the inability of Muslims to conceive of a Protestant-style reform in Islam. Those Muslim scholars who have suggested to their fellow Muslims the need of such a reform have become the darlings of Western institutions, which demonstrates Western eagerness to bring about such a reform so that Islam can be diluted and rendered ineffective from within, much the same way as Christian Europe.

From the Muslim point of view, the West led by Trump's America appears to be the champion of an economic and political system that is responsible for increasing distributive injustice within and among nations. Particularly the United States government, corporations, and certain agencies are seen as morally corrupt forces that want to lift all ethical fetters on social, political, and economic life. The modern world system is seen by Muslims as anti-spiritual and antithetical to the spirit of justice that is considered central in the message of Islam. Trump, on the other hand, greases the wheels of the Islamophobia leviathan operating inside the United States. He said:

> Remember this, radical Islam is anti-woman, anti-gay, and anti-American. I refuse to allow America to become a place where gay people, Christian people, Jewish people are targets of persecution and intimidation by radical Islamic preachers of hate and violence. This is not just a national security issue. It's a quality of life issue. It we want to protect the quality of life for all Americans, women, children, gays and straight, Jews and Christians, then we need to tell the truth about radical Islam. . . . We need to tell the truth about radical Islam and we need to do it now. We need to tell the truth also [about] how radical Islam is coming to our shores. With these people, folks, it's coming. We're importing radical terrorism into the West through a failed immigration system and an intelligence community held back by our president. Even our own FBI director has admitted that we cannot effectively check the backgrounds of people we're letting into America. (Golshan, 2016)

While addressing India's Modi government and the gangs of RSS fascists who routinely murder and rape Muslim women from Kashmir to Delhi, Trump spoke about Islamic terrorism much the same way he addressed the Christian fundamentalists of the 700 Club. He said: "Well, I'll tell you what. The Koran is very interesting. A lot of people say it teaches love and there is a very big group of people who really understand the Koran far better than I do. . . . But there's something there that teaches some very negative vibe" (Brody, 2011). During Trump's election campaign and in the first four years of his administration, Trump has not hidden his animosity toward Islam, and this is perhaps the most important reason why Trump is ridiculed and despised in Pakistan. His style of conducting Islamophobia is different from George Bush's or Obama's. He is less knowledgeable than his predecessors and speaks very frankly, which appeals to his Zionist constituents in America and takes away his credibility in Pakistan. It may be necessary to take assessment of Pakistani and Islamic perceptions of pre-Trump America in order to demonstrate that Trump is not the sole reason for negative perceptions of the United States in Pakistan; rather, the Trump administration is a dramatic continuation of it.

PAKISTANI PERCEPTIONS OF PRE-TRUMP AMERICA

Like many other nations/regions that exhibit a typical pattern of love-hate relationship with the United States, so does Pakistan. The reason for such a relationship is to a large extent the geostrategic accommodation of mutual interests at the state level. However, at the civilizational/regional level, Pakistan is an important part of the Muslim world and harbors the same critical animosity toward American policies as many other Muslim nations do. A pivotal reason for this is the US hostile foreign policy toward nations that comprise the Muslim world. The central feature of American foreign policy that is bothersome for Muslim countries such as Pakistan is the tacit support of Indian atrocities in Kashmir and unrelenting support for Israel in the form of massive military aid as well as perceivable misuse of its UN veto power in favor of Israel.

Background: History of Relations with the United States

The Cold War and Pakistan

Any discussion of US-Pakistan relations in isolation from the India-Soviet relationship during the Cold War is likely to yield an incomplete picture. Pakistan's entry into the comity of nations as a struggling state occurred at a time just when the United States of America was emerging as a superpower. At the time of Pakistan's birth, the United States had already assumed leadership of the anti-communist bloc. On the eve of independence, the United States showed interest in India, but because of Indian neutrality, Pakistan became an obvious choice for the United States to counter the growing Soviet influence in the region. In the subsequent course of events during the Cold War, given the Indian tilt toward socialism, the USSR lent support to India. To counter American influence in the region, the USSR-India partnership engendered military ties between Moscow and New Delhi.

According to the envisioned grand Soviet strategy, to balance America in the Middle East, it became important for the USSR to achieve naval supremacy in the Indian Ocean. To accomplish that, the USSR would extend into Afghanistan and exert pressure on Pakistan from the north, while India would do the same from the South. The United States and Soviet Union competed for influence in the subcontinent for almost four decades. The US-Pakistan strategic partnership was thus a natural result of a geostrategic predicament. The US-Pakistan relationship culminated in the Baghdad Pact (1954–1958), the Central Treaty Organization (CENTO) in 1954, and the Southeast Asian Treaty Organization (SEATO, 1955–1971), all of which gave Pakistan an American security shield against the Soviet Union, and by default, Pakistan protected itself against India. During this time, Pakistan also moved close to China to further defend itself from the Soviet Union. It has been argued that until the collapse of the Soviet Union "the United States and Pakistan were broadly on the same wavelength during the Eisenhower, Nixon, and Reagan presidencies. During the Kennedy, Johnson, Carter, Bush, and Clinton administrations, however, policy differences have been significant" (Kux, 2001, p. 359). This overall direction became even more pronounced when the Soviet Union invaded Afghanistan in 1979. Even though India was ostensibly committed to the Non-Aligned Movement (NAM) and championed neutrality in the third world, it failed to condemn the Soviet Union when it invaded Afghanistan (Tahir-Kheli & Council on Foreign Relations, 1997). This was a time when no one anticipated that the Soviet Union would invade a neutral country such as Afghanistan. In defiance of world opinion against the Soviet invasion, India provided the only non-Soviet air link to facilitate its operation in Afghanistan. The Soviet invasion of Afghanistan pushed the United States and Pakistan into an ever-closer relationship, with Pakistan emerging as a front-line American ally. China too, worried about the growing Soviet presence in the region, lent its diplomatic and material support to Pakistan.

Soviet Invasion of Afghanistan and the Role of Pakistan

During the height of the Cold War between the United States and the USSR and in the aftermath of the Soviet invasion of Afghanistan, Pakistani leaders, especially General Zia believed that Afghanistan alone was of no strategic value for Soviet Union. Pakistanis also worried about the Indo-Soviet treaty of 1971. Zia convinced the Americans that the Soviet assault in South Asia would continue in the form of the invasion of Pakistan and made a plea for American military aid. The Carter administration's lukewarm response to his appeal was rectified during Reagan's administration, whose key priority was to give the "evil empire" a payback for the American defeat in Vietnam. Until Zia's death in a mysterious plane crash in 1987, the second half of his 11-year rule characterizes the US-Pakistan alliance as a close military alliance that eventually defeated the Soviet Union in Afghanistan and may have helped cause the subsequent implosion of the Soviet Union.

During the time of the Afghan war, the United States helped the Pakistani Inter-Services Intelligence (ISI) to help funnel American funds to the Afghan mujahideen (the freedom fighters). The ISI played a key role in planning and orchestrating the war effort as the mujahideen did not constitute a professional army such as that of Pakistan. The mujahideen undertook the jihad effort and sought to dispel the Soviet "disbelievers" from Afghanistan. America fanned the Afghan jihad with moral and material support. Once the Soviets were defeated, the United States abandoned Afghanistan. With no clear party of mujahids having emerged to form a central Afghan state, Afghanistan plunged into a civil war. Thus, several Afghan factions such as those belonging to Gulbuddin Hekmatyar, Burhanuddin Rabbani, Ahmed Shah Masood, and Abdul Rashid Dostum, all governed or formed coalitions to govern different parts of the country. Until 1996, there seemed no consensus as to how the state-formation in Afghanistan would take place. The ISI sought to bring a Pakistan-friendly state in Afghanistan into power.

Afghanistan's prewar relations with Pakistan were never smooth, as the Afghans, whose majority constitutes the Pashtun, laid irredentist claims on the then Northwest Frontier Province (NWFP, but now Khyber-Pukhtunkhwa or KP Province). This always provided India an opportunity to establish relations with the nationalist Afghans to keep Pakistan under pressure. In the aftermath of the American pullout from Afghanistan, Islamabad hoped to create a Pakistan-friendly Afghan state backed by the Taliban who took over Kabul by 1996. Although there was criticism around the world about the Islamic motivations of the Taliban, the United States did not actively undertake any measures to destabilize the Taliban until after 9/11. Moreover, the direct result of supporting Pakistan during the Afghan jihad was an enormous stockpile of weapons, which transformed Pakistan and Afghanistan into one of the most heavily armed civil societies of the world. Amid civil war in Afghanistan, Pakistan had to host a heavy toll of 6 million Afghan refugees, which impacted Pakistan's fragile economy. The Taliban were the second generation of the Afghan mujahideen, youngsters who grew up in war: "As the principal provider of the means for armed resistance, the United States shares the blame for the ascendancy of the 'fundamentalists' in Afghanistan. Only after the Soviets left in defeat and some of the very same 'fundamentalists' began to appear threatening to American interests elsewhere did the United States objectively acknowledge some of the costs of its Afghan strategy" (Tahir-Kheli & Council on Foreign Relations, 1997, p. 47).

Pakistan's Nuclear Program

In 1974, India did its first nuclear tests that led to direct acceleration of Pakistan's nuclear program. During the Zia regime, with a hefty aid package from America, indigenous enterprise, and the possible help of China, Pakistanis were successful in enriching Uranium to a bomb-grade level. Despite the American support of Pakistan during the Afghan war, the US Congress had reservations about the nuclear program of Pakistan. While the Reagan administration worked to get congressional approval for aid to Pakistan, it could not avert the course of congressional lobbying that had begun against Pakistan's nuclear program. Pakistan was and still remains the only nuclear power of the Muslim world, and the American press expressed its fear of an "Islamic Bomb." During this period Indo-Israel friendly American senators sought to initiate legislation that would help halt Pakistan's nuclear program: "Congressional concern about the nuclear issue inevitably meant that Pakistan's failure to provide acceptable guarantees about its nuclear program would provoke congressional strictures. These came as amendments to the assistance legislation requiring a cutoff of US aid to Pakistan should it engage in activities such as enrichment, reprocessing, manufacture, or illegal acquisition of materials for the nuclear program, including violating American export laws. Senators Stuart Symington, John Glenn, and Larry Pressler and Congressman Stephen Solarz put their names on the legislation that called for penalties if Pakistan undertook these prohibited actions" (Tahir-Kheli & Council on Foreign Relations, 1997, p. 44).

In 1990 the United States announced the Pressler Amendment which became the basis of stopping American aid to Pakistan. Pakistanis saw this as the fulfillment of the American objective of defeating the Soviets and the abandonment of the US relationship with Pakistan. In the US-Pakistan relationship, Afghanistan was now on the backburner, while Pakistan's contentious nuclear program began making headlines in the American press. The Pakistani press, on the other hand, portrayed America as an unreliable ally that had used Pakistan to penetrate Afghanistan at a tremendous social cost to Pakistan in the form of refugee load, and also led to the amplification of drugs and Kalashnikov culture. Moreover, in the Pakistani perspective the United States did not share Pakistan's security concerns, given India's perceivably hostile posture, a state with nuclear weapons which had gone to war with Pakistan three times. Pakistan in the American public perceptions remains an undemocratic state that harbors fundamentalists and terrorists.

Pakistan between Zia and Musharraf

It is ironic that only during military dictatorships in Pakistan are US-Pakistan relations in full swing. The intermittent democratic regimes of Pakistan have mostly seen fractured relations with the United State. Zulfiqar Ali Bhutto's democratically elected administration was socialist, whose slogan was to provide "bread, clothing, and housing" for all on one hand, and *nizam-i-mustafa*—that is, the system of Prophet Muhammad—on the other. It was during the same administration that Pakistan moved very close to certain key Islamic states by hosting the Islamic Summit Conference in 1973. After Zia's military rule, the Benazir Bhutto as well as Nawaz Sharif administrations experienced a period of isolation from the United States. This post–Cold War era was also a period when India, cognizant that the socialist model was now passé, undertook economic reforms and made a swift transition toward a market economy. With an enormous population open for foreign direct investment, the United States saw India as a great market with abundant opportunity for American business. Pakistanis eyed the thawing of US-India relations with suspicion. Moreover, it was during the civilian administrations of Sharif and Bhutto when the United States received money to deliver 40 F-16 fighter jets, but neither delivered the aircrafts nor remitted the money to Pakistan. The F-16s issue aggravated both the state and the people of Pakistan who viewed America's broken promises as an unethical way of dealing with allies.

The culmination of friction in US-Pakistan relations came about in the aftermath of the nuclear tests of May/June 1998. When India conducted its nuclear tests in May 1998, Nawaz Sharif's democratically elected administration came under intense pressure to respond. Pakistan's nuclear program, which was heretofore only known by American intelligence, now became official when Pakistan in response to the Indian tests, successfully exploded its own nuclear devices in the Baluchistan desert in May 1998. Following the nuclear tests by both countries, there was condemnation and uproar from the world community, which was then followed by American sanctions on Pakistan and India. Sanctions on India were lifted in a matter of months and they hit India much less than they did Pakistan, given the nature of the Indian economy in comparison to that of Pakistan. This also led to a feeling of anger and resentment in Pakistan against the United States. The following year saw the ouster of Nawaz Sharif's government through a military coup d'état by General Pervez Musharraf. The following summer saw a further plummeting of US-Pakistan relations when India accelerated its efforts to have Pakistan's name put on the list of nations exporting terrorism. This was mostly due to Pakistan's unrelenting support to the Kashmiri Muslims' movement who had wanted to secede from India since 1990. Although the United States did not put Pakistan on the list of terrorist states, it reprimanded its war with India in Kargil, the highest battleground of the world in the lofty Himalayan range.

Pakistan's image in the United States then gradually deteriorated as a dictatorship that America no longer needed until September 11, 2001. In the wake of 9/11, the focus of the whole world once again shifted to Afghanistan and Pakistan. The attacks on the World Trade Center and Pentagon were known to be the work of Osama bin Laden and his organization, al-Qaeda. Bin Laden, who was wanted by the United States for bombing American Embassies in Africa and the American warship USS *Cole*, had sought refuge with the Taliban in Afghanistan. Afghanistan is a landlocked country, and out of all its neighbors, Pakistan is the most strategic route of entry for military operations in Afghanistan. This meant that the United States once again needed Pakistan. However, this time around the enemy was not the Soviet Union but the second-generation mujahideen—that is, the Taliban, the by-product of an earlier US-Pakistan war strategy in Afghanistan. Pakistan, which had supported the Taliban in quest of a friendly government and strategic depth vis-à-vis India, was now under intense pressure to choose sides. The choices were either to support the Taliban and risk American assault from Indian bases, leading to a complete annihilation of the Pakistani military machine, or to side with America by making a complete U-turn on its Afghanistan policy by abandoning the Taliban and jumping on the American bandwagon in its fight against terrorism. Surely, General Musharraf chose the latter route, seeking the preservation of his country. This drew another anti-American response from the Pakistani public, who suspected that Pakistan would be used once again by America to kill its own brethren, the Muslims in Afghanistan.

Pakistan-US Relations Since 9/11

The Pakistan-US relationship after 9/11 did not bear the stamp of the broad theme of Cold War power relations; rather, the new relationship was based on a break from the old pattern. During the Cold War, Pakistan was a junior partner of a superpower in an unequal relationship. Still, Pakistan was in a position to highlight the "red menace" and get American attention. Since 9/11 that relationship has changed more from a "partner that Americans need" to an "enemy that Americans need." Just because Pakistan cooperated with the United States in its war against terror does not mean that US policy makers now view Pakistan's nuclear program as it does those of France, Britain, India, or Israel. The frequency of negative American media coverage on Pakistan's nuclear program has increased since 9/11.

The Pakistani public on the other hand is more restive than ever. Except for those who were in charge of governance in Pakistan (during the Zardari-Nawaz years), it is hard to find people who can be called pro-American. One can only find shades of anti-Americanism. From the secular nationalists to a small intellectual elite (mostly journalists) of left-leaning individuals, to the downright fundamentalists, American foreign policy is responsible for the estrangement of the entire Muslim world, of which Pakistan is a very identity conscious part. Paradoxically, the elite from the above-mentioned groups are ever eager to send their children to the United States for education, and imbibe the American pop culture. This can be misleading for Americans who look at the Muslim youths' proclivity toward American culture as a sign of pro-Americanism.

Most Pakistanis remain Muslims first, then Pakistanis, and then come their provincial identities. Pro-Americanism does not constitute any part of that identity. It merely remains a tool of professional grooming in the quest for a better job. Not even 1% of the entire society has the wherewithal to send their children to America to pursue the American dream.[3] However, the financially well-off minority come back as "America returned" and are very visible in the society due to their flashy look. Since most people lack the capacity to imitate them, they develop resentment and swing to the opposite extreme—that is, the growing constituency of the fundamentalists. Even the America-returned group of young Pakistanis does not love America to death, because China is fast replacing America in fields of higher education applications from Pakistan.

The spiritual bankruptcy of modern societies has also prompted Muslims to relapse to their religious tradition. Since 9/11, Pakistanis feel more alienated from the United States because Pakistan in American perception continues to aid terror groups. Pakistanis like many other Muslims believe al-Qaeda, ISIS, and their links with the private military companies (PMCs) based in Western corporations have co-created such terror groups using Saudi Wahabi ideol-

---

3. Given the biophysical limits of the globe, this dream has turned into an ecological nightmare. Most environmentalists, scientific community, and development experts now believe that it is neither possible nor desirable for the rest of the world to mimic the American or even the European level of consumption and waste. Xi Jinping's China dream, in contrast, is a lot more realistic and parsimonious, and to be learned from. See Ejaz Akram, *Xi Jinping's Thought from Islamic Point of View: Its Relevance for the Muslim World.*

ogy with CIA money and expertise. The anti-foreigner mood pervasive in America since 9/11 has also affected Pakistanis negatively. The Council of American-Islamic Relations (2004) noted that 63% of Pakistanis reported that they were mistreated and profiled by local police, a figure that is considerably higher than Arab Americans' experience of profiling and mistreatment. Consequently, there has been a considerable flight of Pakistani families from the United States, despite most of them having lived in the United States as American citizens for decades. This has also affected state relations between Pakistan and the United States, because the dollar remittances by Pakistani-Americans from the United State were crucial for keeping afloat Pakistan's foreign reserve. In early 2020, the Saudis under Trump's pressure threatened to send home four million Pakistani expats who are an important source of dollar remittances to Pakistan, and to take out a few billion dollars of Saudi deposits from Pakistani state bank.

All this is not to suggest that there exists a monolithic disdain of Trump and America in Pakistan, but to point out the pervasiveness of this trend albeit with nuances. Due to a culture of general anti-Americanism in the Pakistani masses, Pakistani administrations are always under pressure to keep their dealings with the United States furtive. If Pakistani administrations openly subscribe to American policies, they are threatened by the masses, and if they openly defy American policies, they are intimidated by the United States.

PAKISTANI PERSPECTIVES ON POST-TRUMP AMERICA

A European expert of Pakistan Studies, Hermann Kreutzmann, remarked that Pakistan is one of the most misrepresented of all the Muslim countries of the world. While that may be true, it is equally true that just as the leadership from the Muslim world has often had unrealistic expectations from the West, Pakistani leadership, too, has misjudged the motives of the United States. It is important to analyze factors that constitute these (mis)perceptions.

Dennis Kux (2001) argues that friction in Pakistan-US relations is hardly surprising and it stems from lack of congruence in their security goals: "US-Pakistan ties have lacked a solid underpinning of shared national interests. Major differences and consequent disputes were probably inevitable. The partnership was likely to prove a fragile structure. The tendency of Americans and Pakistanis to gloss over this basic problem has only served to sharpen the sense of frustration and disappointment about the actions of the other" (p. 359). The British left the subcontinent without resolving the territorial award of agreed-upon Muslim majority areas to Pakistan. Kashmir was one such state that was overwhelmingly Muslim but its Hindu maharaja (prince) was swayed by New Delhi and undemocratically ceded the whole state to India. Kashmir has thus been a disputed territory over which Pakistan and India have fought three wars. The Kashmir issue constitutes the core of Pakistan's security policy. Most recently, upon Prime Minister Imran Khan's visit to Washington, D.C., President Trump offered to mediate between India and Pakistan over the Kashmir issue. However, India was quick to state that no such understanding took place between President Trump and Indian prime minister Modi. By August 5, India had illegally annexed Indian Occupied Kashmir (IOK) and the United States was as cozy toward India as it had been before. This led the Pakistani administration to adopt a view that Trump's bluff on the Kashmir issue mediation was only to soften the Pakistani stance on the American exit from Afghanistan. Since Pakistan still wields considerable influence and trust with the Afghan resistance, Trump offered the bait to Pakistan in the form of Kashmir mediation. Furthermore, the recent visit of Trump to India on February 24, 2020, is the manifestation of the close ties of the United States of America with India. During his visit, he concluded many military agreements and promised to provide military weapons to India regardless of Pakistan's security concerns. He also lauded Modi's administrative policies at home and abroad. During his speech at the famous Motera Stadium in Ahmedabad, he restated the term "radical Islamic terrorism" and mentioned Pakistan in the context of elimination of terrorist organizations operating within and outside Pakistan (ABP News, 2020). All this shows that Trump has a deep and strong strategic partnership with India, whereas Pakistan enters this picture only when the American administration has to use it for its own selfish interests in the region.

The Afghan conflict has been at the core of Pakistani-American relations for the past two decades since 9/11. After spending almost two decades on Afghan soil, America's Afghanistan mission is on the brink of collapse. The American army and NATO have incurred heavy losses and now want to extract themselves from this fruitless military effort. For a safe exit from Afghanistan, the Americans need Pakistan's help. Since Trump's coming into power, Pakistan has been pressurized on many occasions to aid America's safe passage out of Afghanistan on its own conditions. Pakistan was labeled as an untrustworthy ally in the war against terrorism. However, recently the dominant feeling in the power circles of Washington is that without Pakistan's considerable help it will be difficult to convince the Taliban to negotiate peace. In 2017, during Arab-Islamic-US summit in Riyadh, president Trump's speech infuriated Pakistani officials as he mentioned India as a victim of terrorism without even mentioning the sacrifices of the Pakistan Army and civilians. Since then, the popular sentiment among most of the Pakistani society has been that of total humiliation of a Muslim country that played the role of front-line ally of America during its GWOT. Moreover, Trump's blatant offer to India to increase its involvement in Afghanistan has further aggravated Pakistan-US relations on the issue of the Afghan peace process. Trump's policy of seeking help to peacefully exit Afghanistan on one hand, and continuously giving threats and more to-do lists on the other is not helping the dialogue process; rather such policies are fanning anti-American sentiments in the policy circles and general masses of the society. As mentioned earlier, Trump's recent visit to India is controversial because he lauded India as a close strategic partner, which has perturbed Pakistan. Trump's speech in India is just diplomacy. Pakistan and the Taliban are looking closely at Trump's actions, not his words.

It is due to the Kashmir issue and illegal American occupation of Afghanistan that Pakistan had to incur heavy defense expenditures to counter its much larger and powerful enemy India and its proxies operating out of Afghanistan. The United States neither shares nor cares for this concern of the Pakistanis. The American aid to Pakistan has not helped offset the economic pressure that Pakistanis incur due to its heavy defense burden especially due to GWOT. The recipients of American aid are the political administrations of Pakistan, not the people or the state. The American aid has only exaggerated the disparity between the state and its people. This growing disparity has led to state-civil society opposition in Pakistan.

RISE OF CHINA, DECLINE OF TRUMP'S AMERICA: IMPACT ON PAKISTAN

Since the rise of China, the relative decline of the West and the process of One Belt One Road (OBOR), the US-Pakistan relationship has assumed even higher importance because the success of OBOR and CPEC depends on peace in the Muslim world. Success of CPEC is vital to the success of OBOR, and CPEC depends on peace in Pakistan. Peace in Pakistan depends on peace in Afghanistan and the reason there is no peace in Afghanistan is because of the illegal American occupation of Afghanistan.

Pakistani strategists are well aware of the American and Indian opposition to CPEC because it promises to extricate Pakistan from the American zone of influence into the nascent China-led world system of trade and finance. Similarly, the rise of China provides opportunity for Pakistan's politico-intellectual independence from America. Whereas the American empire wants the world locked into a backward system of nation-states, China contends that it is not a nation state but a civilization state. Pakistan too is a nation state, but as mentioned earlier, it is part of a transnational union of several nations, and Muslims know well that before the era of nation states imposed by the colonizers, the entire Muslim world was a system of sub-civilization states. This means that if peace comes to landlocked Afghanistan, its development and rebuilding will require Chinese firms that will offer to rebuild the country at the cheapest cost, which would have to take place through Pakistan. China-led Eurasian connectivity can hence provide an opportunity to the Muslim world to overcome the divisiveness of the nation-state system and restoration of inter- and intra-civilizational connectivity. The United States does not want that at any cost because it threatens the manipulative and extractive status quo which it has parasitically spawned on much of humanity. US involvement in Baluchistan has been precisely to deny China this space by igniting violence in Pakistan and allowing Afghanistan to simmer so as to make sure the region does not return to peace and harmony.

It is very important to understand the past because it has clues for the future. Outside of Europe, the Eurasian land mass has four predominant clusters of civilizations: Eastern Orthodox Christianity, Islamic, Chinese, and Indian. The recent millennial histories of Christian, Chinese, and Indian civilizations are incomplete without the contributions of Muslims in their intellectual, economic, and political life. A significant amount of English-language literature has covered Islam in the Indian subcontinent, but there is a dearth of literature on the mutual collaboration of Islamic and Chinese civilizations. Due to the initiative of the Chinese state, there is recent interest in researching the peaceful interface of the Chinese and Islamic civilizations, because the future of the Chinese state and civilization once again depends on what happens in the Muslim world. The economic future of China now hinges to a large extent on OBOR, which has to go through many parts of the Eastern Islamic lands before it reaches Western Islamic lands, Europe, and Africa. This was a historical norm that was scuttled by the forces of colonialism, supported by American neocolonialism. With the irreversible decline of the West, particularly America, this historical norm is poised to reestablish itself. However, since the decline of the West is in its early stages, the West is still a power to reckon with, at least militarily, and the United States of America still has a lot of assets in Pakistan, which it established since the post 9/11 infiltration in the country. These American assets are liberal and Saudi-style Wahabi fundamentalists, who are two sides of the same coin.

Pro-America Pakistani liberals often exhort that China is not a liberal democracy and is therefore a dictatorship. Pakistani liberals are bought-out politicians, journalists, and intellectuals who rant about how Western liberal democracy is the only legitimate form of government. The Chinese as well as by Islamic scholars contest this notion, which needs to be analytically debunked because it fails to understand China on its own terms and is espoused by a generation of Pakistanis who have seen nothing other than American hegemony, which prevents them from considering sensible alternatives. The Trump administration has endorsed this point of view and remains wary of Chinese entry in the Indian Ocean via Gwadar, the opening of the CPEC artery in the Arabian Sea, too close to the world hub of global oil ex-

Figure 17.1 National Highway Network in Pakistan
Source: Cpek.gov.pk

port. In early 2018, the CPC (Communist Party of China) adopted a recommendation that the two-term limit for the president and vice president should be lifted. The Western media is looking at this as a "dramatic shift" from the existing Chinese norm because it allows President Xi Jinping to remain in power after his term is due to end in 2023. From a Chinese point of view, it is hardly dramatic that the president is given a long administrative tenure, even though it may be a significant change in the existing practice of CPC norms. This was done because it was the need of the Chinese system. Xi Jinping also made CPEC a part of the Chinese constitution that cannot be changed by any future president.

The history of modern China tends to suggest a pattern that the Chinese approach to its politics, economy, and law is flexible, pragmatic, and responsive to changes in its exogenous environment. From Marxism, to Maoism, to Dengism, now we may be witnessing Xi-ism. This is normal for China. The CPC is not emotionally attached to one idea, like the Western attachment to the idea of liberal democracy as the only legitimate form of government. Intelligent thinking calls for rational pragmatism without violating the principle. China's attachment to one-party rule with multiple parties underneath it is by no means challenged by this newest political arrangement. China is facing certain challenges at home and abroad, which have necessitated this move. If it works for China, the world should remain relaxed and focus on their own problems. From the American point of view, if there is a systemic shift in Pakistan's political system, the United States is likely to lose influence in Pakistan because the new system will roll back American infiltration which is currently underway but slow and cumbersome because of bottlenecks that exist in the old system of parliamentary democracy, which has never worked satisfactorily anywhere outside of Britain. Even in Britain this system is experiencing hiccups because it is based on a centuries-old system that is incapable of responding to current realities of the world. China wants Pakistan to reform its political system according to its current needs using some aspects of the China model, but America is dead opposed to any such change and insists that Pakistan continue to govern itself according to the centuries-old defunct British system of so-called "enlightenment values."

However, it is important what this shift signifies for China's allies, particularly for China's closest ally, Pakistan, and how it will impact its relationship with today's America. We have observed something quite phenomenal over the last couple of decades. Ever since the West unleashed wars of fascism in the Muslim world since 9/11, China and Russia have risen to gain a more respectful place on the world negotiating table. If it were not for the sagacious leadership of Vladimir Putin, Russia may not have achieved what it has. The Russian public and Kremlin are of the view that Putin should be allowed to continue, because his sudden dislocation from the position of leadership could alter the internal balance of power and leave Russia susceptible to American infiltration and sedition, which Putin has tried to weed out successfully. Similarly, like Russia, China is also facing political and military threats by Trump in the form of a trade war and alleged germ warfare. At this dangerous juncture in world politics, it is extremely important that China has the most experienced leader at the helm of its affairs, as a new president can take time to settle in such a position. President Xi will be 69 in 2022, and possibly in good health to continue. During President Xi's tenure, some very important decisions were taken, and to assure the continuity of these decisions, it may be very important that such a possibility of a continuum of leadership should exist in the system. Etching CPEC as a part of the Chinese constitution was one such landmark decision over which the Trump administration is upset.[4] Similarly, in the Asian region, we see President Erdoğan of Turkey playing the same role in Turkey, the Iranian system is steadfast on its own path, and Pakistan is likely to adopt a similar path under the leadership of Prime Minister Imran Khan with support from the military.

From a Pakistani point of view, what people see is that China launched Asian Infrastructure Investment Bank (AIIB); reclaimed important areas in the South China Sea to bolster Chinese security; and signed the most important initiative in the history of developing states, the CPEC—all signed off during President Xi's tenure. Further, China's western regions' development, a record number of Pakistani students getting higher education scholarships in China, and an increase in the number of Pakistanis in China and Chinese in Pakistan have all occurred during President Xi's tenure. All these developments have made President Xi popular among the Pakistani masses, notwithstanding a very tiny fringe of pro-India/pro-America

---

4. In the backdrop of the current situation, it may be observable that there are certain inward-looking elements in China that are of the opinion that China should not worry about OBOR and CPEC and not take on a fight with the West by adopting a Japanese or South Korean posture. The sympathizers of such a view within the upper echelons of CPC may be under the influence of the West who may roll back the OBOR and CPEC due to the West's war threats. If such elements are amplified with external support, it can derail China from its current trajectory. Therefore, it makes sense that the policy of political continuum should be supported. As far as the Western media is concerned, one cannot expect positive media coverage on countries such as China, Russia, Pakistan, and Iran because of the discursive resistance these countries offer to global injustice, lies, and wars of fascism.

liberal elite who are in habitual subservience to the West. So, it seems that the Trump administration's assets in Pakistan and the role that the CIA played in this region are atrophying.

CONCLUSION

The last two decades of Pakistani history can be called the rule of the liberals. During this period, there has been the reckless administrations of Musharraf and his so-called enlightened Islam; Zardari, the most corrupt ruler in Pakistani history; and Nawaz Sharif, a serious rival of Zardari, who almost equaled him in corruption, nasty politics of extortion, murder, money laundering, mega-embezzlement, and treason. Zardari and Sharif (along with other perceived traitors such as Asfandyar Wali, Fazl-Ur-Rahman, Achakzai and Altaf Hussain) were political leaders of mainstream political parties who had sworn to the Zionist and Hindu right-wing elites to finish Pakistan by assuming the role of the enablers of the hybrid warfare spawned by American agencies to hollow out the state institutions one by one through corruption. However, the fortunes of Pakistan have reversed since August 2018, when Imran Khan's government, against all odds, struggled to fight against the corrupt mafia mentioned above. Khan is known to be upright and unpurchaseable compared to his predecessors. In addition, he is also known to enjoy the support of the military in the accountability process of his predecessors. Here too, the Trump administration and Xi Jinping administration are at loggerheads with each other. Khan got this hard-won victory after 20 years of struggle against these fraudulent democrats who were the minions of America for a long time. In barely two months after Khan's victory, a slow but legitimate process of accountability has begun. Zardari and Sharif and all the other cronies are either in jail, exiled, or headed for permanent incarceration. Almost US$300 billion are yet to be recovered that were looted only within a decade. Having handed over an empty exchequer, Khan was destined to fail according to Pakistani liberals, IMF, and Trump's political elite, but a fortunate series of events prevented that from happening. Saudi Arabia's young leader became implicated in Jamal Khashoggi's murder in Istanbul's Saudi embassy. This estranged Saudi Arabia on an international level. With a dearth of international support, the Saudis did not want to lose Pakistan, and hence doled out US$6 billion. Khan's second visit was to China, where something earth-shattering happened. Pakistan decided to ditch the dollar and went for direct convertibility with the Chinese Renminbi (or Yuan). This move is likely to have important ramifications not only for Pakistan and China but for the entire region. Turkey burned dollars publicly, Iran is out of the dollar loop, Russian and Chinese currencies with gold backing have been bartering and thereby bypassing the dollar for a long time. This process of de-dollarization has begun, and after China and Russia, Pakistan and Turkey are two key countries that are likely to move out of their decades-old American embrace.

If one compares the Western hypocrisy, double standards, oppression, injustice, and continuous deception with our experience with the rising Asian powers, one finds a sharp contrast. China can understand the Muslim world better because it went through a similar predicament: what China calls the century of humiliation at the hands of the West. For the Muslim world it was two centuries of humiliation. China has pulled itself out of that test of destiny and Muslims would like to learn from China how it did that. Westernization is designed to keep Muslims subjugated. Easternization by contrast, may offer hope. President Trump has inherited a declining America, which shows the "wounded tiger syndrome," and hence today's America is a danger for the world as well as a danger for its own welfare and security.

REFERENCES

ABP News. (2020, February 24). Namaste Trump: "America loves and respects India," says Trump. YouTube. https://www.youtube.com/watch?v=RtWZfDH1ADM&t=1172s

Brody, D. (2011, December 4). Brody file exclusive: Donald Trump says something in Koran teaches a "very negative vibe." CBN News. https://www1.cbn.com/thebrodyfile/archive/2011/04/12/brody-file-exclusive-donald-trump-says-something-in-koran-teaches

Council for American Islamic Relations (CAIR). (2004, August 27). CAIR news briefs.

Golshan, T. (2016, June 13). Read Donald Trump's most inflammatory speech yet on Muslims and immigration. Vox. https://www.vox.com/2016/6/13/11925122/trump-orlando-foreign-policy-transcript

Irshad, M. (2003). Mahathir's call to awaken the Muslim Ummah. *Defence Journal, 7*(4), 84–88.

Kux, D. (2001). *The United States and Pakistan, 1947–2000: Disenchanted allies.* Woodrow Wilson Center Press.

Nasr, S. H. (1987). *Traditional Islam in the modern world.* K. Paul International.

Tahir-Kheli, S. R., & Council on Foreign Relations. (1997). *India, Pakistan, and the United States: Breaking with the past.* Council on Foreign Relations Press.

18

Poland and the United States Now Serve Each Other as Mirrors

The Trump Effect

Tomasz Płudowski, Cardinal Stefan Wyszyński University, Warsaw

INTRODUCTION

This chapter argues that much of the Polish conservative press and political right have found in Trump a means of legitimizing their own populist tendencies, and in so doing they have shifted the foundations of both countries' bilateral relations—despite a wealth of shared history—from being based on shared values to being transactional, with one result being that Trump's America defends its interests but has not joined the EU in sending Poland's ruling Law and Justice party a clear message about the importance of maintaining the separation of powers and the rule of law. From the aspect of communication, politics in both countries has become largely concerned with distributing social dignity based on two, new populist social cleavages—in-groups vs. out-groups and the people vs. the elite.

As this book is going to press, international confidence in Trump remains consistently low around the world, especially in Europe, with Poland being the only exception: 51% have confidence, followed by Ukraine, 44%; Slovakia, 34%; Hungary, 33%; and Italy and UK, 32% (Pew Research Center, 2019; see Figure 18.1). Even though in Europe this confidence is consistently greater among populist party supporters, in Poland the difference between national populist party supporters and non-supporters is one of the lowest, which means Trump gets some credit simply for being an American president in a pro-American country. Unsurprisingly, Trump chose Poland as a location for his first major international speech, knowing he would receive a warm welcome there before facing the riots and demonstrations that greeted him in Germany and the UK.

Confidence in Trump remains low internationally

% who have confidence in U.S. President Donald Trump to do the right thing regarding world affairs

Source: Spring 2019 Global Attitudes Survey. Q38a.
"Trump Ratings Remain Low Around Globe, While Views of U.S. Stay Mostly Favorable"

PEW RESEARCH CENTER

Figure 18.1   Confidence in Trump remains low internationally
Pew Research: https://www.pewresearch.org/global/2020/01/08/trump-ratings-remain-low-around-globe-while-views-of
-u-s-stay-mostly-favorable/pg_2020-01-08_us-image_0-02/

POLISH-US RELATIONS: BACKGROUND

Historically speaking, Poland has had a special place in its heart and mind for the United States and there are many good reasons for this (Pastusiak, 1992, 2010; Szlajfer, 2009). Close parallels between the two countries' histories are immediately apparent, but nothing builds friendship like commiseration, charity, military camaraderie, and common enemies (Smoliński, 2004). After all, in the same decade that Americans were winning their sovereignty, Poles for 123 years were losing theirs. As a result, Kościuszko and Pułaski fought in the American war for independence and in both nations became national heroes. Poles understood the American desire to shed British rule, having themselves been so eager to gain independence from Russia, Prussia, and the Austro-Hungarian Empire during the three partitions. Then, in 1918, Poland regained its statehood, which was, to a large extent, due to the support of President Wilson in his speech to Congress on January 8, 1918, when in America's Fourteen Points for Peace regarding upcoming negotiations to end World War I he included: "XIII. An independent Polish state should be erected which should include the territories inhabited by indisputably Polish populations, which should be assured a free and secure access to the sea, and whose political and economic independence and territorial integrity should be guaranteed by international covenant."

In no small part President Wilson's move was a result of the friendship between Polish pianist Ignacy Paderewski and the president's advisor for foreign affairs, Edward House. Impressed with stories of Poland's democratic traditions, including its writing of the first European Constitution, Paderewski was also instrumental in creating another great America-Poland connection. While on his second American tour in 1892, he was approached by a Stanford student by the name of Herbert Hoover to give a concert on the university campus. Since the attendance was very poor that day, Hoover could not pay royalties to the piano star, but 27 years later he repaid Paderewski's kindness after he was elected Poland's first prime minister and Hoover, now head of President Wilson's American Relief Administration, provided assistance to Poland and the rest of postwar Europe. In 1919, Hoover personally arrived in Warsaw and met with Paderewski. To this day, one of Warsaw's central squares is named after Hoover.

During the post–World War II period, America's Polish legend grew even greater. First, America was instrumental in liberating Europe, in contrast to Britain and France—Poland's allies in 1939—which did declare war on Nazi Germany after it invaded Poland, but then failed to act (during so-called phony war). Later, America's status as a promised land, already strong at the turn of the century when Eastern Europeans constituted a large American immigrant group, was strengthened by Cold War binary dynamics. Specifically, Ronald Reagan's presidency, which still enjoys in Poland a semi-legendary status, is considered a decisive factor in ending Communism through its arms race with the Soviet Union and its sanctions on Communist Poland. In the aftermath of the 1989 transition to a free market economy and a liberal democracy, the two countries' bilateral relations were further strengthened. First, George H. W. Bush visited Poland in the summer of 1989 and was instrumental in ushering in a peaceful political transition by having Poland's Solidarity opposition accept General Jaruzelski as the country's first post-communist president, albeit a short-lived, interim solution. Second, George H. W. Bush saw to it that Poland's Paris Club, communist-era, debt was reduced by half. In turn, during the summer of 1997 when President Clinton spoke in Warsaw's Old Town, he personally announced that Poland would be joining NATO, which officially took place in March 1999. On a lighter note, President George W. Bush deflected John Kerry's presidential debate criticism of his semi-unilateral action in Iraq during America's war on terror (an action supported only by Britain, Australia, and some smaller countries) by saying: "You forgot about Poland." Admittedly, anti-American sentiments have increased in Eastern Europe after the United States organized secret and illegal prisons for supposed Muslim terrorists, but until Donald Trump's presidency, major Polish parties remained unanimous in their strong pro-American stand.

Under Trump, however, many Polish party leaders have started to separate the person from the office or the country, which certainly has not helped America's image.

FOREIGN POLICY: FROM SHARED VALUES TO TRANSACTIONAL CLIENT RELATIONS

In fact, one of the most readily visible changes to accompany the transition from Obama to Trump was reflected in the language of American diplomacy toward Poland. All American presidents from George H. W. Bush to Barack Obama had seen Poland as moving from the status of an Eastern European country, a former, if unwilling, Warsaw Pact member, to a member of the Western family, joined by common values and interests, if somewhat vaguely defined and not entirely unanimously. Still, George H. W. Bush, Bill Clinton, George W.

Bush, and Barack Obama spoke as if our mutual cooperation was a natural consequence of who we were, of how we two nations defined ourselves.

As a result, the United States was widely viewed by Poles as their helpful, bigger brother, so to speak. Even though slightly less popular in Poland than in other European countries, President Obama visited the country three times and on the 25th anniversary of Poland's first free post-Communist elections, promised: "Poland, you will never stand alone." On June 4, 2014, Obama said in Warsaw:

> History was made here. The victory of 1989 was not inevitable. It was the culmination of centuries of Polish struggle, at times in this very square. The generations of Poles who rose up and finally won independence. The soldiers who resisted invasion, from the east and the west. . . . I know that throughout history, the Polish people were abandoned by friends when you needed them most. So I've come to Warsaw today—on behalf of the United States, on behalf of the NATO Alliance—to reaffirm our unwavering commitment to Poland's security. Article 5 is clear—an attack on one is an attack on all. And as allies, we have a solemn duty—a binding treaty obligation—to defend your territorial integrity. And we will. We stand together—now and forever—for your freedom is ours. [Applause.] *Poland will never stand alone.* [Applause.] But not just Poland—Estonia will never stand alone. Latvia will never stand alone. Lithuania will never stand alone. Romania will never stand alone. [Applause.] These are not just words. They're unbreakable commitments backed by the strongest alliance in the world and the armed forces of the United States of America—the most powerful military in history.

During the 2016 NATO Summit in Warsaw, Obama announced the deployment of 1,000 US soldiers in Poland, calling it "the most important moment" for the alliance since the Cold War. He talked of Brexit in terms of maintaining the US-European solidarity. The gathering of 18 presidents and 21 heads of government was held in the new national stadium on the East side of the Vistula river, where in the summer of 1944 Stalin halted the Soviet troops long enough for Hitler to annihilate the Warsaw uprising. Then, the Soviets came into Poland as glorious liberators and imposed Communism until 1991 when their troops finally left the country. The location naturally gave the gathering an important international and historic context. During the summit, NATO and the EU issued their first joint declaration, pledging to cooperate in the areas of hybrid and cyber warfare, as well as in preventing illegal migration on sea.[1]

In contrast, during his election campaign Trump called NATO "obsolete." With his slogan "America First," he promised to make America's allies pay more so that America can pay less. Although Trump did have a point about some European allies being free-riders, NATO was originally created in 1949 as a mutually beneficial system. Not only did countries such as Great Britain, Greece, Estonia, and Poland (on top of the United States itself) meet the expected 2% of the national GDP spent on national defense in 2016, but Europe was providing a network of infrastructure for American soldiers. Additionally, during the next three years—perhaps partly in response to Trump's criticisms—four more NATO members (Bulgaria, Lithuania, Latvia, and Romania) met the agreed-upon quota. Rather tellingly, of the nine reliables only Great Britain and Greece (apart from the United States itself) are not former Eastern Bloc members. Clearly, the EU border countries, especially former Soviet allies, are particularly dedicated to NATO, putting their money where their mouth is. Still, Trump stood out from his predecessors in terms of his crudeness and matter-of-factness about the expenses, as if NATO were merely a business operation, and the United States did not end

---

1. Regardless of veiled criticism from Obama, the right-wing PiS was eager to take credit for the NATO Summit even though its preparations and decisions were set in place by the previous government and president. As a result, the summit was framed as clear evidence of the rising international importance and recognition of Poland under the PiS government and Andrzej Duda's presidency.

up covering a lion's share of the overall expenses anyway given the disparities in the member countries' budgets. Moreover, if NATO did not exist, America would have to spend more to maintain its international presence, provided it wanted to maintain its global domination.

More importantly, when Trump finally agreed to raise the number of American non-combat troops stationing in Poland by a 1,000, he framed it again mostly as a great business deal for America. "The Polish government will build these projects at no cost to the United States," Trump said. "The Polish government will pay for this."[2]

In short, while Obama spoke the language of shared values, Trump spoke mostly in transactional terms, mostly of American benefit, and mostly to his own voters, in accordance with his campaign slogan: "America first." Interestingly, both President Duda and PiS expressed their approval, saying the American president *should* put America first, *just like* Poles put Poland first. The possible conflict of interests stemming from those nationalist preferences did not seem to bother populist minds, political, academic, or otherwise. The potential threat was particularly pressing from the Polish point of view, given the country's geopolitics: its location between powerful and historically aggressive Russia and Germany and the resulting centuries of some of the world's bloodiest conflicts. In short, Poland needs America (and other strong allies) more than the other way around.

CONSERVATIVE ATTITUDES: FROM CHOOSING BETWEEN PLAGUE AND CHOLERA TO BEING EACH OTHER'S MIRRORS

It is worth noting that initially—during the American presidential campaign stage—Donald Trump was not seen by Poland's ruling Law and Justice (PiS) party as their immediate ally, just a crude American, upwardly mobile opportunist who happened to get undeservingly far in life, a personage akin to Chance from Jerzy Kosiński's *Being There*, seemingly modeled after the title character of *The Career of Nicodemus Dyzma* (1932), a successful Polish political novel by Tadeusz Dołęga-Mostowicz. In fact, it is not hard to find examples of high PiS officials equally critical of both Hillary Clinton and her competitor. In May 2016, the soon-to-be prime minister, then minister of development, Mateusz Morawiecki, a former high bank executive, when asked which of the two main US candidates would be better for Poland, said it is "like a choice between plague and cholera." The dislike for Clinton can be easily explained by the Democrats' criticisms of the first year of the PiS rule and the two parties' generally clashing social views. The butt of criticism was Poland's emerging problems with the rule of law, discussed later on in this chapter.

However, soon the Polish conservative media and politicians warmed up to Donald Trump, arguing that great social and political change first happened in Poland, only to be followed by America, as opposed to the other way round, thus claiming credit for leading the international anti-elite shift. Specifically, in its coverage of Trump's victory, the Polish right-wing press deployed several themes. One was anti-elitism, which is built around the populist social cleavage: *the people vs. the elite*. In other words, it basically repeats the candidate's campaign message (Płudowski, 2018, pp. 297–304), which attests to its power, or at least to Trump's recognition

---

2. Additionally, over two months later, Trump's visit to Poland on the 80th anniversary of the outbreak of World War II was canceled at the last minute under the pretense of Hurricane Dorian about to hit the United States. Trump told Polish television: "I do have a great message for Poland, that we have Mike Pence, our vice president is just about landing right now, and he is representing me. I look forward to being there soon. But I just want to congratulate Poland and it's a great country with great people. We also have many Polish people in our country. It could be eight million. We love our Polish friends and I will be there soon." However, on the 75th anniversary of the liberation of the Nazi-operated concentration camp of Auschwitz, Trump decided to go to Israel rather than Poland.

that the body politic was plagued with social cleavages. The people vs. the elite frame has its variations, for example, simplicity (of the people) vs. corruption (of the elites). The right-wing weekly *Do Rzeczy* summarizes the conflict in several cover-story pieces gathered under the common headline "Why Are They Afraid of Him?" (2016): "Americans have chosen vitality and simple values against the demoralized oligarchy of the Democrats" (Piotr Semka); "The salon is terrified of his victory. The bastion it has deemed untouchable has fallen" (Rafał Ziemkiewicz).

The editor-in-chief of *Newsweek Poland*, Tomasz Lis (2016), who is one of the PiS's most vocal opponents and one of the stars of liberal journalism, attributes Trump's victory to how he linked anti-elitism with xenophobia: "Two [reasons] clearly stand out. First, showing the middle finger to the hated elites. Second, screaming out aversion toward immigrants, Muslims, Afro-Americans, gays, and women."

The *W Sieci* weekly asked "What does Trump's victory mean for us, Europe, and the world?" in a series of articles by Wildstein, Kostrzewa-Zorbas, Pawlicki, and other conservative pundits (2016). What might have come as a surprise, some of them initially held that it constituted a disruption of the post-WWII world order: "The U.S. election has shaken the ideological and political architecture of the West, shaped after the collapse of Communism. Donald Trump's victory seems to constitute its end. Naturally, we do not know what the next chapter of world history will look like. It is likely that we enter an era of turbulence, even chaos, and have no idea what will emerge from it. This is going to be a dangerous time" (Bronisław Wildstein).

Some right-wing commentators even argued that Trump should take back some of his Europe-related campaign promises: "European NATO members and Canada should help Trump realize that he has crossed the red line. They must agreeably demand that he forget his campaign-time anti-Atlantic declarations and make contrary declarations—to sustain collective defense. . . . It is even more crucial that he maintain the orders to place American troops on the Eastern flank of the Alliance, including in Poland. Simultaneously, there is a need to start creating a European center of power, capable of America-independent and self-sufficient defense, including deterrence. The only kind certainly effective in a grand global game is nuclear deterrence (Grzegorz Kostrzewa-Zorbas).

With some exaggeration, Maciej Pawlicki concluded that the Trump win would boost the patriotic spirit of Polish conservatives and legitimize the PiS government by linking Kaczyński's and Trump's political rhetoric and equating both countries in terms of similar social and political processes at work: "Americans, like Poles, rejected the hypocrisy of the cliques and a subordination to muddy mechanisms. And rightly so. . . . Poland and the U.S. now serve each other as mirrors."

This mirroring tendency has continued throughout the two leaders' overlapping terms in office and is well represented by the right-wing *Sieci* weekly pre-election cover story that likened Kaczyński and Trump to "Statesmen under Fire" (2019). Both are framed as having numerous similarities, starting with "a certain political incorrectness of both gentlemen, a specific and rare among politicians' naturalness." Also, in both countries the opposition is said by *Sieci* to use the same rhetoric, "summed up as three R's: Russia, racism, and recession." This trinity is said to misrepresent both Trump's and Kaczyński's rule as their likely and inevitable consequences. In the meantime, says the paper, both economies prosper, Joe-the-Plumbers not only get noticed but symbolically elevated while its only mention of xenophobia is represented in both countries by Hillary Clinton's consequential put-down, "basket of deplorables," and its Polish equivalent—the elite's contempt for those receiving the government's assistance, in particular the so called "500+," the monthly cash handout in excess of 100 euros to the parents of all children under 18 who are typically thought of as disadvantaged. Though initially announced as a fertility-encouraging instrument, this disbursement ended up being merely a social and electoral program that speaks to the populist appeal of the PiS government. Like Trump, PiS may not be perfect, but it stands for the little guy, or "the people," according to *Sieci*'s perspective.

Tellingly, the more inward-looking, conservative section of the Polish press occasionally uses the historically American term *silent majority* to refer to the new Polish populist social cleavage: *people vs. elite*. Namely, both Trump and Kaczyński are said to have "recognized the power of the initially forgotten, then openly despised by the liberals, "silent majority." While Hillary Clinton called it "a basket of deplorables," argue conservatives, a Cannes Film Festival award-winning Polish actress represented the elites when she posted on her Facebook account a popular drawing representing the supposed relationship between PiS and its voters: a dressed up man holding a bank note over the head of an elderly babushka kneeling in front of him as he calls on her to "give your voice" [double meaning: vote for me/bark]. However unrepresentative or taken out of context, such public communications have come to be framed as representing the new, populist social cleavage: people vs. the elite. Politics have become—to a large extent—concerned only with managing the social distribution of dignity (see Figure 18.2).

Figure 18.2   Cartoon
Reprinted by permission from the artist, Tomasz Wiater.

IN BED WITH TRUMP: BUSINESS OR PLEASURE?
CONTENTIOUS ISSUES

There is no country that Andrzej Duda has visited more often during his presidency than the United States (during the five years of his first term, as of February 2020)—11 times. At the same time, no Polish president waited as long as Andrzej Duda for his first invitation to the White House after the election of a new American president. There were several contentious issues at stake that kept the relations at bay during the initial stages, particularly involving Polish-Jewish history, the rule of law, and American-owned media freedom in Poland.

Polish-American-Jewish Relations

To begin with, in early 2018 President Duda signed into law an amendment to the Act of the Institute of National Remembrance, making those who publicly ascribe to the Polish nation's collective responsibility for Holocaust-related acts punishable with up to three years in prison. The main declared intention of the law was to suppress the widespread use of the phrase "Polish death camps" in international media, even if applied thoughtlessly, ignorantly, or simply geographically to refer to Nazi-occupied Poland, which did not exist as a state. Admittedly, the law was poorly written and unenforceable. Also, some of the rationale behind it was probably purely propagandistic, meant to beat a patriotic drum for election purposes. However, some Jewish organizations saw the law as a form of censorship to prevent research into and discussion of individual responsibility of individuals during the Holocaust. Polish and Israeli authorities finally reached an agreement rephrasing the law and cosponsoring newspaper ads with their shared statement that stressed both Jewish and Polish victims of the Nazi occupation, rejected any collective responsibility of the Polish people, and criticized anti-Semitism and anti-Polonism as well as the phrase "Polish death camps," which, they said, diminished the responsibility of the Germans.

Another factor that provides an important context for the negative statements regarding Poland by the Israeli prime minister was that he was up for reelection at the time. Also, American Congress was working on a law that would encourage the passing of heirless Jewish property to American Jewish organizations. "The Justice for Uncompensated Survivors Today" Act became effective May 9, 2018. Admittedly, the law was not applicable in Poland, and even in the United States it did not even provide for any enforcement. All it did was require the State Department to report to Congress on the steps taken by the 47 European signatories of the 2009 nonbinding Terezin Declaration, which in turn had called on all the corresponding countries to take measures to "right economic wrongs" committed to Holocaust victims, Jewish or otherwise, by property restitution, where possible, or "genuinely fair and adequate" payment or property substitution. Other proposed steps included funding education that worked toward enhancing mutual understanding.[3]

The Rule of Law

Another possibly contentious issue was America's response to the PiS-imposed, messy, overnight series of controversial changes to the country's legal system, which violated its separation

---

3. On the 75th anniversary of the liberation of Auschwitz, Trump went to Jerusalem, where Putin was given voice along with the leaders of France and Great Britain and President Duda decided not to attend since he was not given the opportunity to speak. In contrast, the following week, the Polish celebrations in Auschwitz/Oświęcim itself were attended by Nancy Pelosi, who made a point of meeting with Senate majority leader, opposition's Professor Tomasz Grodzki, a target of state television's personal attack politics due to the Senate being Poland's only major national political institution not in the hands of PiS (by a margin of two votes).

of powers and made the judiciary, including the Constitutional Tribunal, subject to political influence by the ruling party (Sadurski, 2019).

First, in November 2015 President Duda pardoned four Law and Justice politicians who had not yet been found guilty, which stopped the legal procedure well underway and prevented the public from ever finding out if the politicians were in fact guilty or not.[4] A month later, he refused to appoint three judges elected by the Sejm (lower House of the Parliament). In 2016, Prime Minister Szydło refused to publish the verdict of the Constitutional Tribunal. In effect, on various occasions, the executive power represented by the Law and Justice government and the president has been exerting influence over the judiciary; most legal scholars, all major Polish university law departments, and EU institutions view this influence as breaches of the Constitution. Zbigniew Ziobro, the minister of justice, is on record publicly confirming that in his view the 2015 parliamentary victory of the Law and Justice party legitimized the executive branch's actions, resulting in exerting more political influence on nominating judges, assigning cases, and other legal system matters. During the second half of this decade, this disagreement has become a critical issue in Polish-EU relations.

The first American criticisms came from Democrats. During a New Jersey rally in support of his wife running for president, Bill Clinton delivered a sound condemnation of the early PiS government. While warning of populists like Trump, Hillary Clinton's challenger at the time, the former president criticized Poland, along with Hungary, comparing their new governments to Putin's: "Poland and Hungary, two countries that would not be free but for the United States and the long Cold War, have now decided this democracy is too much trouble. . . . They want Putin-like leadership: Just give me an authoritarian dictatorship and keep the foreigners out." Jarosław Kaczyński's prompt response was even more undiplomatic: "If someone feels that there is no democracy in Poland, they should be medically examined."

President Barack Obama was also vocal in his disapproval of the changes on his third and last visit to Poland during the final months of his presidency. On the opening day of the June 2016 NATO Summit in Warsaw, following a private meeting with President Duda, Obama publicly, and much to the surprise of his interlocutor, joined the Clintons and the EU in chiding Polish leaders, though in diplomatic terms: "I expressed to President Duda our concerns over certain actions and the impasse around Poland's constitutional tribunal. . . . I insisted that we are very respectful of Poland's sovereignty and I recognized that Parliament is working on legislation to take important steps, but more needs to be done."

In contrast, President Trump has been much more evasive. While his office expressed concern on several occasions, saying the American administration was monitoring the situation closely, the president himself avoided direct criticism: he either remained silent or provided reassurance. In fact, during the Duda visit to the White House in June 2019, where a new defense agreement was signed, Trump said: "I'm not concerned at all." Duda added in his presence to the journalist asking the question: "Someone cheated you. There is no problem with democracy in Poland, really. Everything is excellent."

Former US ambassador to Poland Stephen Mull said on the eve of the 2020 primaries: "If there is a change of government in Washington, Poland will not be "punished" for close relations with Trump. However, if the Law and Justice government undermines the rule of law, it will have a problem in relations with Washington, regardless of who wins the election" (Wirtualna Polska, 2019). However, the fact of the matter is that so far PiS does not have much problem with Trump in this area, as he is willing to pursue America's business interests at the expense of standing by international democratic standards.

---

4. Unlike American law, Polish law did not provide for an innocent person (i.e., one without a valid court verdict) to be pardoned, at least according to most interpretations and previous presidential practice.

AMERICAN BUSINESS'S HANDS-ON
APPROACH TO SECURITY AND MEDIA

In the meantime, Duda has managed to have relatively frequent and seemingly amicable personal relations with Trump, mostly business oriented, with a particular focus on military and energy security issues. According to liberal observers, both politicians get along so well because they share their nationalism and their dislike for international organizations and international ostracism. Duda has been willing to deploy psychological devices that, whether staged or authentic, appeal to Trump's ego, widely considered to be substantial, as evidenced by his habit of naming his tallest buildings after himself. Not only was Duda highly praising of Trump at his side, more informal, and less presidential (the infamous photo depicting Duda standing up at Trump's Oval Office desk while signing an agreement with the US president sitting down and looking on approvingly); but he suggested at a White House press conference that the desired American military base in Poland be named "Fort Trump." Consequently, the two countries tightened their cooperation in areas of energy and military security. Although Fort Trump predictably did not happen, Poland bought American military equipment and made a long-term commitment to buy gas, mostly to become independent from Russia. As a result, Poland was not in a position to refuse an offer to organize a Middle-Eastern conference in early 2019. Unfortunately, not only did the international diplomatic gathering target Iran but the country itself was not invited and the decision to hold the conference in Warsaw was announced by Mike Pompeo solo on Fox News rather than standing together with representatives from the Polish side.

Attesting to President Trump's desire to have a trusted representative in Poland, he replaced a professional ambassador with his close friend, a successful businesswoman and a New York socialite, Georgette Mosbacher. In late August 2018, she posted a special video saying that Poland and the United States have been friends for over 240 years and remain the closest of allies, adding that the United States is satisfied with the bilateral cooperation in the area of defense and expressing a desire to support American private investment in Poland (Wieliński, 2018).

Supporting American business in Poland did remain Ambassador Mosbacher's primary concern but she has had minor conflicts with Polish politicians over instances when she has exerted direct personal pressure on behalf of specific interests. For example, she has not shied away from lobbying personally and in writing on behalf of particular pharmaceutical companies or products. Even though the Trump-nominated ambassador was initially warmly welcomed by the governing party as a representative of its perceived strategic and ideological ally, the United States, other American business interests also soon came in conflict with Law and Justice's expansive policies and intentions, especially in the area of media freedom. Namely, several PiS deputies expressed their expectation to be able to exert a stronger influence in other formerly independent branches of power, not just the judiciary but also the media. The public broadcast media (TVP and PR), strong, longtime players in the country's media system, were immediately taken over and politicized along party lines, especially via aggressive and manipulative on-screen, framing-based, evening news propaganda, with a corresponding rationale of bringing a much-needed balance to Poland's supposedly liberal media mix; while the private media, remained out of government reach. Given a high concentration of local newspapers and magazines in the hands of German companies, the government announced a willingness to "Polonize" the media by curbing foreign investment. However, the main political media in the country are still considered to be three television stations: TVP, Polsat, and TVN, and their own specialized 24-hour news channels: TVP Info, Polsat News, TVN24 (and TVNBiŚ). With public television (TVP, TVP Info) already under political control, the remaining independent stations were Polish-owned Polsat and TVN, which was recently purchased by America's Discovery Corporation.

The ruling party's former spin doctor and deputy Adam Hoffman announced that apart from public television, "Law and Justice needs public television light," because you cannot convince all Polish people with the same message (Dąbrowska, 2018) and the new objective was to have a TV station targeting persuadable voters, not just hardcore supporters. As a result, economic pressure was exerted through state-owned companies that serve as significant revenue providers to all media through advertising. According to the official state Supreme Audit Office (NIK) report, during the first two years of the new government, between 2015 and the first half of 2017, the percentage of state companies' advertising expenses going to TVN went down from 22.3% to 1.6%, while for Polsat, it increased from 15.8% to 33.9%. At the same time, Polsat restructured its journalistic team, taking over one of TVN's anchors and softened its critique of the government starting mid-2018, which was linked to the likely prospect of its owner's other business ventures being threatened through government regulation. The station's middle-ground approach, sometimes referred to by the media as "soft propaganda" was aimed at the undecided voter who finds the public station's narrative (e.g., "The opposition is jealous of the Polish people's New Year's Eve Festivities") too crude, silly, and manipulative.

However, American-owned TVN remained the most critical TV station, and the ruling party was reported to be considering several options, mostly economic, to influence its coverage. First, it approached the station's owners with an offer to buy it out. Faced with a refusal, it imposed steep fines for supposed breaches in programming. Finally, following Ambassador Mosbacher's intervention, the Law and Justice eased its pressure, recognizing that with Trump, business trumps ideology and the American hands-off approach to the media is expected, at least in reference to privately owned American outlets.

As far as the Polish print media is concerned, the bulk of the funding coming from state companies, also in the shape of advertising revenue, previously going to center-left/liberal titles such as *Gazeta Wyborcza* daily or *Polityka* weekly, was now redirected to newer, more government-friendly, more right-wing or even populist titles, such as *Gazeta Polska*, *Sieci*, and *Do Rzeczy*; even if they foster a much lower and less business-oriented readership, their advertising support essentially constitutes a form of subsidizing the government's own ideological press by this misspending of public business funds. None of those new beneficiaries was American owned; but, coincidentally, all of them have been much more sympathetic to Donald Trump personally, his policies, and the United States as Poland's ally of preference, even—or maybe especially—at the expense of good relations with the European Union.[5]

Axiological Allies?

The axiological sphere was assumed to be shared, given both executive branches' declared conservative party ideologies. For example, during his 2017 Warsaw speech, Donald Trump devoted a good deal of attention to Poles' perceived conservatism, choosing to go back to Pope

---

5. The right-wing press was particularly enthusiastic about Brexit and framed it as evidence of the weakness of the European project, even placing personal responsibility on the shoulders of Kaczyński's nemesis—Donald Tusk—who in the years 2014–2019 served as president of the European Council and was widely expected to return to Poland to run against President Duda as the candidate of the whole opposition. However, this would have taken the country back to the main political and personal conflict behind Polish politics since 2005. Having recognized this, Donald Tusk decided not to run, which constituted a major setback for the ruling party, suddenly left without a political enemy of preference, but with war chests full of negative campaign material.

John Paul II's 1978 visit to his homeland. Rather than quote the best-known passage from Cardinal Wojtyła's speech: "Let the spirit descend and renew the face of the earth, the face of this land," which preceded the fall of Communism, he seemed intent on making that historic visit relevant to contemporary global identity-based culture wars, both in Poland and in America:

> Through four decades of communist rule, Poland and the other captive nations of Europe endured a brutal campaign to demolish freedom, your faith, your laws, your history, your identity—indeed the very essence of your culture and your humanity. Yet, through it all, you never lost that spirit [Applause]. Your oppressors tried to break you, but Poland could not be broken [Applause]. And when the day came on June 2nd, 1979, and one million Poles gathered around Victory Square for their very first mass with their Polish pope, that day, every communist in Warsaw must have known that their oppressive system would soon come crashing down [Applause]. They must have known it at the exact moment during Pope John Paul II's sermon when a million Polish men, women, and children suddenly raised their voices in a single prayer. A million Polish people did not ask for wealth. They did not ask for privilege. Instead, one million Poles sang three simple words: *"We Want God"* [Applause]. In those words, the Polish people recalled the promise of a better future. They found new courage to face down their oppressors, and they found the words to declare that Poland would be Poland once again. As I stand here today before this incredible crowd, this faithful nation, we can still hear those voices that echo through history. Their message is as true today as ever. The people of Poland, the people of America, and the people of Europe still cry out "We want God" [Applause]. Together, with Pope John Paul II, the Poles reasserted their identity as a nation devoted to God. And with that powerful declaration of who you are, you came to understand what to do and how to live. You stood in solidarity against oppression, against a lawless secret police, against a cruel and wicked system that impoverished your cities and your souls. And you won. Poland prevailed. Poland will always prevail [Applause].

Trump's conservatism was certainly visible in his domestic political policies, not so much in his personal life, which might have been an issue with his born-again voters, but they managed to reduce their cognitive dissonance by changing their expectations of him rather than withdrawing their support. Despite Trump being married three times and having paid a former porn actress to keep secret their encounter during his third wife's pregnancy, his conservative voters did not abandon him, which only speaks to the strength of political affiliations. In any case, PiS had every reason to expect the two parties to share a conservative, Christian, pro-family, anti-minority rhetoric. In reality, both sides shared an anti-immigrant rhetoric in particular. It first helped PiS win in 2015 on the wave of the European refugee crisis that never reached Poland as PiS's sentiment coincided with that of the public by criticizing how the previous government agreed to admit a small number of displaced foreigners. A year later during his presidential election, Trump repeated the maneuver with the Mexicans and the Muslims.

Thus, it did come as a bit of a surprise that the Polish government's next xenophobic rhetoric met with an American response of a lower level that seemingly questioned shared conservative values over gay rights. Namely, in the 2019 Polish election cycle, a new Polish party ran on a progressive social agenda. Presided over by the first openly gay Polish MP, Robert Biedroń, Wiosna (Spring) demanded, among other things, a clearer separation of church and state. Throughout the year, pride marches were organized all over Poland, in many towns for the first time ever. Public attitude to gay partnerships, which have not yet been institutionalized in any shape or form in Poland—making it one of the last Western countries not to do so—became a political issue, if not an election criterion. In the summer of 2019, during a pride parade in the eastern city of Białystok, known for its high levels of nationalism, heavy violence erupted. Consequently, hordes of stocky nationalists attacked and beat up marchers, many of them teenage girls and boys.

In response, the American Embassy in Warsaw put out rainbow flags, which aggravated a number of PiS MPs as "an interference in domestic issues." It is not clear to what extent Donald Trump knew of this symbolic support or approved. On the one hand, Trump did not deem this issue important, judging by the removal or absence of any pro-LGBT rhetoric from his national strategy document. By contrast, Barack Obama's National Security Strategy stated in 2015: "We will advance respect for universal values at home and around the world by . . . leading the international community to prevent and respond to human rights abuses and mass atrocities as well as gender-based violence and discrimination against LGBT persons." No such passage can be found in Trump's 2017 National Security Strategy. Indeed, Trump's approach to international relations, however difficult to decipher, is consistently not as ambitious or active as the Democrats'. Rather than being thought of as the leader of the indispensable nation, Donald Trump, like neoconservatives before him, chooses to engage internationally but only to the extent that it serves American interests, mostly economic and security. Spreading human rights values has lost its immediacy, if not rationale. Still, the American Embassy in Warsaw did send a minor symbolic sign at a crucial moment in Poland's struggle for human rights.

CONCLUSION

In the areas of domestic and foreign policy, Trump shared with Poland's ruling Law and Justice a large amount of political messaging and style. Domestic economic policy differences had to be put aside, but this has not been a problem in bilateral relations. For example, PiS-initiated cash-handout policies targeting parents, seniors, and others were in fact to the left of Obama's fiscal policies, which could have rendered them "Communist" in Trump's fighting words. Certainly, the core of the overlapping areas consisted of the my-country-first, nationalistic, anti-elite populist rhetoric. Both sides were not foreign to a somewhat crude rhetorical style, but then both were internationally ostracized and considered undignified. In a way, both parties were bound to get along, although PiS certainly needed Trump more than the other way around. In bilateral relations, Poland under PiS was willing to be more lenient and unconditional than under the previous government, an attitude that fitted well with Trump's transactional approach, which he had carried over from the world of business negotiations to that of international relations in most areas and especially in military and energy security.

As far as the Polish media coverage is concerned, this study finds—as expected—a relatively high salience of American issues, including special issues of opinion weeklies devoted to Trump. It also finds a correlation between the tone of coverage of a given medium and its domestic political leaning: the more pro-Law and Justice the medium, the more pro-Trump its coverage, especially in *(W)Sieci* and *Do Rzeczy*. In addition, it has found a high degree of salience of pro-nationalistic and anti-liberal themes in right-wing media, as well as content critical of Trump's foreign policy in liberal media (*Gazeta Wyborcza*, *Polityka*, *Newsweek Polska*, *Kultura Liberalna*). There is a high salience of positive, "brotherly" frames in right-wing media, which serve to project an enthusiastic image of both Trump and Kaczyński as genuine statesmen representing the people vs. the elites (*Sieci*, *Do Rzeczy*). Interestingly, there is a virtual absence of discussions related to economic policies, particularly social welfare policies, in most media, stemming from the active-state policies adopted by Law and Justice, which are more akin to Democrats' proposals. Finally, there is to be found an enthusiastic image of Polish-U.S. relations in right-wing media (an increase in military and energy security cooperation) and a negative image to be found in liberal and left-wing media (unpredictability of Trump's administration, his undermining of the EU, and a transition from value-based to transactional bilateral relations).

Overall, Poland's ruling conservatives and populists have made progress in their attitudes toward Trump in a way that is similar to that of America's Republicans: slowly, they have warmed up to him. Initially, the Republican Party was hostile to him and possessed an independent agenda, but gradually he and his agenda have taken over, turning it into the party of Trump. Likewise, many Polish self-declared conservatives disapproved of Trump but now see his agenda as analogous to that of Duda and Law and Justice in putting their countries first and being anti-elite.

Internationally, confidence in Trump has especially risen among representatives of the self-identified ideological right. Poland is no exception here: but it is notable in terms of its degree. As many as 61% of self-identified, right-wing respondents expressed confidence in him in 2019, up from 48% the year before (Pew Research Center, 2019). In other words, support for Law and Justice is correlated with confidence in Trump "to do the right thing in world affairs" and the difference is statistically significant. In Poland, as everywhere else, Trump gets a premium from local populists for being a populist himself.

On November 11, 2019, the 101st anniversary of Polish independence, Donald Trump announced that Poland was joining the US Visa Waiver Program as a seal of the close relations between himself and President Duda, especially in regard to their own personal influence and achievement in bringing this 30-year-long process of visa waiving to completion with the help of the ambassador's significant personal engagement—even though America's decision to include Poland is based on the percentage of US visa rejections recently falling to below 3%. In 2019, PiS won three campaigns in a row—local, European, and parliamentary. In 2020, both Donald Trump and Andrzej Duda are standing to get reelected. Will the nation-first, anti-elite agenda work for both again? The recent global virus pandemic adds another layer of complexity. In theory, it gives incumbents an edge, particularly during election time, as they have more tools at their disposals to remedy the situation. Besides, citizens tend to unite around leaders in times of national crises and outside threats anyway, unless radical incompetence transpires. Whatever the outcome, there has been a significant shift in the tone of US diplomacy toward more transactional relations, and Donald Trump's presidency has legitimized and strengthened populist tendencies worldwide.

REFERENCES

Dąbrowska, A. (2018, November 27). Polsat skręca w prawo [Polsat turns right]. *Polityka*. https://www.polityka.pl/tygodnikpolityka/kraj/1772994,1,polsat-skreca-w-prawo.read

Dołęga-Mostowicz, T. (1932). *Kariera Nikodema Dyzmy*. Tow. Wydawnicze "Rój."

Do Rzeczy. (2016, November 13). Dlaczego się go boją? [Why are they afraid of him?]. No. 46.

Kosiński, J. (1970). *Being There*. New York: Harcourt Brace Jovanovich.

Lis, T. (2016, November 13). Terapia zbiorowa [Group Therapy]. *Newsweek Polska*. https://www.newsweek.pl/tomasz-lis-terapia-dla-demokracji-felieton/x6s21n6

Pastusiak, L. (1992). *Polacy w zaraniu Stanów Zjednoczonych* [Poles at the onset of the United States of America]. Wiedza Powszechna.

Pastusiak, L. (2010). *400 lat stosunków polsko-amerykańskich (1608–2008)*, vols. 1–2. Oficyna Wydawniczo-Poligraficzna Adam.

Pew Research Center (2019). *Global Attitudes Survey.* https://www.pewresearch.org/global/wp-content/uploads/sites/2/2020/01/PG_2020.01.08_US-Image_FINAL.pdf .

Płudowski, T. (2018). *American political issue ownership and framing: A functional theory of advantage-seeking in presidential advertising from Eisenhower to Trump.* Collegium Civitas, Fulbright Polska, Aspra.

Sadurski, W. (2019). *Poland's constitutional breakdown.* Oxford University Press.

Sieci (August 24, 2019). Mężowie stanu pod ostrzałem. [Statesmen under fire].

Smoliński, J. (2004). *Polsko-amerykańskie stosunki wojskowe 1776–1945.* Bellona.

Szlajfer, H. (2009). *My naród . . . : 90 lat stosunków dyplomatycznych między Polską a USA* [We the people . . . : 90 years of Polish-US diplomatic ties]. US Embassy in Poland.

Wieliński, B. (2018, August 28) Nowa ambasador USA Georgette Mosbacher już w Warszawie. [New American ambassador already in Warsaw]. *Gazeta Wyborcza* https://wyborcza.pl/7,75399,23836208,nowa-ambasador-usa-georgette-mosbacher-juz-w-warszawie.html.

Wirtualna Polska. (2019, December 26). Były ambasador USA ostrzega: Jeśli rząd PiS będzie podważał praworządność, mogą być problemy. [Former ambassador warns: If the Law and Justice government undermines the rule of law, problems may arise]. https://wiadomosci.gazeta.pl/wiadomosci/7,114884,25546485,byly-ambasador-usa-ostrzega-jesli-rzad-pis-bedzie-podwazal.html

W Sieci (2016, November 13). Wielka zmiana—najpierw Polska, teraz USA. Co wygrana Trumpa oznacza dla nas, Europy i świata? [Great change—first Poland, now USA. What does Trump's Victory mean for us, Europe and the world?].

RUSSIA

19

The US Image and Donald Trump Through Russian Eyes

Rovinskaya Juliana, Russian State University for the Humanities
Greydina Nadezhda, Pyatigorks State University

INTRODUCTION

The purpose of this work is to describe the mediatized image of US President Donald Trump and the country he leads—the United States of America. A mediatized image is understood as a media picture of the world, formed on the basis of the implementation of a set of verbal and nonverbal means that can convey attitudes and values. The mediatized image receives a research interpretation based on content analysis and discourse analysis.

This study captures the stereotypical core of knowledge, opinions, and perceptions of Donald Trump and the United States determined by Russian quality press and television, and public opinion. As a result, an ethnic stereotype is built as the basis for the broadcast media image of the current US president.

The image of the United States and the Donald Trump factor have been the subject of various studies done by researchers and journalists. As Yelena Shestopal (2018) indicates, the image is an impression constructed purposefully and consciously. In some other studies (Greidina, 2019), the image is treated as a reflection of a leader's personality or of the state in mass or individual consciousness, but it is of specifically constructed and replicated character.

The political image, while being an aspect of the general image, is determined as a display of real characteristics of the perception object—that is, the political power of the leader's personality, on the one hand, and the projection of expectations of the perception subject, that is, citizens, on the other hand (Smirnova, 2017). Consequently, the image of political power reflects knowledge, ideas, opinions, expectations, emotions, and demands of the mass consciousness for power.

One long-term political study resulted in the development of the concept of "I-state" (Kiseleva, 2018, p. 8). According to this concept, the image of the state corresponds to the unity of three components: identification of the political leader of the nation with common values, awareness of the status of the country, and understanding the role that the country plays in the international arena. The institutionalization of the country image is reproduced in the approval of various doctrines and foreign policy concepts when the image becomes an information filter.

In studying the influence of the media on the perceptions of countries, the concept of the media image was introduced (Bogdan, 2017). It refers to the media-transformed representations of a country and its leader, created to control the audience in order to change the perception of the country.

Currently, relations between Russia and the United States are in a rather challenging time. But everyone in Russia is asking about the prospects for bilateral cooperation, which determines human well-being and world peace in many ways. Established in 1809, diplomatic relations between the countries are going through some difficulties at present. There have been different periods in the relationship between the countries in the past—from the willingness of Russia and the United States to cooperate to mutual disappointments and gradual distancing from each other. In the current circumstances, the political dialogue between the leaders of Russia and the United States is of particular importance. The relationship between the Russian leader Vladimir Putin and the US leader Donald Trump is the hallmark of Russia-US ties.

THE US IMAGE IN RUSSIANS' PERCEPTION

The US image in Russians' perception consists of different dimensions: national symbols, geographic, cultural, ethnic, political, economic, and other peculiarities. In this paper the US image is treated by different social layers of the Russian society and analyzed by both representatives of the political elite and ordinary people who having nothing to do with professional politics.

The issue of American democracy is frequently touched upon by the Russian political elite. Russian politicians (Zhirinovsky, Mironov, Kosachev) have often doubted the use of democratic principles when the candidate with the highest number of votes is not elected for the post of president of the United States. It has been noticed that no serious steps have been taken in that direction, though the reform of the electoral college system is discussed at every presidential election. In this regard, Vladimir Putin expressed the following idea about the US political system published in *Komsomolskaya Pravda*:[1]

> Do you think that there are democratic presidential elections in the US? Look. Twice in the history of the United States, the President was elected by a majority of electors, and those electors were represented by fewer voters. Is this a democracy? (Kotsur, 2016, p. 3)

The views of Vasily Likhachev, who oversaw international issues at the Central Election Commission of Russia, criticizing American election legislation that did not meet international standards, were reflected in *Izvestia*:[2]

> There are carousels voting [a type of vote rigging in elections, consisting in the circular movement made by the voters who are transported from one polling station to the next to cast multiple

---

1. *Komsomolskaya Pravda* is a Russian sociopolitical daily newspaper established in March 1925 as an official print body of the All-Union Leninist Young Communist League, usually known as *Komsomol*.

2. *Izvestia* is a Russian sociopolitical and business daily newspaper established in January 1917 (during the Soviet era, it was the official organ of the governing bodies of the Soviet government). In February 2005, the *New York Times* selected *Izvestia* as a partner for publishing the *New York Times* in the *Izvestia* supplement in Russia.

votes—auth. comm] in the US, there are restrictions on detainees voting in the US, and there is no control over the compilation of a single national list of voters in the US. Only three states provide for international surveillance, whereas in Russia this is a norm of Federal Law and is taken into account at the regional level. Seven hundred and seventy-four foreign observers from 63 countries came to Russia for the previous election. (Likhachev, 2016, p. 4)

The American election procedure itself was also analyzed by the Russian politicians. The head of the Central Election Commission of Russia Ella Pamfilova drew attention to a number of distinctive features of American elections, "What would be an off-scale abuse of administrative resources in our view, the United States treat it as normal" (Toropov, 2016, p. 3).

The same article reflected Ella Pamfilova's views on a number of electoral procedures (Toropov, 2016). The politician considered it unacceptable for the US president to campaign for a candidate from his party during working hours. It was also considered illegal to offer the only possibility of monitoring the American elections—within the OSCE ODIHR (Office for democratic institutions and human rights).

Some articles reproduce the most extreme, sometimes absurd, points of view that are accepted by Russian politicians. The deputy of the State Duma Alexey Zhuravlev linked the abnormally warm winter in Russia in 2020 with the use of climate weapons of the United States (Treskova 2020). Dmitry Stefanovich, an expert on the Russian Council on International Affairs, and Roman Vilfand, scientific director of the Russian Hydrometeorological Center, denied that possibility and warned that such statements should be taken with irony (Treskova, 2020). The leading specialist of the Weather Center "Phobos," Eugene Tishkovets, reminded that in 2019 the United States had suffered the largest losses, up to $12.5 billion from weather phenomena (Treskova, 2020).

No less curious were the cases when the coronavirus was interpreted conspiratorially. That point of view was expressed on *Channel One*[3] when etymological theory was used as an argumentative concept of the reasons for the appearance of the coronavirus (Vernitsky, 2020). It was explained that the name "coronavirus" came from two words: *corona* (meaning "crown" in the Russian language) and *virus*. They asked what Donald Trump, the resident of the country that was China's main rival on the world stage, did before becoming US president. The answer pointed to the fact that Trump was handing out crowns at a famous world beauty pageant. So, the origin of the coronavirus was clear.

We also analyzed the US image perceived by ordinary Russian people and found unprecedented interest in the 2016 presidential election campaign. The reasons for it were related to election excitement and intrigue until the last moment (Ishchenko, 2016).

In this regard, the results of the public opinion polls were the most obvious examples. In the poll conducted by *VTSIOM*[4] on October 21, 2016, and published in *Kommersant*[5] (Dupin, 2016, p. 4), there were Russians aged 18 and over who participated in the surveys. On average, for the given information the maximum size of the statistical error (i.e., the deviation of the measured value from its true—actual—value) with a probability of 95% did not exceed 2.5%. The poll showed that Russians were more interested in the US presidential

---

3. Channel One is a Russian TV company, positioned as the main Russian TV channel, and a member of the European Broadcasting Union.

4. VTSIOM (All-Russian Center for Public Opinion Research) is the oldest Russian research organization that regularly conducts sociological and marketing research based on public opinion polls; one of the largest Russian companies in this market, established in 1987, in which 100% of the company's shares are owned by the state.

5. *Kommersant* is a Russian daily sociopolitical newspaper established in December 1989. Based on the results of the leading media monitoring company "TNS Media Intelligence" report, *Kommersant*, along with three other Russian newspapers, was recognized as a key source of business and political news in the Russian information space.

election which took place on November 8, 2016, than in the elections to the State Duma of the Russian Federation held in September 2016. Approximately one-third of the respondents claimed that a victory for the Republican candidate Donald Trump would be useful for Russia (Dupin, 2016). The study presented the range of the data (Dupin, 2016, p. 4). The number of Russians interested in the American elections reached 53%. At the same time, 41% of the respondents admitted that they were only interested in the presidential campaign from time to time, while 12% of the respondents were constantly following it, and another 46% did not follow it at all. More than half of the respondents (57%) believed that the outcome of the US vote was important to Russia; 39% of those who believed that the outcome of the election was important were confident that relations between the United States and Russia would improve if Donald Trump won. Another 35% of the Russians considered that Trump's victory was "more in line with Russia's national interests" (Dupin, 2016, p. 4) (only 6% held this opinion about Hillary Clinton). At the same time, even those who believed that the outcome of the US election was not important to Russia would not like to see Hillary Clinton as president: 34% of them believed that relations between the two countries would deteriorate if she won (Dupin, 2016).

As for the image of the United States among Russians, it was not attractive (Dupin, 2016)—the country was aggressive and interfering in other people's affairs. The majority of Russians believed that the United States "interferes in the affairs of other states" (86%) and "behaves aggressively" (76%) (Dupin, 2016, p. 4). Fewer Russians considered that the United States was "trustworthy" (13%), "open to the world" (26%), and "democratic" (37%) (Dupin, 2016, p. 4). As far as positive aspects were concerned, a significant percentage of respondents actually admitted that the United States had "the most modern science and technology" (73%), that it was "influential" (66%), had a "high standard of living" (57%) (Dupin, 2016, p. 4). The polls by *the Levada Center*[6] and *the Analytical Center "LIK PRO"*[7] showed a similar situation (Dupin, 2016).

THE IMAGE OF DONALD TRUMP IN RUSSIANS' PERCEPTION

The first mentioning of Donald Trump as president of the United States in the Russian press appeared in the Russian News Agency TASS[8] on November 9, 2016, immediately after the announcement of the results of the presidential election. The information was released based on exit polls and preliminary vote counts submitted by a number of local media outlets.

The first official Russian press analytical article about Donald Trump appeared in *Izvestia* on November 10, 2016 (Firsov, 2016), a day after the victory of the Republican Party representative (who received 306 electoral votes—56.88%) for the US presidency over the Democratic candidate Hillary Clinton. In this article, Alexey Firsov analyzed the reasons for the victory of Donald Trump, who was not taken seriously at first, even by his own party, against whom the entire US political machine really worked, who was subjected to the expected accusation of populism, and whose chances in the American presidential election seemed minimal.

---

6. The Levada Center is one of the largest nongovernmental research organizations in Russia that regularly conducts its own and commissioned sociological and marketing research. The Center partners and customers are international institutions, Russian and foreign companies, research, educational and non-profit organizations. In 2016, the Center was awarded the status of a "foreign agent."

7. The Analytical Center "LIK PRO" is the Russian Information Consulting Laboratory.

8. Russian News Agency TASS is the largest news agency in Russia (founded in 1904, registered as a Federal State Unitary Enterprise, owned by the Government of Russia, with its 68 bureaus around the world).

According to Firsov, the reasons for Donald Trump's victory in the 2016 presidential election included the following:

- growth of right-wing movements in Europe,
- failure of the Republican primaries and the Democratic primaries,
- need for a radical change in the situation in the country,
- mass need for a counter-elite in the American society,
- dissatisfaction of the white population of the United States,
- mistakes of sociologists who predicted Hillary Clinton's victory,
- the decline of media influence in American society.

The journalist Andrey Ontikov (2018) considered the phenomenon of Donald Trump to be based on the contradictions in his image (a rebel, political bully, on the one hand, a man of business, natural leader, on the other hand).

The image of Donald Trump was also interpreted through the eyes of Russian politicians and researchers as well as of ordinary people. At the height of the presidential race in the United States, Vladimir Putin described Donald Trump as "a very bright and talented man" (Firsov, 2016, p. 3). But half a year after the 2016 US elections, Vladimir Putin answering questions from American film director Oliver Stone for his film *The Putin Interviews*, which aired on Channel One on June 19, 2017, in the midst of an unprecedented hysteria around Moscow's alleged interference in the US election, gave some indirect opinions about Donald Trump: "Presidents in the USA change, but politics does not" (Stone, 2017).

Vladimir Zhirinovsky, the leader of the Liberal Democratic Party of Russia, compared the victory of Donald Trump to a holiday: "The victory of Donald Trump will be a holiday for Trump, for America, and for the whole world" (Makarychev, 2016, p. 3). These ideas were published in *Rossiyskaya Gazeta*.[9]

Senator Aleksey Pushkov also commented on the victory of Donald Trump: "Trump was an out-of-system candidate, challenged the traditional ruling elite and presented a disaffected and even outraged America with the omnipotence of the traditional establishment" (Zabrodin, 2016, p. 4).

The Russian media (Baikova, 2017) analyzed the efficiency of the candidates' presidential campaigns. Donald Trump was such a strong candidate that he managed to impose his own style and methods of political struggle on his rivals. As a comparison, his main opponent— Hillary Clinton—was forced to copy his methods of working with the electorate and even political rhetoric. It was Trump who first struck Americans with his statement that he would not fight with Russia, but would make friends with this country.

There were some witty comparisons of Trump's image—a businessman and a politician (Manoilo, 2016), which is why Trump's thoughts, plans, and behavior are viewed not only through a political lens, but a business one as well. Correspondingly, Trump treated politics as a project activity: for him, the presidential election was nothing more than another business project. One of the articles (Galanina, 2017) reflected metaphorically upon the consequences of the dual character image of Trump: if the United States seemed hopeless in terms of restoring statehood, Trump would deal with it the same way as in business with unprofitable projects, divide and sell it off in parts.

---

9. *Rossiyskaya Gazeta* is a Russian official government daily newspaper, publishing government-related affairs such as official decrees, statements, documents, and announcements of the state bodies; established in 1990.

Some political scientists, such as Rostislav Ishchenko (2016), characterized Trump as a non-standard personality and a complicated negotiating partner, predicting the complexity of the inter-American political and financial-economic situation, coupled with the need to defend US interests in vital regions (Europe, the Middle East, South-East Asia, Latin America), which would require unconventional solutions and unexpected moves from America.

The Russian journalists Alexey Zabrodin and Angelina Galanina (2017) stated that ordinary Russians liked Trump immediately because he was very different from the vast majority of American politicians and assured that he would get along with Moscow and negotiate with Vladimir Putin.

Trump's popularity in Russia was also reflected in various quizzes and tests about the American politician. Some of the questions dealt with Trump's favorite sport, the school where Trump studied, and the name of a beauty pageant Trump owned.

Over time the attitude of the Russians toward Donald Trump became worse (Pushkov, 2019). More than a third of Russians (37%) began to assume that Donald Trump's actions aggravated relations between Russia and the United States. Only about one in ten (8%) Russians suggested that Donald Trump sought to improve relations between the countries—according to the materials of the VTSIOM survey (Pushkov, 2019, p. 6). The polls increasingly showed a negative perception of the American leader: 43% of Russians—indifference, 23%—distrust, 12%—antipathy, 12%—skepticism, 10%—disappointment (Pushkov, 2019, p. 6).

The common idea of the articles and videos studied was that it would be neither boring nor easy to deal with the new US president. However, Russia's dealings with the United States have never been easy with any American president.

TRUMP AND THE RUSSIAN LANGUAGE

Russian journalists noted an interesting phenomenon: the word "trumpism" had appeared. Its meaning varied depending on the political preferences of the addresser. In the case of a pro-Western orientation, it meant a new American system based on isolationism, greater populism, risk, unpredictability, uncertainty in domestic and foreign policy, and Washington's friendship with Vladimir Putin which led to weakening NATO and cold relations with the European Union. In the case of pro-Russian leanings, this concept covered the policy and ideology of the current US president based on mixing elements of Jacksonianism (after President Andrew Jackson) and neoconservatism: the first notion reflected the elements of protectionism in the economy as well as pragmatism and selfishness in international affairs; the second notion reproduced the slogan "America First," calling for the return of the conservative Goldwater-Reagan model and a change of course from a democratic world to a multipolar world. It meant not only the return of national interests, but also a significant blow to the supranational factor.

International journalist Mikhail Taratuta (2019) explained why trumpism, with all its chaos and shortcomings, was popular in the United States. First, Trump was the only politician with whom many voters associated the urgent need for change. Second, Trump remained the most consistent of all American presidents in almost all of his promises. Third, the economy as a business card of Donald Trump was an objective thing, the success of which was felt by Americans.

In the Russian humorous context, there appeared a lot of jokes and parodies about the guile of Trump's election campaign in 2016 and his presidential term. It is important to note that parody in Russian national cultural is an indicator of a warm and friendly relationship.

For example, on the television channel Russia-1[10] a typical Russian joke has Trump saying, "I have always promised to improve relations with Russia, and I do not deny my words, never, no. Only my actions, not my words" (Shirokov, 2018). Another has Trump remarking, "I was spending much time thinking where to go for the New Year: Miami, Hawaii, and the Maldives. Where am I now? [everyone shouts, "Russia!"] Oops, it seems Russia again has influenced the American choice!" (Shirokov, 2017).

VERBAL BEHAVIOR OF DONALD TRUMP AS IMAGE CONSTITUENT

A whole layer of publications and media analytics has been devoted to the rhetoric of Donald Trump, including both the form (intonation of speeches, types of words used, stylistic means) and the content (logic and thematic focus of speeches). Since not only information, but also meanings are transmitted through communication, political rhetoric analysts and researchers are interested in Trump's public speech. A number of Russian journalists called Donald Trump a master of classical rhetoric (Koretskaya, 2017).

In general, researchers and journalists have noted that Trump is one of those politicians who can captivate the audience. They emphasize the advantages of Trump speeches: he does not use prompters, arranges a small show, and leads a casual conversation with the audience—supporters or opponents.

Russian researchers (Koretskaya, 2017; Novikova, Esmurzaeva, Marus, & Shkaiderova, 2017) in the field of political rhetoric noted the rhetorical figures actively used by Donald Trump in his public speeches. One of these rhetorical figures was hyperbole, which the US president called "true exaggeration" (Koretskaya, 2017, p. 352). According to the researcher, that was an obvious oxymoron, since by its definition, hyperbole is an untrue exaggeration. Trump used hyperbole when speaking about building a wall between the US and Mexico, eradicating radical Islamic terrorism, and global warming. One of the researchers (Koretskaya, 2017, p. 352) illustrated that the wall was hyperbolically called "great" by analogy with the Great Wall of China, Islamic terrorism had to be "completely wiped off the face of the Earth," and global warming "was invented by the Chinese and for the Chinese." Some other figures of speech used by Trump were the combination of parceling with syntactic repetition ("I always win. . . . I win. . . . I win") (Koretskaya, 2017, p. 352), syntactic parallelism ("They're bringing drugs. They're bringing crime") (Koretskaya, 2017, p. 352), the antithesis ("We're not talking about . . . we're talking about . . .") (Koretskaya, 2017, p. 352).

Not of less interest to the researchers (Novikova et al., 2017) was the rhythm of Trump's speeches: one-beat and two-beat rhythmic groups prevailed, which gave the statements a sharp and abrupt character and made the impression of determination, irrevocability, courage, energy, and effectiveness.

Another rhetorical device characteristic of Trump was aposiopesis, or default. Its use in Trump's speeches meant emphasizing what the speaker wanted to hide. The researcher (Koretskaya, 2017, p. 353) gave an example: "I refuse to call Megyn Kelly a bimbo because that would not be politically correct" (the phrase "refuse to call" indicated, on the one hand, the speaker's refusal to criticize, on the other hand, calling a spade a spade).

---

10. Russia-1 is an all-Russian public state TV channel owned by the all-Russian State Television and Radio Broadcasting Company.

Trump's lexicon was of importance as well. The researchers (Novikova et al., 2017, p. 132) found that Trump's speeches were addressed primarily to his middle-class voters: a large amount of informal-style vocabulary ("I want," "okay"), with word shortening (for example, word clipping: "congrats" instead of "congratulations"). The computer program used by them calculated the number of one-syllable, two-syllable, and three-syllable words in Trump's speeches. As it turned out, one-syllable words were dominant—79%, two-syllable words—18%, three-syllable words—3% (Novikova et al., 2017, p. 134). The authors concluded that the recipients of Trump's speeches were fifth-graders (in contrast to Barack Obama and Bill Clinton whose speeches corresponded to the vocabulary of seventh-graders or eighth-graders). There was a witty remark of the researchers (Novikova et al., 2017, p. 134) that out of 3% of three-syllable words, the word "America" became the most frequent one in Trump's speeches, but that word was unavoidable.

NONVERBAL BEHAVIOR OF DONALD TRUMP AS IMAGE CONSTITUENT

Some political analysts and political psychologists (Idzikovsky, 2017) interpreted the non-verbal aspects (facial expressions, gestures, etc.) of Donald Trump's behavior and made some comments about it for the website of *Zvezda* TV channel.[11]

According to Yevgeniy Idzikovsky (2017), at the nonverbal level, the fact that Trump tapped Putin on the elbow indicated his human sympathy for the Russian president. In general, a handshake could be described as a manifestation of positive relations. Thus, Trump was experiencing or demonstrating an obvious sympathy.

The nonverbal analysis done by Roman Golovanov (2017) stated the fact that Trump was the first to offer his hand, with the palm up. That could be evaluated as a gesture of openness, and as the role of the petitioner. Trump's speech partner reacted with some irony.

There was a professional interpretation of Trump's handshake made with Putin on the eve of the G20 Summit in Hamburg (Pototsky, 2017). The observation showed that the handshake was of a formal nature. It was noteworthy that Trump's palm was lower and Putin won the handshake.

Along with this, the research (Maslov, 2017) reflected that Donald Trump held his hands between his knees, they were directed downward, his index fingers and thumbs were folded so that they resembled a vagina. The interpretation demonstrated a subconscious level understanding of the situation: Trump showed the world that he could not resist Putin. The conclusion of the research explicated that Putin dominated over Trump regardless of the consent of the latter.

The researcher (Maslov, 2017) drew attention to some other elements of the nonverbal communication of the two presidents. In particular, when greeting, Donald Trump tried to pull the hand of the Russian president sharply, but his typical attempt to demonstrate force only caused Putin to smile. Slowing down the videotape, it was easy to see that the experienced judoka Vladimir Putin immediately reacted—an extra step compensated for the jerk of Trump's hand. Such a greeting might throw one off balance, but not the Russian leader, who was well aware of Trump's mannerisms.

---

11. Zvezda TV channel is an all-Russian state federal socio-patriotic TV channel owned by the Zvezda media group, which is overseen by the Ministry of Defense of the Russian Federation.

The general conclusion based on Trump's nonverbal communication was as follows: "Trump wants to become for America what Putin has become for Russia. The American leader is trying to understand how the head of Russia managed to achieve stability in his country" (Maslov, 2017, p. 3).

THE US PRESIDENT AND AMERICAN MEDIA

The Russian quality papers and special political television programs reported that in American media after the inauguration, liberal reporters vied with each other to comment on Trump's remarks as completely unprecedented, presenting his attacks as a threat to free speech and American democracy. The focus of the Russian media was the tone of American media toward Trump: harsh statements about the guarantor of the American Constitution who was called a "hater" and a "threat to national security" (Bolotnitskiy, 2018, p. 16).

The Russian media showed that the US liberal media had become a weapon in the hands of the system. The goal of the information war against Trump was to introduce a negative attitude about people's lives under the elected president.

Russian journalists recognized the victory of Trump in the battle with the American media. First, Trump won the election. Second, he demonstrated that the importance of influencing the minds of the "fourth estate" was much exaggerated. In this regard, Trump could mock the media with impunity, and in general, facts did not affect his ratings in any way.

The Russian media concluded that the American press and television began to fight not with Donald Trump as they tried to show, but for their own survival (Bolotnitskiy, 2018). It is doubtful whether the American media will be able to maintain its position in society after defiantly sacrificing standards in the name of a corporate interests, personal hostility, or political views. After all, the longer and more fiercely the US media attacked Trump, referring to its professional duty to hold the administration accountable, the more obvious its bias looked. One could see a drop in the circulation of publications and the ratings of TV channels that had attacked the American president. The former greatness of the traditional American media is a thing of the past, and the media itself has had a hand in it.

METHOD

This research is based on qualitative methods: content and discourse analyses of the Russian media reflecting official press commentaries, television programs, and opinion surveys covering common views of ordinary people contrasted to the opinions of the Russian politicians, journalists, and researchers.

Using a search algorithm, any article or video with a headline or major content having the word "Trump" and "the US" became parts of the research. A ciphering procedure included the process of coding each article (or video) for the paper (or television channel), topic, year and month of issue, the length of the article in paragraphs or video in minutes, the rating of *approval*, *disapproval*, and *mixed* (both *approval* and *disapproval*) of Donald Trump and the United States. Two coders coded each article or video. When there were contradictions between the two coders, the third coder chose one of the two first codes.

FINDINGS

The information published in the Russian quality papers (*Izvestia, Rossiyskaya Gazeta, Komsomolskaya Pravda,* and *Kommersant*), presented in some leading Russian News Agencies (TASS, Rossiya Segodnya), and reflected on three of Russia's highest-rated television channels (Channel One, Russia 1, Zvezda) was examined for a period of three and a half years (September 2016 to February 2020).

The total number of the articles analyzed was 635. The length of the articles was 15 paragraphs (28% out of the total number), 10–15 paragraphs (32%), 6–10 paragraphs (36%), up to 6 paragraphs (4%). Consequently, the issues dealing with Donald Trump and the United States were considerably long, representing heavy press coverage.

The total number of the videos interpreted was 479. The length of the videos was 80 minutes (16% out of the total number), 40–60 minutes (38%), 20–40 minutes (26%), up to 20 minutes (20%). In this regard, the points analyzing Donald Trump and the United States were numerous and corresponded to the importance of the problem.

The years and months of the heaviest coverage in the Russian press (three publications a day in every above-mentioned newspaper) and television (four programs a day on every above-mentioned channel) were November 2016 and January 2017. This period coincided with the election of the US president and inauguration of Donald Trump as the 45th president of the United States. December 2016 was the period that lay below, but still was very high in the press (three publications a day) and video coverage (two programs a day) of the issues studied. This span reflected the punitive measures imposed on Russia for the alleged interference of President Putin into the US presidential election.

Out of all the paper articles 96% interpreted Trump's verbal behavior and the means of communication while 4% of press materials treated Trump's nonverbal parameters.

Trump's rhetoric was built on comprehensible words and simple logical structures, and his verbal image as a clear-cut and convincing politician was based on the simplicity of his thoughts and speeches.

Donald Trump's personality was presented in a humorous way in 1.8% out of all the publications and videos.

The Russian ethnic stereotype of the image of Donald Trump and the United States was demonstrated by the combination of *approval* (see Table 19.1), *disapproval* (See Table 19.2), and *mixed* (both approval and disapproval) (See Table 19.3) ratings of Russian media coverage. The topics discussed were given in descending order, depending upon the main criterion (*approval, disapproval,* or *mixed* character of Russian media coverage).

From a qualitative standpoint, this study found a high degree of association between the topic of media coverage and the tone (approval, disapproval, and mixed) toward the United States and Donald Trump: $\chi^2 = 21.59$, $p < .09$ for approval; $\chi^2 = 19.68$, $p < .08$ for disapproval; $\chi^2 = 23.78$, $p < .10$ for mixed character.

The articles and videos reflecting the prospects for the development of Russian-American relations were positive at the beginning of Trump's presidency and negative by the end of his presidential term. That was reflected in the mixed character of information materials analyzed. The issues covering the US relations with the EU were also treated dually: positively (at the beginning of Trump's term when the EU theme took a back seat for the American president) and negatively (when Trump outlined the need to increase the defense spending of European NATO member countries in the face of Russia's unfriendly behavior). The next issue of mixed nature was relations with Ukraine. It was interpreted positively when Trump came to power

Table 19.1. Topics (of Approval Character) in the US and Trump Coverage by the Russian Media

Topics	Izvestia (%)	Rossiyskaya Gazeta (%)	Komsomolskaya Pravda (%)	Kommersant (%)	Channel 1 (%)	Russia 1 (%)	Zvezda (%)	Total (%)
Trump's personal image	16	23	28	26	14	12	8	127
US economic policy	12	16	8	18	8	6	7	75
Trump family	6	15	26	9	4	2	3	65

Table 19.2. Topics (of Disapproval Character) in the US and Trump Coverage by the Russian Media

Topics	Izvestia (%)	Rossiyskaya Gazeta (%)	Komsomolskaya Pravda (%)	Kommersant (%)	Channel 1 (%)	Russia 1 (%)	Zvezda (%)	Total (%)
Russian collusion	29	32	21	16	36	34	28	196
Special counsel investigation of Russian interference in the 2016 US elections	28	26	12	22	32	36	27	183
Impeachment	28	29	14	16	23	21	18	149
Relations with Syria	26	27	9	14	24	21	26	147
Media's war on Trump	26	24	18	23	16	14	11	132
Relations with Iran	24	18	8	16	23	19	23	131
Foreign policy	16	18	6	12	26	28	24	130
Sexual misconduct	4	2	12	8	19	24	14	83
Racial views	6	14	8	12	9	8	4	61
Presence on social media	8	4	16	14	6	7	3	58

Table 19.3. Topics (of Mixed Character) in the US and Trump Coverage by the Russian Media

Topics	Izvestia (%)	Rossiyskaya Gazeta (%)	Komsomolskaya Pravda (%)	Kommersant (%)	Channel 1 (%)	Russia 1 (%)	Zvezda (%)	Total (%)
Relations with Russia	28	23	21	24	38	36	32	202
Relations with Ukraine	24	26	21	23	36	32	31	193
Relations with the EU	12	14	8	9	18	14	17	92
Immigration policy	14	12	6	16	9	8	6	71

and aimed his foreign policy at minimizing participation in international affairs. Then the tone changed to a negative one when Trump focused his attention on the fact that the money he had saved on NATO would go to support Ukraine. The point of immigration policy was considered differently by the Russian media—positively at the beginning of Trump's presidency as he limited the influx of refugees, took tough measures against illegal immigrants; negatively by the end of Trump's presidential term when there was a rejection of international agreements on refugees and migration, commitments, and, as a result, a reduction in the amount of refugees and refusal to participate in the International conference aimed at setting up an international legal framework for ensuring safe and regular migration.

CONCLUSION

The study of the coverage of Donald Trump and the United States in Russia shows that the Russian media treat the United States and President Donald Trump as important players in the world political arena. At the same time, President Trump is differentiated from the rest of the government, mainly for the reason of his unusual nature, views, opinions, and actions.

It should be mentioned that in recent years, the relations between Russia and the United States, which are a system-forming factor in ensuring global security and stability, have seriously deteriorated due to different approaches to resolving a number of international problems. At the present stage, the Trump administration continues the course initiated by the previous president on "systemic containment" of Russia taking steps to destroy the foundation of interaction.

President Donald Trump has repeatedly stated his desire to return the Russian-American dialogue to a more stable state. However, in practice, Washington continues its confrontational line using economic, military-political propaganda, and other tools against Russia. At the end of 2019, 288 Russian citizens and 485 legal entities were subject to various American restrictions. The atmosphere of the relations is negatively affected by the domestic political situation in the United States. Its component was the use of Russophobia in the inter-party struggle and the spread of baseless insinuations about the so-called Russian interference in American elections. The Russian side is taking the necessary measures, both mirror and asymmetric, to protect national interests in connection with Washington's unfriendly actions. At the same time, Russia does not close the possibility of normalizing relations if the United States actually shows its readiness for equal and mutually beneficial cooperation.

Despite the difficulties in interstate relations, the positive dynamics of Russian-American contacts, including trade, is being recorded. For example, the official website of the Russian Ministry of Foreign Affairs (www.mid.ru) indicates that Russia considers it important to develop a wide range of bilateral social and humanitarian contacts that contribute to strengthening mutual understanding between the peoples. One of the most promising topics in this context that arouses an interested response from Russians and Americans is the common history and cultural and historical heritage, including the preservation of the memory of Russian America and our allied relations during the World War II.

The political forecast, including the presidential election, for 2020 in the USA, is hard to make. No matter how the candidates are treated and how negative they are about Russia in this context, the outcome of the confrontation between the Republicans and the Democrats will undoubtedly affect the world agenda. But we will most likely feel this only by 2021. In any election outcome, the significance of the Russian theme in the domestic American political realities will decrease slightly. Partly because the relationship between the countries at the present stage is probably the worst.

REFERENCES

Baikova, T. S. (2017, January 20). The day of changes. *Izvestia*, 2993, p. 3.

Bogdan, Y. N. (2017). *Media image of Russia as consolidation society means: Structural and functional characteristics*. Slovo.

Bolotnitskiy, A. S. (2018). *American mass media*. Nauka.

Dupin, S. T. (2016, October 21). Russians are interested in the US election. *Kommersant*, 2639, p. 4.

Firsov, A. K. (2016, November 10). Springboard to a new world. *Izvestia*, 2932, p. 3.

Galanina, A. T. (2017, April 7). Neither intriguing nor boring. *Izvestia*, 3068, p. 4.

Golovanov, R. P. (2017, July 7). What Putin and Trump say through their gesture language. *Komsomolskaya Pravda*, 6389, p. 2.

Greidina, N. L. (2019). Conflict and fake information in American political discourse. *Modern Communication Studies, 6*, 28–34.

Idzikovsky, Y. P. (2017). *Nonverbal behaviour of political leaders*. Moscow: Russkaya rech.

Ishchenko, R. K. (2016, November 10). Trump has broken the system. *Izvestia*, 2932, p. 3.

Kiseleva, S. P. (2018). *Image of the country: Ideas and concepts*. Logos.

Koretskaya, O. V. (2017). Linguistic specificity of Donald Trump's political rhetoric. *Professor of XXI Century*, 349–355.

Kotsur, V. S. (2016, June 16). Putin won the CNN reporter. *Komsomolskaya Pravda*, p. 3.

Likhachev, V. K. (2016, November 10). US election system. *Izvestia*, 2932, p. 4.

Makarychev, M. A. (2016, December 9). More opportunities. *Rossiyskaya Gazeta*, 2678, p. 3.

Manoilo, A. V. (2016, May 31). Effects of the Trump victory. *Izvestia*, 3124, p. 7.

Maslov, V. I. (2017, July 8). Did Trump surrender? *Rossiyskaya Gazeta*, 2887, p. 3.

Novikova, Y. V., Esmurzaeva, Zh. B., Marus, M. L., & Shkaiderova, T. V. (2017). Donald Trump's media image in German media texts. *Philological Sciences: Issues of Theory and Practice, 5*(1), 130–135.

Ontikov A. K. (2018, November 30). Seven tweets within a week. *Izvestia*, 2952, p. 3.

Pototsky, F. T. (2017, July 8). Hands speak. *Izvestia*, 3159, p. 3.

Pushkov, A. K. (2019, January 26). World leader. *Izvestia*, 3008, p. 6.

Shestopal, Y. B. (2018). *Images of the states, nations, and leaders*. Flinta.

Shirokov, S. T. (Director). (2017, December 31). *New Year Parade of Stars '17* [Musical film]. Russia: Russia-1. Retrieved from https://www.youtube.com/watch?v=9jfEMW-cHvM

Shirokov, S. T. (Director). (2018, December 31). *New Year Parade of Stars '18* [Musical film]. Russia: Russia-1. Retrieved from https://www.youtube.com/watch?v=_OofThtR0_Q

Smirnova, A. G. (2017). *Image of the state and factors in making foreign policy decisions*. Slovo.

Stone, O. W. (Director). (2017, June 19). *The Putin Interviews* [Documentary film]. USA: Channel 1. Retrieved from https://www.yandex.ru/video/preview/?filmId=4416976402060537805

Taratuta, M. K. (2019). *America and Trump*. Moscow: Progress.

Toropov, K. S. (2016, November 10). Election in Russian and the US. *Izvestia*, 2932, p. 3.

Treskova, P. F. (2020, January 14). Warm winter in Russia and the US climate weapons. *Komsomolskaya Pravda*, 6817, p. 4.

Vernitsky, A. V. (2020, March 3). *Face of coronavirus and the US*. Retrieved from https://www.youtube.com/watch?v=V9jmyrqmTTM

Zabrodin, A. S. (2016, November 10). Trump phenomenon. *Izvestia*, 2932, p. 4.

Zabrodin, A. S., & Galanina, A. T. (2017, January 23). Russia is looking forward to the US news. *Izvestia*, 3005. p. 6.

TURKEY

20

Long Time Allies No More?

How News Media in Turkey Covered the United States in 2019

Banu Akdenizli, Northwestern University, Qatar
Burak Özçetin, Istanbul Bilgi University
Nazlı Çetin Gündoğdu, Yeditepe University, Istanbul

INTRODUCTION

The relations between countries have never been more volatile and slippery than they are today. In an age of insecurity, the persistent global economic, political, military, and environmental crises make international actors prone to shifting and reassessing their alliances and strategic partnerships on a constant basis. The relations and alliances between nations are now determined by a myriad of variables that are hard to evaluate. Even alliances with deep-rooted histories are being tested in this dynamic environment. The relations between Turkey and the United States are no exception.

Since the end of the Second World War Turkey has been an important geopolitical partner for the United States (Atmaca, 2014). However, in the last two decades, the alliance between the two countries has gained new dimensions. The USA's "War on Terror" and determination to control the region; Turkey's ambitious foreign policy shift to become a regional power; the political turmoil and civil war in Syria and the United States' alliance with the Kurdish forces in the region; Russia's alliance with Syrian regime forces; Iran's nuclear deal framework; and, last but not least, Fethullah Gülen's sheltering in the United States have been the elements of an equation with multiple variables. However, we must note that covering these points is beyond the aims and scope of this study. Our contribution aims at analyzing the way the United States and Donald Trump were framed and evaluated by the Turkish press throughout 2019. Our study is based on a thorough and systematic analysis of news items from six national newspapers that represent the political, ideological, and structural diversity of the Turkish press.

In our analysis, we sought answers to the following questions regarding the US coverage in the Turkish press: (1) What were the major storylines or big stories in the news? (2) How was the storyline developed? (3) What was the story informing the readers about? (4) What was the tone of coverage—positive, negative, or neutral? and (5) Did the news sources analyzed differ in their coverage of US-related news?

In the following sections, this chapter will offer some brief historical information of Turkey-US relations, together with some theoretical underpinnings of the study. After a brief note on methods, we will present the main findings of our research. Our study will argue that the newspapers' political and ideological stances and their distance from the government sometimes influence the way they frame the United States and Trump-related news stories.

HISTORICAL AND THEORETICAL BACKGROUND

First a brief look into the history of US-Turkish relations. If there are two words that exemplify US-Turkish relations since the 1950s, it would be *love* and *hate*. In the period after the Second World War, the United States depicted Turkey as a strategically important ally. In the postwar geopolitical context, this was regarded as part of the US containment policy (Bilgiç, 2015). In the 1950s, the close political, economic, and cultural engagement between two countries was clearly manifested in Prime Minister Adnan Menderes's objective of "creating a little America" (Güney, 2008, p. 472). There is a general conviction that anti-Americanism in Turkey started after the Cyprus Crisis in the 1960s when Turkey decided to invade Cyprus, but Bilgiç (2015) notes that the roots of the phenomenon must be sought actually in postwar Turkey. The Truman Doctrine and Marshall Plan aid led to critical voices and objections being raised against the form of this alliance. Turkey's sovereignty and independence and the American imperialist agenda was at the heart of these objections (Bilgiç, 2015, p. 256). According to the critics, American aid was aimed at colonizing the country.

A series of events and developments in the 1960s strained the relationship between Turkey and the United States even further: the Cuban Missile Crisis,[1] the opium issue,[2] and Johnson's letter following the 1963 Cyprus crisis.[3] Anti-American sentiments in the country started to strengthen. The rise of the socialist left at the time was an additional influence in this process. With an anti-American discourse, the Turkish Workers' Party (Türkiye İşçi Partisi, TİP) and other socialist organizations were successful in articulating nationalist concerns with Marxist rhetoric (Hale, 2013, p. 107). These developments made Turkey question the reliability of the American commitment to Turkey and "made Turkey realize that in future a decision by Washington might jeopardize her safety and even her existence" (Güney, 2008, p. 472).

In the multipolar post–Cold War setting, the strategic relations between Turkey and the United States had a short-lived renewal and revival. Turkey's participation in the Gulf War in 1990 was part of this close alliance between the two countries—an alliance that ended up with dire costs for Turkey both in economic and geopolitical terms (Grigoriadis, 2010, p. 53). The American invasion of Iraq in 2003 brought a wind of change when on March 1, 2003, the Turkish parliament rejected a government motion regarding the use of Turk-

---

1. In 1962, as part of the deal between the United States and Soviets, the United States removed Jupiter missiles installed in Turkey without prior consultation with the Turkish government.

2. In 1969, the Johnson administration demanded Turkey eradicate opium cultivation, since relevant US authorities believed that a considerable portion of heroin illicitly introduced into the United States originated from Turkey. Washington achieved a complete ban on opium production by compensating Turkey with $35 million over a three-year period (Spain, 1975; Güney, 2008).

3. The condescending and threatening letter sent by President Johnson to the Turkish government in 1964 following the tension between Turks and Greeks over Cyprus in 1963 stirred a huge reaction in Turkish public opinion.

ish soil in the US military campaign. A considerable majority of the Turkish population (88%) was against Turkey's involvement with the conflict (Güney, 2008, p. 378). The famed "Hood Incident" (Çuval Olayı)[4] in July 2003 led to public indignation and increased anti-American sentiments: two public opinion polls of that time show that 82% of the population defined themselves anti-American (Güney, 2008, p. 481). A 2006 *Pew Global Attitudes and Trends Survey* shows the gradual decline in the number of Turkish citizens who held a positive view of the United States. From 32% approval in 2004 to 23% in 2005 and a mere 17% approval in 2006 (Grigoriadis, 2010, p. 58).

Looking into the recent decade, especially with the arrival of the Trump administration, it would be safe to say relations are not improving. The United States' strategic partnership with the Kurdish forces in Syria and the residency of Fethullah Gülen (a Turkish Muslim cleric and alleged leader of Fethullah Gülen Terrorist Organization FETO held responsible by the Erdoğan government for the failed coup attempt in July 2016) in the United States are among the two key topics that strain the relationship between the two countries (Soylu, 2019). According to a poll, in 2018, 82% of Turkey's population saw the United States as a threat to Turkey. This would decrease to 64.5% in 2019 (TEA, 2020). Most recent data from the Pew Research Center's *Global Attitudes and Trends* survey shows only 11% of Turkey's population has confidence in US President Donald Trump to do the right thing regarding world politics (Pew, 2020), an indication that President Trump has a more negative standing than that of the United States in general.

WHY LOOK AT NEWS COVERAGE?

Framing in news is defined as "the activities of the mass media as they select, emphasize and present some aspects of 'reality' to audiences while ignoring others" (Bateson, 1972, p. 277). According to Entman, "to frame is to select some aspects of a perceived reality and make them more salient in a communicating text" (1993, p. 52). News and news frames are important, since they continuously redefine, constitute, and reconstitute social phenomena (Tuchman, 1978, p. 278). News frames invite people to think about issues and events in certain ways through establishing associations between concepts (Tewksbury & Scheufele, 2009, p. 11). Some prominent reasons and dynamics behind this selection process are the political and socioeconomic context in which news media are operating; media ownership; varying codes of journalistic profession and level of professionalism; and the relations between the media and the state (Bourdieu, 1996; Hallin & Mancini, 2004; Herman & Chomsky, 1988; Schlesinger, 1991).

Another important concept to keep in mind is the influence of media structure and ownership on news narrative. The interaction of media organizations as economic foundations with other fields and power relations arising from economic relations produce an economical and political structure of news. As Hall (1977) states, the political and economic context in which the mass communication organizations take place; ownership structure of mass media organizations; organization style and objectives; means of production; production process; and "mass" to which the product is delivered becomes extremely important. In news-making processes the rules of the capitalist market economy and the social structure formed by it, the con-

---

4. On July 4, 2003, 11 Turkish soldiers were captured in Sulaimaniya by the US military, led away with hoods on their heads, and interrogated. They were released 60 hours later.

tent produced by the mass communication organizations in the social structures shaped by the capitalist market economy; economic and political power structures due to their importance in this social structure; and organizational ownership and professional practices are decisive.

Media organizations have an ideological function in building and transforming individuals' perceptions of the world, shaping worldviews, and defining the social sphere. To claim that the media are ideological is to say that they work in the social human field of meaning (Hall, 1977). However, while ideological production is a constant for media institutions, the size, form, and appearance of this product may vary according to the ideological atmosphere to which each media institution is connected (Özer, 2011, p. 60). Therefore, news media may adopt different discourses in the presentation of national and international incidents in line with their ideological positioning. This positioning may vary according to ownership and business strategies of the media institution but it certainly affects the ideological presentation of the news. So, the news discourses may vary according to the ideological window of the mass media organization.

Press-party parallelism, uneven access to media for different political actors, interference from state authorities, commercial pressures, concentration, and state-induced transfer of media ownership are some of the main characteristics that define the media landscape in Turkey (Akser & McCollum, 2018; Hansen, 2019). According to the *Media Ownership Monitor* project (MOM, 2020) in Turkey 2,474 daily newspapers, 3,650 magazines, 899 radio stations, and 196 TV channels are active, and 71% of media followers are owned by four media groups. These four media groups have investments in at least three media types out of the four types studied in the research, which are radio, TV, newspapers, and online web portals. Cross-media ownership in Turkey is 71%, meaning high concentration of the Big Four (Turkuvaz/Kalyon Group, Ciner Group, Demirören Group, and Doğuş Group) in these four areas. Furthermore, Turkey ranks at 157 out of 180 countries in terms of freedom of the press, a continual negative trend since 2002, when the country ranked at 99. According to RSF, Turkey, facing a severe crackdown on the press and media freedom, is the biggest jailer of professional journalists (Reporters Without Borders, 2019). The Committee to Protect Journalists' 2018 prison census notes that 68 journalists are jailed in Turkey in direct relation to their work. Freedom House classifies Turkey as "not free" in both press and internet freedoms.

A WORD ABOUT METHOD

The analysis of how the USA has been covered in the Turkish press in 2019 comes from an in-depth analysis of 1,261 new stories published from six online newspapers between January 1 and December 31, 2019. Accordingly, "USA" was used as a keyword in the search made on the online platforms of newspapers and unrelated news was eliminated, reaching a total of 1,261 USA-related news items. The sample of our study is comprised of six newspapers: *Cumhuriyet*, *Hürriyet*, *Sabah*, *Sözcü*, *Yeni Akit*, and *Yeni Şafak*. These newspapers were chosen according to the following criteria: circulation, click rates, ownership, and political stance.

The average circulation of all newspapers in Turkey for the month of January 2019 was about 2.27 million, and for the month of December 2019 about 1.9 million (*Gazete Tirajlari*, 2020). Within the year 2019, it is seen that although the ranking may change from time to time, the top three were still the same: *Sabah*, *Hürriyet*, and *Sözcü*.

Within this time frame, we see that in the month of January 2019 Sabah, with an average circulation rate of 275,000, ranked at the top, *Hürriyet* was second with 258,000, *Sözcü* was third with about 251,000. In the month of December 2019, *Sözcü* with an average circulation rate of 244,000 ranked at the top, *Sabah* was second with 243,000, *Hürriyet* was third with about 212,000. In the overall ranking, *Yeni Şafak* was at seventh place with an average circulation of 110,000 in the month of January and 102,000 in the month of December. Similarly, *Cumhuriyet* was at eighteenth place with an average circulation of 32,000 in the month of January and 28,000 in the month of December. Unlike others, *Yeni Akit* moved from seventeenth to fourteenth place with an average circulation of 50,000 in the month of January and 56,000 in the month of December. For the online platforms of these national daily newspapers, a similar frame is valid. The highest click rate belongs to *Hürriyet*, third is *Sözcü*, fifth is *Yeni Akit*, sixth is *Yeni Şafak*, seventh is *Sabah*, and nineteenth is *Cumhuriyet* in overall rankings among online platforms of newspapers (Alexa, 2020).

Another criterion of newspaper selection was political stance and ownership structure. With the exception of *Yeni Akit*, the selected newspapers can be labeled as mainstream outlets, yet they have relatively different ideological positions. *Cumhuriyet* and *Sözcü* tend to appeal to the secular middle class but differ from each other ideologically. *Cumhuriyet* identifies itself with social democratic interpretation of Kemalism, the founding ideology of the Turkish Republic as outlined by Mustafa Kemal Atatürk (1881–1938). Founded in 1924, the newspaper is currently owned by Cumhuriyet Foundation. In 2015, *Cumhuriyet* was awarded the Freedom of Press Prize by Reporters Without Borders. *Sözcü*, on the other hand, sticks to a hardline nationalist interpretation of Kemalism. The newspaper was founded in 2007 by a businessman, Burak Akbay, who owns two other national newspapers and a humor magazine. Until its acquisition by pro-government Demirören Holding in 2018 and adopting a pro-government stance, *Hürriyet* was considered as the bedrock of the Turkish mainstream press, appealing to the secular, liberal, nationalist masses.

Owned by a close associate of President Erdoğan, Ahmet Çalık, the pro-government daily *Sabah* functions as a mouthpiece of the AKP governments and Erdoğan. Likewise, Islamist conservative daily *Yeni Şafak* is identified by its explicit pro-government stance. The newspaper started publication as a venture of Albayrak Holding, which is owned by an ardent supporter of Erdoğan. *Yeni Akit*, on the other hand, distinguishes itself from other pro-government newspapers with its Islamic-fundamentalist stance. A longtime supporter of the AKP, the newspaper is owned by Akit Medya Group. The newspaper is often criticized on several grounds: disinformation, hate speech, anti-Semitism, anti-LGBT, censoring of women, and targeting of journalists.

News stories were collected from the online archives of these six newspapers and were coded for content according to categories created by the Pew Research Journalism Project for the News Index Project.[5] We give detailed information on the coding categories below.

THE UNITED STATES: A CONSTANT NEWS STORY

A look into the overall timeline reveals that coverage of the news is constant with episodic spikes. Studies on international news have shown that rich countries with elite status enjoy more coverage in comparison to other countries (Galtung & Ruge, 1965; Kim & Barnett, 1996; Grasland, 2019). There were certain weeks when coverage of the United States was

---

5. Banu Akdenizli is a former methodologist and analyst for Pew Research Center's Journalism Project, and was one of the developers of the original News Index Project codebook.

relentless. The week of May 16, 2019; the period from July 29 to August 6; the first week of September and the week of September 23; the week of October 7; and the period from November 25 to December 15 were particularly busy.

The week of May 16, 2019, stories in newspapers focused particularly on ongoing tensions between Iran and the United States, the world economy and its repercussions for the dollar, and the US government's decision to block sales to China's Huawei. Among developed nations, the United States is an outlier when it comes to gun violence. Mass shootings in California, Texas, and Ohio were the main stories covered during late July and the first weeks of August 2019. The week of September 23 was the week of Trump. The impeachment trial news dominated when it came to the news about the United States. The war in Syria has fed tensions between the United States and Turkey. An ongoing big story that is covered both from national and international angles in the Turkish press, Syria was a constant story. The weeks of October, and particularly November 25 to December 15, stories in relation to the United States focused on the entrance of Turkey's military (and allied Syrian opposition groups) into northeastern Syria after President Trump ordered a pullback of US special forces. When the Trump administration imposed sanctions on some Turkish cabinet ministries and ministers in response to Turkey's operation decision in Syria, news on growing tensions between the two countries skyrocketed.

THE MAJOR STORYLINES

A major power player in world politics with a populist and at times unpredictable leader, the United States more than any other country enjoys international coverage. Furthermore, when it comes to coverage of world leaders, President Trump eclipses them all. So, what were some of the major stories in the press in Turkey when it came to world leader Trump and the United States?

Major storylines or big stories are defined here as stories on topics that occur often in news media, featured in multiple news outlets during the time period under study. While stories on the ongoing conflict in Syria, contentious relations between the United States and Iran, and the S-400 missile crisis emerged as the top three stories (see Table 20.1), 17.6% of all stories

Table 20.1.   The Major Storylines on the United States in the Press in Turkey Overall

News Story	Percent of Stories Analyzed
Syria	13.6
Iran	8.4
S-400	8.2
Economy	6.1
China	5.3
PKK	4.5
Sanctions	4.4
Russia	3.3
Efforts to combat terrorism	3.2
Shootings in the United States	2.9

Note: The breakdown of major news stories does not add up to 100% because 17.6% of the news stories analyzed did not belong to any major news story and thus were excluded from the table.

coded did not fall under a specific big story. These were brief stories like President Erdoğan's visits to the United States and the US delegation visits to Turkey that lacked information or detail to be coded as an ongoing big story, developments in the Julian Assange trial, and human-interest stories involving Turks living in the United States.

The war in Syria and Turkey's relation to the United States in that war was the major storyline that dominated 2019 when it came to news that involved the United States (13.6%). Turkish-led forces have occupied and administered some parts of Syria since 2016. One of the main concerns for Turkey has been to prevent the PKK-linked Syrian Kurdish People Protection Units (YPG) from establishing an autonomous area along the border with Syria and Turkey. And one of the main tensions between Turkey and the United States has been the US alliance with Syrian Kurds against Turkey's wishes. Stories such as logistical support of the United States to the YPG by providing them with 600 trucks; Trump's tweet "sending regards to Kurdish people and looking forward to see Mazloum Kobani soon" and the reaction to this tweet not only in the political circles but also in the Turkish press; and meetings of Turkish officials with their American counterparts, such as Hulusi Akar, Şahin Cilo, and Mark Esper, James Jeffrey, and Patrick Shanahan.

Iran, a neighboring country with close historical and cultural ties to Turkey comes in as the second most covered storyline (8.4%). Relations between the United States and Iran have been tricky, to say the least. With the overthrow of Prime Minister Mohammed Mossadeq in 1953, the 1979 revolution in Iran, the 1979–1981 Iran hostage crisis, former President George W. Bush declaring Iran as a member of the "axis of evil," and Iran's nuclear weapons development fears, the relationship between Iran and the United States can be at least described as adversarial. In 2019 according to our study, stories in the Turkish press in relation to the United States and Iran were mainly about highlighting military and political tensions and conflict between those countries. Some of the main stories were Iran declaring US activity in the Middle East as terrorism, US sanctions on Iran, Iran's statement that they will not negotiate with the United States before the sanctions end, drone activity in the region; and oil tanker standoffs at the Strait of Hormuz.

A close third were stories on the S-400 crisis (8.2%). Turkey's decision to purchase the Russian S-400 air defense system, and thus its removal from the F-35 fighter jet program was another issue of contention between the United States and Turkey in 2019. Stories such as the United States declaring, "If Turkey gets S400, the Patriot process will stop" and General Curtis Scaparotti's statement that F-35s should not be given if Turkey completes the S400 purchase, the United States threatening Turkey with sanctions, admission in the US Assembly of Turkey's removal from the program, and subsequently Turkish firms' moving the F-35 process to the international court were some of the major sub-storylines emphasizing a political battle. The global economy connects markets and also nations. News on the general economy in the United States has repercussions and ripple effects in many markets, news on interest rate cuts or increases by the Federal Reserve in the United States would make their way into the news agenda. The Turkish market is heavily reliant on the exchange rate. Thus, stories on the US dollar value against the Turkish lira are very common and appear on a daily basis. Other stories under the category were stories alluding to a fruitful relationship between Turkish and American businesses. Statements by Minister of Economy Ruhsan Pekcar aiming for a $100 billion trade with the United States and meetings among Turkish and American businesses were some examples.

China made the headlines in relation to US-oriented stories in particular ways. The ongoing trade war between the two countries was one of the major substory lines. One company in particular was the focus: Chinese tech giant Huawei. The United States' and specifically President Trump's allegations were that the company's close ties to the Chinese government and military put American national security at risk. The Trump administration blacklisted Huawei in May 2019, banning US firms from selling its components or software. Stories on Huawei officials' response to these sanctions and companies cutting cooperation ties with the tech giant were some of the other angles. Nuclear weapon tensions and distrust between the United States and China are not new stories. TikTok, the new social media phenomenon app that has become popular was a sub-storyline in this. Stories on how the US government called for a formal investigation of whether the app poses a national security threat were popular in the third period of 2019.

There were other storylines that had their moment but overall ended up only occupying 2% or less within the stories analyzed for this study. Among them were the decision of the US Senate to recognize the Armenian genocide; US policy toward Venezuela; diplomatic relationships between North Korea and the United States; and stories on the refusal to extradite Fethullah Gülen, leader of what Turkey considers to be a terrorist group (FETO) behind the attempted coup of July 2016.

HOW WERE THE STORIES FRAMED?

In addition to the major storylines of how the United States was covered in the Turkish press, another question to consider is how these stories were framed. A story involving the United States could focus on what the leaders said, strategy, and more. To get at this, this study looked into how a storyline was developed, what the story was informing the readers about, and what point(s) it was making.

Data show that news on and about the United States was predominantly framed as diplomacy and foreign military stories (see Table 20.2). The top three big stories that were framed as diplomacy were Syria (12%), S-400 Crisis (10.7%) and Iran (9.8%). Meetings between President Erdoğan and Mike Pence; statements of Mike Pompeo stating that there are positive developments in Syria; and various political leaders' comments in regard to the crisis were some of the stories in relation to Syria that were framed from a diplomacy angle. Stories on the S-400 crisis varied from evaluating how the crisis would influence the diplomatic relationship between Turkey and the United States to announcements from the foreign minister of Turkey and his counterpart in the United States. The possibility of a conversation/meeting between

Table 20.2.   The Top 10 Topics on US News in Turkey Overall

Topic	Percent of Stories Analyzed
Foreign affairs/diplomacy	29.0
Foreign affairs/military	26.2
Economy	7.9
Politics	6.8
Government/executive	5.1
Crime	4.8
Terrorism	3.7
Trial proceedings	3.2
Business	2.5
Press and media	2.2

Trump and Rouhani; Macron's meeting with Rouhani and what that might mean for Iran's relationship with the United States; and the United States' decision to impose sanctions on Iran were some of the diplomacy frames when it came to Iran stories.

The top three stories framed as military stories were the same as diplomacy stories. However, military stories predominantly centered around stories on Syria. Almost one-third of all military-framed stories belonged to that storyline (31.1.%). Typical angles would be military tactics and strategy, confrontations, attacks, human loss, and death tolls.

Stories on China tech giant Huawei; trade between Turkey and the United States, the volatile dollar exchange rate, and US sanctions on countries were some of the typical stories covered from an economics angle. There were also some individual stories that did not fit under an ongoing big story that could still be approached in an economy frame. News stories on multinational investment bank JP Morgan and success stories such as that of Turkish-American Muhtar Kent, former CEO and Chairman of Coca-Cola would be examples.

POSITIVE? NEGATIVE? MAINLY NEUTRAL

Products produced by media organizations, which are located in social structures shaped by the capitalist market economy and are established to carry out an economic activity, are not neutral (İnal, 1996). Daily professional practices are implemented without being questioned, and public understanding practice is directed. Through selective resource use, uniform news tempo, and choice of story title, the news media decide which news actors will be represented to the public, what to say about them, and especially how to say it (van Dijk, 1989, p. 367).

To examine tone, this study employed the Pew Journalism Project's cautious and conservative approach. The study examined not just whether assertions in stories were positive or negative, but also if they were inherently neutral. For a story to be deemed as having a negative or positive tone, the negative assertions in a story had to outweigh positive assertions by a margin of at least 1.5 to 1. All comments that have either a negative or positive tone in reporting, as well as direct and indirect quotes were counted along with the assertions made by the journalists themselves.

The findings of this analysis suggest that, overall, the Turkish press when reporting on US-related news adopted a neutral tone: 68.5% of the stories analyzed were neutral in tone (see Table 20.3). Yet negative stories outweighed the positive ones by more than three times.

Negative stories focused especially on two main issues: US-YPG relations and Turkey's official statements about US sanctions. Apart from these, news about Israel and Palestine, the United States and Russia, the Trump impeachment, and trade "wars" between China and the United States all were also framed negatively. As mentioned above, positive stories were relatively few. These were mostly about Turkey's statements on international/military/economic affairs, such as Erdoğan's visit to the United States, Syrian border operations, and the trade agreement between the United States and Turkey. When it came to neutral stories, we saw that they were in the majority. In general, news about the foreign policy of the United States not

Table 20.3. Tone of News Stories Overall

Tone	Percent of Stories Analyzed
Positive	7.4
Negative	24.1
Neutral	68.5

related to Turkey, natural disasters such as Hurricane Dorian, and crime incidents like mass shootings in Texas and Ohio were reported in a neutral tone in Turkish newspapers.

HOW COVERAGE OF THE UNITED STATES VARIED BY OUTLETS

The evidence in this study suggests that while overall the coverage of US-related news was neutral across newspapers, there were differences when it came to individual outlets and storylines. Keohane and Katzenstein (2007, p. 10) present a useful framework for evaluating varieties of critical attitudes toward the United States. The authors propose a distinction between negative attitudes based on "what the United States *is*" and "what the United States *does*." Negative (and in some cases positive) attitudes toward the United States in Turkey oscillate between *is* and *does*. Hence, the way negativity and positivity are constructed by the newspapers is worth a closer analysis.

The breakdown of stories analyzed for this study shows *Hürriyet* and *Cumhuriyet* were the newspapers that had the most stories published (Table 20.4). *Yeni Akit* and *Cumhuriyet* were the ones with the most negative coverage. More than one-third of news stories that were analyzed from the *Yeni Akit* sample were negative in tone (Table 20.5).

The majority of US-related stories in *Hürriyet* were on Syria (12.2%), followed closely by stories on the economy (11.8%) and then China (8.1%). The tone of *Hürriyet*'s coverage, one of the more populist-nationalist pro-state newspapers, was more negative than it was positive. More than a quarter of the articles analyzed from this newspaper (26.4%) were negative, while 12.6% were positive. The negative stories were predominantly stories on Syria, Iran, and China. Statements by Turkish leaders such as Foreign Minister Mevlüt Çavuşoğlu in regard to US strategy and military operations in Syria and stories emphasizing the "cold reception" of comments by US officials such as Lindsey Graham by their Turkish counterparts were some examples. Iran stories in *Hürriyet* would more often be negative, highlighting tensions between Trump and Rouhani and the developments in the Strait of Hormuz.

Syria was also one of the top stories for *Cumhuriyet*, but not the top. Unlike other newspapers, the top story for this newspaper was the S-400 crisis with a high percentage of 17.8%. (another anomaly would be *Sabah* with its focus on US-Iran relations as the top story). The tone of the news was mostly neutral, but negative ones outweighed the positive ones by seven

Table 20.4.   News Stories Breakdown by News Outlet

News Outlet	Percent of Stories Analyzed
Yeni Akit	11.9%
Sabah	13.9%
Sözcü	14.0%
Cumhuriyet	19.1%
Hürriyet	19.5%

Table 20.5.   Tone of News- by Source

Tone	Yeni Akit	Cumhuriyet	Hürriyet	Sabah	Sözcü	Yeni Şafak
Positive	2.0%	4.6%	12.6%	8.0%	2.3%	11.0%
Negative	36.0%	29.9%	26.4%	19.4%	7.9%	23.9%
Neutral	62.0%	65.6%	61.0%	72.6%	89.8%	65.1%

times. The news covered stories mostly about foreign affairs and diplomatic issues as well as campaign news. Syria was also the top story in *Yeni Akit* with the highest percentage (16.7%) followed closely by stories about the S-400 crisis (13.3%).

Yeni Şafak also covered mostly the news about Syria (15.4%) followed by stories about the PKK, with a percentage of 9.6%, and then stories on Iran (6.3%). In our sample, stories on the PKK were mostly covered by *Yeni Şafak*.

Syria and Iran were top stories in *Sözcü* with the same percentage (13.6%), then came stories on US sanctions with 10.7%. News on and about the United States were predominantly conveyed with a neutral tone (89.8%) in *Sözcü*. The stories covered were predominantly framed as diplomacy and foreign politics.

When it came to negative framing of the United States in the news, fundamentalist *Yeni Akit* occupied first place, with 36% of *Yeni Akit* news stories on the United States being negative in tone. According to *Yeni Akit* the United States "is" an evil force constantly "doing" evil things against Turkey. A news story dated August 12, 2019, accused the United States of assaulting the Turkish economy ("Ekonomiye ABD saldırısı"). In covering the United States, *Yeni Akit* would highlight United States' role in arming terrorist organizations in Syria against Turkish armed forces: a June 18, 2019, story headline read: "Shocking confession from Syrian terrorist: The Americans gave artillery training" (Suriyeli teröristten şok itiraf! Ağır silah eğitimini ABD'liler verdi). A July 9, 2019, story would accuse the United States of being arrogant and making insolent threats ("ABD'den Türkiye'ye bir küstah tehdit daha"). The United States would also be portrayed as a bully imposing its policies on Turkey; on August 18 a story ran with the headline revealing—for the first time—the secret plan and maps imposed on Turkey by the US forces ("İlk kez paylaşıldı! İşte ABD'nin Türkiye'ye dayattığı 3 harita"). It is evident that *Yeni Akit* clearly had no love for the United States, framing the United States as (1) A greedy occupant force (August 17, 2019, story titled "ABD'nin gözünü toprak doyursun!" [Nothing on earth can satisfy the United States]); (2) the "great devil" (October 12, "Büyük şeytan ABD, Halkbank davasında yeni oyun peşinde!" [The great devil United States is after something in Halkbank case!]; (3) the "supporter of terrorists" (December 2nd, ABD'den 'ilginç' Türkiye uyarısı [An "interesting" attack warning from the United States]); (4) a "global murderer" (August 6, "ABD'nin katliamı hala hafızalarda" [The United States' massacre is still remembered]); (5) a country with secret plans on Turkey (August 19, "Amerika'nın gizli Türkiye planı!" [America's secret Turkey plan!]); and (6) aiming at containing Turkey all around (September 30 "ABD dört bir koldan Türkiye'yi kuşatma peşinde!" [The United States is after containing Turkey from all corners]). Moreover, the newspaper would frequently use condescending language stressing the "cowardliness" of the United States and US soldiers: November 29, "ABD'li komutanların ödü koptu" (The US Commanders are Scared to Death). The newspaper would at times openly wish evil upon the United States. On October 8, *Yeni Akit* would carry popular Turkish singer Yıldız Tilbe's words to the headlines: "Yıldız Tilbe'den ABD'ye sert sözler: Allah belanızı versin" (Strong words from Yıldız Tilbe to the United States: God damn you all").

Almost a quarter of the US-related news stories analyzed on *Yeni Şafak* were negative in tone. Yet, unlike *Yeni Akit*, negative frames were mostly based on what the United States does rather than is. Constant "threats" and "scandalous" statements made by the United States against Turkey were also a recurrent theme in *Yeni Şafak* news: October 5, "ABD ile Yunanistan'dan skandal Türkiye açıklaması" (Scandalous statement from the United States and Greece); October 11, "ABD'den küstah açıklama" (Arrogant statement from the United States). Stories accusing the United States of aiding and supporting the PKK would also be covered in negative tone, such as on September 23: "BD teröristlere sevkiyata devam ediyor" (The United States continues military shipment to terrorists). And on October 19: "3 bin tır silah ve cephane PKK'ya teslim edildi" (3,000 trucks loaded with weapons were delivered to the PKK). The United States' imperialist agenda, reactions regarding the S-400 crisis, and US resolutions recognizing the Armenian Genocide were other American misdeeds according to *Yeni Şafak*.

Sözcü is the least negative and most neutral newspaper in terms of its attitude toward the United States. Only 7.9% of the news stories were negative and 89.8% were neutral. The negative news focused on economic sanctions (December 17, "ABD'den Türkiye'ye yaptırım kararı" [The United States sanctions Turkey]); Trump's close relations with YPG officers (October 23, "Trump'ın YPG yöneticisine mention twiti" [Trump mentions YPG officer in tweet]); and the United States' interference with Turkey's foreign policy moves.

Cumhuriyet mainly criticizes the United States for violating the sovereignty of the Turkish Republic. The interventionist attitude of the United States in Syria, the United States' objections to establishing security zones, and the S-400 conflict are among the most covered subjects. However, in negative framing *Cumhuriyet* refrained from using a defamatory language. In a news item on July 5, 2019, on security zones in Syria, *Cumhuriyet* asks, "Suriye'de 'güvenli bölge': Türkiye ne istiyor, ABD neden sıcak bakmıyor?" (Security zone in Syria: What does Turkey want, why is the United States so reluctant?). Armenian Genocide resolutions were frequently and negatively covered by *Cunhuriyet*: November 3, 2019, "MSB'den ABD ve Fransa'ya sert tepki" (Harsh Reaction from Ministry of Defense to the United States and France); December 12, 2019, "ABD'nin 'Ermeni Soykırımı' tasarısına ilk tepki" (First reaction to the United States' 'Armenian Genocide' resolution).

Likewise, the sovereignty of the Turkish Republic and US interventionist policies were at the heart of *Hürriyet*'s critical attitude toward the United States. *Hürriyet* gave wide coverage to official authorities' responses to US actions and statements. The Turkish Grand National Assembly's reaction to the Armenian Genocide resolution on October 30, 2019, is an example: "TBMM'de, ABD Temsilciler Meclisi'nin kararına tepki tezkeresi kabul edildi" (Turkish Parliament approves memorandum as a reaction to House of Representatives' resolution). Official authorities' statements on Syria, S-400 or on economic sanctions were frequently quoted by *Hürriyet*.

Sabah adopted a more neutral language in its news on the United States. Of news items on the United States 72.6% were neutral, and 19.4% negative. Negative news items were based on governmental figures' statements about (1) the United States' support to PKK-YPG (October 10, 2019, "ABD'nin YPG/PKK'ya verdiği silah mühimmatları ele geçirildi" [Weapons and ammunition given by the United States to the YPG/PKK are captured]), (September 18, 2019, "ABD'den terör örgütü YPG/PKK'ya skandal güvence" [Scandalous guarantee given by the United States to terrorist organization YPG/PKK]); (2) the United States's recognition of Armenian Genocide (October 30, 2019, "Bakan Çavuşoğlu'ndan ABD'nin skandal tasarısına sert tepki" [Strong reaction from Minister Çavuşoğlu to scandalous US resolution]); (3) economic and military sanctions on Turkey (December 12, 2019, "ABD'den skandal hamle! Trump Türkiye'ye yönelik yaptırımları bugün imzalayacak" [Scandalous move from the United States! Trump will approve sanctions against Turkey today]); and (4) the S-400 deal (June 16, 2019, "Türkiye'de ABD'ye sert S-400 tepkisi" [Strong S-400 reaction from Turkey to the United States]). Unlike *Hürriyet*, *Sabah* adopted a more dramatic language that frequently highlighted the irrational and unexpected ("scandalous") character of US actions, and rational but strong responses given by Turkish authorities.

CONCLUSION

As longtime allies, and now increasingly foes, Turkey and the United States' relationship is and continues to be marked by ups and downs. Syria, Northern Iraq, tensions with Russia, Iran, Kurdish and Armenian issues, as well as global trade are some of the issues that have from time to time put pressure on the rapport of these two countries. Analysis of 1,261 news articles related to the United States in six prominent newspaper overall suggests:

- United States as a storyline in the Turkish press was a constant in 2019, a trend that will continue likely in 2020 given the relations between the two countries and the United States' political and economic presence within the world system.
- The coverage of the United States in the Turkish press was a political one. The coverage mostly centered around analyzing what the ongoing crises (Syria, S-400, sanctions) meant for the relationship between the United States and Turkey, and on a larger scale seemed to concentrate on the compatibility of US and Turkish future goals and objectives.
- Not all newspapers devoted the same amount of coverage to US-related news. Of the newspapers analyzed, *Yeni Şafak*, explicitly pro-government; *Hürriyet*, the once bedrock of mainstream press in Turkey; and *Cumhuriyet*, with a social-democratic stance, were the top three. As evident in our data, their political stance would frame how stories were covered and presented.
- The storyline that received the most coverage overall when it came to US-related news was the ongoing crisis in Syria. With multiple stakeholders such as the United States, Turkey, Northern Iraq, and Russia, this was also the story that was analyzed mostly from a diplomacy and military frame with more or less negative undertones.
- When it comes to tone of coverage, there were some differences among the news outlets. But there were stories that they all framed as negative: the relationship between the United States and the YPG, with a particularly negative and critical approach to US forces offering logistical support to YPG forces, and also meetings among senior officials from both of these sides.
- This study also emphasized the importance of the way negativity is constructed. While newspapers with more religious orientation (conservative *Yeni Şafak* and fundamentalist *Yeni Akit*) focused on what the United States "is" by stressing its inherently evil character; other sources, through using a different language, focused more on the "actions" of the United States.
- There were few positive stories, which mostly focused on either fruitful economic cooperation between Turkish and American companies or human-interest stories that involved Turkish Americans.
- This analysis shows that despite a more populated mediascape, some patterns for foreign news coverage still hold true. Foreign news is mostly political news and is associated with mostly military actions, diplomatic activity, and economics. Disruptive events, such as unusual weather (Hurricane Dorian) and crime (shootings in Texas and Ohio) get coverage, but are not the only ones. Positive news exists.

In a globalized world, everything is connected. Every economic, political, or military move affects another. The developments that have taken place since the beginning of 2020 show that the balance of the world can change at any time. The developments in Syria today may be the harbinger of a return to a post–Cold War era.

The power struggle between Russia and the United States within the Syrian territory, Turkey's position in this triangle will likely continue to be important. And news relating to the United States will likely continue to rise in Turkey.

REFERENCES

Akser, M., & McCollum, V. (eds.) (2018). *Alternative media in Turkey: Sustainability, activism, and resistance*. Rowman & Littlefield.

Alexa (2020). Top Sites in Turkey. Last accessed December 24, 2019. https://alexa.com/topsites/countries/TR

Atmaca, A. Ö. (2014). The Geopolitical origins of Turkish-American relations: Revisiting the Cold War years. *All Azimuth: A Journal of Foreign Policy and Peace, 3*(1), 19–34.

Bateson, G. (1972). *Steps to an Ecology of Mind*. Ballantine Books: New York.

Bilgiç, T. Ü. (2015). The roots of anti-Americanism in Turkey 1945–1960. *Bilig, 1*(73), 251–280.

Bourdieu, P. (1996). *On television*. The New Press.

Entman, R. M. (1993). Framing: Toward clarification of fractured paradigm. *Journal of Communication, 43*(4), 51–58.

Galtung, J., & Ruge, M. H. (1965). The structure of foreign news: The presentation of the Congo, Cuba and Cyprus Crises in four Norwegian newspapers. *Journal of Peace Research, 2*(1), 64–90.

Gazete Tirajları (2020). Ocak 2019 *Gazete Tirajları*. Last accessed December 24, 2019. http://gazetetirajlari.com/

Grasland, C. (2019). International news theory revisited trough a space-time interaction model. *International Communication Gazette*, https://doi.org/10.1177/1748048518825091

Grigoriadis, I. N. (2010). Friends no more? The rise of anti-American nationalism in Turkey. *Middle East Journal, 64*(1), 51–66. https://doi.org/10.3751/64.1.13

Güney, A. (2008). Anti-Americanism in Turkey: Past and present. *Middle Eastern Studies, 44*(3), 471–487. https://doi.org/10.1080/00263200802021632

Hale, W. (2013). *Turkish foreign policy since 1774*. Routledge.

Hall, S. (1977). Culture, the media and the "ideological effect." In J. Curran, M. Gurevitch, & J. Wollacott (Eds.), *Mass Communication and Society* (pp. 315–348). Edward Arnold.

Hallin, D. C., & Mancini, P. (2004). *Comparing media systems: Three models of media and politics*. Cambridge University Press.

Hansen, S (2019). What Remains of the Turkish Press? *Columbia Journalism Review*. https://www.cjr.org/special_report/turkish-press.php

Herman, E. S., & Chomsky, N. (1988). *Manufacturing consent: The political economy of the mass media*. Pantheon Books.

İnal, A. (1996). *Haberi okumak*. Temuçin Yayınları.

Keohane, R. O., & Katzenstein, P. J. (2007). Varieties of anti-Americanism: A framework for analysis. In R. O. Keohane & P. J. Katzenstein (Eds.), *Anti-Americanisms in world politics* (pp. 9–38). Cornell University Press.

Kim, K., & Barnett, G. A. (1996). The determinants of international news flow: A network analysis. *Communication Research, 23*(3), 636–653.

MOM. (2020). Media ownership matters. https://turkey.mom-rsf.org/en.

Özer, Ö. (2011). *Haber söylem ideoloji: Eleştirel haber çözümlemeleri*. LiteraTürk.

Pew Research Center. (2020). Confidence in Trump remains low internationally. Global Attitudes and Trends. https://www.pewresearch.org/global/2020/01/08/trump-ratings-remain-low-around-globe-while-views-of-u-s-stay-mostly-favorable/pg_2020-01-08_us-image_0-02/

Reporters Without Borders (2019). 2019 World Press Freedom Index. https://rsf.org/en/ranking

Schlesinger, P. (1991). *Media, State and Nation*. SAGE.

Soylu, R. (2019). Anti-US sentiment in Turkey reaches a new high, poll shows. Middle East Eye. https://www.middleeasteye.net/news/anti-us-sentiment-turkey-reaches-new-high-poll-shows

Spain, J. W. (1975). The United States, Turkey and the poppy. *Middle East Journal, 29*(3), 295–309.

TEA. (2020). *Türkiye Eğilimler Araştırması (TEA) 2019 Sonuçları Açıklandı.* Kadir Has University. https://www.khas.edu.tr/tr/haberler/turkiye-egilimler-arastirmasi-tea-2019-sonuclari-aciklandi

Tewksbury, D., & Scheufele, D. A. (2009). News framing theory and research. In B. Jennings & M. B. Oliver (Eds.), *Media effects: Advances in theory and research* (pp. 17–33). Routledge.

Tuchman, G. (1978). *Making news: A study in the construction of reality.* Free Press.

van Dijk, T. A. (1989). Structures of discourse and structures of power. In J. A. Anderson (Ed.), *Communication yearbook 12* (pp. 18–59). SAGE.

Suggested Reading

Achen, C. H., & L. M. Bartels. (2017). *Democracy for realists: Why elections do not produce responsive government*. Princeton University Press.

Adams, N. (2020). *Trump and Churchill: Defenders of Western civilization*. Post Hill Press.

Anonymous. (2019). *A warning*. Twelve Publishing.

Anthony, J. (2018). *The Constitution needs a good party: Good government comes from good boundaries*. Neuwoehner Press.

Asia Foundation (2001). *America's role in Asia: American views*. The Asia Foundation.

Bergen, P. (2019). *Trump and his generals: The cost of chaos*. Penguin Press.

Bernstein, A. (2020). *American oligarchs: The Kushners, the Trumps, and the marriage of money and power*. W.W. Norton.

Bolton, J. (2020). *The room where it happened: A White House memoir*. Simon & Schuster.

Bongino, D. (2018). *Spygate: The attempted sabotage of Donald J. Trump*. Post Hill Press.

Bongino, D. (2019). Exonerated: The failed takedown of President Donald Trump by the swamp. Post Hill Press.

Booth, M. (2016). *The almost nearly perfect people: Behind the myth of the Scandinavian utopia*. Picador.

Bozell, B. III, and T. Graham. (2019). *Unmasked: Big media's war against Trump*. Humanix Books.

Brakke, P. (2019). *Fractured America: The many divisions in the U.S. and how to fix them*. Changemakers Publishing.

Braun, J. (2019). *Democracy in danger: How hackers and activists exposed fatal flaws in the election*. Rowman & Littlefield.

Brewer, M. D., & L. S. Maise. (2020). Parties and elections in America: The electoral process. Rowman & Littlefield.

Burnham, J. (2014). *Suicide of the West: An essay on the meaning and destiny of liberalism*. Encounter Books.

Chaffetz, J. (2018). *The deep state: How an army of bureaucrats protected Barack Obama and is working to destroy the Trump agenda*. Broadside Books.

Chaffetz, J. (2019). *Power grab: The liberal scheme to undermine Trump, the GOP, and our Republic*. Broadside Books.

Cohen, A. (2020). *Supreme inequality: The Supreme Court's fifty-year battle for a more unjust America.* Penguin Press.

Cohen, B. C. (2016). *Trump politically incorrect: The top 100 tweets & quotes of Donald J. Trump.* CreateSpace Independent Publishing Platform.

Corsi, J. R. (2018). *Killing the deep state: The fight to save President Trump.* Humanix Books.

Daniels, G. R. (2020). *Uncounted: The crisis of voter suppression in America.* New York University Press.

Denker, A. (2019). *Red state Christians: Understanding the voters who elected Donald Trump.* Fortress Press.

Dionne E. J. Jr. (2020). *Code red: How progressives and moderates can unite to save our country.* St. Martin's Press.

Drezner, D. W. (2020). *Toddler-in-chief: What Donald Trump teaches us about the modern presidency.* University of Chicago Press.

Eliasson, L. J. (2010). *America's perceptions of Europe.* Palgrave Macmillan.

Enrich, D. (2020). *Dark towers: Deutsche bank, Donald Trump, and an epic trail of destruction.* Custom House.

Foley, E. B. (2020). *Presidential elections and majority rule: The rise, demise, and potential restoration of the Jeffersonian electoral college.* Oxford University Press.

Gingrich, N. (2017). *Understanding Trump.* Center Street Publishing.

Gingrich, N. (2018). *Trump's America: The truth about our nation's great comeback.* Center Street Publishing.

Gingrich, N. (2019). *Trump vs. China: Facing America's greatest threat.* Center Street Publishing.

Giridharadas, A. (2018). *Winners take all: The elite charade of changing the world.* Knopf.

Goldberg, J. (2018). *Suicide of the West: How the rebirth of tribalism, populism, nationalism, and identity politics is destroying American democracy.* Crown Forum.

Goldstein, J., J. Israel, and H. Conroy (Editors). (1991). *America views China: American images of China, then and now.* Lehigh University Press.

Gorka, S. (2019). *The war for America's soul: Donald Trump, the Left's assault on America, and how we take back our country.* Regnery Publishing.

Green, J. (2017). *Devil's bargain: Steve Bannon, Donald Trump, and the storming of the Presidency.* Penguin Press.

Hall, T., & B. Sinclair. (2018). *A connected America: Politics in the era of social media.* Oxford University Press.

Hanson, V. D. (2019). *The case for Trump.* Basic Books.

Hasen, R. L. (2020). *Election meltdown: Dirty tricks, distrust, and the threat to American democracy.* Yale University Press.

Heldman, C., et al. (2016). *Sex and gender in the 2016 presidential election.* Praeger.

Hennessey, S., & B. White. (2020). *Unmaking the presidency: Donald Trump's war on the world's most powerful office.* Farrar, Straus and Giroux.

House Intelligence Committee & J. Meachan. (2019). *The impeachment report: The House Intelligence Committee's report on its investigation into Donald Trump and Ukraine.* Broadway Books.

Isikoff, M. (2018). *Russian roulette: The inside story of Putin's war on America and the election of Donald Trump.* Twelve Publishing.

Jackson, V. (2018). *On the brink: Trump, Kim, and the threat of nuclear war.* Cambridge University Press.

Jarrett, G. (2019). *The Russia hoax: The illicit scheme to clear Hillary Clinton and frame Donald Trump.* Broadside Books.

Jarrett, G. (2019). *Witch hunt: The story of the greatest mass delusion in American political history.* Broadside Books.

Kamalipour, Y. R. (1998). *Images of the U.S. around the world: A multicultural perspective.* State University of New York Press.

Kamalipour, Y. R. (2019). *Global communication: A multicultural perspective,* 3rd edition. Rowman & Littlefield.

Karl, J. (2020). *Front row at the Trump show.* New York: Dutton.

Katyal, N., and S. Koppelman (2019). *Impeach: The case against Donald Trump.* Mariner Books.

Kelley, D. (2019). *Truth and toleration*. The Atlas Society.

Klein, E. (2017). *All out war: The plot to destroy Trump*. Regnery Publishing.

Kolhatkar, V., and W. Donway. (2020). *Media wars: The battle to shape our minds*. Independently published.

Kovalik, D. (2018). The plot to control the world: How the US spent billions to change the outcome of elections around the world. Hot Books.

Krugman, P. (2020). *Arguing with zombies: Economics, politics, and the fight for a better future*. W. W. Norton & Company.

Levin, M. R. (2018). *Rediscovering Americanism: And the tyranny of progressivism*. Threshold Editions.

Levin, M. R. (2019). *Unfreedom of the press*. Threshold Editions.

Lewandowski, C. R., and D. N. Bossie. (2017). *Let Trump be Trump: The inside story of his rise to the presidency*. Center Street Publishing.

Lithgow, J. (2019). *Dumpty: The age of Trump in verse*. Chronicle Prism.

Lopez, I. H. (2019). *Merge left: Fusing race and class, winning elections, and saving America*. The New Press.

Markay, L., & A. Suebsaeng. (2020). *Sinking in the swamp: How Trump's minions and misfits poisoned Washington*. Viking.

Mayer, J. (2017). *Dark money: The hidden history of the billionaires behind the rise of the radical right*. Anchor Books.

McFarland, K. T. (2020). *Revolution: Trump, Washington and "We the people."* Post Hill Press.

Meddaw, R. (2019). *Blowout: Corrupted democracy, rogue state Russia, and the richest, most destructive industry on earth*. Crown.

Medved, M. (2019). *God's hand on America: Divine providence in the modern era*. Crown Forum.

Mitchell, C. (2020). *Cyber in the age of Trump: The unraveling of America's national security policy*. Rowman & Littlefield.

Morris, D., & E. McGann. (2016). *Armageddon: How Trump can beat Hillary*. Humanix Books.

O'Reilly, B. (2019). *The United States of Trump: How the president really sees America*. Henry Holt and Co.

Payton, T. (2020). *Manipulated: Inside the cyberwar to hijack elections and distort the truth*. Rowman & Littlefield.

Pfeiffer, D. (2020). Un-Trumping America: A plan to make America a democracy again. Twelve.

Pirro, J. J. (2019). *Radicals, resistance, and revenge: The left's plot to remake America*. Center Street Publishing.

Post, J., and S. Doucette (2019). *Dangerous charisma: The political psychology of Donald Trump and his followers*. Pegasus Books.

Reilly, R. (2020). *Commander in cheat: How golf explains Trump*. Hachette Books.

Rohde, D. (2020). *In deep: The FBI, the CIA, and the truth about America's "Deep State."* W. W. Norton & Company.

Rucker, Ph. and C. Leonnig. (2020). *A very stable genius: Donald J. Trump's testing of America*. Penguin Press.

Samuels, T. (2019). *Future man: How to evolve and thrive in the Age of Trump, mansplaining, and #MeToo*. Arcade Publishing.

Schenker, J. (2019). *The dumpster fire election: Realistic dystopian expectations for the 2020 presidential election*. Prestige Professional Publishing.

Schoultz, L. (1998). *Beneath the United States: A history of U.S. policy toward Latin America*. Harvard University Press.

Schweizer, P. (2020). *Profiles in corruption: Abuse of power by America's progressive elite*. Harper.

Schweizer, P. (2019). *Secret empires: How the American political class hides corruption and enriches family and friends*. Harper.

Sirvent, R. (2019). *American exceptionalism and American innocence: A people's history of fake news—from the revolutionary war to the war on terror*. Skyhorse.

Smith, L. (2019). *The plot against the President: The true story of how Congressman Devin Nunes uncovered the biggest political scandal in U.S. History*. Center Street Publishing.

Stent, A. (2019). *Putin's world: Russia against the West and with the rest.* Twelve.

Stone, R. (2019). *The myth of Russian collusion: The inside story of how Donald Trump REALLY won.* Skyhorse.

Strang, S. E. (2020). *God, Trump, and the 2020 election: Why he must win and what's at stake for Christians if he loses.* Frontline.

Tausch, A. (2015). *The political algebra of global value change: General models and implications for the Muslim world.* With Almas Heshmati and Hichem Karoui. Nova Science Publishers.

Troy, T. (2020). *Fight house: Rivalries in the White House from Truman to Trump.* Regnery History.

Trump, D. J. (1987). *Trump: The art of the deal.* Random House.

Trump, D. J. (2015). *Crippled America: How to make America great again.* Threshold Editions.

Trump, D. J., & M. McIver. (2008). *Trump never give up: How I turned my biggest challenges into success.* Wiley.

Trump, D. Jr. (2019). *Triggered: How the Left thrives on hate and wants to silence us.* Center Street Books.

Trump, D. Jr. (2019). *Figgered: My dad is bigger than your dad.* Center Street Publishing.

Wead, D. (2019). *Inside Trump's White House: The real story of his presidency.* Center Street Books.

Wilson, R. (2019). *Everything Trump touches dies: A Republican strategist gets real about the worst president.* Free Press.

Wilson, R. (2020). *Running against the devil: A plot to save America from Trump.* Crown Forum.

Index

Afghanistan: Greek media on US invasion of, 149–50; Pakistan relations with, 232–33; Pakistan-US relations tied to, 227, 228, 237–38; refugees in Pakistan, 233; resistance to foreign occupation, 228, 228n2, 237; Soviet Union conflicts with, 228n2, 232–33; US exit from, 237; US invasion and occupation of, 149–50, 155, 227–28, 235, 237; US public views on, 30

Africa: Chinese investment in, 218, 222; global workforce from, 222; Middle East and Islam ties with North, 25; South, 25, 106; Trump verbal attack on, 25; US policy toward, 221–22; US public views on, 25. *See also* Egypt; Nigeria

agenda-setting theories, 128–29, 139, 190–91, 215–16

Allen, Richard V., 1

America First stance: Australian media on, 60; Chinese media on, 70; history and evolution of, 109, 112–13, 115; Iranian media on, 167; Ku Klux Klan relation to, 113; Nigerian media on, *220*, 221, 223; Poland response to, 247; Russian media on, 264

American dream: Colombian media on Trump impacting, 86–87; Colombian public belief in, 83, 86; German media on Trump

destruction of, 138; Pakistani perspective on, 235, 235n3

Anthropocene, 12, 13

The Apprentice, 3, 120

Arabian Gulf, 29, 29n1, 32, 155

Arab Spring, 25, 155, 190, 216

Armenian genocide, 280, 284, 285

Arnold, Matthew, 110

arrogance, of Trump: Chinese media views on, 77, 78; Colombian media views on, 83, 84, 93; Iranian media on, 167–68; Nigerian perception of, *220*, 223, 224

Assange, Julian, 57, 57n8, 279

atomic bombs. *See* nuclear weapons

austerity, politics of: citizen action against, 52; global expansion of, 38, 50, 51; impacts of, 41; Trump Effect and, 50–51; Trump policies supporting, 37, 40

Australia: Clinton, H., support in, 56; in FVEY alliance, 63n43; populism in, 60, 65n50; Trumpism adoption in, 60; Trump relations with, 59, 59nn24–25; UK relations with, 55, 55n1; US relations historically with, 55–56, 55nn1–2, 65

Australian media, 56n5; on America First stance, 60; anti-competitive laws repeal impact on, 57; anti-Trump bias criticism, 62, 64, 64n46;

About the Editor and Contributors

Yahya R. Kamalipour (PhD, University of Missouri) is a professor of media and communications and former chair of the Department of Journalism and Mass Communication, North Carolina A&T State University. Previously, for 28 years, he served as professor and head of the Department of Communication and Creative Arts, Purdue University Northwest. His areas of interest and research include globalization, media impact, international communication, Middle East media, and new communication technologies. Profiled in *Contemporary Authors* and *Who's Who in the World*, he has published 18 books, including *Global Communication: A Multicultural Perspective*, in its third edition; *Digital Transformation in Journalism and News Media*; and *Communicating Through the Universe*. Kamalipour has served as an international academic consultant for several colleges and universities and on advisory/editorial boards of a dozen prominent communication journals. He is the founding manager of the *Global Media Journals* network and founding president of the Global Communication Association. Kamalipour has visited 65 countries and has been interviewed by major newspapers and broadcast media, including the BBC, Reuters, ABC, VOA, RFL/RL, National Public Radio, Radio France International, Chinese TV, Turkish TV, Indian TV, Iranian TV, Egyptian TV, the *Indianapolis Star*, *Quill*, and the *Washington Post*. Kamalipour earned his PhD in communication at the University of Missouri–Columbia, his MA in mass media at the University of Wisconsin–Superior, and his BA in mass communication–public relations at the Minnesota State University. For additional information visit www.kamalipour.com.

Banu Akdenizli (PhD, Temple University) is associate professor of communication at Northwestern University in Qatar. Prior to joining Northwestern-Qatar, Banu Akdenizli was an associate professor of communication at Yeditepe University in Istanbul, Turkey. She formerly worked as a methodologist and analyst for the Pew Research Center's Journalism Project in Washington, D.C. She is the editor and contributor of *Digital Transformations in Turkey: Current Perspectives in Communication Studies* (2015), author of *Toward a Healthier Understanding of Internet Policy Development, The Case of Turkey* (2007), and coauthor of *Democracy in the Age of New Media: A Report on the Media and the Immigration Debate* (2008). She has also authored book chapters and numerous periodical articles both in English and Turkish. She holds a BA in sociology and an MA in translation studies from Boğaziçi University, Turkey. Akdenizli is the 2016–2018 University of Southern California (USC) Center for Public Diplomacy Fellow. She is one of the principal investigators representing Turkey for the Journalistic Role Performance Project. Her areas of interest and research include international communication, political communication, public diplomacy, media in the Middle East and Turkey.

Topic Peremobowei Akoje is a PhD candidate majoring in communication at the University of Benin, Benin City, Nigeria. He obtained his master's degree in communication from Limkokwing University of Creative Technology, Malaysia, and was a lecturer in the International Institute of Journalism (IIJ), Asokoro Abuja, Nigeria, from May 2015 to May 2019. While pursuing his doctoral degree, he is an English-language lecturer at the Nigeria Maritime University, Okerenkoko, Delta State, Nigeria.

Ejaz Akram (PhD, Catholic University of America, Washington, D.C.) is a professor of world politics, Southwestern University of Politics and Law, Chongqing, China. Formerly, he was an advisor with the Faculty of Contemporary Studies in National Defense University Islamabad. He served as an associate professor in the Faculty of Humanities and Social Sciences at LUMS from 2005 to 2016, and at American University in Cairo as an assistant professor from 2003 to 2005. Akram has also taught as summer faculty at Franklin College, Switzerland, and as adjunct faculty at Franklin & Marshall, Pennsylvania, USA. He was nominated as the Outstanding Visiting Scholar of 2017 at Tsinghua University, Beijing. Akram specializes in the field of comparative religion and world politics with a focus on the Muslim world and China. He also writes on the religio-political issues of Judaism, Christianity in the West, and Hinduism and Confucianism in the East. He has taught a large variety of courses, including Comparative World Religions, Religion and World Politics, Islamic Civilization and the West, East Asia and the Muslim World, Islamic Political Philosophy, Chinese Political Thought, and Philosophy, and Politics of Global Ecology. He has published several scholarly books, articles, reviews, and editorials, and has conducted and appeared on several radio and television programs in Pakistan, North America, China, South Asia, and the Middle East.

Rasha Allam (DBA, Maastricht School of Management) is an assistant professor and associate chair at the Department of Journalism and Mass Communication. She is an Honorary Alumni of the Annenberg school for Communication, University of Pennsylvania, and a graduate of the Oxford University program of Media Laws and Regulations. She received her doctorate in business administration with specialization in media management. Allam's research interests include Egyptian and Arab media management systems, Arab broadcast media laws and regulations, media monitoring, media and elections, and freedom of speech and of the press in the Middle East. Among other publications, she has a weekly column at *Al Masry Al Youm*, where she introduced the Twitter debate, "Engaging with Your Readers on Twitter."

Jesus Arroyave (PhD, University of Miami) is a professor at the Department of Communication and Journalism at Universidad del Norte, in Barranquilla, Colombia. His professional interest focuses on journalism and media studies, health and social change communication, and communication and gender. His research has appeared in journals such as *Feminist Media Studies*, *Journalism*, *Journalism Studies*, *Palabra Clave*, *Revista Diálogos*, and *Chasqui*. He holds position as visiting scholar in Spain, Germany, Great Britain, and the United States.

Lee Artz (PhD, University of Iowa), a former machinist, is professor of media studies at Purdue University Northwest, teaching courses in political economy, popular culture, and international communication. He has published more than 50 articles and book chapters and 10 books including: *Pink Tide: Media Access and Political Power in Latin America*, *Global Entertainment Media: A Critical Introduction*; *Bring 'Em On! Media and Politics in the Iraq War*; *The Globalization of Corporate Media Hegemony*; and *Cultural Hegemony in the United States*. Artz is director of the Center for Global Studies at Purdue Northwest.

Kadir Jun Ayhan (PhD, Seoul National University) is a professor of international relations at Hankuk University of Foreign Studies Graduate School of International and Area Studies. Ayhan's main research interests include public diplomacy, power in world politics, active learning pedagogy for international relations, and Korean foreign policy. He serves on the board of various academic journals and NGOs. Ayhan writes regular columns for *Donga Ilbo* newspaper. Ayhan earned his bachelor of commerce in economics and international trade at the University of Auckland and his master of international studies at Seoul National University.

Abbas Ghanbari Baghestan (PhD, University Putra Malaysia) is an assistant professor in the Department of Communication, Faculty of Social Science, University of Tehran (UT) and an adjunct professor at Universiti Sains Malaysia (USM). Previously he was a scientific counsellor of Iran in East Asia, based in Malaysia (2015–2018). Also, since 2005, he has worked as an international journalist with Malaysian media. He is the author of *Islamic Understanding of Information Society: Interview with Muslim Communication Scholars* (2010) and also served as a guest editor of *Current Issues and Challenges Facing Iran through the Lens of the Social Sciences* (*Pertanika Journal of Social Sciences and Humanities*, vol. 26, February 2018).

Antonio Castillo (PhD, Western Sydney University) is a Latin American academic, journalist, and activist and a senior journalism lecturer at Western Sydney University. As a researcher, Castillo is interested in Latin American journalism history and politics, reportage and literary journalism, and international comparative news, journalism, and democracy. In the past, he has conducted research in ethnic and social media representation.

Regina Cazzamatta is a doctoral candidate at the University of Erfurt, Germany. She holds a master's degree in media studies and communication and was a visiting scholar in the German Institute of Global and Area Studies (GIGA) in Hamburg.

Noam Chomsky (PhD, University of Pennsylvania), considered the founder of modern linguistics, is one of the most cited scholars in modern history. Among his groundbreaking books are: *Syntactic Structures*, *Language and Mind*, *Aspects of the Theory of Syntax*, and *The Minimalist Program*, each of which has made distinct contributions to the development of the field. He has received numerous awards, including the Kyoto Prize in Basic Sciences, the Helmholtz Medal, and the Ben Franklin Medal in Computer and Cognitive Science. Chomsky introduced the Chomsky hierarchy, generative grammar and the concept of a universal grammar that underlies all human speech and is based in the innate structure of the mind/brain. Chomsky has not only transformed the field of linguistics, his work has influenced fields such as cognitive science, philosophy, psychology, computer science, mathematics, childhood education, and anthropology. Chomsky is also one of the most influential public intellectuals in the world. He has written more than 100 books, one of his most recent being *Requiem for the American Dream: The 10 Principles of Concentration of Wealth and Power*. Chomsky joined the University of Arizona in fall 2017, coming from the Massachusetts Institute of Technology, where he had worked since 1955 as professor of linguistics, then professor of linguistics, emeritus.

Hart Cohen (PhD, McGill University, Canada) is a professor in the School of Humanities and Communication Arts, a member of the Institute for Cultural and Society, and deputy leader of the Digital Humanities Research Group at Western Sydney University, Australia. Dr. Cohen is author of *The Strehlow Archive: Explorations in Old and New Media* (2018), coauthor of *Screen Media Arts: An Introduction to Concepts and Practices* (2009), and editor of the *Global Media Journal/Australian Edition*: 2007–present. Dr. Cohen collaborates with a research team on a SSHRC-funded project, *Patterns That Connect: Re-curating the Anthropological Media Studies of Edmund Carpenter*.

Nazlı Çetin Gündoğdu (PhD, Yeditepe University Istanbul) is an assistant professor within the Public Relations and Publicity Department, at Yeditepe University, Istanbul. Her doctoral degree was in radio, TV, and cinema. She holds a BA and MA in public relations and publicity from Yeditepe University. She had been a research assistant since 2013 at Yeditepe, and prior to that she worked in the industry as a brand manager. Çetin Gündoğdu is also one of the principal investigators representing Turkey for the Journalistic Role Performance Project.

Myra Gurney (PhD, Western Sydney University) is a lecturer in the School of Humanities and Communication Arts at Western Sydney University and teaches in the key Bachelor of Communication program. Along with Professor Cohen, she has been a member of the editorial committee of *Global Media Journal/Australian Edition*: 2007–present and has edited several editions of the journal. She is coauthor of *Communicating as Professionals* (third edition, 2012). Her research interests relate to the language, discourse, and media representation of climate change politics and policy in Australia since 2007 and she has authored several research papers on aspects of this issue as part of her PhD. She maintains a critical interest in American politics and media.

Kai Hafez (PhD, University of Hamburg) is professor and chair of International and Comparative Media and Communication Studies at the University of Erfurt, Germany. He was also a guest professor/researcher at the University of Oxford, Cambridge, Bern, and Cairo. Hafez is the author of *Islam and the West in the Mass Media* and *Politics and Society in the Middle East*. Hafez earned an additional doctoral degree at Habilitation. His recent books include, as coeditor *The Blackwell Handbook of Political Economy of Communication* (2011), *Money Talks: Media, Markets, Crisis* (2015), *New Media and Metropolitan Life: Connecting, Consuming, Creating* (2015) (in Chinese); and *Carbon Capitalism and Communication: Confronting Climate Crisis* (2017). His writings have been translated into 21 languages.

Cees Hamelink (PhD, University of Amsterdam) is an emeritus professor of international communication at the University of Amsterdam, where he also studied philosophy and psychology. He worked as journalist, policy advisor, and researcher in many different institutions and countries. He was consultant to several intergovernmental organizations and national governments and guest-lectured in some 40 countries. Additionally, Hamelink was an Athena professor of human rights and public health at the Vrije Universiteit in Amsterdam. He is an honorary president of the International Association for Media and Communication Research and editor-in-chief of the *International Communication Gazette.* He has published 19 books on human rights, culture, and technology and numerous other academic writings. He is also a passionate jazz musician.

Seulgi Jang is a PhD candidate at Seoul National University. Her major research interests are political communication, especially related to elections, polls, and voting behavior, and she has a strength in big data. She worked in several political tech or data projects with the Korea National Election Commission and other governmental agencies. She also coauthored *Seeing the New Trend in Korean Politics Through Big Data* (2016), and it was translated into Japanese. With her strong data analytic skills and journalistic perspective, she collaborated with major networks and newspapers in Korea for five years before she works as a data journalist at MBC.

Rovinskaya Juliana (PhD, Russian State University for the Humanities) is a professor of communication studies at the Russian State University for the Humanities. Juliana is the author of *Universal and Ethnic Patterns of Communication* (2016) and *Communication in the New Russian Era* (2018) and a team member of the RFFR-funded research project on specificity of Russian communication.

Ayesha Khan is a PhD student in the Department of Global Studies, Shanghai University China. She holds a MPhil degree in international relations from the National Defense University Islamabad. She has served as a research assistant to the advisor to the president (Dr. Ejaz Akram), National Defense University.

Hyelim Lee is a PhD candidate at Seoul National University. Her major research interests are political communication, public diplomacy, and gender in media. She has a tremendous interest in social communication regarding societal intergroup conflicts such as ideological polarization, nationalism, and the battle of the sexes. She worked as a researcher at the Korea Women's Development Institute and wrote many reports for the Korean government's gender equality policy. She also participated in writing a review report, *Participatory Surveys for Public Deliberation on Shin Gori Nuclear Reactors No. 5 and 6* in 2018. Also, her original enthusiasm in elections has led her to work on several projects funded by the Korea National Election Commission. She has contributed three book chapters and published articles in prominent Korean and international academic journals.

José Carlos Lozano (PhD, University of Texas at Austin) is a Research Fellow at Tecnológico de Monterrey, México. He has published extensively on media flows between the United States and Latin America, and on the reception of foreign television and films in Mexico.

Francisco J. Martínez-Garza (PhD, Universidad de Sevilla, Spain; MA, Universidad Autónoma de Nuevo León, México) is a professor of communication and director of the master's in communication program at Universidad Autónoma de Nuevo León, México. His research is on political communication and media policies in Mexico.

Saeedeh Moradifar is a PhD candidate in international relations, Department of Political Science, Faculty of Administrative Sciences and Economics, University of Isfahan, Isfahan, Iran. She is also a visiting research fellow at the Institute for Middle East Strategic Studies, Tehran, Iran. Ms. Moradifar is coauthor of "Social Media and Its Effects on Political Participation: A Case Study of Political Participation in the Province of Mazandaran," *Global Media Journal—Persian Edition* (2019); and "Explaining the Impact of Telegram Messenger on the Political Participation Approach" (Case Study: University of Isfahan), *Rasaneh Journal* (2018). Her doctoral dissertation is on "A Comparative Analysis Twiplomacy of the US and Russia 2014–2019."

Graham Murdock is professor emeritus of culture and economy at the Department of Social Sciences at Loughborough University. He has held the Bonnier Chair at the University of Stockholm and the Teaching Chair at the Free University of Brussels and been a visiting professor at the Universities of Auckland, California at San Diego, Mexico City, Curtin Western Australia, and Bergen and a visiting fellow at the Fudan University in Shanghai. He is currently vice president of the International Association of Media and Communication Research (IAMCR) one of the two major international professional associations in the field with members from over 90 countries.

Greydina Nadezhda (PhD, Pyatigorsk State University) is professor of intercultural communication at the Pyatigorsk State University, director of Ethnolinguistics and Communication Studies Research Institute (Russia), and president of the Russian Branch of Global Communication Association. Her research interests include political and cross-cultural communication and gender studies.

Ali Omidi (PhD, University of Tehran) is an associate professor of international relations at the Department of Political Science, Faculty of Administrative Sciences and Economics, University of Isfahan, Isfahan, Iran. He has authored a dozen peer-reviewed articles on Iranian foreign policy and is coauthor of articles such as "The Cultural-Identical Roots of Confrontation between the US and Islamism," "Iran's Narrative of Security in Afghanistan and the Feasibility of Iranian–US Engagement," "Social Media and the Arab Spring," and "How ISIS Employs Three Generations of the Web," and "A Constructivist Analysis of Iranophobia in U.S. Foreign Policy in the Post-JCPOA Era." He is regularly interviewed by the Iranian national and local media on Iranian foreign policy. He writes short pieces for political outlets such as *Al-Monitor*, *Foreign Policy Journal*, *Iran Review*, and *Iranian Diplomacy*.

Mohd Nizam Osman (PhD, University of Sussex) is an associate professor in the Department of Communication, Faculty of Modern Languages and Communication, Universiti Putra Malaysia. He obtained his master's and undergraduate degrees from Western Michigan University in 1996 and 1994, respectively. He is currently the deputy director at the University Community Transformation Centre (UCTC). He is also the secretary general of the Pacific and Asian Communication Association (PACA), a communication association based in Seoul, South Korea. Osman has authored and coauthored several books in the communication discipline.

Burak Özçetin (PhD, Middle East Technical University) is associate professor of communication at Istanbul Bilgi University Faculty of Communication. Graduated from Middle East Technical University (METU) Department of International Relations in 2001, Özçetin received his master's degree from the Department of Political Science (METU) in 2005. As a Fulbright Scholar, he visited The New School for Social Research Political Science Department between 2006 and 2007. Özçetin received his PhD in political science from METU in 2011. He has worked at METU, Akdeniz University, and Kadir Has University. Özçetin took part in several national and international research projects. Most recently he supervised a nationwide audience study titled *Television Viewing among Conservatives: Identity, Popular Taste, and Boundaries* (funded by TUBITAK). Currently he is working on a book on the history of populism in Turkey, with a specific focus on the media and popular culture. He is one of the principal investigators representing Turkey for the Journalistic Role Performance Project. His latest book, *Mass Communication Theories: Concepts, Schools, Models* (in Turkish) was published in 2018.

John V. Pavlik (PhD, University of Minnesota) is a professor in the Department of Journalism and Media Studies in the School of Communication and Information at Rutgers University. Pavlik has written widely on the impact of new technology on journalism, media, and society, with a particular interest in the role of the press in society in the United States and globally. His books include *Journalism in the Age of Virtual Reality*, *Converging Media*, with Shawn McIntosh, *Mobile Disruptions in the Middle East: Lessons from Qatar and the Arabian Gulf Region in Mobile Media Content Innovation*, with Everette E. Dennis, Rachel Davis Mersey, and Justin Gengler, *Masterful Stories: Lessons from Golden Age Radio*, *Media in the Digital Age*, *Journalism and New Media*, and *The People's Right to Know*. He is codeveloper (with Prof. Steven Feiner, Computer Science, Columbia University) of the Situated Documentary, a form of location-based storytelling using the emerging mobile and wearable platforms of Augmented Reality and 360-degree video. He has previously written for CNN.com. He is former associate dean for research and professor, Northwestern University in Qatar. He was the inaugural Distinguished Fulbright Chair in Media Studies at the Academy of Fine Arts, Vienna, Austria (2008).

Tomasz Płudowski (PhD, University of Łódź) is assistant professor in the American Studies Department, Cardinal Stefan Wyszyński University in Warsaw, Poland, an academic book translator, and a political media commentator. He has studied Russian in Finland, taught US students at a Japanese University in Holland, and was a Fulbright senior scholar at Stanford and a Kosciuszko Foundation junior scholar at New York University. His research focuses on American studies, media and communication, and politics. He has co-translated the Polity Press series New Media and Society, as well as *The Oxford Handbook of Political Behavior*. His recent monograph is *American Political Issue Ownership and Framing: A Functional Theory of Electoral Advantage-Seeking in Presidential Advertising from Eisenhower to Trump*.

Fei Song (PhD, Carlos III University of Madrid) is an assistant professor at the School of Foreign Languages of Henan University of Technology with a main research direction in cross-cultural language and Latin American region research. Song has eight years overseas study experience, is proficient in Spanish and English, has published three papers and presided over a provincial scientific research project, and has made several speeches at international conferences.

Jane Stokes (PhD, University of Southern California) is an academic and writer who has lived and worked in the United States and the United Kingdom. Jane's PhD in communications theory and research is from the Annenberg School at USC, where her doctoral thesis explored the shifting transatlantic representations of television. She has taught media, cultural, and communication studies at the University of Westminster, the University of Kent at Canterbury, London South Bank University, and the University of North London. Her most recent post was as programme leader of the Illustration BA at the University of East London. She is the author of *On Screen Rivals: The Cinema and Television in the Britain and the US* and *How to Media and Cultural Studies* (third edition, 2020).

Lizhou Sun (PhD, University of Peking University) is an assistant professor at Southwest University of Political Science and Law. He worked as a researcher for CITIC Foundation for Reform and Development Studies. Sun has translated and published three books and published more than 200 papers and articles in academic journals, newspapers, and magazines in the fields of international relations, global communications, Himalaya studies, and military history.

Thimios Zaharopoulos (PhD Southern Illinois University–Carbondale) has served as the provost of Deree–The American College of Greece since 2013. Previously he served in a variety of positions, including dean, interim provost, and vice president for global and lifelong learning at Park University, Missouri, USA. Zaharopoulos has also served as professor and chair of the Department of Mass Media at Washburn University (USA) and as the director of graduate studies in communication and later as assistant dean in the College of Arts and Sciences at Pittsburg State University in Kansas (USA). In 1994, he was a Fulbright visiting lecturer at Panteion University in Athens. Zaharopoulos has published two books: *Mass Media in Greece: Power, Politics and Privatization* (1993) and *Sports and Media* (in Greek, 2008). In addition, he has published 13 book chapters, 20 refereed journal articles, four book reviews, and over 45 conference paper presentations. He also served on the Editorial Review Board of the *Journal of Radio Studies* from 1993 to 2010.

Kourosh Ziabari is an award-winning Iranian journalist and reporter. He is the Iran correspondent of Fair Observer, a San Francisco–based online publication. He is also the Iran reporter of Asia Times, a Hong Kong–headquartered news media publishing group. Kourosh's writings have appeared in *Al-Monitor*, *openDemocracy*, *International Policy Digest*, *Al-Arabiya*, the *Huffington Post*, *Middle East Eye*, *Your Middle East*, and other publications. He has interviewed more than 500 prominent world leaders, politicians, diplomats, public intellectuals, academicians, and Nobel Prize laureates. He is the recipient of an American Middle Eastern Network for Dialogue at Stanford (AMENDS) Fellowship. He also received a Senior Journalists Seminar Fellowship from the East-West Center in 2015. Kourosh is an alumnus of Chevening Scholarships awarded by the UK's Foreign and Commonwealth Office.

Lightning Source UK Ltd.
Milton Keynes UK
UKHW030609220622
404761UK00001B/33

9 781538 142417